Law and Regulation of Aerodromes

Ruwantissa Abeyratne

Law and Regulation of Aerodromes

Springer

Ruwantissa Abeyratne
Montreal
Québec
Canada

ISBN 978-3-319-04779-9 ISBN 978-3-319-04780-5 (eBook)
DOI 10.1007/978-3-319-04780-5
Springer Cham Heidelberg New York Dordrecht London

Library of Congress Control Number: 2014935059

Printed on acid-free paper

Springer is part of Springer Science+Business Media (www.springer.com)

Preface

I began writing this book in mid-November 2013. At that time, super typhoon Haiyan had already caused landfall in the central Philippines. The typhoon hit landfall on Friday, November 8, killing several thousand people and leaving over a million homeless. The huge scale of death and destruction from the storm became clearer as reports emerged of thousands of people missing, and images showed apocalyptic scenes in towns that were not even reached by rescue workers in time. One of the most powerful storms ever recorded, typhoon Haiyan, levelled Basey, a seaside town in Samar province about 10 km across a bay from Tacloban in Leyte province, where at least 10,000 people were killed. Overall United Nations figures reflected that more than 11 million people were believed to have been affected and some 673,000 were displaced.

Many States pledged support and assistance, which the United Nations estimated at 300 million or more. Aircraft kept coming with food, medical aid, and water, but to the wrong airport of Cebu, quite a distance away from Tacloban, where there was an airport but with a shorter runway than what Cebu International Airport had. If donor States had used C-130 aircraft which could land in Tacloban, the food, water, and other supplies could have got through to those in need in much less time. But the supplies were stranded in Cebu, with no internal infrastructure to get them in time to the starving and the thirsty who were drinking contaminated water just to survive. It is worthy of note that the 38th Session of the Assembly of the International Civil Aviation Organization (ICAO), held at ICAO's Headquarters in September/October 2013 adopted a Resolution which said, *inter alia*, that there is a need for future generations of aircraft to be designed so that they are capable of being operated efficiently, and with the least possible environmental disturbance, from aerodromes used for the operation of present-day aircraft.

No one doubts that airports promote growth and development. They also provide connectivity with the outside world, particularly when tragedy hits. However, it is one thing to have an airport where aircraft could land bringing much needed supplies, but it is another thing entirely to ensure that the airport is close enough to the people of the community to be of some use. Regrettably, an earlier example of the Haiti earthquake in January 2010, where supplies sent in by generous donor States languished on the tarmac of the airport for several weeks, has seemingly not served as a planning tool for: those involved in ensuring disaster relief infrastructure; those in the airport business; those providing relief flights who should have the foresight to send the proper aircraft types laden with supplies; and those expected to bring the aid to the destitute, and therefore are responsible for having land transport ready.

In 2011 John Kasarda and Greg Lindsay published their book "*Aerotropolis*" which argues that cities of the future as well as their economies will be built and will function in close proximity to airports. Aerotropolis is a new urban economic phenomenon which is on the rise in the airport industry. It is an airport city which has a core and outlying area of aviation-oriented businesses and associated residential developments. Being very similar to the traditional "metropolis" which is a contrived formation of a central city and commuter-linked suburbs, the aerotropolis will respond to a society's demands for communications through speed and agility of multimodel transportation systems and sophisticated telecommunication systems. A functional aerotropolis will be optimized by corridor and cluster development of high-volume commercial activity facilitated through aero-lanes such as expressway links and aero trains linking the airport city to the airport itself. Infrastructure has also to be created for the smooth flow of buses, taxis, and trucks between the two points.

Despite this uplifting vision the 38th Session of the ICAO Assembly (September/October 2013) noted that there was a low level of implementation of aerodrome certification, including Safety Management Systems (SMS) at airports among States. This was further corroborated by an analysis of the ICAO Universal Safety Oversight Audit Programme audit results that showed that a large number of audited States had not yet certified or established a process for the certification of aerodromes. Many audited States have not ensured that aerodrome operators implement an SMS as part of their aerodrome certification process.

The title of this book involves aerodromes and not "airports." In practical parlance and in usage these two terms are referred to interchangeably in this book, although there is a subtle difference in terminology since an airport is an area of land or water where aircraft land and take off and an aerodrome is defined in the ICAO Aerodromes Manual as "a defined area on land or water (including any buildings, installations and equipment) intended to be used either wholly or in part for the arrival, departure and surface movement of aircraft." One could come to the conclusion that an aerodrome is an area of land or water where aircraft land or take off and where aircraft are serviced and maintained. The inconsistency of usage is blatant and inexplicable where in the Convention on International Civil Aviation—the multilateral treaty which governs civil aviation—the word "airport" is used whereas Annex 14 to the Convention deals with "aerodromes." However, for convenience and easy readership, this book will follow common practice and refer to the terms interchangeably to mean one and the same thing.

As the title denotes, this book will address legal and regulatory issues pertaining to the various aspects of the structure and functioning of an aerodrome and the complexities involved. This is my second book on airports. The first—*Airport Business Law*—was published in 2009.

Montreal, QC, Canada
April 2014

Ruwantissa Abeyratne

Contents

Table of Cases

M

N

O

P

Q

R

S

T

U

V

W

Y

Chapter 1
The Airport and the State

1.1 Introduction

Annex 9 (Facilitation) to the Chicago Convention defines an international airport as "*Any airport designated by the Contracting State in whose territory it is situated as an airport of entry and departure for international air traffic, where the formalities incident to customs, immigration, public health, animal and plant quarantine and similar procedures are carried out*". Annex 15 to the Chicago Convention has a similar definition. The main functions of an airport are activities concerned with: administration and finance; operation of airport facilities; engineering, construction works and maintenance; marketing and public relations; ground handling; air traffic operations; security, immigration, health and customs.

The functions and responsibilities of an airport will vary according to its size, type of traffic and areas of responsibility. For example, some airports are responsible for air traffic control as well as for meteorological services, while at most other airports such services are provided by separate government entities. Many airports are involved in security functions in varying degrees and in providing facilities for customs, immigration and health authorities. Ground-handling services for the airlines, including terminal handling or ramp handling, or both, are provided by some airports, while at others they are provided by the airlines or by specialized agents or companies. Certain airports also perform functions that exceed the scope of conventional airport activities, such as consultancy services, public works, construction, and real estate development.

The primary consideration is the relationship between the airport and the State. Article 28 of the Convention on International Civil Aviation (hereafter referred to as the Chicago Convention)[1] provides *inter alia* that each contracting State undertakes, so far as it may find practicable, to provide, in its territory, airports, radio services, meteorological services and other air navigation facilities to facilitate

[1] Convention on International Civil Aviation signed at Chicago on 7 December 1944. See ICAO Doc 7300/8: 2006. See also Abeyratne (2012).

R. Abeyratne, *Law and Regulation of Aerodromes*, DOI 10.1007/978-3-319-04780-5_1,

international air navigation, in accordance with the standards and practices recommended or established from time to time, pursuant to the Convention. This provision leaves no room for doubt that the ultimate responsibility for an airport rests within the State in which it is situated.

However, the airport has been misunderstood over the years. One recent example was in the case of Edward Snowden, who attracted much attention in mid 2013 and continues to do so. The Snowden saga[2] brought to bear issues such as, how is an offender treated at the transit lounge of an international airport? Is the transit lounge a "no man's land" pertaining to which the State in which the airport is located has no control or jurisdiction? What does international law have to say on these issues? Snowden, who leaked critical security information of the United States to the international press, ran off to Hong Kong and onwards to the Russian Federation with the US authorities in diplomatic pursuit. The Russians denied that Snowden had "entered" Russia since he was in an airport transit hotel and had not passed through immigration and customs, which the United States refused to acknowledge as a valid and legal premise.

There are some States that apply the principle that a passenger, upon arrival is considered as not having entered the country until he or she passes through immigration and is legally accepted by that country. Snowden, who travelled to Moscow from Hong Kong, was in this situation and the Russian authorities clearly stated to the international media that he had not entered Russia, although knowing full well that Snowden was holed up in the transit lounge at Moscow airport. The Russian authorities claimed that an airport transit lounge is not subject to the authority of the country in which it lies, because the passengers there are not required to pass through that country's immigration process. One is reminded of others who sought refuge in an airport transit lounge in the same manner as did Snowden, such as Iranian refugee Mehran Karimi Nasseri, who lived for almost 18 years (from 26 August 1988 until July 2006), in terminal one of Charles de Gaulle Airport in Paris, the victim of a bureaucratic nightmare.[3] Nasseri only left after falling sick and having to undergo hospital treatment.

Irrespective of the status of the airport transit lounge, and whether, in certain jurisdictions the law recognizes that such an area is outside the territory of the State, treaty law prescribes some responsibility on those who bring a person into a country by air. The Chicago Convention stipulates, in Article 13 that the laws and regulations of a contracting State as to the admission to or departure from its territory of passengers, crew or cargo of aircraft, such as regulations relating to entry,

---

[2] In June 2013, Edward Snowden, a former technical contractor to the National Security Agency (NSA) and the Central Intelligence Agency (CIA) leaked to the media (The Washington Post and The Guardian newspaper) details of top secret American and British mass surveillance programmes. The leaked material included a variety of classified intelligence programmes containing *inter alia*, intercepted telephone metadata and internet surveillance programmes. This act constituted a breach of United States law, making Snowden a felon.

[3] The film *The Terminal*, directed by Steven Spielberg and starring Tom Hanks, is partly based on the real-life story.

clearance, immigration, passports, customs, and quarantine shall be complied with by or on behalf of such passengers, crew or cargo upon entrance into or departure from, or while within the territory of that State. Article 13 does not specify as to who is responsible for compliance with the provision and one can presume it is the carrier.

There is also specific provision in Annex 9 (facilitation) to the Chicago Convention to the effect that the carrier transporting the passenger to a State is responsible for his care and custody until he/she is accepted by the immigration and customs authorities of the receiving State.[4] If a person is found inadmissible, the carrier has the responsibility of transporting the passenger back to his State of origin or any other State that would accept the passenger.[5]

The link between the airport and the carrier which operates into the airport was made clear in the case of *Vumbaca* v. *Terminal One Group Association L.P.*[6] decided in April 2012 by the United States District Court, E.D. New York. Vivian Vumbaca—the Plaintiff—an Italian citizen who was a permanent resident of the United States who arrived in New York during the snow storm of 26–27 December 2010 from Rome, alleged that she was kept locked in an aircraft on the ground without food, water, or adequate sanitary facilities for 7 h, suffering mental distress. She sued Terminal One Group Association, L.P. (TOGA), which operates Terminal One, and sought to represent similarly situated passengers claiming emotional harms resulting from negligence, false imprisonment, and intentional infliction of emotional distress under her contract of carriage on the ground that Terminal One Group Association did not afford her the facility of disembarking at her destination and kept her on board the aircraft for seven hours causing her mental distress.[7]

In terms of jurisdictional competence of the court, the court recognized Article 33 of the Montreal Convention[8] which stipulates that an action for damages must be brought, at the option of the plaintiff, in the territory of one of the States Parties, either before the court of the domicile of the carrier or of its principal place of business, or where it has a place of business through which the contract has been made or before the court at the place of destination. The Convention goes on to say that In respect of damage resulting from the death or injury of a passenger, an action may be brought before one of the courts mentioned in paragraph 1 of Article 33, or in the territory of a State Party in which at the time of the accident the passenger has

[4] Annex 9, Chapter 3 Section E, Standard 3.38.1.

[5] *Id.* Standard 3.39.

[6] 859 F Supp. 2d. 353 (E.D.N.Y).

[7] From December 26th to 27th, 2010, during the height of the holiday travel season, the New York metropolitan area was—somewhat unexpectedly—blanketed with over a foot of snow. John F. Kennedy International Airport (JFK) was closed to air traffic for the worst of the storm. When it reopened, there were continuing problems. Passengers on arriving flights were forced to endure substantial waits after landing before they were able to disembark. Difficulties appear to have been particularly severe at terminals serving international flights.

[8] Convention for the Unification of Certain Rules for International carriage by Air, 1999. The Convention entered into force on 4 November 2003. It has been ratified by 105 State Parties.

his or her principal and permanent residence and to or from which the carrier operates services for the carriage of passengers by air, either on its own aircraft or on another carrier's aircraft pursuant to a commercial agreement, and in which that carrier conducts its business of carriage of passengers by air from premises leased or owned by the carrier itself or by another carrier with which it has a commercial agreement.

The court held that the Montreal Convention is an international treaty to which the United States is a party, and which establishes a uniform system of liability for international air carriers.

The plaintiff averred that her claim was based on Article 30 of the Montreal Convention which stipulates that if an action is brought against a servant or agent of the carrier arising out of damage to which the Convention relates, such servant or agent, if they prove that they acted within the scope of their employment, shall be entitled to avail themselves of the conditions and limits of liability which the carrier itself is entitled to invoke under this Convention. It was the contention of the plaintiff that Terminal One Group Association, L.P. (TOGA) was an agent of the carrier and therefore could be held liable under the Montreal Convention.

The court held *inter alia* that The Convention does not define "agent" and that the Supreme Court has provided no guidance. It also observed that the Court of Appeals for the Second Circuit had held that the airline employees are agents covered by the Convention[9] and that the Convention's "basic principle" required that air carriers be "protected from having to pay out more than a fixed and definite sum for passenger injuries sustained in international air disasters."

The Court held:

> As a general rule, whenever one person is by circumstances placed in such a position with regard to another that every one of ordinary sense who did think would at once recognize that if he did not use ordinary care and skill in his own conduct with regard to the circumstances he would cause danger of injury to the person or property of the other, a duty arises to use ordinary care and skill to avoid such danger.[10] The court's power to modify this rule "is reserved for very limited situations. . . .In determining whether a defendant had a duty of care toward the plaintiff, courts look to morality, logic, and the social consequences of imposing the duty".[11]

The Court found that the defendant TOGA had acted as an agent of the carrier. Despite the fact that TOGA was a terminal operator, its services were vital to the performance by the carrier of the contract of carriage with the plaintiff and therefore formed an integral part thereof and that TOGA had a common law duty to ensure that passengers on arriving flights had safe and prompt access to Terminal One. It provided a necessary link in the chain of transportation, facilitating the common carrier airline's service of its passengers. The defendant's duty to passengers extended beyond merely ensuring that stairs are not slippery, or that gates are properly maintained. It must ensure that those stairs and gates are made available

---

[9] Quoting *Reed* v. *Wiser*, 555 F.2d. at 1089–1093.

[10] *Havas v. Victory Paper Stock Co.*, 49 N.Y.2d. 381 (1980).

[11] *Eiseman v. State of New York*, 70 NY.2d. 175 (1987).

in a timely manner when needed for use by the passengers, and that adequate ground handling staff is present to facilitate access. The Court further observed that TOGA should have foreseen that a breach of this duty would cause passengers to remain trapped on their aircraft in cramped and increasingly unpleasant or dangerous conditions. Imposing on defendant this duty was neither novel nor undesirable as a matter of public policy.

The court concluded:

> In the instant case, the defendant was in a favorable position to prevent harm to the plaintiff. TOGA—arguably, unlike the air carrier, Alitalia—was fully aware of the situation on the ground and its inability to handle incoming flights. It should have taken a robust position, ordering Alitalia not to let its flights to JFK take off since no disembarkation facilities were available. Instead, it made a soft, timid suggestion that it might not be able to handle incoming flights adequately, creating no strong sense of the serious dangers in letting planes take off for New York.[12]

The Court also held that TOGA had sole responsibility for managing the gates by which passengers moved between the terminal and an airplane. This included the duty and discretion to select a ground handling provider to move planes to and from the gates.

The recognition that an airport operator could be considered an agent of the airline establishes an inextricable link between the two—a link hitherto not recognized—and places airports in a new light and widens the scope of their liability and responsibility.

Furthermore, in an earlier case decided in 1992 by the United States Supreme Court, Rehnquist C.J., said that an airport terminal operated by a public authority is a non-public forum. Neither by tradition nor purpose can the terminals be described as public fora.[13] The terminals are generally accessible to the general public, and contain various commercial establishments such as restaurants, snack stands, bars, newsstands, and stores of various types. Virtually all who visit the terminals do so for purposes related to air travel. These visitors principally include passengers, those meeting or seeing off passengers, flight crews, and terminal employees[14] His Lordship also said that airports are funded by user fees and operated to make a regulated profit[15] and that most space at the three airports coming within the purview of the New York and New Jersey Ports Authority is leased to commercial airlines, which bear primary responsibility for the leasehold.

When the *Vumbaca* principle is applied to airports as an extension to the contract of carriage, their liability in other areas become clearer. For instance, when the aircraft is landing and touches the runway, inadequate lighting and dangers posed thereby and accidents that follow could follow the same agent analogy. Inadequate signs and lighting and the paucity of emergency plans at airports would all make for

---

[12] *Supra* note 6 at 371.

[13] *International Society for Krishna Consciousness, Inc.* v. *Lee*, 505 U.S. 672 at 673.

[14] *Id.* 678.

[15] *Id.* at 581.

bringing the airport under the purview of the contract of carriage, as agent of the carrier. This makes it all the more important for the players concerned to exercise extreme caution. The operative criterion in determining whether the key players exercise due diligence would depend on a judicial determination of prudent practice in the application of acceptable weather information systems, availability of adequate aerodrome facilities, effective contingency and emergency plans and overall professional conduct of all concerned

From a legal perspective, an airport would be analogous to an occupier and liability principles could be common to both categories The leading case which expands the definition of "occupier" is the House of Lords decision in *Wheat* v. *E. Lacon & Co. Ltd.*[16] In this case the defendants owned a public house of which R was their manager. R and his wife were allowed by agreement to live in the upper floor, access to which was by a door separate from the licensed premises. Mrs. R was allowed to take paying guests on the upper floor. An accident was sustained by a paying guest on the staircase leading to the upper floor. It was held that the defendants were occupiers of the upper floor. Mr. R was only a licensee of that part, and the defendants had enough residuary control to be treated as occupiers. In fact the defendants, Mr. R and Mrs. R, were all occupiers. The case recognizes three instances that there may be two or more occupiers at one time[17]; that exclusive occupation is not required; and that the test is whether a person has some degree of control associated with and arising from his presence in and use of or activity in the premises. The following principles, enunciated by earlier decisions, that a concessionaire without a lease in a fairground is an occupier[18]; a contractor converting a ship into a troopship in dry dock occupies the ship[19]; and a local authority which has requisitioned a house[20] is an occupier (even in respect of those parts of the house in which it is allowing homeless persons to live)[21] are also good examples of occupiers.

---

[16] [1966] AC 552, [1966] 1 All ER 582, HL.

[17] In *Fisher* v. *CHT Ltd.* (*No 2*) [1966] 1 All ER 88, CA, the owners of a club and the defendants who ran a restaurant in the club under licence from the club were both held to be occupiers. In *AMF International Ltd.* v. *Magnet Bowling Ltd.* [1968] 2 All ER789, a contractor (as well as the owner) was an occupier of the whole building although part of the building was separated by a screen beyond which he went only to attend to heating and lighting. It is doubtful whether someone who has granted a right of way occupies that right of way: See *Holden* v. *White* [1982] QB 679, [1982] 2 All ER 328, CA. A highway authority which owns the land but has not adopted the highway is not an occupier of the highway. See *Holmes* v. *Norfolk County Council* (1981) 131 NLJ 401. A highway authority does not occupy a footpath on land owned by another although it has a statutory obligation to maintain it. See *Whiting v. Hillingdon London Borough Council* (1970) 68 LGR 437.

[18] *Humphreys v. Dreamland (Margate) Ltd.* [1930] All ER Rep 327, HL.

[19] *Hartwell v. Grayson Rollo and Clover Docks Ltd.* [1947] KB 901, CA. However, a contractor merely painting a house is not an occupier. See *Page v. Read* (1984) 134 NLJ 723.

[20] *Hawkins v. Coulsdon and Purley UDC* [1954] 1 QB 319, [1954] 1 All ER 97, CA.

[21] *Greene v. Chelsea Borough Council* [1954] 2 QB 127, [1954] 2 All ER 318, CA. See also *Harris v. Birkenhead Corporation* [1976] 1 All ER 341, CA where a local authority, having acquired a house by compulsory purchase, occupies it even before its staff enter it.

In a more recent case it was held that:

> Whenever one person is by circumstances placed in such a position with regard to another that every one of ordinary sense who did think would at once recognize that if he did not use ordinary care and skill in his own conduct with regard to the circumstances he would cause danger of injury to the person or property of the other, a duty arises to use ordinary care and skill to avoid such danger.[22]

The *Vumbaca* principle, enunciated by the court was that TOGA had a common law duty to ensure that passengers on arriving flights had safe and prompt access to Terminal One. It provided a necessary link in the chain of transportation, facilitating the common carrier airline's service of its passengers. The Court held that Terminal One was designed for the express purpose of permitting passengers to wait for their arriving aircraft and to safely and comfortably board and disembark their flights. TOGA is responsible for all of the facilities and equipment necessary to perform this function, as well as for providing adequate staffing in order to do so. The most noteworthy pronouncement of the Court was that:

> The defendant's duty to passengers extends beyond merely ensuring that stairs are not slippery, or that gates are properly maintained. It must ensure that those stairs and gates are made available in a timely manner when needed for use by the passengers, and that adequate ground handling staff is present to facilitate access. TOGA should have foreseen that a breach of this duty would cause passengers to remain trapped on their aircraft in cramped and increasingly unpleasant or dangerous conditions. Imposing on defendant this duty is neither novel nor undesirable as a matter of public policy.
>
> TOGA knew that it was short-staffed following the snow storm, and that, as a result, it was having difficulty timely clearing empty planes from terminal areas in order to remove snow and to permit arriving planes to disembark. The potential for harm foreseeably increased as more and more international flights continued to arrive at Terminal One. TOGA had a duty to take appropriate firm steps to prevent or delay the arrival of those flights[23]

1.1.1 The Nature and Future of Airports

In the past an airport was simply a terminus, much the same as a bus terminus of that time, assigning it as the focal geographical point at which people gathered to embark on a plane for a journey by air, or disembark after an air journey. However, the traditional definition of an airport is being reshaped and refined to accord with the fact that airports are now complex industrial enterprises. Quite apart from the essential air side support given by airports to landing and departing aircraft, there are commercial facilities provided for both passengers and the public within the terminal building by concessionaires who are specialists in their own fields of

---

[22] *Havas v. Victory Paper Stock Co.*, 49 N.Y.2d 381, 426 N.Y.S.2d 233, 402 N.E.2d 1136, 1138 (1980).

[23] *Supra* note 6 at 371.

business. The airport authorities collect concession fees (non aeronautical revenues) from the concessionaires and in numerous airports around the world, the income derived from such resources are significant, often exceeding traditional income derived through the provision of landing fees and airport and air navigation services charges (aeronautical revenues) to incoming and outgoing aircraft.

According to Airports Council International, worldwide total airport income in 2010 reached US$101.8 billion, including an estimated US$4.6 billion for the Middle East region. Hence, compared to 2009 survey results, industry revenue was roughly 7 % up in 2010 which is broadly in line with industry growth.

In 2010, aeronautical revenue from passenger and airline user charges accounted for 53.5 % of industry-wide income, a similar proportion to 2009. The global airport industry generated US$54.5 billion in aeronautical revenues in 2010 (including ground handling). Aeronautical revenue from passenger and airline user charges accounted for 53.5 % of industry-wide income, a similar proportion to 2009.

Non-aeronautical revenues worldwide made up 46.5 % of industry revenue in 2010, however this category includes non-operating income of US$6.9 billion.

Airports worldwide in 2010 incurred operating expenses in the amount of US$56 billion or 55 % of revenues. The largest expense item reported was personnel cost, accounting for 36 % of operating expenses, followed by contracted services (outsourcing cost to third parties) as the second biggest cost item at 19 % of total operating cost.

Capital expenditure at airports worldwide in 2010 was almost a third lower than predicted for 2010, with US$26 billion were spent on airport upgrades or expansions of existing airport infrastructure. The markedly reduced capital expenditure is clearly a consequence of the global financial crisis which led many airports to scrap or cut down on capital programmes. Also, the crisis entailed tighter credit markets, lower commodity costs and more competitive bids that made financing harder to obtain or made construction cheaper, both putting pressure on expenditure.

The prognosis for 2012 was that, while there was considerable uncertainty in financial markets as to whether governments will be able to contain the sovereign debt crisis in Europe, the consumer was seemingly unaffected. ACI noted that consumer confidence was a resilient and spending is still growing year on year as the current crisis had not been adding to unemployment yet.

Therefore, the prognosis was that another year of growth lay ahead of the industry. Growth rates could be smaller, especially in the first half of the year, but ACI expected overall airports to be in a good shape to grow revenues further. As far as the individual regions are concerned, the significant spreads in growth rates among the regions were expected to homogenize further as economic growth in China and Brazil cools and the continuing political uncertainty in North Africa will continue to limit its growth opportunities. The bottom line was that Asia-Pacific would continue to remain the fastest growing region followed by Latin America, and North America and Europe will be rather stultified in growth.

In the context of these trends, it is evident that more and more, airports are evolving from being basic aeronautical infrastructures into complex multi-functional enterprises serving the travelling public while at the same time catering to their commercial needs and those of others who visit the airport. Such enterprises include duty free shops, specialty retail and brand name shops, restaurants, hotels and accommodation, banks, business and office complexes, leisure, recreation and fitness centres just to name a few.

In the present context, the major hubs are facing a non-aeronautical boom in their commercial activities which are not directly related to air travel. For instance Chek Lap Kok, Hong Kong's international airport, has more than 30 high end designer shops. Singapore's Changi International pampers the human's physical fitness cravings and the continuing need for entertainment by hosting cinemas, saunas and even a swimming pool in the airport itself. Frankfurt has the world's largest airport clinic having the facilities to serve 36,000 patients annually while Detroit Metropolitan Wayne County has a 420 bedroom hotel in its main concourse. Munich airport has its own hospital while Amsterdam Schipol has a Dutch master's gallery. Beijing has quite a few banks carrying on business within the terminal building while Stockholm's Arlanda airport solemnized marriages and officiated over 450 weddings in 2008 in the vast chapel located within the terminal.

All this is of course due to the fact that the average air traveller is more affluent than the non-traveller (they have higher incomes, typically three to five times the average) and a busy airport has scores of them continuously flowing through the airport. This has prompted airport managers to re structure their operational management. For example, many airports have established separate real estate management and property units and divisions to capitalize on their landside commercial activities and enhance real estate values. One of the foremost in this area is Aeroports de Paris which established its real estate division in 2003 to manage landside commercial activities coming under the purview of the airport both in Paris and Orly. Some others have aggressively put in place free trade zones, customs free zones, golf courses, child and day care centres, factory outlet stores and fitness centers. Amsterdam Schipol is also doing the same and developing its real estate potential to build large office complexes, meeting and entertainment facilities logistics parks, shopping and other commercial activities.

Beijing, which is coming up as one of the busiest airports in the next few years, has gone ahead with its Capital Airport City, which will provide shopping, entertainment, education, sports and leisure activities while accommodating activities related to commerce, finance trade and housing. Dallas Fort Worth (US) has concentrated its activities in the field of real estate development as a profitable adjunct to its traditional airport activities. Hong Kong airport's SkyCity is a colourful and fabulous project, which will contain a million square meters of retail, exhibition, business, office and hotel complex very near to the terminal. This complex will also accommodate cinemas and mini theme parks.

Yet another spectacular development is the new airport city of Kuala Lumpur International Airport which will be commercially held together by its large Gateway Park. This Park will host office complexes retail stores, an automotive hypermarket and leisure venues which will cater to the aviation and non aviation market in the city. In Seoul, Incheon International Airport would have its own mega complex in its "Winged City" which provides for large business areas, shopping and tourism districts, housing and medical services for airport workers and residents.

While still in Asia, Suvarnabhumi, the new Bangkok International Airport, has an entire airport city within the boundaries of the airport that houses an international business centre, international conference and exhibition complex, shopping malls, car parks, hospitals, restaurants and a large entertainment centre.

It is clear that what these airports are doing is merely anchoring their strategically placed airport resources and potential on a metropolitan commercial business district (CBD) formula to create employment and generate revenue. This is a highly lucrative and eminently strategic commercial practice among the major airports of the world that are aware of the trends with regard to passenger movements in their terminals.

The airline and airport business are interlinked and inter-connected and, since air transport is a growth industry, so is the airport industry. According to the global market forecast of Airbus Industrie forecasts that from 2009 to 2028, some 25,000 new passenger and freighter aircraft valued at US$3.1 trillion will be delivered. This rapidly evolving demand is driven by emerging economies, evolving airline networks, expansion of low cost carriers and the increasing number of mega-cities as well as traffic growth and the replacement of older less efficient aircraft with more eco-efficient airliners. These are factors driving demand for new aircraft.

The forecast also attributes the demand for larger aircraft to the compelling need to ease aircraft congestion and to accommodate growth on existing routes and to achieve more with less. Needless to say, this exponential growth in air traffic will place a burden on airport capacity and consequent demands upon the airport industry.

Airports are a complex, big business. The first element in the airport business equation is the customer and it is therefore a good starting point to determine who the customers of the airport are. It is incontrovertible that airline passengers generate the bulk of the concession revenue and that the airlines who bring them would normally generate most of the rental or lease income. However other market groups are by no means inconsequential.

Airport employees who work for airlines, the airport authority, the concessionaires and other enterprises within the airport premises form a substantial customer category although their *modus vivendi* in purchasing goods and services, particularly from the concessionaire stores could be different from those of the passenger. While the former would look for convenience in buying goods in house during their work breaks without having to travel to the local stores and supermarkets in their neighbourhoods, the latter would buy gifts to take home. A good example of an airport which caters to the airport employee is Frankfurt Airport which has released the statistic that employees working at the airport spend approximately 15 % of their net household income at the airport's shops and service facilities.

Airline crews are another category of customer, particularly at larger airports where crew movement is prolific. Their needs are mostly work related and they may look primarily for clothes stores, dry cleaning, shoe repairs, hair-dressing salons and tailors in addition to some goods that are in demand for airport employees. Another category of customer is the person who goes to meet and greet an arriving passenger or one who goes to drop off a passenger. The meeter who comes in early and finds himself with time on his hands until the arrival of the flight in which the passenger whom he meets is travelling, could well stroll around and purchase goods that he needs or is attracted by. The same goes for the person who accompanies a departing passenger and hangs about until the passenger is admitted to security clearance. A prime attraction in this regard is the restaurant as well as other catering outlets.

Airport shops would usually have much longer opening hours than other shops offering goods and services to local residential areas, which could in turn attract visitors to the airport who would come in for the convenience of shopping after hours. Although not as significant as the ones already mentioned, this category of customer could include local residents who are attracted to the airport by the convenience of late shopping hours at airport shops, unlike those of their neighbouring supermarkets and shops. Today's airport, in its typical form, is primarily a commercial entity and operates as a business oriented entity. Most airports provide retail shops and parking facilities not only for airline passengers and their visitors but also to residents of the area. They are, in this sense, as much profit centres as are such retail outlets as K-Mart and Walmart. In addition, there are also airport free zones which are bonded areas, adjacent to the airport premises which, as the name suggests, are duty free areas promoting industry and other commercial activity.

The airport, like any other autonomous business enterprise, has to exploit inherent resources optimally; compete with other businesses of the area on quality of services offered; and reinvest funds in developing its business interests. The Council of ICAO recognizes the continuing importance to airports of income derived from such sources as concessions, rental of premises and "free zones". The Council recommends that, with the exception of concessions that are directly associated with the operation of air transport services, such as fuel, in-flight catering and ground handling, the full development of revenues of this kind be encouraged having regard to the need for moderation in prices to the public, the requirements of passengers and the need for terminal efficiency. The fact that the general public are recognized as customers of airports by ICAO policy leaves room to attribute to the wisdom of the policy statement the acknowledgment that airports do not only cater to airline passengers and their visitors, but to shoppers who may wish to pick up a bargain at the airport.

Airports are compelled to compete with each other to attract air traffic and business flowing therefrom and from the general public. To this end, many airports are now privatized and operate as autonomous entities. Privatization brings not only fiscal benefits, but also legal liability (as the discussion below will show) which is a possible cost factor that should be taken into account. More importantly, privatization connotes a business-like approach that requires a certain involvement with market forces and competition that would necessitate reinvestment in the airport business for the commercial sustainability of the airport.

Airports are complex businesses which are subject to both external and internal factors with regard to revenue generation and their cost-benefit equation. The most significant external factors are current and projected traffic levels, global and local economic fluctuations and currency exchange rates, taxes and charges imposed on airports by governments and authorities as well as charges that can be exercised by airports on their users. Internally, strategic planning in terms of air and terminal space, slot allocation and the nature and effect of taxes. A large number of factors will influence an airports' ability to maximize its commercial revenues. There are first of all certain external factors, which are crucially important in affecting revenue generation or strategic options but which are largely outside the control of individual airport managements. These include the airport's traffic levels and its proportion of international traffic, exchange rates and the level of taxes or duties imposed on alcohol or tobacco. Then there are a variety of factors which can be influenced directly by management. These are the area and the location of terminal space allocated to commercial activities, the nature of the contracts negotiated with the concessionaires and the quality of the concessionaires themselves. In order to understand how commercial revenues might be maximized, all these factors are discussed in the next chapter.

Airports have a range of goods, services and facilities to offer. Their income comes from rents and concession fees. Rental income is earned primarily from the renting or leasing of space and the customers are direct users of what airports have to offer, such as users airlines, freight forwarders and handling agents. The indirect users are hotels, catering firms, manufacturing companies and other similar business enterprises. Concession fees are earned from, payments made to the airport by the providers of various services for the right to offer their services in the airport premises. These fees are generally based on the volume of business generated by the concessionaires and not usually on the dimensions of space occupied, although it is not uncommon for some concession agreements to include a straightforward ground-rent criterion.

Duty-and tax-free shops are arguably the most attractive to airports in terms of non-aeronautical revenue. These shops are ready to pay competitive rents since consumers find them more attractive than city centre shops as the prices in the former are substantially low. An added attraction for concessionaires to pay high rents is that since the profit margins earned by the concessionaires are considerably high, airports can negotiate a contract that is advantageous in obtaining for the airport a large share of the profits earned by such shops

Airports also recognize the need to provide duty and tax free shopping in the landside areas of the passenger terminal since duty-free shopping is only accessible to passengers who have entered the departure or transit lounges. A wide range of duty-and tax-paid shopping needs to be provided in the public landside areas of terminals. Such shops will be of three kinds. These shops could sell goods such as travel goods, tobacco, books, sweets, drugs and toiletries, food, flowers, fashion goods souvenirs, glassware, clothing, videos and records. As I any place where humanity gathers, the airport also needs food and drink outlets. The provision of these services would depend on market demand as determined by the type of passenger who frequents the area in question. Another revenue generating source is through bill board advertising and other types of promotional sources business enterprises might wish to have in the premises of an airport.

Another important element in airport business caters to the financial transactions a passenger or visitor to the airport might need and his transport needs when he leaves the airport on arrival. These services are essentially related to those provided by banks, post offices, travel agents, car hire and hotel reservations. While car rentals produce most of the revenue, banks are the most popular. Car parks are clearly another source of revenue generation for airports, particularly where there are no regular public transport services. Finally, leisure facilities, which is a growing need for a generation acutely aware of the travails of air travel and the need to stay in shape has proved popular. This category begins with health spas and health clubs but extends to swimming pools, and entertainment facilities such as cinemas, discotheques, night clubs and billiard rooms.

The ICAO Council Statements (Doc 9802/5) leave it wide open for airports to optimize their revenue to exceed all direct and indirect operating costs, including general administration etc., and so provide for a reasonable return on assets (before tax and cost of capital) to contribute toward necessary capital improvements.[24] This policy statement encourages commercial autonomy of airports and the practice of deviating from being instrumentalities of the State. *A fortiori*, it urges airports to optimize revenues in order to boost capital investment toward improvement, which would not necessarily mean such revenues should subsidize airport and air navigation service charges. The *Airport Economics Manual*, which was first produced and issued by ICAO in 1991 stated:

It should be noted that revenues from non-aeronautical activities are in fact the principal means by which a growing number of airports are able to recover their total costs because their profits from these activities more than cover the losses most of them incur on their air side operations[25] . . . and in so far as ICAO cost recovery policies are concerned, not subject to the same limitations that it is recommended apply to charges on air traffic.[26]

It is arguable in the context of the above mentioned policy that, if two different criteria are applied, one strictly on the basis of recovery of costs of services provided which would essentially be a non-profit operation, as in the case of charges levied for the provision of airport and air navigation services, and another strictly on a profit making business basis, whether the latter, applicable to non-aeronautical revenues, is mutually exclusive from the former. If this argument were to prevail, one could maintain that charges for airport and air navigation

---

[24] Doc 9082/6 Id. paragraph 14 vii).

[25] *Airport Economics Manual*, First Edition—1991, Doc 9562, Chapter 6, para 6.3 at p. 50.

[26] *Id.* paragraph 4.60 at p. 40. It should also be noted that certain concession type facilities are established at an airport to provide services considered necessary for passengers, visitors and/or persons working at the airport. Such facilities may include cafeterias, post offices and tourist information counters. See *Airport Economics Manual*, note 37 in Chap. 2, at paragraph 6.11.

services need not as of necessity be minimized as a result of capital injection towards facilities providing such services if such capital were to be derived from the non-aeronautical activities of the airport. Of course, this does not mean that an airport which wishes to inject some capital derived from one source to another should be precluded from doing so in the best interests of aviation.

Airports, like any other business enterprises, are compelled to compete with each other to attract air traffic and business flowing therefrom and from the general public. To this end, many airports are now privatized and operate as autonomous entities. Privatization brings not only fiscal benefits, but also legal liability (as the discussion below will show) which is a possible cost factor that should be taken into account. More importantly, privatization connotes a businesslike approach that requires a certain involvement with market forces and competition that would necessitate reinvestment in the airport business for the commercial sustainability of the airport.

The attractiveness of airports to the average shopper is largely due to the range of shops and services available in the airport premises. In this regard, local residents and airport employees share common interests and many airports have expanded the range of their shops to meet the demand posed by these categories. It has been known that those items which do not fall into the category of daily purchases, such as furniture, electrical goods, hardware are popular consumer items at some airports.

The local business community, which would find it more cost effective and productive from a sales perspective to conduct their business at the airport, could be another important customer of the airport. They could require office space, conference and meeting facilities which can enable them to take advantage of the airport's strategic location, inter-connectivity and diversity of nationalities which an airport attracts. Businesses may also need large storage and warehouse space for freight and therefore may seek space close to the passenger terminal. There needs may extend to land, warehouses, hangars or office buildings from which the airport can generate substantial rental income.

One of the best examples of prolific non aeronautical commercial activity is Changi International in Singapore. The seventh busiest international airport today, it serves some 100 airlines flying to over 220 cities in about 60 countries and territories worldwide. Changi Airport handled more than 46 million passenger movements in 2011 (that's more than 9 times the size of Singapore's population. Incheon at the Republic of Korea is another example. It has a museum and provides in its vicinity a traditional Korean Cultural Experience Zone which allows users of the airport to make handcrafts of their own and watch Korean traditional performances. Also, there are mini concerts and Royal Court parades to entertain the senses.

As far back 1992, Rigas Doganis noted that airports such as Frankfurt airport had sophisticated services to offer passengers and users. He emphasized leisure activities in the following manner:

> Non-passengers at the airport may also value a range of leisure facilities such as cinemas, discotheques, night clubs, billiard rooms, a gym or health care and even a swimming pool. They might even want a golf course between the runways as at Bangkok's Don Muang airport. Some of these facilities may be used by passengers especially if they are provided within the airport hotel. But they are not primarily targeted at passengers.[27]

Don Muang airport has since been replaced by Suvarnabumi. The airport offers the following facilities: hair salon; spa and massage; information desks; medical care (provided by Samitivej Srinakarin Hospital and Bumrungrad International); pharmacies and mini-marts; tour service; Muslim prayer rooms; monks' reception room; luggage wrapping service; book and magazine kiosks; souvenir shops; meeting points; smoking areas; transit hotels; VAT refund for tourists; and lost and found.

In view of the current trends in the airport business model, airports have to make strategic decisions to be financially self-sufficient and be run like businesses. There should therefore be a commercial airport model which maximizes revenue, whether such is generated through aeronautical revenues (such as airport charges from airlines) or non-aeronautical revenues (such as from concessionaires). They should also have a reasoned view on who their target clients are and who their most attractive customers are.

1.1.2 Corporate Foresight

The chaos at European airports in the winter of 2010, particularly London Heathrow, wrought by pummelling snowstorms and ice, not only was caused by cancelled flights and stranded passengers but also resulted in the tremendous cost involved for the airport authorities. Airports operator BAA has released the figure of 24 million pounds sterling ($38 million) as the cost incurred by the Spanish owned firm which operates six airports in Britain. These costs included reduction in profit as a result of the decrease in passenger numbers by 11 % over a few days.

The handling of the crisis by BAA drew large criticism by both legislators and airlines, the former considering the adoption of legislation against airports and the latter threatening to withhold charges due to the airports. Another issue is whether airports should be held responsible for service failure brought about by a natural phenomenon; and whether should airports have had, what in modern business parlance is called "corporate foresight" to deal with the natural phenomenon. This leads to a discussion on the kind of foresight an airport should have to deal with such situations as well as the obligations of a State to provide functional airport services in its territory.

Another question is, as regards corporate foresight, does an airport have to start with a culture of corporate foresight and adopt a dynamic and comprehensive

[27] Doganis (1992) at 119.

emergency management process. More importantly, should airports work jointly and in partnership with airlines and air navigation service providers in developing their corporate foresight.

The judicial focus in *Vumbaca* of corporate foresight attributed to the defendant terminal brings to bear the compelling need for airports to act with foresight when providing services to its users. It is a known fact that not many industries face the same challenges with regard to combining social responsibility and business as the airport industry. One of the challenges faced by airports is to cope with adverse weather conditions and ensure that the airport industry remains a safe place to work in. The success of an airport depends on a delicate balance between safety and punctuality and always remains a critical operational challenge for airports. Aviation and weather are strange and unwilling bedfellows and the former has never underestimated the latter and has treated it with respect.

Other hazards that might seriously affect those working on the airside are windstorms (which have, in certain instances lifted baggage containers off the ground) and ice and snow which pose a serious threat of injury to passengers climbing aircraft steps who could slip on accumulated black ice. Catastrophic events such as tsunamis[28] tropical cyclones, snow storms, floods and dust and sand storms are real threats to airports, requiring vigilance and responsibility of both the State concerned and the airport authorities. Early warning systems and emergency and contingency response plans have to be in place, which have to be implemented with precise communications. Aerodrome emergency planning is addressed in detail in Chapter 9 of Annex 14 to the Chicago Convention which provides that every aerodrome must have established an aerodrome emergency plan commensurate with aircraft operations and other activities conducted at an aerodrome.[29]

One of the most critical functions of airports is de-icing of aircraft, since if aircraft have ice on their wings they must be de-iced and protected with anti-icing fluids. An insignificantly small accumulation of ice on the upper structure of the wing could considerably reduce the lift of that surface and all ice must be removed before takeoff.[30] Airports providing ground handling services have to constantly

---

[28] It is noteworthy that, in response to a request received from the International Air Transport Association (IATA), the Secretariat of ICAO (ICAO) has included "tsunami" in the draft amendment to Annex 3 to the Convention on International Civil Aviation which addresses meteorological services, as a phenomenon which should prompt the issuance of an aerodrome warning. It may be expected that within the global warning system for tsunami being established under the Intergovernmental Oceanographic Commission of UNESCO (IOC), the meteorological authorities will receive tsunami warnings in a timely manner and that they will be in a position to implement the proposed amendment, as far as aerodrome warnings are concerned, in time for its applicability date. See AN-WP/8086, *Preliminary Review of a Proposed Amendment to Annex 3 and Consequential Amendment to the PANS-ABC.*

[29] Standard 9.1.1. Annex 14 to the Convention on International Civil Aviation (Aerodromes), Fourth Edition, July 2004, at pp. 9–1.

[30] Stuart and Isaac (1994), at 5. See also, Rusmussen et al. (1995–1996), pp. 24–26 at 24. See also Captain Wagner (1994–1995), pp. 21–25. Wagner (1995–1996), pp. 3–11.

monitor the de-icing process as the fluids applied to de-ice an aircraft are only effective in holding off re-icing for a limited time, after which ice could accumulate again, requiring de-icing. The period between de-icing and re-icing is called the holdover time and would be critical, particularly in the case of a departing aircraft delayed on takeoff.

There are also attendant problems for aircraft stemming from extreme cold temperatures. These could include fuel and hydraulic leaks; difficulty starting the Auxiliary Power Unit (APU); difficulty starting the engines; landing gear tire "cold set"; and difficulty in opening doors. To counter these problems, State regulation[31] and accurate weather forecasts[32] are now provided in many States through computer aided forecasting systems. These modern weather observation systems help the air navigation service provider to improve the quality of weather data and partly replace the human observer in the weather forecasting process.[33]

With regard to looking after passengers stranded at airports due to the cancellation of flights, the airport, as occupier of the premises (be it a lessee or lessor) could be *prima facie* liable on two counts: liability for inadequately maintained property which may cause an accident; and liability for an unsafe premises. Liability under negligent entrustment, be it that of the lessor or lessee, should usually be concurrent with an act of negligent on the part of the entrustee.[34] The fundamental principle under this head of liability is based on the line of argument that one who entrusts his property to another, knowing that such other is incompetent or having the duty to ascertain whether the entrustee is competent or not, is negligent and liable for injury.[35]

1.1.3 Airport Planning

The necessity for corporate foresight stems from the continuing and rapid development of science and technology which are the drivers of social and economic change. Using these two knowledge based and fact intensive fields, airports would

---

[31] Frank Carlson (1995), p. 9. The author discusses United States FAA regulations and certain regulations in the CIS States which apply standards for certification of aircraft to ensure they are equipped against extreme cold weather. See also generally, Woolley (1999), pp. 23–26; McKenna (1994), pp. 46–47; and Freedman (1994), pp. 53–78.

[32] Arpino (1994).

[33] Steinhorst and van Dijk (1994), pp. 12–14, at 13. Also, Dan Manningham (1996), pp. 60–62.

[34] See *Hood* v. *Dealers Transport Co.*, 459 F.Supp. 684. It is also noteworthy that one jurisdiction in the United States has followed the approach that the lack of a licence of competence *per se* does not give rise to liability if the absence of licence was not the proximate cause of the injury. See *Laughlin v Rose*, 200 Va. 127, 104 S.E. 2d 782 (1958) and *White v Edwards Chevrolet Co.* 186 Va. 669, 43 S.E. 2d 870 (1947).

[35] *Department of Water and Power of City of Los Angeles v Anderson* 95 F.2d 577. See also, *Cox v Dubois*, 16 F.Supp. 2d 861, *Brantley v Vaughn*, 835 F. Supp. 258.

be able to obtain a clear picture of challenges and opportunities confronting them. Airports are a complex, big business and their business environment is highly dynamic. Therefore they need proactive measures to respond to the uncertainties of their business as well as a long term orientation to remain stable amidst imponderables. Airports need think tanks to mesh their technology trends and market trends to meet a growing demand for air travel. Foremost in this process is a far reaching and forward looking communications strategy as well as a good team of scientific and economic forecasters.

The first step to corporate foresight is to know what the future is going to be like by adopting a foresight-awareness culture. If, as Airport Council International (ACI)[36] Director Angela Gittens said at the 20th World Annual General Meeting of ACI in Bermuda in October 2010, airports should transition from the public utility model to the entrepreneurial business model, the key would be customer service excellence. Research and innovation strategies should necessarily be developed through foresight activities. "Foresight" has been defined as:

> [a] participatory, future intelligence gathering and medium-to-long-term vision-building process that systematically attempts to look into the future of science, the economy and society in order to support present-day decision-making and to mobilise joint forces to realise them.[37]

Corporate foresight is a process of formulation and should not be confused with a set of techniques. Through a sustained consultative process, corporate foresight involves the examination of a series of future scenarios and ideally prescribes solutions. Foresight shares common ground with risk management and evaluation of risk,[38] and addresses the nature of the particular business and the uncertainties of the business environment. For example, in the airport industry, a grave uncertainty is the weather, as in the context of an unexpected winter storm or the eruption of a volcano which spews ash into the atmosphere. Both these events occurred in 2010 in Europe.

In every instance of a natural disaster the focus revolves around those who are affected by such events. Therefore, it is difficult not to discuss the merits and demerits of a strategy that would bring about the least damage based on a balance of probability. The process of foresight should commence with airport builders and managers who should look at airports as business enterprises that contribute to efficient air travel. The terminal is used to enable passengers and freight to connect

[36] Airports Council International is the only global trade representative of the world's airports. Established in 1991, ACI represents airports interests with Governments and international organizations such as ICAO, develops standards, policies and recommended practices for airports, and provides information and training opportunities to raise standards around the world.

[37] Becker (2002), at 7.

[38] Blaise Pascal, in his book *Ars Cogitandi* states that fear of harm ought to be proportional not merely to the gravity of the harm but also to the probability of the event. It is also a fact of risk management that, under similar conditions, the occurrence (or non-occurrence) of an event in the future will follow the same pattern as was observed in the past. For a discussion on risk assessment and risk management see Ferguson (2008) at 188 and Bobbitt (2008) at 98–179.

with aircraft for their transportation on departure and to connect with ground transportation on arrival. As such airport business planners must take into account elements that are not only exclusively related to the carrying on of a business, but also those principles that are essential for the safer, secure and efficient running of an airport. In this context airport planning becomes a necessary element to the airport business. An airport administration should take into account when planning for the injection of additional aircraft capacity in an airport the responses of the international community in the form of Standards and Recommended Practices as promulgated by ICAO, in order that international civil aviation retains a certain consistency and uniformity in its global activity. For instance, ICAO has in use an Airport Planning Manual[39] in two parts setting out in detail, all aspects of airport planning. ICAO has in this document developed a master planning process which involves plans, programmes and stringent policy that go to make a viable airport. The document serves as a basis for providing for the orderly and timely development of an airport adequate to meet the present and future air transportation needs of an area or State.[40] The manual starts from the fact that early aviation history recognized the need for some public control of land in the vicinity of an airport[41] and bifurcates this need to reflect airport needs i.e. obstacle limitation areas and future airport development etc. and the need to ensure 60 minimal interference with the environment and the public.[42] By this dual approach ICAO has introduced a whole new area of thought into airport development. What was once a concern to merely provide easy facilities for the fluid movement of air traffic has now become in addition an ecological concern. By this process, airport development now falls into three main areas which are:

a) the development of airport capacity and facilities;
b) the balancing of airport development with necessary security measures; and,
c) the balancing of airport development with ecology i.e. city planning, noise pollution avoidance etc.

The ICAO Airport Planning Manual ensures a balance between airport development and ecological considerations.

Cooperation in technical and economic areas would have to be further expanded to include safety and ecological factors in the technical field and all economic research in city planning and infrastructural development in the economic field. These studies would have to be done in the form of committed and in depth country studies by individual States taking into consideration futuristic studies of a country's outlook and the financial outlay that the country would be prepared to make for an airport expansion programme. The outcome of these studies could then form legislation for the planning of airports in a State. Such legislation would

[39] *Airport Planning Manual*, Doc. 9184-AN/902, Parts 1 and 2.

[40] *Id.* Part 1, 2.9.1 (a).

[41] Doc. 9184-AN 902 Part 2, 1.3.1.

[42] *Id.* 1.3.2.

present, for the first time, a cohesive and enforceable set of laws in that State that would meet the airport congestion problem.

Although the concept of airport planning laws can be summed up easily as above, the three broad areas of ecology, safety and infrastructural planning need a sustained approach of study before such are incorporated into laws. For a start, ICAO's *Airport Planning Manual* is geared to provide information and guidance to those responsible for airport planning,[43] where information on a comprehensive list of planning subjects such as sizes and types of projects[44] task identification,[45] preparation of manpower and cost budgets,[46] selection of consultants[47] and standard contract provisions[48] are given. With these guidelines each State can start its planning process.

1.1.4 Link with Air Transport

The airline and airport business are interlinked and inter-connected and, since air transport is a growth industry, so is the airport industry. According to the global market forecast of Airbus Industrie forecasts that from 2009 to 2028, some 25,000 new passenger and freighter aircraft valued at US$3.1 trillion will be delivered.[49] This rapidly evolving demand is driven by emerging economies, evolving airline networks, expansion of low cost carriers and the increasing number of mega-cities as well as traffic growth and the replacement of older less efficient aircraft with more eco-efficient airliners. These are factors driving demand for new aircraft.

The forecast also attributes the demand for larger aircraft to the compelling need to ease aircraft congestion and to accommodate growth on existing routes and to achieve more with less. Needless to say, this exponential growth in air traffic[50] will

[43] Airport Planning Manual, Doc 9184-AN/902, Part 3.

[44] *Id.* 1.3.1–1.3.5.

[45] *Id.* Chapter 2.2.1.

[46] *Id.* 2.4.

[47] *Id.* 3.1.

[48] *Id.* Appendix.

[49] http://www.airbus.com/en/gmf2009/appli.htm?onglet=&page=. The forecast anticipates that in the next 20 years, passenger traffic RPK's will remain resilient to the cyclical effects of the sector and increase by 4.7 % per year or double in the next 15 years. This will require a demand for almost 24,100 new passenger aircraft valued at US$2.9 trillion. With the replacement of some 10,000 older passenger aircraft, the world's passenger aircraft fleet of 100 seats or more will double from some 14,000 in 2009.

[50] *Id.* The forecast states that the greatest demand for passenger aircraft will be from airlines in Asia-Pacific and emerging markets. The region that includes the People's Republic of China and India accounts for 31 % of the total, followed by Europe (25 %) and North America (23 %). In terms of domestic passenger markets, India (10 %) and China (7.9 %) will have the fastest growth over the next 20 years. The largest by volume of traffic, will remain domestic US.

place a burden on airport capacity and consequent demands upon the airport industry.

Therefore, in a manner of speaking, the future of airports is linked with the future of airlines. Naval Taneja, academic and industry strategist is of the view that the airline business model will change in the future and game changing strategies will have to be in place in the air transport industry. Taneja ascribes to unconventional thinking and innovative technology the foremost place and states that these two that will bring about change management. One example he gives is the enhancement by airlines of the customer experience on their websites by offering a virtual assistant to answer questions and direct travellers to the information that they are seeking.[51] Another expert is of the view that airports will invariably follow suit by preparing for similar technological innovations such as the maximizing the use of the internet, and the provision and availability of information on passengers' connecting flights, airport maps, information on their destinations and other phone or PDA applications which will all be built into their eyeglasses.[52]

Corporate foresight hinges on the early identification of markets and technologies. However, it takes a long time to restructure a corresponding system along the lines of market forecasts and the development of technology. Building competence to a level that would correspond to effective risk management. One commentator identifies a period of 10 years as preparatory for effective corporative foresight to be built.[53] A salient feature in foresight is leadership, which is linked inextricably to the quality of not being surprised at any unexpected event or circumstance. Essential to this process is the prompt identification of developments in the areas of science, technology and society that are likely to ensure future benefits both from a business and social perspective. Foresight has been categorized as (a) *anticipatory intelligence*, *i.e.* providing background information and an early warning of recent developments; (b) *direction-setting*, *i.e.* establishing broad guidelines for the corporate strategy; (c) *determining priorities*, *i.e.* identifying the most desirable lines of R&D as a direct input into specific (funding) decisions; (d) *strategy formulation*, *i.e.* participating in the formulation and implementation of strategic decisions; and (e) *innovation catalysing*, *i.e.* stimulating and supporting innovation processes between the different partners.

From an airport perspective, *anticipatory intelligence* should be extended to the various disaster scenarios that could be: (a) inability to accommodate flights due to frozen runways; (b) straining of infrastructure in accommodating a passenger influx greater than the airport could handle at any given time; (c) a possible security threat that would slow down traffic and clog the system; and (d) adverse weather systems (such as storms) that could halt ground handling systems. In this context, most

---

[51] See Naval Taneja, Technology enabled game changing models, http://www.airlineleader.com/_webapp_1098704/Technology-enabled_game-changing_airline_business_models.

[52] Michael Rogers' Commentary on the 20th ACI World Annual General Assembly at http://www.airtransportnews.aero/analysis.pl?acateg+reports.

[53] Patrick Becker, *Corporate Foresight in Europe*: A First Overview, *supra* note 37 at 8.

problems that an airport could face are weather related. In *direction setting* the airport management should have a corporate strategy that would also be an adequate contingency plan. Such a plan should include adequate staff training for contingencies; providing back-up support staff who have pre-organized schedules for exigencies and adequately compensating staff who have to cope with a stressful situation and irate customers. The most important factor in such situations is an effective method of communicating with everyone and providing extra services. A major factor in *determining priorities*, is the assurance at all times, whether good or bad, of an effective and efficient safety and security system at the airport. *Strategy formulation* would include developing a range of alternative routes and timings and alternative means of transport; having adequate and additional accommodation ready to make customers comfortable; having joint plans with airlines for the provision of meals through ground handlers or other caterers at the airport; and ensuring that constant contact be maintained with the Consulates involved, and the local police.

Innovation catalyzing is arguably the most creative element of corporate foresight. Here, the starting point is to look at existing planning documentation. ICAO's *Airport Planning Manual* is geared to provide information and guidance to those responsible for airport planning,[54] where information on a comprehensive list of planning subjects such as sizes and types of projects[55] task identification,[56] preparation of manpower and cost budgets,[57] selection of consultants[58] and standard contract provisions[59] are given. With these guidelines each State can start its planning process. Regrettably, a study conducted on corporate foresight reflects that the transportation sector does not consider innovations as important in corporate foresight.[60] It is all the more reason that, as further action, corporate foresight in the airport industry needs an un-fragmented process of corporate development and strategic planning. An initiative could be taken by ACI to gather a team of forecasters, technical experts and airport planners to develop guidelines for disaster management.

The above discussion focuses on the incontrovertible fact that there are two aspects to the issue of preparedness for natural disasters by airports. The first is airport responsibility and the second is the need for corporate foresight. As for airport responsibility, in addition to the overall responsibility of the State for the provision of airport services in Article 28 of the Chicago Convention, Annex 14 to the Chicago Convention, pertaining to aerodromes and their operations also contains requirements which devolve responsibility on States to provide weather

[54] *Airport Planning Manual*, Doc 9184-AN/902, Part 3.

[55] *Id.* 1.3.1–1.3.5.

[56] *Id.* Chapter 2.2.1.

[57] *Id.* 2.4.

[58] *Id.* 3.1.

[59] *Id.* Appendix.

[60] *Supra* note 37 at p. 22.

information and take necessary steps. For example, there is an umbrella provision requiring States to provide information on the condition of the movement area and the operational status of related facilities to enable units to provide services to arriving and departing aircraft.[61] Recommendation 2.9.9. of the Annex suggests that whenever a runway is affected by snow, slush or ice and it has not been possible to clear the precipitant fully, the runway should be assessed and the friction coefficient measured. The follow up provision appears in Standard 10.2.8 which requires that the surface of a runway shall be maintained in such a condition so as to provide good friction characteristics and low rolling resistance. Snow, slush, ice, standing water, mud, dust, sand, oil, rubber deposits and other contaminants are required to be removed as rapidly and completely as possible to minimize accumulation. There is also a recommendation in the Annex that a taxiway should be kept clear of snow, slush, ice etc. to the extent necessary to enable the aircraft to be taxied to and from an operational runway.[62] The order of priority for clearance of products of adverse weather, as prescribed by the Annex is: runways in use; taxiways serving runways in use; aprons; holding bays; and other areas.[63]

This notwithstanding, airports also have a responsibility to persons adversely affected by cancellation of flights. Irrespective of the responsibility of a State with regard to airports within its territories, which is founded both at customary international law and at private law for liability incurred by airports, a privately run airport may incur tortuous liability on a private basis, as the occupier of the premises. In the instance of a privately managed airport where the entity charged with managing airport services is located within the airport premises, such an entity would be considered as a legal occupier for purposes of liability.[64]

However, airports remain entitled to levy charges for services rendered irrespective of any inconvenience caused to airlines as a result of a snowstorm or other natural phenomenon which compels an airport to take measures with regard to flights coming in and going out of that airport. Airport charges are based on cost recovery for services provided and States are responsible for policy pertaining to such charges. The fundamental postulate of ICAO's policies on airport charges lies in Article 15 of the Chicago Convention which states that every airport in a contracting State which is open to public use by its national aircraft shall likewise, subject to the provisions of Article 68,[65] be open under uniform conditions to the aircraft of all the other contracting States. The provision goes on to say that like uniform conditions shall apply to the use, by aircraft of every contracting State, of

[61] Standard 2.9.1, Annex 14 to the Convention on International Civil Aviation, Aerodromes, Volume 1 Fourth Edition: July 2004 at 2–4.

[62] Recommendation 10.2.9.

[63] Recommendation 10.2.11.

[64] For a discussion on this subject, See Abeyratne, *Airport Business Law*, *Infra* note 122, at pp. 106–108

[65] Article 68 provides that Each contracting State may, subject to the provisions of this Convention, designate the route to be followed within its territory by any international air service and the airports which any such service may use.

all air navigation facilities, including radio and meteorological services, which may be provided for public use for the safety and expedition of air navigation. Any charges that may be imposed or permitted to be imposed by a contracting State for the use of such airports and air navigation facilities by the aircraft of any other contracting State shall not be higher: as to aircraft not engaged in scheduled international air services, than those that would be paid by its national aircraft of the same class engaged in similar operations, and; as to aircraft engaged in scheduled international air services, than those that would be paid by its national aircraft engaged in similar international air services.

Article 15 sets out the following three basic principles:

- uniform conditions shall apply to the use of airports and air navigation services in a Contracting State by aircraft of all other Contracting States;
- the charges imposed by a Contracting State for the use of such airports or air navigation services shall not be higher for aircraft of other Contracting States than those paid by its national aircraft engaged in similar international operations; and
- no charge shall be imposed by any Contracting State solely for the right of transit over or entry into or exit from its territory of any aircraft of a Contracting State or persons or property thereon.

Specific regulatory provisions applicable to charges levied by airports have their genesis in ICAO and are contained in Doc 9082.[66] Some fundamental principles relating to these charges have particular relevance in the context of the cost basis for airport charges and charging systems are that:

- airports should maintain accounts that provide a satisfactory basis for determining and allocating the costs to be recovered, and should provide adequate financial information to the users
- the proportion of costs allocable to the various categories of airport users should be determined on an equitable basis, so that no users shall be burdened with costs not properly allocable to them according to sound accounting principles;
- airports may produce sufficient revenues to exceed all direct and indirect operating costs and so provide for a reasonable return on assets at a sufficient level to secure efficient financing in capital markets for the purpose of investing in new or expanded airport infrastructure and, where relevant, to remunerate adequately holders of airport equity;
- any charging system should, so far as possible, be simple and suitable for general application at international airports;
- charges should not be imposed in such a way as to discourage the use of facilities and services necessary for safety, such as lighting and navigation aids;
- consistent with the form of economic oversight adopted, States should assess, on a case-by-case basis and according to local or national circumstances, the

[66] *ICAO's Policies on Charges for Airports and Air Navigation Services* Doc 9082/8 Eighth Edition-2009.

positive and negative effects of differential charges applied by airports. States should ensure that the purpose, creation and criteria for differential charges are transparent. Without prejudice to modulated charging schemes, the costs associated with such differential charges should not be allocated to users not benefiting from them. Charges offered for the purpose of attracting or retaining new air services should be offered on a temporary basis only;

- to avoid undue disruption to users, increases in charges should be introduced on a gradual basis; however, it is recognized that in some circumstances a departure from this approach may be necessary and;
- airport charges levied on international general aviation, including business aviation, should be assessed in a reasonable manner, having regard to the cost of the facilities needed and used and the goal of promoting the sound development of international civil aviation as a whole

According to ICAO's policies concerning security charges any charges or transfers of security costs should be directly related to the costs of providing the security services concerned and should be designed to recover no more than the relevant costs involved.

As regards corporate foresight, an airport has to start with a culture of corporate foresight. Emergency management is a dynamic process. Planning, though critical, is not the only component. Training, conducting drills, testing equipment and coordinating activities with the community are other important functions. More importantly, airports should work jointly, and in partnership with airlines and air navigation service providers in furthering their corporate foresight.

1.1.5 Airports and Facilitation

At the 38th Session of the ICAO Assembly, a separate Resolution A38-16 on facilitation of air transport was adopted by the Assembly. Regrettably, there was only one mention in the Resolution (in passing) on airports which urged Member States, aircraft operators and airport operators to continue to cooperate intensively as regards: (a) identification and solution of facilitation problems; and (b) developing cooperative arrangements for the prevention of illicit narcotics trafficking, illegal immigration and other threats to national interests. However, Annex 9 to the Chicago Convention compensates for this lapse. There is a separate chapter—Chap. 6—dedicated to airports. This chapter contains several provisions in the Annex including Recommended Practice 6 which provides that each Contracting State should, in consultation with airport operators, ensure that the design, development and maintenance of facilities at international airports provide efficient and effective flow arrangements. Further provisions in the Annex seek to ensure that airport and aircraft operators provide for the expeditious processing of passengers, crew, baggage, cargo and mail.

The Annex also calls for efficient customs, immigration, quarantine and health border clearance services to be provided at international airports. Contracting States are also required to ensure, in consultation with airport operators, that facilities and services provided at international airports are, where possible, flexible and capable of expansion to meet traffic growth, an increase in security requirements arising from increased threat, or other changes to support border integrity measures.

The Annex in Standard 6.2 calls for consultation and consensus in airport planning when it requires each Contracting State to ensure that, in the planning of new facilities or major modifications to existing facilities, including cargo facilities, at international airports, the entity or entities responsible for such planning consult with public authorities, aircraft operators and appropriate bodies representing airport users, at the earliest stages of planning. There is also Recommended Practice 6.3 which suggests that Aircraft operators should inform airport operators and relevant government agencies, in commercial confidence, of their service, schedule and fleet plans at the airport, to enable rational planning of facilities and services in relation to the traffic anticipated. If the airport operator is constrained for space the Annex gives the flexibility to the airport operator to choose how, and by whom, their ground handling operations should be carried out.

Further impetus to consultation can be seen in Recommended Practices 6.3 and 6.4 which provide that airport operators, aircraft operators and public authorities should exchange, in a timely manner, all relevant operational information, in order to provide for a smooth and expeditious passenger flow and efficient resource allocation and that Contracting States, airport and aircraft operators, where appropriate and after consultation, should implement automated facilities for passenger and baggage processing.

The Annex also has a provision addressing the issue of the provision of accurate flight information at the airport. Recommended Practice 6.11 provides that each Contracting State should ensure that an airport or aircraft operator, as appropriate, installs flight information systems capable of providing up-to-the-minute information on departures, arrivals, cancellations, delays, and terminal/gate allocations. According to this provision, the onus of providing information to the passenger of his flight vests with the airport. This issue deserves more discussion, particularly since the distinction between the responsibilities and duties of the air carrier and the airport are blurred in this context. If the *Vumbaca* principle of agency were to apply, the provision of Annex 9 may have to be interpreted in favour of the airline.

1.1.6 Flight Information Displays at the Airport

The Flight Information Display System (FIDS) is an integral component of airport information management and passenger service. FIDS[67] provides automated

[67] FIDS communicates and supports most any type of display device such as CRT monitors, LCD flat panels, plasma displays, split flap boards and LED signage.

control in the distribution and display of critical information to the travelling public, airport tenants, and airport operational staff. FIDS has evolved over the years from the display of airline departure information through rapid board changes to a dynamic digitalized format to facilitate the changing operational environment. This migration has catered to the increasing traffic by providing an efficient information exchange to the many users of the airport, whilst at the same time effectively coordinating directional signage at the terminals, check-in desks, gates, and baggage carousels. Additionally FIDS has introduced an efficient visual paging system for the hearing impaired, while also supporting the display of weather information, promotional and advertising information.

While FIDS is mainly of importance to the departing passenger, the Baggage Information Data System (BIDS) is of importance to the passenger arriving at an airport. BIDS advises the passenger as to what carousel his baggage would arrive at. Airports generate additional revenue from both FIDS and BIDS by selling space to advertisers in their systems.[68]

Modern FIDS is a key systemic component[69] that is connected to the operational database and resource management of the airport's integrated operational systems. FIDS has a direct link to the airport, providing an automated display of necessary information mainly to departing passengers. FIDS is composed of a control centre which drives distribution servers and input terminals through the most sophisticated display technology. The control centre acts as the repository for storing, processing and transferring all data (flight and general information) and conveys information through a local area network (LAN) to distribution servers. Information in FIDS is updated to the minute so that users are ensured of accurate information that is provided with regularity and consistency.

The following discussion addresses and analyzes principles of airport accountability for management of flight information, will address FIDS as the reference point since principles of management and accountability addressed herein would apply to both FIDS and BIDS.

1.1.7 Regulatory Aspects of FIDS

It is the right of a passenger to expect accurate and up to date flight information that would enable him to board his flight on time. There is no formal and internationally recognized definition as to what a passenger right is. However, ICAO recognizes that:

> The term passenger right has been used to generally refer to the entitlements of passengers to protection from or compensation for certain actions by airlines and/or airports that are

[68] Carey (2010).

[69] FIDS can also be accessed through the internet. For example see the FIDS at Hong Kong International airport at http://www.hongkongairport.com/flightinfo/eng/chkfltdep.html.

adverse to their interests, which are specified in government regulations or in the airline's contract of carriage and or other published commitments.[70]

Annex 9 (Facilitation) to the Chicago Convention recommends that each Member State of ICAO, in consultation with airport operators, ensure that the design, development and maintenance of facilities at international airports provide efficient and effective flow arrangements.[71] The Annex also exhorts ICAO member States to ensure that an airport operator or aircraft operator, as appropriate, installs flight information systems capable of providing accurate, adequate and up-to-the-minute information on departures, arrivals, cancellations, delays, and terminal/gate allocations[72] and consistently maintains a flight information system and follows the standard layout recommended in Doc 9249, *Dynamic Flight-Related Public Information Displays*.[73]

Both the Recommended Practices encourage the greater use of flight-related public information display systems in order to provide up-to-the-minute information on departures, arrivals, cancellations, delays and terminal/gate allocations and also to assist in maintaining smooth passenger flow patterns through airport terminal buildings. The airport operator has the dual flexibility of freedom to choose the most suitable display and freedom to choose what form of information to display.

Doc 9249 prescribes that the time indication on any public display should always be the local time and that each flight should be indicated by its two letter airline code in conjunction with the flight number. In order to save space in the TIME column, there should be no spaces, dots or commas separating the hours and minutes and all four digits are presented in the same size. Although the heading Departures would be sufficient, in the absence of any general headings, the terms *Flight Departures* should be used. Doc 9249 also provides that, since people are used to reading from left to right in a large majority of countries throughout the world, logic demands that three identifying items be placed on the left, with the gate information and remarks on the right.

It is recommended that there be five columns in the FDIS: TIME; TO; FLIGHT; GATES; REMARKS. In the TIME column, the scheduled time of departure should always be indicated. If there is any deviation from the scheduled departure time, this should be included in the REMARKS column. The TO column may be waived in situations where the cost of displaying all the points is excessive. The REMARKS column is normally needed on both the Departure and the Arrival Display. The following standard remarks should be used and kept to minimum, such as: Boarding; Check in at Gate; Wait here; Delayed; New Time (followed by four-figure time group); New Gate; Cancelled; Not Operating; Ask Agent; Diverted; Landed; Non-stop; Charter; Extra Flight.

---

[70] *Manual on the Regulation of International Air Transport*, ICAO Doc 9626, Second Edition: 2004, at 4.9-1.

[71] Annex 9 to the Chicago Convention, Recommended Practice 6.1.1.

[72] Annex 9 to the Chicago Convention, Recommended Practice 6.11.

[73] Annex 9 to the Chicago Convention, Recommended Practice 6.12.

With regard to the location of FDIS at airports, Doc 9249 recommends that the following points should be observed as a general rule when providing public information displays in airport buildings. They should be placed: (a) so that they can be simultaneously observed and read by the largest number of viewers for which that display was designed; (b) at such locations where passengers have to make a decision as to the direction in which to proceed; (c) at such height that they are never hidden by circulating people; (d) away from other signs and from advertisements; (e) away from highlighted backgrounds unless there is a continuous strong front lighting; (f) away from points where they may create congestion or restrict circulation of people; and (g) at places where it is relatively simple to carry out any maintenance and repair.

Another ICAO Document—*Airport Planning Manual*[74] recommends that FDIS should be considered at the same time as the check-in concourse and waiting areas are being planned. They should be located so that flight information is visible from all principal parts of these areas, and also to ensure that they do not create visual obstruction or cause passengers to obstruct the primary flow routes.[75]

1.1.8 Legal Aspects of FIDS

The airport operator who provides flight information on an FDIS would have to ensure that accurate information is provided to the passenger so that he could embark on his flight through the appropriate gate and at the time indicated in the display. A misstatement, particularly if negligently made, that misdirects the passenger leading to his missing his flight would entail legal liability for the airport operator. An airport is prima facie a business and a misstatement to a client (passenger) which would be relied upon by that client and which would cause him some damage or injury would be actionable at law. The British House of Lords in the 1963 case of *Hedley Byrne* v. *Heller & Co.*[76] first recognized the possibility of liability for pure economic loss, not dependent on any contractual relationship, for negligent statements. The basis of this liability was variously held to be an "assumption of responsibility" to the claimant, a "special relationship" between the parties, or a relationship "equivalent to contract". The facts of the case were that the bankers for Hedley Byrne (an advertising partnership) telephoned the bank of Heller & Partners Ltd. inquiring about the financial state and credit record of one of Heller's client companies, *Easipower Ltd.* Hedley Byrne was about to undertake some significant advertising contracts for them, and wanted to be sure of their financial security. Heller vouched for their client's record but qualified it by waiving responsibility, stating that the information was: "for your private use and

[74] Airport Planning Manual, Doc 9184-AN/902 Part 1, Master Planning, Second Edition, 1987.

[75] *Id.* at Section 9.4.25 at pp. 1–92.

[76] [1964] A.C. 465.

without responsibility on the part of the bank and its officials." Hedley Byrne relied on this information and entered into a contract with *Easipower* which went bankrupt soon afterwards. Unable to obtain their debt from the bankrupt, Hedley Byrne sued Heller for negligence, claiming that the information was given negligently and was misleading.

The court found that the relationship between the parties was "sufficiently proximate" as to create a duty of care. It was reasonable for them to have known that the information that they had given would likely have been relied upon for entering into a contract of some sort. This would give rise, the court said, to a "special relationship", in which the defendant would have to take sufficient care in giving advice to avoid negligence liability. However, on the facts, the disclaimer was found to be sufficient to discharge any duty created by Heller's actions.

In *White* v. *Jones*,[77] a solicitor was told to draw up a new will, splitting the testator's estate between the two plaintiffs, his daughters. He negligently failed to do this by the time of the testator's death, and the estate passed in accordance with the testator's wishes expressed in a previous will. The daughters sued the solicitor in negligence. It was held that the solicitor had assumed a special relationship towards them, creating a duty of care which he had carried out negligently, and therefore had to indemnify them for their loss. Once again this extended Hedley Byrne liability to a proximate third party.

The *White* case brought to bear an interesting fact that, even if a professional cannot foresee the possible future appearance of an intended beneficiary or plaintiff who could suffer damage by that professional's act, that person who suffered injury or damage must have some form of redress. Lord Goff of Chieveley stated:

> Certainly, again in the absence of special circumstances, there will have been no reliance by the intended beneficiary on the exercise by the solicitor of due care and skill; indeed, the intended beneficiary may not even have been aware that the solicitor was engaged on such a task, or that his position might be affected...
>
> The Hedley Byrne principle cannot, in the absence of special circumstances, give rise on ordinary principles to an assumption of responsibility by the testator's solicitor towards an intended beneficiary. Even so, if seems to me that it is open to your Lordships' House...to fashion a remedy...and so prevent the injustice which would otherwise occur on the facts of cases such as the present ...
>
> ... In my opinion, therefore, your Lordships' House should in cases such as these extend to the intended beneficiary a remedy under the Hedley Byrne principle by holding that the assumption of responsibility by the solicitor towards his client should be held in law to extend to the intended beneficiary who (as the solicitor can reasonably foresee) may, as a result of the solicitor's negligence, be deprived of his intended legacy in circumstances in which neither the testator nor his estate will have a remedy against the solicitor.[78]

---

[77] [1995] 1 AER 691.

[78] *Id.* 671.

In Canada and in many others jurisdictions, a distinction is drawn between commercial services and professional services. Professionals such as architects, accountants and lawyers have traditionally claimed special status and freedom from State control on the argument that professional firms primarily offer a service to the community and that they are not merely profit making enterprises. These professions, it is argued, are bound by strong professional ethics that seemingly bind members of such professions to stringent ethical conduct, the breach of which would result in inquiry by disciplinary committees and other governing bodies. By the same token, a higher standard of care is expected of surgeons, physician's who provide diagnoses of illnesses, pilots, lawyers and accountants to name but a few categories representing professions of expertise. It is arguable that an airport operator, who is expected to provide information that the user of the airport would depend on, would fall into the same category.

British Airports Authority (BAA) Airports Limited has the following disclaimer in its flight information web page:

> BAA Airports Limited does not verify the accuracy or completeness of this flight information and disclaims any implied warranties with regard to it. BAA Airports Limited shall have no liability for any loss or damage suffered as a result of relying on flight information on this site which may prove to be inaccurate or incomplete[79]

As a general rule, such a disclaimer of responsibility for the accuracy of information will preclude the person relying on such information from suing the airport on the ground that the establishment of a duty of care of the airport towards the passenger has not been established. The legal principle is that it is not normally foreseeable that a reasonable person would place complete reliance on information that is subject to a disclaimer. However, in exceptional circumstances, a disclaimer will not effectively remove responsibility nor preclude liability. There are two reasons for this: first, if there had been insufficient notice of such disclaimer or notice of such disclaimer, particularly in the instance of a passenger who has already checked in and is dependent on the FDIS at the airport; and second, and more compellingly, common law courts usually construe such disclaimers stringently against the defendant.[80]

The decision rendered by the British Columbia Court of Appeal in Canada in 2001 in the case of *Micron Construction Ltd.* V. *Hong Kong Bank of Canada*,[81] unlike the *Hedley Byrne* case (where the court held that a disclaimer was sufficient for the defendant to avoid liability), held that although Hong Kong Bank had issued a disclaimer to its client (the plaintiff), the bank was aware that the plaintiff would pass on the information provided by the bank to its sub-clients and the reliance of the plaintiff on the information provided by the bank was justifiable. Furthermore,

---

[79] http://www.baa.com/portal/page/BAA+Airports%5EMisc%5EHelp%5EFlight+information +help/8365e288d7639210VgnVCM10000036821c0a____/ 448c6a4c7f1b0010VgnVCM200000357e120a____/.

[80] See *Queen* v. *Cognos Inc.*, [1993] 1. S.C.R. 87.

[81] (2001) 184 D.L.R. (4 Th) 75 (B.C.C.A.).

the criteria of "special relationship" and the assumption of responsibility recognized by the courts in the *Hedley Byrne* case were not considered as a point of emphasis in the 1997 decision by the Canadian Supreme Court in the case of *Hercules Management Ltd.* v. *Ernst & Young*[82] where the court emphasized the importance of the concept of foreseeable and reasonable reliance by the plaintiff. Based on these principles, it is arguable that the disclaimer of BAA Airports Limited would be regarded by the courts as ineffectual and destitute of legal effect as it would be counter-intuitive for an airport to provide information that it does not verify or check, particularly when that information is critical to the passenger and his interests.

If one were to argue that there is no contract between the passenger and the airport and therefore there is no nexus between the two, it has to be made clear that liability in this instance is solely under tort law. Accordingly the above discussion could be subsumed by two fundamental judicial pronouncements: The case of *McAlister* (*Donoughue*) v. *Stevenson*[83] established three fundamental premises in tort liability. They were: that a person was liable for an unintentional act if he owed a duty of care to another; there was a breach of that duty; and the act or omission in question caused damage to the person to whom that duty of care was owed. The case also destroyed the myth that contractual duty and tort liability are mutually exclusive and could not apply together. The *Hedley Byrne*[84] decision handed down by the House of Lords exploded the misconception that all damage must be of a pecuniary nature. It also established the fundamental postulate that there would be negligence on the part of a person who, when in a special relationship with another (such as a relationship between airport and passenger) made a representation which was untrue, inaccurate or misleading on which the other relied, and such reliance was detrimental to his interests.

As discussed, the liability of the airport, within the parameters of this article is based on principles of tort law pertaining to negligent misstatements. It must be mentioned that the popular misconception that an error or deficit of judgment does not amount to negligence is no longer accepted by courts. The House of Lords in the 1988 case of *Whitehouse* v. *Jordan*[85] rejected the idea that mere errors of judgments cannot amount to negligence. Lord Fraser observed:

> Merely to describe something as an error of judgment tells us nothing about whether it is negligent or not. The true position is that an error of judgment may, or may not, be negligent; it depends on the nature of the error. If it is one that would not have been made by a reasonable competent professional man professing to have the standard and type of skill that the defendant held himself out as having, and acting with ordinary care, then it is negligent.[86]

---

[82] [1997] 2 S.C.R. 165.

[83] [1932] A.C. 562. See also Fleming (1977), p. 176.

[84] *Supra* note 76.

[85] [1981] 1 All E.R. 267.

[86] *Id.* at 276.

Managers of airports have to bear in mind that principles of executive liability are now veering towards imposition of liability on a strict principle of implied or extended responsibility that would preclude denial of responsibility merely on the basis that the airport was just a conduit in conveying flight information to the passenger as provided by the airline. The FIDS is a service provided by the airport inasmuch as the serving of food and beverages on board an aircraft is a service provided by the airline, even though the goods are provided by an outside caterer. In a case of food poisoning on board, the airline cannot hide itself behind a disclaimer. Neither should an airport be allowed to invoke a disclaimer as a defense where it conveys incorrect information to the passenger through its FIDS, unless there are compelling reasons.

1.2 Airports and Aviation System Block Upgrades

The ICAO Assembly, at its 38th Session in 2013, adopted a consolidated statement of policies in the air transport field which requests the ICAO Council *inter alia* to develop guidance on funding of air transport infrastructure, appropriate oversight functions and financing of the air transport system, including mechanisms to support operational improvements as described in the aviation system block upgrade modules (ASBUs).

At its 12th Air Navigation Conference (AN-Conf/12) held in Montréal, from 19 to 30 November 2012, ICAO introduced its Global Air Navigation Capacity and Efficiency Plan (GANP) for the period 2013–2028. The Plan is meant to be approved by the ICAO Assembly at its sessions every 3 years. This is the fourth such Plan adopted by ICAO over the years and is based on operational objectives agreed upon by States and the aviation industry. It provides for a rolling15 year strategic methodology and introduces Aviation System Block Upgrades (ASBUs), each of which has a 5 year time scale. The ASBUs are not overarching, nor are they an umbrella system but remain flexible modules that can be used by States in accordance with their individual operational needs. One of the salient characteristics of ASBUs is that they define technologies and procedures that are calculated to improve operational performance, particularly when the need arises for an operational problem to be solved. The ultimate aim is to achieve global harmonization and interoperability of air navigation.

ASBUs are based on flexibility and collaboration and as such are not mandatory requirements imposed on States. The precursor to AN-Conf/12 was the Global Air Navigation Industry Symposium (GANIS) held in Montreal from 20 to 23 September 2011 in preparation for the 12th Air Navigation Conference. The purpose of the Symposium, entitled "Towards One Sky", was to provide a platform for global and regional industry partners to share their latest developments, discuss emerging issues and to chart the next steps to achieve a seamless global air navigation system. It gathered industry and stakeholders from all over the world and served as a unique opportunity to reinforce the importance of global interoperability in air traffic management. GANIS responded to a request of the 37th Session of ICAO Assembly held in 2010 that the Organization double its efforts for meeting the global needs for airspace interoperability while sustaining its focus on safety.[87] GANIS therefore was the initial forum that discussed ASBUs as having the essential characteristics of: a clearly-defined measurable operational improvement and success metric; necessary equipment and/or systems in aircraft and on ground along with an operational approval or certification plan; standards and procedures for both airborne and ground systems; and a positive business case over a clearly defined period of time.

GANIS was based on ICAO's vision of air traffic management,[88] which is to achieve an interoperable global air traffic management system, for all users during all phases of flight that meets agreed levels of safety, provides for optimum economic operations, is environmentally sustainable and meets national security requirements.[89] Another influencing factor at the Symposium was ICAO's Performance Based Navigation (PBN)[90] system which provides for more direct and precise flight paths, increased safety, reduced fuel burn, more efficient traffic flows and reduced ATC communications. This includes the implementation of area navigation (RNAV) and required navigation performance (RNP) in accordance with the PBN concept, integration of the ICAO Global Air Navigation Plan in performance-based transition planning, collaboration on establishing performance indicators, use of ICAO-defined key performance areas for performance management, and application of the ICAO Global Aviation Safety Plan (GASP) as a basis for meeting safety performance objectives.

GANIS provided an opportunity for participants to share information on latest developments and best practices, identify commonalities and differences among existing or planned systems, discuss emerging issues and chart out the next steps to achieve a seamless and interoperable global air navigation system. Feedback from participants helped refine the "block upgrades" concept, which ICAO incorporated into fourth Global Air Navigation Plan that was presented to and adopted by Member States at AN-Conf/12.

---

[87] Air transport plays a major role in driving sustainable economic and social development worldwide. It directly and indirectly supports the employment of almost 60 million people today, while contributing over $2 trillion to global gross domestic product (GDP) and carrying over 2.5 billion passengers and $5.3 trillion worth of cargo annually.

[88] Air traffic management is the dynamic, integrated management of air traffic and airspace—safely, economically and efficiently—through the provision of facilities and seamless services in collaboration with all parties. See Doc 9854 *infra* note 89, *ibid.*

[89] *Global Air Traffic Management Operational Concept*, Doc 9854, AN/458, First Edition—2005, Chapter 1 at 1-1.

[90] Performance-Based Navigation (PBN) is a framework for defining navigation performance specifications for an aircraft along a route, during a procedure, or in airspace. These navigation performance specifications have been defined and have specific operational performance requirements. PBN provides a simple basis for the design and implementation of automated flight paths, as well as for airspace design, aircraft separation, and obstacle clearance. PBN comprises both Area Navigation (RNAV) and Required Navigation Performance (RNP).

1.2.1 GANP

GANP is defined by ICAO's Global Air Navigation Policy which establishes a framework for standardization, implementation, and monitoring and performance management of the air navigation system. GANP offers a transparent strategic process that would manage future air traffic growth in a safe and efficient manner and be annually monitored both by ICAO and other aviation stakeholders. This monitoring process will be done through the ICAO Air Navigation Commission,[91] which is charged with considering, and recommending to the Council for adoption, modifications of the Annexes to the Convention on International Civil Aviation (Chicago Convention)[92]; establishing technical sub commissions on which any contracting State may be represented, if it so desires; and advising the Council concerning the collection and communication to the contracting States of all information which it considers necessary and useful for the advancement of air navigation.

The review of GANP at the 38th Session of the ICAO Assembly in September/October 2013 provided States with a comprehensive aviation system appraisal. Regional planning and reporting is key to the process of air navigation planning and implementation and ICAO has devised a standardized air navigation reporting system in commonality with the approach adopted by the Planning and Implementation Regional Groups (PIRGs).[93] Central to GANP is the establishment and maintenance of a seamless, truly global air traffic management (ATM) system through an agreed structure of homogeneous ATM areas and major traffic flows/routing areas. It is on the basis of these areas and flows that the global Air Navigation community will be able to organize the disparate legacy elements of the worldwide aviation infrastructure into a single, global system. According to GANP, Homogeneous ATM areas feature shared ATM interests and requirements, based on similar levels of traffic density, complexity, required Air Navigation

---

[91] The Air Navigation Commission is composed of members appointed by the Council from among persons nominated by contracting States. These persons are required to have suitable qualifications and experience in the science and practice of aeronautics. The Council requests all contracting States (to the Convention on International Civil Aviation) to submit nominations. The President of the Air Navigation Commission shall be appointed by the Council. See *Chicago Convention*, Article 56. Members of the Commission are deemed to have suitable qualifications and experience in the science and practice of aeronautics. The President of the Air Navigation Commission is appointed by the Council.

[92] The Chicago Convention (supra note 1) was signed on 7 December 1944 at Chicago and its provisions are contained in Doc 7300/8: 2006.

[93] PIRGs work in close conjunction with ICAO's regional offices and Headquarters as it carries out its work programme responsibilities. The six ICAO PIRGs are: (a) APANPIRG (Asia/Pacific Air Navigation Planning and Implementation Regional Group); (b) APIRG (Africa-Indian Ocean Planning and Implementation Regional Group) ; (c) EANPG (European Air Navigation Planning Group); (d) GREPECAS (Caribbean/South American Planning and Implementation Regional Group) ; (e) MIDANPIRG (Middle East Air Navigation Planning and Implementation Regional Group) ; (f) NAT SPG (North Atlantic Systems Planning Group).

system infrastructure or other specified considerations. Homogeneous ATM areas may extend over States, specific portions of States, or groupings of States. They may also extend over large oceanic and continental areas. The identification of distinct, homogenous ATM areas has been the first step towards the development of globally interoperable air navigation systems.

Proper linkage between operational improvements and technology enablers forms the basis for the efficiency objectives of the GANP. Implementation is also facilitated by the clear understanding of technological constraints in relation to a specific operational improvement. Therefore, ICAO will further develop technology roadmaps in alignment with the ASBU modules for communication, navigation, and surveillance and information management. An avionics roadmap and frequency spectrum strategy will also be developed to ensure full coherence of global strategy and support synchronized implementation.

The evolution of the GANP to a strategic policy-level document will provide greater levels of transparency and investment certainty to States and industry as they continue to address capacity and sustainability challenges over the coming decades. The GANP's close strategic links to the policies and priorities established by ICAO for safety, air transport economy and environment will also ensure closer integration between related work programmes, minimizing duplication and enabling new efficiencies.

1.2.2 ASBUs

Following the 37th Session of the ICAO Assembly in 2010, ICAO increased its efforts to meet global needs for airspace interoperability while maintaining its focus on safety. To this end, a planning framework for global harmonization and interoperability named the aviation system block upgrade (ASBU) was proposed to AN-Conf/12 for incorporation into the Fourth Edition of the *Global Air Navigation Plan*. The ASBU framework[94] includes modules describing operational improvements over a series of blocks, supported by technology roadmaps, which serve to progressively enhance many aspects of civil aviation operations.

At AN-Conf/12 GANP introduced to the aviation community ICAO's Block Upgrade strategy, a systems engineering planning and implementation approach which has been the result of extensive collaboration and consultation between ICAO, its Member States and industry stakeholders. ICAO developed the Block Upgrade global framework primarily to ensure that aviation safety will be maintained and enhanced, that ATM improvement programmes are effectively

[94] For a detailed discussion on the nature and framework of the ASBUs see *Working Document for the Aviation System Block Upgrades*, The Framework for Global Harmonization, Issued by ICAO on 17 July 2012.

harmonized, and that barriers to future aviation efficiency and environmental gains can be removed at reasonable cost.

The basic difference between the current methodology and the ASBU methodology is that the scope of the current methodology covers ground equipment for air navigation services providers and planning is based on short and medium term, while in the ASBU methodology the scope extends to airspace users and regulators. Planning is based on short, medium and long term and the implementation process is through blocks and corresponding modules.

The Block Upgrades incorporate a long-term perspective matching that of the three companion ICAO Air Navigation planning documents.[95] They coordinate clear aircraft- and ground-based operational objectives together with the avionics, data link and ATM system requirements needed to achieve them. The overall strategy serves to provide industry with wide transparency and essential investment certainty for operators, equipment manufacturers and ANSPs.

The core of the Block Upgrade concept is linked to four specific and interrelated aviation performance areas, namely: (a) airport operations; (b) globally-interoperable systems and data; (c) optimum capacity and flexible flights; and (d) efficient flight paths.

The ASBU modules are organized into flexible and scalable building blocks that can be implemented depending on the operational needs, while recognizing that implementation of a particular module is not mandatory in all areas or circumstances. The approach adopted is not limiting and recognizes that deployment in addition to the material described in the ASBUs may also take place or be necessary. The broad timescales associated with the ASBU framework (Block 0 = 2013, Block 1 = 2018, Block 2 = 2023, Block = 2028) are intended only to depict the initial readiness of all components, including ICAO Standards and Recommended Practices (SARPs), needed for deployment and do not imply a mandated State or regional implementation timeframe. The ASBU framework with supporting technology roadmaps ensures that State and regional implementation planning and deployment activities can be undertaken with the confidence that all components necessary for a particular deployment will be available within the ASBU dates mentioned.

1.2.3 Airport Capacity

In relation to airport operations, carefully considered medium- and long-term airport planning to improve the efficacy of runway and taxiway infrastructure by optimizing surface movement, and the implementation of safety management to control safety risks and mitigate hazards such as those that contribute to runway

[95] GANP, GASP (Global Aviation Safety Plan) and Global Air Traffic Management Operational Concept.

excursions and incursions, remain essential. At the same time, taking advantage of technical developments in air navigation and aircraft systems may also assist in improving airport capacity and efficiency. In order to contribute to an overall strategy enhancing airport capacity, five significant planning threads are proposed for inclusion in the ASBU framework: (a) integration of arrival/departure/surface management; (b) increasing use of GNSS[96]-based instrument procedures; (c) optimized management of wake turbulence separation; (d) enhanced surface surveillance, and (e) airport collaborative decision-making.

By working on some of today's capacity constraints using the planning threads shown above, worthwhile gains in airport capacity have been demonstrated by deployment of one or more of the Block 0 modules.[97] Transitioning over time towards the Block 3 outcomes should see the operational use of aircraft capabilities and the synchronization of collective traffic flows to optimize the use of runways and the airport surface. Increasing use of traffic planning tools, advanced instrument procedures and all-weather operations should realize greater predictability of operations without undue reliance on ground based navigation infrastructure.

The ASBU concept facilitates the step by step deployment of operational improvements within the boundaries of an overall planning framework. Looking towards the end state, following the deployment of the airport capacity elements of Block 3 each aircraft should be capable of exchanging information regarding its 4D trajectory profile and be able to adhere fully to an agreed 4D trajectory. The air traffic and airport management systems should support time-based interval management, integrated sequencing and augmented surveillance capabilities.

The initial steps on this path (Block 0) implement a combination of wake turbulence re-categorization, approach procedures making optimal usage of GNSS-based PBN approaches and traffic flow improvements through the management of arrival and departure runway sequencing. New technology is available to enhance the surveillance of aircraft surface movement, and may also provide information on suitably equipped vehicles. Improved processes are offered to support Collaborative Decision Making (CDM) involving all stakeholders on the airport.

Block 1 continues the evolution of the Block 0 planning threads to, where possible; reduce approach minima, potentially to CAT II/III[98] capability by using

---

[96] Global Navigation Satellite System (GNSS) is a key element of the Communications, Navigation, and Surveillance/Air Traffic Management (CNS/ATM) systems as well as a foundation upon which States can deliver improved aeronautical navigation services is fundamentally different from traditional navigational aids (NAVAIDs). It has the potential to support all phases of flight by providing seamless global navigation guidance. This could eliminate the need for a variety of ground and airborne systems that were designed to meet specific requirements for certain phases of flight. See *Global Navigation Satellite System Manual*, Doc 9849, AN/457, 5th Edition—2005 at Foreword and 1.1.

[97] ASBUs are divided, on a 5 year segment through the 15 years of their application into four blocks. Block 0 is for 2013–2018; Block 1 is for 2018–2023; Block 2 is for 2023–2028 and Block 3 is for 2028 onwards. See *Global Air Traffic Management Operational Concept*, *supra* note 95, at 26.

[98] GNSS specifications for precision approach operations.

GNSS. Developments in managing wake vortex separation build on a new, more detailed, wake turbulence categorization to create static leader/follower pair matrices of aircraft type wake separation pairings for application on a pair-by-pair basis, with the aim to increase arrivals on closely spaced parallel runways. Airport capacity may also be increased by extended arrival metering and departure/surface integration to facilitate efficient and flexible departure all-weather operations. Procedures and technology, such as enhanced visualization systems, are provided to enhance safety and efficiency of surface operations. Associated with these improvements, airport CDM is brought to another level by establishing a collaborative airport operations plan and performance framework, enabling airport stakeholders to communicate and coordinate through interconnected systems. This sharing of the available resources and information should increase real-time capability. At this level of maturity, it should also be possible to provide remotely operated control tower services at suitable aerodromes.

With Block 2, aircraft equipage and the interconnection of systems become increasingly important. The leader/follower pair matrices of aircraft wake separation become dynamic, using real-time weather observations to allow the air navigation service provider (ANSP) to minimize the wake turbulence distance between aircraft. At the same time, the synchronization of departures, arrivals and surface movements, adjusted dynamically to accommodate any change in the arrival/departure flow patterns, allow optimization of airspace and airport resources. Enhancement of airport surface surveillance, with implementation of safety nets, and the extended use of enhanced vision systems for taxi operations may also contribute to increased capacity.

1.2.4 Legal Issues

From a legal and regulatory perspective, ASBUs should be viewed in the context of their main purpose—as modules that are developed and designed to achieve harmonization and interoperability that result in improvements in the provision of air navigation services globally. Harmonization in this context is consistency in procedures and practice. Since not all ASBUs are intended to be implemented everywhere simultaneously, they have to be prioritized in terms of their implementation to assist in the determination as to the circumstances, places and timeframes in which they should be implemented.

Such prioritization has to be done firstly at State level and then on a regional basis through the PIRGs in coordination with ICAO, particularly when the latter is in the process of updating the Regional Air Navigation Plans which drive the PIRGs. The planning process of the PIRGs should be paramount over implementation of the ASBUs on a State by State basis and eventually the regional process should be extended harmoniously to a global application. The global applicability should be based on PBN.

PBN is elaborated in ICAO Assembly Resolution A37-11[99]which urges all States to implement Area Navigation (RNAV) and Required Navigation Performance (RNP) air traffic services route and approach procedures in accordance with the ICAO PBN concept.[100] The Resolution requires States to complete a PBN implementation plan as a matter of urgency to achieve: implementation of RNAV and RNP operations (where required) for en route and terminal areas according to established timelines and intermediate milestones; implementation of approach procedures with vertical guidance (APV) for all instrument runway ends, either as the primary approach or as a back-up for precision approaches by 2016 with intermediate milestones as follows: 30 % by 2010, 70 % by 2014 for instrument runways at aerodromes where there is no local altimeter setting available and where there are no aircraft suitably equipped for APV operations with a maximum certificated take-off mass of five 700 kg or more. ICAO is required to develop a coordinated action plan to assist States in the implementation of PBN and to ensure development and/or maintenance of globally harmonized SARPs, Procedures for Air Navigation Services (PANS) and guidance material including a global harmonized safety assessment methodology to keep pace with operational demands.

The first legal principle which applies to ASBUs and their implementation is that ASBUs are meant for harmonization and interoperability and not necessarily for standardization. Here the distinction between harmonization and standardization is important, where the former relates to consistency and the latter relates to compliance. Article 37 of the Chicago Convention applies to ASBUs and their implementation in that it provides that each contracting State undertakes to collaborate in securing the highest practicable degree of uniformity in regulations, standards, procedures, and organization in relation to aircraft, personnel, airways and auxiliary services in all matters in which such uniformity will facilitate and improve air navigation. This imposes an obligation on States to make their best efforts to implement ASBUs when improvements to the air navigation systems are needed.

However, there is no mandatory obligation as prescribed by Article 38 of the Chicago Convention,[101] which requires that States unable to comply with Standards

---

[99] See Assembly Resolutions in Force (as of 8 October 2010), Doc 9958at II-32.

[100] The ICAO PBN Concept is laid down in the *Performance Based Navigation (PBN) Manual*, Doc. 9613.

[101] Article 38 provides: "Any State which finds it impracticable to comply in all respects with any such international standard or procedure, or to bring its own regulations or practices into full accord with any international standard or procedure after amendment of the latter, or which deems it necessary to adopt regulations or practices differing in any particular respect from those established by an international standard, shall give immediate notification to ICAO of the differences between its own practice and that established by the international standard. In the case of amendments to international standards, any State which does not make the appropriate amendments to its own regulations or practices shall give notice to the Council within 60 days of the adoption of the amendment to the international standard, or indicate the action which it proposes to take. In any such case, the Council shall make immediate notification to all other states of the difference which exists between one or more features of an international standard and the corresponding national practice of that State".

of the Annexes should report such inability to ICAO. Consequently the implementation of ASBUs would not come within ICAO's Universal Safety Oversight Audit Programme (USOAP) and safety audits.

Furthermore, the Council of ICAO does not have the authority of Article 54 j) of the Chicago Convention which is extremely clear in identifying the Council's mandatory function to report to any Contracting State any infraction of the Chicago Convention as well as any failure to carry out recommendations and determinations of the Council.

1.2.5 ASBUs and the Council of ICAO

Given the above, it is clear that the Council has no coercive power over States in their implementation of ASBUs. The Council, under the Convention, has only functions (which are in essence duties) and no powers.[102] On the other hand the Assembly has powers and duties accorded to it in the Chicago Convention,[103] one of which is to delegate to the Council the powers and authority necessary or desirable for the discharge of the duties of the Organization and revoke or modify the delegations of authority at any time.[104]

Article 54 n) provides that the Council can consider any matter relating to the Convention which any Contracting State refers to it, giving the Council the capacity to make its own determination and recommendations pertaining to a matter referred to it. In this context, the Council may invoke Article 44 which identifies as one of the aims and objectives of ICAO the developments of techniques and principles pertaining to air navigation, and discuss States' implementation of ASBUs in the context of the GANP.

A significant issue in the determination of ICAO's effectiveness as an international organization is the overriding principle of universality and global participation of all its 191 Contracting States in the implementation of ICAO policy. This principle, which has its genesis in the Chicago Conference of 1944, has flowed on, gaining express recognition of legal scholars. This is what makes ICAO unique as a specialized agency of the United Nations and establishes without any doubt that ICAO is not just a tool of cooperation among States.

The ICAO Symposium on Global Runway Safety,[105] which was held from 24 to 26 May 2011, brought to bear this global leadership role of ICAO, together with the

[102] Although Jacob Schenkman, in his well documented and logically reasoned treatise on ICAO states that "The Council has been entrusted with duties, powers and functions..." he does not give a single example of such a power. See Capt. Schenkman (1955) at 158.

[103] Article 49 of the Chicago Convention.

[104] Article 49 h) of the Chicago Convention.

[105] See Abeyratne (2011), pp. 427–440.

fact that it is time to define roles and have the legislative courage to give effect to a safety reporting culture and the legal legitimacy given to ICAO by the Chicago Convention. In this context, there are a few home truths one has to consider with regard to the Council. The first is that the 36 members of the Council are voted in by the Assembly of 191 States. Therefore the Council members, who are not sent in by their States on the States' own accord, are obliged to act in the best interests of their constituents, which are all States comprising ICAO. It would therefore be morally reprehensible for a member of the Council to act in the interests of its own.

Notwithstanding the Council's limited scope on the implementation of ASBUs, the Council could robustly monitor their implementation. Article 55 (c) requires the Council to:

> Conduct research into all aspects of air transport and air navigation which are of international importance, communicate the results of its research to the Contracting States, and facilitate the exchange of information between Contracting States on air transport and air navigation matters.

This could be tied to the objective of ICAO to meet the needs of the people of the world for safe, regular, efficient and economical air transport. In this regard the Council should initiate studies that involve research into safety of air navigation, which is of paramount international importance. This is provided for in the Chicago Convention. Such studies, taking into account global, regional and national implementation trends, could analyse their effects on the improvements on safety regionally and globally. This in turn could result in a compendium of implementation of safety measures for States.

1.2.6 ASBUs and States

The first question that has to be asked is, is non-implementation of ASBUs by a State which has a need for their implementation, a breach of a legal obligation? In other words, do ICAO member States have legal obligation to implement ASBUs? As already discussed, ASBUs come under Article 37 of the Chicago Convention where States undertake to collaborate in harmonizing regulations with each other, and in the case of ASBUs would do so using the PBN concept. PBN is governed by Assembly Resolution A37-11. Therefore it would be too simplistic to conclude that States could totally ignore ASBUs and consider their implementation unnecessary. ASBUs are tools whereby States would ensure that ICAO performs its functions under Article 44 of the Chicago Convention.[106] To ICAO has been attributed

[106] Article 44 provides: "The aims and objectives of the Organization are to develop the principles and techniques of international air navigation and to foster the planning and development of international air transport so as to: (a) Insure the safe and orderly growth of international civil aviation throughout the world; (b) Encourage the arts of aircraft design and operation for peaceful purposes; (c) Encourage the development of airways, airports, and air navigation facilities for

international personality and therefore it is not merely an aggregate of its member States and it has a right to expect performance of its practices and procedures. The International Court of Justice, in the *Reparations for Injuries Case* held:

> There is an undeniable right of the [sic] Organization to demand that its members shall fulfil the obligations entered into by them in the interest of the good working of the Organization.[107]

This obligation in the context of ASBUs is reflected in ICAO Assembly Resolution A37-15 (Consolidated statement containing ICAO policies and associated practices related specifically to air navigation) Appendix L of which relates to implementation of regional plans. The Appendix recognizes that in accordance with Article 28[108] of the Chicago Convention, Contracting States undertake, insofar as they may find practicable, to provide air navigation facilities and services necessary to facilitate international air navigation. It also acknowledged that the Regional Plans set forth the requirements for facilities and services for international civil aviation; and any serious deficiencies in the implementation of Regional Plans may affect the safety, regularity and efficiency of international air operations and therefore should be eliminated as quickly as practicable.

The Assembly resolved that priority should be given in the implementation programmes of Contracting States to the provision, including continuing operation, of those facilities and services the lack of which would likely have a serious effect on international air operations; the identification and investigation of and action by the Organization on serious deficiencies in the implementation of Regional Plans be carried out in the minimum practicable time; and regional planning and implementation groups shall identify problems and shortcomings in Regional Plans and in the implementation thereof, along with suggested remedial measures.

ASBUs are a compelling and critical link to implementing regional plans implemented through the PIRGs. In this context the Assembly resolved that the Council take into account the requirement to improve still further existing safety levels, should inform fully and promptly each Contracting State of the

international civil aviation; (d) Meet the needs of the peoples of the world for safe, regular, efficient and economical air transport; (e) Prevent economic waste caused by unreasonable competition; (f) Insure that the rights of contracting States are fully respected and that every contracting State has a fair opportunity to operate international airlines; (g) Avoid discrimination between contracting States; (h) Promote safety of flight in international air navigation; (i) Promote generally the development of all aspects of international civil aeronautics.

[107] 1949 ICJ Reports at 184.

[108] Article 28 provides: "Each contracting State undertakes, so far as it may find practicable, to: (a) Provide, in its territory, airports, radio services, meteorological services and other air navigation facilities to facilitate international air navigation, in accordance with the standards and practices recommended or established from time to time, pursuant to this Convention; (b) Adopt and put into operation the appropriate standard systems of communications procedure, codes, markings, signals, lighting and other operational practices and rules which may be recommended or established from time to time, pursuant to this Convention; (c) Collaborate in international measures to secure the publication of aeronautical maps and charts in accordance with standards which may be recommended or established from time to time, pursuant to this Convention".

recommendations for the provision of air navigation facilities and services that are applicable to that State under the Regional Plans. Contracting States are required to prepare and keep up to date suitable plans, including the requirements for personnel, for the orderly implementation of the parts of Regional Plans applicable to them.

Furthermore, the Council is requested by the Resolution to arrange for the monitoring of the status of implementation of the Regional Plans and for the issue of periodic progress reports which should include information on serious shortcomings in implementation of the Regional Plans. The users of air navigation facilities and services are required to report any serious problems encountered due to the lack of implementation of air navigation facilities or services required by Regional Plans. The reports should be addressed to the Contracting States responsible for implementation. These States should act on such reports to resolve the problems, but when remedial action is not taken users should inform ICAO, through the medium of an international organization where appropriate. Finally Appendix L requires that the Council arrange for periodic review of serious problems encountered by users due to the lack of implementation of air navigation facilities or services and, when appropriate, for measures to be taken to facilitate elimination of the problems as quickly as practicable.

An earlier Resolution of the ICAO Assembly, adopted at the 22nd Assembly (Montreal, 13 September-4 October 1977), brings to bear the importance of ASBUs (which were not envisioned at the time). Resolution A22-19 (Assistance and advice in the implementation of regional plans) resolved that ICAO give high priority to fostering and implementing regional plans and called on member States to Contracting States should note the possibility of using operating agencies as a means of fulfilling their international obligations under Article 28[109] of the Convention. It also calls upon States to examine with other States in the region whether the implementation of the particular Regional Plan could be facilitated through bilateral or multilateral agreements; and to hold informal meetings, whether initiated by Contracting States or convened by the Secretary-general, which are confined to implementation problems affecting two or more States, should be encouraged where no other effective and timely means are available to resolve the problems.

The ICAO Council is required to render assistance to Contracting States in planning and developing those portions of national implementation programmes

[109] Article 28 provides: "Each contracting State undertakes, so far as it may find practicable, to: (a) Provide, in its territory, airports, radio services, meteorological services and other air navigation facilities to facilitate international air navigation, in accordance with the standards and practices recommended or established from time to time, pursuant to this Convention; (b) Adopt and put into operation the appropriate standard systems of communications procedure, codes, markings, signals, lighting and other operational practices and rules which may be recommended or established from time to time, pursuant to this Convention; (c) Collaborate in international measures to secure the publication of aeronautical maps and charts in accordance with standards which may be recommended or established from time to time, pursuant to this Convention".

related to the provision of facilities and services called for by Regional Plans; and promote implementation of those parts of the Regional Plans with which they are concerned, and, furthermore, the Council should ensure that the Regional Offices are utilized to the fullest extent possible in the carrying out of these tasks.

The Council is also called upon to ensure that all the activities of the Organization that can contribute to the implementation of Regional Plans are carefully coordinated, in particular at the regional level. This provision is directly applicable to the implementation by States of ASBUs. The Resolution also provides that when a Contracting State, having explored all methods and means for implementing the Regional Plans with which it is concerned pursuant to Article 28 of the Convention, experiences difficulties which hinder such implementation, it should report accordingly to ICAO and, with respect to those items that might become serious deficiencies if not implemented, it should request assistance from ICAO; and the Council should continue, as a matter of priority, to assist and encourage Contracting States to meet their responsibilities under Article 28 of the Convention, and to investigate the practicability of any other solutions for obtaining implementation of specific facilities and services determined by the Council to represent serious deficiencies in the world air navigation network. What was established and adopted as a Resolution by the Assembly in 1977 has seen the light of day in the form of ASBUs and it is the obligation of States to implement ASBUs when necessary, so that their ultimate obligation of adhering to Standards and Recommended Practices (SARPs) of the technical Annexes to the Chicago Convention is met.

In the ultimate analysis, ASBUs are an integral part of safety management. Safety Management Systems (SMS) are processes which proactively manage the projected increase in aircraft incidents and accidents brought about by the increase in air traffic movements, and ASBUs are calculated to achieve this goal. The upcoming 38th ICAO Assembly Session in late 2013 should, in formulating and adopting an Annex on ASBUs to the Consolidated statement containing ICAO policies and associated practices related specifically to air navigation, ascribe a compelling role to the ASBU, thus avoiding presenting it to the aviation community as a mere option to be applied at the discretion of States. The Resolution should be so contrived and structured that a compelling link is drawn between ASBUs on the one hand and SARPs, PBN the GANP, GASP and the Global Air Traffic Management Operational Concept on the other.

It is inevitable that some states may lack the necessary resources to implement ASBUs when the need arises. Therefore some degree of assistance or a mechanism must be in place. At the airport or the ANSP level, ICAO's policies[110]state that costs directly related to the safety oversight function for airport services or for air navigation services may be included in the airport or ANSP cost basis for user charges at the States' discretion and provided that such costs are imposed on the providers of services.[111] It is also stated in ICAO policies that policies and charging

[110] *ICAO's Policies on Charges for Airports and Air Navigation Services* (Doc 9082).

[111] *Id.* paragraph 2 x) of Section II and paragraph 3 vii) of Section III.

principles contained therein can be applied in other circumstances, such as for funding of the safety oversight function at the national and the regional level. In all circumstances the four key charging principles of non-discrimination, transparency, cost-relatedness and consultation with users, as well as the requirement that users should only pay for services received, should be observed with respect to funding for safety oversight. This principle should be extended to ASBUs on the valid basis that ASBUs would enhance and ensure proper safety oversight.

It is therefore highly recommended that ASBUs should be accorded the legal legitimacy they deserve on two fronts: a strong and compelling Assembly Resolution and an efficient and effective assistance mechanism based on ICAO policy.

1.3 State Responsibility for Airports

It has already been mentioned that the State has ultimate responsibility for the provision and running of its airports. However, does that mean that the State can build, run and operate airports at will, based on the concept of sovereignty of a State? Technically, although the Chicago Convention provides that Member States of ICAO recognize that every State has complete and exclusive sovereignty over the air space above its territory,[112] the general consensus of contemporary international law is that this is not an absolute and pristine principle anymore. One commentator states very aptly:

> The role of the State in the modern world is a complex one. According to legal theory, each State is sovereign and equal. In reality, with the phenomenal growth in communications and consciousness, and with the constant reminder of global rivalries, not even the most powerful of States can be entirely sovereign. Interdependence and the close knit character of contemporary international commercial and political society ensures that virtually any action of a State could well have profound repercussions upon the system as a whole and the decisions under consideration by other States.[113]

[112] Chicago Convention, *supra* note 1, Article 1. The Convention applies only to State aircraft and not to military aircraft. However, it states, in Article 3 that no aircraft used in military, customs or police services shall fly over the territory of another State or land thereon without authorization by special agreement or otherwise, and in accordance with the terms thereof. It must also be borne in mind that United Nations General Assembly Resolution *A/RES/46/18*2 of 19 December 1991 provides, in resolving clause 3 that the sovereignty, territorial integrity and national unity of States must be fully respected in accordance with the Charter of the United Nations. In this context, humanitarian assistance should be provided with the consent of the affected country and in principle on the basis of an appeal by the affected country. In April 1992, the Secretary-General established the Department of Humanitarian Affairs (DHA), incorporating UNDRO, various UN units that had been dealing with specific emergency programs, and the secretariat for the International Decade for Natural Disaster Reduction. The Secretary-General appointed an Emergency Relief Coordinator to head the new department. The DHA has its headquarters in New York and an office in Geneva.

[113] Shaw (2003) at 120.

Therefore, although sovereignty is the basic constitutional doctrine of the law of nations, modern exigencies of international relations, particularly in the case of disasters, whether man made or natural, have not regarded this principle as inflexible. The essence of intervention is compulsion. The legal question with regard to the inviolability of the sovereignty of a State is not whether the intervention concerned was an armed or unarmed one, but whether it was effected unilaterally under compulsion or threat by the intervening State.[114] Starke is inclined to stretch the principle of sovereignty to accommodate external involvement by a State in the affairs of another in special circumstances:

> ..."Sovereignty" has a much more restricted meaning today than in the eighteenth and nineteenth centuries when, with the emergence of powerful highly nationalised States, few limits on State autonomy were acknowledged. At the present time there is hardly a State which, in the interests of the international community, has not accepted restrictions on its liberty of action. Thus most States are members of the United Nations and the International Labour Organization (ILO), in relation to which they have undertaken obligations limiting their unfettered discretion in matters of international policy. Therefore, it is probably more accurate today to say that the sovereignty of a State means the *residuum* of power which it possesses within the confines laid down by international law. It is of interest to note that this conception resembles the doctrine of early writers on international, law, who treated the State as subordinate to the law of nations, then identified as part of the wider "law of nature".[115]

The Chicago Convention requires States to keep their airports open to all airlines operating into and out of their territories and provide meteorological, radio and other information as well as facilities such as ground services. Of course, one might argue that Article 89 of the Chicago Convention enables Contracting States to have freedom of action irrespective of the provisions of the Convention in case of war, whether belligerents or neutrals. It also allows a State which has declared a state of national emergency (and notifies the ICAO Council of such) to have the same freedom of action notwithstanding the provisions of the Convention. Therefore, unless a State is at war (which the Convention does not define)[116] or has declared a state of national emergency, it would be bound by the provisions of the Convention.

The first duty of a Contracting State not falling within the purview of Article 89 of the Chicago Convention is to keep its airport open to all incoming aircraft. Article 15 of the Convention requires *inter alia* that, uniform conditions shall apply to the use, by aircraft of every contracting State, of all air navigation facilities,

---

[114] de Lima (1971) at 16.

[115] Starke (1977) at 106.

[116] Article 31.1 of the *Vienna Convention on the Law of Treaties* provides that "a treaty shall be interpreted in good faith in accordance with the ordinary meaning to be given to the terms of the treaty in their context and in the light of its object and purpose". See *Vienna Convention on the Law of Treaties 1969*, done at Vienna on 23 May 1969. The Convention entered into force on 27 January 1980. United Nations, *Treaty Series*, vol. 1155, p. 331. The ordinary meaning of war can be considered as a behaviour pattern of organized violent conflict typified by extreme aggression, societal disruption, and high mortality. This behaviour pattern involves two or more organized groups. http://en.wikipedia.org/wiki/War.

including radio and meteorological services, which may be provided for public use for the safety and expedition of air navigation. This condition is subject to Article 9 which stipulates that each contracting State may, for reasons of military necessity or public safety, restrict or prohibit uniformly the aircraft of other States from flying over certain areas of its territory, provided that no distinction in this respect is made between the aircraft of the State whose territory is involved, engaged in international scheduled airline services, and the aircraft of the other contracting States likewise engaged. The provision goes on to say that each contracting State reserves also the right, in exceptional circumstances or during a period of emergency, or in the interest of public safety, and with immediate effect, temporarily to restrict or prohibit flying over the whole or any part of its territory, on condition that such restriction or prohibition will be applicable without distinction of nationality to aircraft of all other States.

The question arises as to whether a State in which there is acute civil unrest is bound to follow the abovementioned principles of the Chicago Convention. States or international organizations which are parties to such treaties have to apply the treaties they have signed and therefore have to interpret them. Although the conclusion of a treaty is generally governed by international customary law to accord with accepted rules and practices of national constitutional law of the signatory States, the application of treaties are governed by principles of international law. If however, the application or performance of a requirement in an international treaty poses problems to a State, the constitutional law of that State would be applied by courts of that State to settle the problem. Although Article 27 of the *Vienna Convention*[117] requires States not to invoke provisions of their internal laws as justification for failure to comply with the provisions of a treaty, States are free to choose the means of implementation they see fit according to their traditions and political organization.[118] The overriding rule is that treaties are juristic acts and have to be performed.

The regulatory process governing air navigation services and aerodromes clearly identifies State responsibility. In terms of standard setting at aerodromes, States are required to undertake certification of aerodromes to standards acceptable to the international aviation community through ICAO.[119] Accordingly, ICAO prescribes comprehensive Standards and Recommended Practices calculated to ensure acceptable levels of airport and aerodrome services. Notable among these are specifications on visual aids[120] and aerodrome maintenance.[121]

[117] *Id.*

[118] Reuter (1989), at 16.

[119] ICAO Assembly Resolution A35-14, Consolidated statement of continuing ICAO policies and associated practices related specifically to air navigation, Appendix Q, Resolving Clauses 1 and 3. See Assembly Resolutions in Force, (as of 8 October 2004) *ICAO Doc 9848* at II-13.

[120] See Chapters 6 and 7 of Annex 14 (Aerodromes) Volume 1 (Aerodrome Design and Operations), Annex 14 to the Convention on international Civil Aviation, Fourth Edition, July 2004, at 6-1 to 8-3. Also Chapter 5 of Annex 14 Volume II (Heliports), Second Edition—July-1995 at pp. 30–48 which has similar provisions for the operation of helicopters.

[121] *Id.* Annex 14, Chapter 10.

The fundamental questions that arise are, should airports be held responsible for service failure brought about by a natural phenomenon; and should airports have had, what in modern business parlance is called "corporate foresight".[122] Firstly, in terms of responsibility, the question could be raised as to whether; irrespective of the business status of the airport (whether it is privatized, autonomous or corporatized) the State in which the airport is situated should bear ultimate responsibility. This responsibility devolves upon the State *in limine* by virtue of Article 28 of the Chicago Convention (as already discussed) which stipulates *inter alia* that each Contracting States to the Convention undertakes, so far as it may find practicable to provide, in its territory, airports, radio services, meteorological services and other air navigation facilities to facilitate international air navigation, in accordance with the standards and practices recommended or established from time to time, pursuant to the Convention. The provision also requires such a State to adopt and put into operation the appropriate standard systems of communications procedure, codes, markings, signals, lighting and other operational practices and rules which may be recommended or established from time to time, pursuant to this Convention. Obviously, the Convention, through an inarticulate premise requires in Article 28 that States provide *functional* airport services among other services prescribed in the provision.

Principally, States bear the ultimate responsibility for aviation safety in their territories. However, airports too owe a duty of care to four categories of users: those in aircraft that are landing and taking off; those in the airport premises; the ground handling staff working on the airside; and other staff employed within the premises of the airport. There is a popular misconception that risks to crew, passengers and staff cease to exist once the aircraft engines are turned off. This is simply not so. One commentator has remarked that it is a common feature at airports that injury and death is caused to ground handling staff during thunderstorms.[123] Adverse weather also portends a serious threat to activities such as refuelling, de-icing and baggage handling operations. There is an increasing burden cast on meteorological information providers to give accurate weather information to airports and many airports are known to have established policy that requires the shut-down of ground handling operations when lightning strikes within 3 miles of the airport.[124]

[122] The functions and responsibilities of an airport will vary according to its size, type of traffic and areas of responsibility. For example, some airports are responsible for air traffic control as well as for meteorological services, while at most other airports such services are provided by separate government entities. Many airports are involved in security functions in varying degrees and in providing facilities for customs, immigration and health authorities. Ground-handling services for the airlines, including terminal handling or ramp handling, or both, are provided by some airports, while at others they are provided by the airlines or by specialized agents or companies. Certain airports also perform functions that exceed the scope of conventional airport activities, such as consultancy services, public works, construction, and real estate development. See Abeyratne (2009) at 13.

[123] Puempol (2006) at 76.

[124] *Ibid.*

Although it was said earlier in the chapter, it is worth reiterating verbatim that the regulatory process governing air navigation services and aerodromes clearly identifies State responsibility. In terms of standard setting at aerodromes, States are required to undertake certification of aerodromes to standards acceptable to the international aviation community through ICAO.[125] Accordingly, ICAO prescribes comprehensive Standards and Recommended Practices calculated to ensure acceptable levels of airport and aerodrome services. Notable among these are specifications on visual aids[126] and aerodrome maintenance.[127]

In addition to the obligation of the State to provide certain services as enumerated in Article 28 of the Chicago Convention, responsibility of the State would also extend to the provision of accurate air traffic control services at the aerodrome. States have to be mindful of the fact that their overall responsibility under the Chicago Convention in providing air navigation services extends to the air traffic controller, whose service is of a unique nature. The special feature in the provision of air traffic control is brought to bear by the nature of the service provided, be it in the relaying of information on meteorology or on traffic. Globally, air traffic control services offer information relayed by people by means of radio communication involving extremely short time periods and using a standard set of terminology in the English language, even in regions of the world where English is not the first language.[128]

The provision of meteorological information to airports and aircraft about to land or take off is also part of State responsibility. Annex 3 to the Chicago Convention provides in Standard 2.1.1. that the objective of meteorological service for international air navigation shall be to contribute towards the safety, regularity and efficiency of international air navigation. This objective shall be achieved by supplying the following users: operators, flight crew members, air traffic services units, search and rescue services units, airport managements and others concerned with the conduct or development of international air navigation, with the meteorological information necessary for the performance of their respective functions.[129]

State responsibility for the provision of meteorological information is provided for in Standard 2.1.4. where each Contracting State is required to ensure that the designated meteorological authority complies with the requirements of the World

---

[125] ICAO Assembly Resolution A35-14, Consolidated statement of continuing ICAO policies and associated practices related specifically to air navigation, Appendix Q, Resolving Clauses 1 and 3. See Assembly Resolutions in Force, (as of 8 October 2004) *ICAO Doc 9848* at II-13.

[126] See Chapters 6 and 7 of Annex 14 (Aerodromes) Volume 1 (Aerodrome Design and Operations), Annex 14 to the Convention on international Civil Aviation, Fourth Edition, July 2004, at 6-1 to 8-3. Also Chapter 5 of Annex 14 Volume II (Heliports), Second Edition—July-1995 at pp. 30–48 which has similar provisions for the operation of helicopters.

[127] *Id.* Annex 14, Chapter 10.

[128] Miyagi (2005), at 143.

[129] Standard 2.1.2.

Meteorological Organization in respect of qualifications and training of meteorological personnel providing service for international air navigation.[130]

It is also provided in the Annex that close liaison shall be maintained between those concerned with the supply and those concerned with the use of meteorological information on matters which affect the provision of meteorological service for international air navigation.[131] Furthermore, States have responsibility establish one or more aerodrome and/or other meteorological offices which shall be adequate for the provision of the meteorological service required to satisfy the needs of international air navigation.[132]

It is incontrovertible that the responsibility of the State is not extinguished merely because an airport is subject to private ownership or private management control. In international air transport, the mere fact that the State has to provide airport services under Article 28 of the Chicago Convention and indeed designate airports within its territory for landing purposes as per Articles 10 and 68 thereof imposes legal responsibility upon the State to be accountable at public international law for any liability incurred as a result of action on the part of airports within its territory. Therefore, legally, neither the State nor the airport can avoid liability even if the latter were privatized. The State entails liability primarily at public international law and also at public law[133] in general, and the airport incurs liability on a private basis in a private action that may be brought, under tort law principles or under contract law, as the case may be.

References

Abeyratne R (2006) State liability for negligent acts of autonomous air navigation service providers. Professional Negligence 22(3):176–192

Abeyratne R (2009) Airport business law. PublishAmerica, Bloomington

Abeyratne R (2011) Ensuring global runway safety: a look at the future. Air Space Law 36 (6):427–440

Abeyratne R (2012) Convention on international civil aviation – a commentary. Springer, Heidelberg

Arpino R (1994) Automated weather observation systems find increasing acceptance at major airports. ICAO J 15

Becker P (2002) Corporate foresight in Europe: a first overview. Institute of Science and Technology Studies, Germany

Bobbitt P (2008) Terror and consent: the wars for the twenty first century. Knopf, New York

[130] Requirements concerning qualifications and training of meteorological personnel in aeronautical meteorology are given in WMO Publication No. 49, Technical Regulations, Volume I—General Meteorological Standards and Recommended Practices, Chapter B.4—*Education and Training*.

[131] Standard 2.2.1.

[132] Standard 3.3.1.

[133] For liability of the State under administrative and tort law principles, see Abeyratne (2006), pp. 176–192 at 183–192.

Carey J (2010) Watch this space. Airport World (April–May 2010), p 39
Dan Manningham G (1996) The keys to using weather radar. Bus Commer Aviation (July 1996) 60–62
de Lima FX (1971) Intervention in international law. Vitgeverij Pax Nederland, Vitgeverij Pax Nederland
Doganis R (1992) The airport business. Routeledge, London
Ferguson N (2008) The ascent of money. The Penguin Press, New York
Fleming JG (1977) The law of torts, 5th edn. The Law Book Company Limited, Sidney, p 176
Frank Carlson E (1995) Brrrr!, Airplanes operating at extremely low ground temperatures. Airliner (October–December 1995) 9
Freedman JE (1994) Applicability of e-scan technology for future airport aviation weather radars. Air Traffic Contr Q 2(1):53–78
McKenna JT (1994) Airlines seek uniform winter safety rules. Aviation Week Space Technol (10 January 1994) 46–47
Miyagi M (2005) Serious accidents and human factors. American Institute of Aeronautics and Astronautics, Virginia
Puempol H (2006) Airports and aviation weather services: a new alliance forming? Int Airport Rev (4) 75
Reuter P (1989) Introduction to the law of treaties. Pinter Publishers, London
Rusmussen R, Cole J, Knight K, Moore RK, Kupperman M (1995–1996) How heavy is that snowfall. Flight Deck 18:24–26
Schenkman J (1955) International Civil Aviation Organization. Librairie E. Droz, Geneva
Shaw MN (2003) International law, 5th edn. Cambridge University Press, Oxford
Starke JG (1977) An introduction to international law, 7th edn. Butterworths, London
Steinhorst G, van Dijk WCM (1994) Modern weather observation systems in use at airports can improve the quality of weather data. ICAO J 49(8):12–14
Stuart RA, Isaac GA (1994) Archived weather data provides new information on ground based icing. ICAO J 49(8):5–7
Wagner GA (1994–1995) Take-off and landing on Icy conditions. Flight Deck 14:21–25
Wagner GA (1995–1996) Rejected take-off in icy conditions results in runway overrun. Flight Deck 18:3–11
Woolley D (1999) Winter operations evolve in Europe. GSE Today (June–July 1999) 23–26

Chapter 2
Certification of Aerodromes

2.1 Introduction

The certification of aerodromes is governed by Annex 14 to the Chicago Convention, in Volume 1 which states that States are required to certify aerodromes used for international operations in accordance with the specifications laid out in the Annex as well as "other relevant ICAO specifications" (my emphasis) through an appropriate regulatory framework.[1] The Annex goes on to recommend that States should certify aerodromes open to public use in accordance with the specifications laid out in the Annex as well as other relevant ICAO specifications through an appropriate framework.[2] The certification process that States should carry out is to be in accordance with an aerodrome manual which would contain information on the aerodrome site, services, equipment, operating procedures, organization and management including a safety management system, and such manual has to be subject to an approval process prior to the certification of an aerodrome.[3]

The safety management system alluded to in the Annex is laid out in Annex 19 to the Chicago Convention, which the Council adopted in 2013. Safety Management Systems (SMS) are processes which proactively manage the projected increase in aircraft incidents and accidents brought about by the increase in air traffic movements. SMS require vigilance in the liberalization of air transport and the correspondent increase in capacity. At the Directors General of Civil Aviation Conference on a Global Strategy for Aviation Safety, convened by ICAO in Montreal from 20 to 22 March 2006, Canada defined a Safety Management System as a businesslike approach to safety. An SMS is a systematic, explicit and comprehensive process for the management of safety risks that integrates operations and technical systems with financial and human resource management, for all activities

[1] Annex 14 to the Convention on in International Civil Aviation (2013). Standard 1.4.1.

[2] *Id.* Recommendation 1.4.2.

[3] *Id.* Standard 1.4.4.

R. Abeyratne, *Law and Regulation of Aerodromes*, DOI 10.1007/978-3-319-04780-5_2,

related to an air operator as an approved maintenance organization's certificate holder.[4]

Any management system, including that which involves aviation safety, would necessarily entail planning, goal setting, performance measurement and accountability. This process is systemic, in that there cannot be one factor without the other to complete the entire system of the safety management process. It also requires a symbiotic relationship between operator and regulator, who are jointly responsible for the determination of the parameters of regulations and their intent. While the regulator's role is to give a clear set of instructions to the operator reflecting the expectations of the regulator, the operator has to ensure their compliance as well as maintain close coordination with the regulator.

At the DGCA Conference, ICAO emphasized that, although the prescriptive aspect of safety management, complied with by adherence to Standards and Recommended Practices (SARPs) of the Annexes to the Chicago Convention were essential, safety management has to transcend the mere compliance with SARPs toward a performance based process.[5] In this context, ICAO suggested a three step management process: firstly, between the operator and the oversight authority where there must be compete agreement between operators and service providers on the one hand and the oversight authority on the other hand on the safety performance to be expected. Performance will be measured by both parties through established safety indicators and safety targets. Secondly, all parties concerned would agree on the safety requirements necessary to achieve the safety performance agreed upon in the first step. Finally, oversight authorities would verify achievement of the agreed safety performance or lack thereof and the operator/service provider would rectify any observed deviations.

At the DGCA Conference, ICAO reiterated the fact that the term safety management conveys the notion that the management of safety is a business process that should be considered at the same level and along the same lines as any other business process. The safety management systems approach, as proposed, would not only be reactive to some triggering event such as an incident or reportable event, but it would also involve a proactive process of ongoing and routine collection and analysis of safety data during the course of a safety oriented work programme that an organization must pursue on a daily basis while in the business of its core functions. Such a system must essentially be performance driven and proactive. Furthermore, the term 'system' involves an integrated and systemic set of processes calculated to actively manage safety transcending departmental boundaries, thus ensuring safety from a broad perspective.

A systemic safety management system would also require a well thought out performance measurement process and indicators of performance which would be determined through organizational structure and accountability established by

[4] DGCA:2006.1—Management of Aviation Safety, Presented by Canada, DGCA/06-WP/15, at 2.

[5] Implementation of Safety Management Systems (SMS in States, Presented by the ICAO Secretariat, DGCA/06-WP/6, 9/01/06, at 1 and 2.

policies and procedures. The accountability in safety management should be enforced throughout an organization including its senior management.

It is incontrovertible that an effective safety management system has to necessarily co-exist with an efficient air transport product. If the former were to affect the latter's development and its capacity to offer services to the consumer, the fundamental purpose of safety management and its supportive role would be lost, as there would be no longer an air transport system that could adequately cater to the exponential demands made on it. The key purpose of the SMS is to adapt the growth in air transport, however evolving the operations of air transport are. A typical approach was exemplified by the United States at the ICAO DGCA Conference when they advised the delegates of four key areas of the SMS which work synergistically to maintain harmony between safety and efficiency, two of which—safety assurance and safety promotion—are critical to the efficiency and continuity of air transport. According to the United States submission the four key elements to effective SMS are: *Safety Policy*, which covers the SMS requirements, responsibilities and accountabilities for system functions; *Safety Risk Management*, which involve procedures used to identify hazards, assess current and future safety risk of the system or operation, manage the safety risk, document the mitigations selected to manage the safety risk and verify and monitor the mitigations throughout its lifecycle; *Safety Assurance*, which calls for the assurance of the safety product or service provider's system, including audits, evaluations and inspections, as well as data tracking and analysis; and *Safety Promotion*, which entails training, communication and dissemination of safety information to strengthen the safety culture and support integration of the SMS into operations.[6]

ICAO has added a unique dimension to safety management which is called the Unified Strategy. At its 35th session, held in September–October 2004, the ICAO. Assembly adopted Resolution A 35-7 which recognizes that transparency and sharing of safety information is one of the fundamental tenets of a safe air transportation system and urges all Contracting States to share with other Contracting States critical safety information which may have an impact on the safety of international air navigation and to facilitate access to all relevant safety information. The Resolution also encourages Contracting States to make full use of available safety information when performing their safety oversight functions, including during inspections as provided for in Article 16 of the Chicago Convention, which empowers State authorities to search aircraft of other States on landing or departure, and to inspect the certificates and other documents prescribed by the Convention. The Resolution also directs the Council to further develop practical means to facilitate the sharing of such safety information among Contracting States and reminds Contracting States of the need for surveillance of all aircraft operations, including foreign aircraft within their territory and to take appropriate action when necessary to preserve safety. A salient feature of Resolution A35-7 is that it touched on Article 54 j) of the Chicago Convention which makes it a mandatory

[6] Safety Management System Concept, DGCA/06-WP/12 at 2.

function of the Council to report to Contracting States any infraction of the Convention, as well as any failure to carry out recommendations and determinations of the Council, and directs the Council to develop a procedure to inform all Contracting States, within the scope of Article 54 j) in the case of a State having significant compliance shortcomings with respect to ICAO safety-related SARPs.

One of the critical elements of the Resolution is that it directs the Council to promote the concept of regional or sub-regional safety oversight organizations, while encouraging States to foster the creation of regional or sub-regional partnerships to collaborate in the development of solutions to common problems to build their individual safety oversight capability. It also requests the Secretary General to continue to foster coordination and cooperation between USOAP and audit programmes of other organizations related to aviation safety, and specifically with the International Air Transport Association (IATA) and the European Organization for the Safety of Air Navigation (Eurocontrol). Furthermore, Contracting States are urged to further develop regional and sub-regional cooperation and, whenever feasible, partnership initiatives with other States, industry, air navigation service providers, financial institutions and other stake holders to strengthen safety oversight capabilities in order to foster a safer international civil aviation system and to better discharge their individual responsibilities.

Many of ICAO's 191 member States are facing problems with respect to safety oversight. A glaring fact emerging from safety audits conducted by ICAO on States is that the findings of the initial safety oversight audit conducted by ICAO relating to Annex 1—*Personnel Licensing*, Annex 6—*Operation of Aircraft* and Annex 8—*Airworthiness of Aircraft*, indicated that of the 181 Contracting States that were audited between March 1999 and July 2004, considerable numbers of States had deficiencies in respect of a number of requirements under these Annexes. Furthermore, audit follow-up missions have revealed that in many cases, significant deficiencies identified during the initial audits remain. Therefore, the ineluctable conclusion is that, when considering liberalization, States should be concerned not merely of the economic benefits that would result but also its potential impact on safety regulation. States must ensure their continued capacity to meet those requirements so that, as prescribed in the Chicago Convention, civil aviation develops in a safe and orderly manner.

Over the past 67 years, significant improvements have been made in the safety of the international aviation system. The decrease in fatalities is tremendous as seen in the figures of 1945 where a rate of 4.48 passenger fatalities per 100 million passenger miles was recorded. In 1995 the rate had dropped to 0.04. Thus, over a period of 50 years, the risk of fatalities to the flying public was reduced by a factor of 100. However, the number of accidents attributed to scheduled commercial flights increased in 2010 to 121, compared to 113 in 2009. This resulted in an accident rate of 4.0 per million departures, a marginal increase compared to the accident rate of 3.9 per million departures in 2009. While the overall number of fatalities in 2010 was below those in 2005 and 2006, there has been an increase in fatalities over the past 3 years. This trend serves as a reminder that cooperation between the various stakeholders is a key part of reducing the number of aviation accidents and related fatalities.[7]

Safety was further improved in more recent years. ICAO recorded that the rate of accidents involving passenger fatalities in scheduled air transport operations (excluding accidents caused by acts of unlawful interference) dropped from 0.12 per 100,000 flights in 1995 to 0.04 in 2004, a reduction of 66 %. In the same time period, the number of fatal accidents in all air transport operations involving fixed wing aircraft dropped from 86 to 62, and the number of fatal accidents in scheduled airline operations decreased from 31 to 12. The number of fatally injured passengers in scheduled air transport operations (excluding fatalities caused by unlawful interference) in 2004 was 208, the lowest number since 1945.

2.2 Annex 19

Annex 19 to the Chicago Convention, which is entitled *Safety Management* became applicable on 14 November 2013 and is the first new ICAO Annex in over 30 years. The Annex complements existing ICAO safety-related programmes and activities, including the recently-revised Global Aviation Safety Plan and ICAO's safety management training offerings. Particular emphasis will be placed on promoting the safety management approach through the network of Regional Aviation Safety Groups around the world.

The adoption of the Annex highlights the importance of safety management at the State level; enhances safety by consolidating safety management provisions applicable to multiple aviation domains; promotes aligned implementation of SMS and State Safety Programmes (SSP) provisions; creates a process to collect and analyse feedback regarding the implementation of SMS and SSP; and facilitates the future evolution of safety management provisions.

Annex 19 requires that each State establishes an SSP for the management of safety in the State, in order to achieve an acceptable level of safety performance in civil aviation. The SSP is required to have four components: State safety policy and objectives; State safety risk management; State safety assurance; and State safety promotion.[8] The Annex prescribes that under an SSP, each State should require *inter alia* operators of certified aerodromes in accordance with Annex 14 to implement SMS.[9]

The key to Annex 19 is the implementation of SMS. The key words to management of safety are coordination, performance and accountability. Of these, performance is the most critical. While coordination ensures global interoperability of

---

[7] *2011 State of Global Safety*, ICAO: Montreal, 2012 at 4.

[8] Annex 19 to the Convention on International Civil Aviation—*Safety Management*, First Edition: 2013, Standard 3.1.1.

[9] *Id.* Standard 3.1.3.

safety measures and performance measurement, accountability ensures the implementation of the safety management system worldwide. Performance measurement is inextricably linked to the most critical factors—the performance indicators. In SMS, performance should be measured within the basic premise that only what is important for safety management should be measured. One must not measure too much; and factors that impact customer satisfaction should also be measured.

A critical first step towards implementing performance management in any organization is to define a set of conceptual, high-level, key performance indicators (KPIs). In view of the level at which they are identified, KPIs do not identify targets to be achieved, deadlines to be met or any other details regarding execution of tasks. They would flow from an organization's strategic objective of ensuring safety and are described at three levels:

- *Outcomes*: through which the decision making bodies of the organization can objectively validate the strategies of the Organization, in other words: "Is the Organization doing the right things and do the overall effects of performance bring on expected results?";
- *Outputs*: through which the senior management of the organization can objectively assess the effectiveness of the Organization, in other words: "How well is the Organization doing what it set out to do?"; and
- *Measurement*: through which those accountable for key activities can independently assess the proper alignment of their resources and timely achievement of outputs.

Once the KPIs have been approved, the organization needs to develop and implement the other key components of its performance management system to enable the indicators to drive better utilization of the available resources. These components include, but are not limited to:

- The infusion of the performance management philosophy into the management culture and practices of the organization;
- The determination of realistic and measurable targets for each of the indicators;
- The alignment of data collection and interpretation mechanisms with the defined indicators and targets; and
- The traceability of operational plans and milestones to the targets.

Once implemented, the performance measurement system will be subject in its entirety to regular monitoring and use by linking it to planned budgetary allocations. The outcomes will also serve as a barometer to redefine measures, targets, outputs and resources if necessary. In order to derive full benefits from the performance measurement system, SMS may have to be realigned periodically with the changing external environment and newly identified critical objectives. This in turn will involve some realignment on the designed performance measurement system and the operational plans that are in place.

The above-mentioned approach will result in a management system where the allocation of resources and measurement of performance will bring about the timely achievement of outcomes that are most valuable to stakeholders.

The key performance indicators in a SMS should be also developed on the basis that the most critically important factor is employee involvement. The first step toward employee involvement is identification of the process flow. The fundamental issue is that if employees cannot agree on their process(es), they could not effectively measure them or utilize the output of what they have measured.

Another important consideration is to identify the critical activity to be measured. The critical activity is that culminating conduct where it makes the most sense to locate a sensor and define an individual performance measure within a process. This should immediately be followed by the recognition that the next step would be to establish performance goal(s) or standards. All performance measures should be tied to a predefined goal or standard, even if the goal is at first somewhat subjective. Having goals and standards is the only way to meaningfully interpret the results of measurements and gauge the success of management systems.

Consequent to establishing goals and standards, it is necessary to establish performance measurement(s). This helps build the performance measurement system by identifying individual measures.

Once measures are identified, the next step would be to identify responsible parties. A specific entity (as in a team or an individual) needs to be assigned the responsibilities for each of the steps in the performance measurement process. Thereafter, collection of data becomes the next consideration. In addition to writing down the numbers, the data need to be pre-analyzed in a timely fashion to observe any early trends and confirm the adequacy of your data collection system.

A corollary to the identification of goals, measurements and the collection of data is analysis of reports of actual performance. The raw data are formally converted into performance measures, displayed in an understandable form, and disseminated in the form of a report. Comparison actual performance to goal(s) is a key step, where the Organization will compare performance, as presented in the report, to predetermined goals or standards and determine the variation (if any).

Finally, to complete the development of key performance indicators, consideration of new goals is important. Even in highly successful safety management systems, changes may need to be revised in order to establish ones that challenge an organization's resources but do not overtax them. Goals and standards need periodic evaluation to keep up with the latest organizational processes. Management of the SMS and in particular the performance measurement side of things is a key factor, bringing to bear the importance of the question as to who will manage the PM system. The person responsible for measurement of performance would have to prepare performance reports and decide on the periodicity of measurement.

Good performance in SMS requires the maintenance of public confidence in the safety of international civil aviation. This is primarily achieved by the decrease in incidents and accidents involving passenger fatalities and fatalities on the ground. The measurements would evaluate the capability of the organization concerned in collection and analysis of safety information, leading to the output of implementation of a global safety data collection and analysis capability. This would in turn lead to the outcome that ensures global resources are aligned to address the most critical safety risks.

Economic liberalization as well as the evolution of business and operating practices may have serious implications for safety regulation, which need to be addressed properly. The most fundamental consideration is that safety of air transport must remain the ultimate responsibility of the State concerned and should not be compromised by economic considerations. While ICAO should continue its monitoring of liberalization within the parameter of safety, all players, including States, service providers and airlines should coordinate well in understanding their responsibilities and providing safety oversight. In this constantly evolving environment, due regard should be paid to the impact of a growing air transport industry's impact on safety so that coherent SMS are developed.

The operative criterion should be that safety of flight is a valid concern of the aviation industry whether or not air transport is liberalized and, as already discussed, liberalization and consequent competition between air carriers should alert States to the potential safety hazards that a highly competitive air transport industry brings to bear. Considering the elaborate work already accomplished by ICAO, in establishing guidance to States on the implementation of Article 83 *bis* to the Chicago Convention. in addition to Articles 12, 30, 31 and 32 a)[10] of the Convention and the up-to-date Standards and Recommended Practices adopted from time to time as necessary in Annexes 1, 6 and 8, there is no room for doubt that the regulatory provisions are in place.

Therefore what remains is for all players concerned to move toward a performance based SMS process where accountability will drive aviation safety to its desired goals.

2.3 Manual on Certification of Aerodromes

The Manual on Certification of Aerodromes[11] is the basic requirement of the certification process. It contains all the pertinent information concerning the aerodrome site, facilities, services, equipment, operating procedures, organization and management including the safety management system and serves as a reference document agreed between the aerodrome operator and the authorities charged with

[10] Article 12 stipulates that each contracting State is required to insure that every aircraft flying over or manoeuvring within its territory and that every aircraft carrying its nationality mark, wherever that aircraft might be, shall comply with the rules and regulations relating to flight and manoeuvre applicable there. It also provides that each Contracting States should keep its regulations consistent with the principles of the Chicago Convention. Over the high seas the rules will be as established under the Convention and States undertake, under Article 12, to prosecute any offender who does not adhere to these principles. Articles 30 and 31 refer to the need for aircraft to carry radio equipment as required and be issued with certificates of airworthiness by the State of Registry, respectively. Article 32 a) requires the pilot and other members of the crew to be provided with certificates of competency and licenses issued by the State of Registry.

[11] Doc 9774—AN/969, First Edition—2001.

the responsibility for the function and operation of the aerodrome with regard to the standards, conditions and the level of service to be maintained at the aerodrome.

The Manual not only serves as a reference document but also contains a checklist of aerodrome certification standards to be followed when providing airside services at the aerodrome. The authorities mandated to overview the operations of an aerodrome are expected to use the Manual to ensure that an aerodrome conforms to the guidelines contained in the Manual in providing services to aircraft operators. Also important is the fact that the provisions of the Manual would assist the authorities to evaluate whether a particular aerodrome has the competence and suitability to hold an aerodrome certificate.

An aerodrome certificate is an official document issued by the regulatory authority and supported by technical documentation demonstrating that the aerodrome for which it was issued meets specific air safety-related criteria. The certificate, once issued by the regulatory authority, provides the airport operator and aircraft operators with documented proof that the facilities they operate or use are safe.

The certificate also leads to risk management in the aerodrome. From the perspective of the aerodrome operator, the Manual contains all instructions, information and guidance material necessary to enable aerodrome management and operational staff to perform their duties according to national regulations and the aerodrome's own requirements. The Manual would also assist the aerodrome operator to convince the authorities the operation of the aerodrome conforms to applicable national regulations.

The Licensing Authority has an obligation to carry out regular site inspections in order to ascertain compliance with standards. The authority carries out planned and coordinated inspections and provides feedback to the aerodrome operator in a report that stipulates required actions. The aerodrome operator is expected, in justifying the certificate issued, to maintain facilities in accordance with the certificate in effect and promptly advise the authorities and aircraft operators concerned of any deviation from the certificate.

The purpose of the manual is to provide guidance to States in establishing their regulatory system for the certification of land aerodromes. The establishment of such a regulatory system is intended to ensure that the facilities, equipment and operational procedures at certified aerodromes are in compliance with the Standards and Recommended Practices specified in Volume I of Annex 14 to the Convention on International Civil Aviation, and to any national standards and practices in force. This manual also provides guidance on aerodrome certification procedures and on the subsequent compliance and enforcement of the aerodrome operator's obligations. Guidance material on the organizational aspects of the regulatory authority is also included.

It is recognized that a State may limit the certification requirement to the operation of certain aerodromes only, distinguishing between factors such as the maximum number of passenger seats in the aeroplanes served by the aerodrome or the maximum take-off weight of the aeroplanes; whether the operations are scheduled or unscheduled; and whether the aerodrome is open for use at night. Since the safety of operations at all aerodromes is the responsibility of the State, the State's regulations may also need to cover the operation of uncertified aerodromes. Such additional regulations are not covered in the Manual.

The Manual has its genesis in Article 15 of the Chicago Convention which provides that every airport in a contracting State which is open to public use by its national aircraft shall likewise, subject to the provisions of Article 68 (which states that each contracting State may, subject to the provisions of the Convention, designate the route to be followed within its territory by any international air service and the airports which any such service may use), be open under uniform conditions to the aircraft of all the other contracting States. The like uniform conditions shall apply to the use, by aircraft of every contracting State, of all air navigation facilities, including radio and meteorological services, which may be provided for public use for the safety and expedition of air navigation.

The basic principle enunciated by both Annex 14 to the Chicago Convention as well as the Manual on Certification of Aerodromes is that when the operation of an airport is delegated by a State to an operator, the State retains its oversight functions with a view to ensuring that the operator adheres to the standardization and harmonization of regulations pertaining to the proper operation of aerodromes. The Manual recommends that a seminal measure towards effective and efficient operation of an aerodrome might be to establish a separate safety oversight entity and a well-defined safety oversight mechanism buttressed by appropriate legislation, coupled with the implementation of an aerodrome certificate procedure by which a State certifies an aerodrome through the submission of an aerodrome manual by the operator.[12]

Even prior to these measures a State must enact legislation that would set the stage for subsidiary aerodrome regulations which would accord in substance with the relevant Annexes to the Chicago Convention. These laws and regulations should apply to every category of aerodrome operator, be the aerodromes run under privatized, corporatized or commercial entities. This requirement is based on the fundamental premise that the safety, regularity and efficiency of aircraft operations at aerodromes are paramount.[13]

Firstly, the basic aviation laws of a State must admit of the development and promulgation of aerodrome regulations. Secondly, there must be an appropriate entity, be it a private entity or instrumentality of the State, vested with authority to ensure compliance with regulations. This entity must be adequately staffed and resourced. Although the Manual calls this entity "Civil Aviation Authority" (CAA) for convenience, any name could be used for such an entity. It is at the discretion of the State concerned to exempt certain airports (say, which have less than a certain number of passengers flowing through them annually) from being certified but alternate provisions must prevail in such instances to ensure safety of air transport within the aerodrome so exempted.

---

[12] *Id.*, paragraph 11.2.

[13] *Id.*, paragraph 1.2.2.

The Manual contains model regulations covering the requirement for aerodrome certification; application for issuance of an aerodrome certificate; grant of the certificate; endorsement of conditions to be included in the certificate; duration of the certificate; surrender of the certificate; transfer of the certificate; grant of an interim certificate and amendment of the certificate.[14]

Every operator of an aerodrome must have a manual that will be known as an aerodrome manual. It will a document typed or printed in a format that could easily be revised from time to time and signed by the aerodrome operator. A copy of the Manual must be deposited with the CAA. It is required to contain general information; particulars of the aerodrome site; particulars that would be required for aeronautical information services; operating procedures and safety measures; and details of aerodrome operations, safety and administration. The Manual should be altered or revised to reflect accuracy and currency of information.

The aerodrome operator is required to comply with both the relevant provisions of Annex 14 as well as the provisions contained in the Manual. If the CAA or other competent authority requires staff in the aerodrome to be certified as necessary and relevant the aerodrome operator is required to ensure that this need is fulfilled. The operation of the aerodrome will be as required by the procedures laid out in the Manual. It is the responsibility of the aerodrome operator to ensure that all regulations, specifications and requirements in the Manual are complied with all those working at the aerodrome, whether they be ground handling staff, fixed based operators or other.

Another responsibility of the aerodrome operator to ensure an audit of the safety management system of the aerodrome. The framework for a safety management system is contained in Appendix 2 to Annex 19 to the Chicago Convention. The Manual identifies a Directorate of Aerodromes Standards and Safety (DASS) that would carry out the audits periodically and on an on-site basis of the safety management system including verification of the aerodrome and data published in the Aeronautical Information Publication (AIP) and inspection of the aerodrome facilities, equipment and operating procedures.[15] The DASS will also review the aerodrome operator's daily audits and special safety audit reports and actions thereon.[16]

Personnel so authorized by the CAA may inspect and carry out tests on the aerodrome facilities, services and equipment, inspect the aerodrome operator's documents and records and verify the aerodrome operator's safety management system before the aerodrome certificate is approved and issued or renewed and, subsequently at any other time, for the purpose of ensuring safety at the aerodrome.[17] Furthermore, an aerodrome operator is required to adhere to the need to notify and report to the CAA, air traffic control and pilots within specified time limits required by the provisions of the Manual.

---

[14] *Id.*, Section B Aerodrome Certification, 1.

[15] *Id.*, paragraph 5.2.3.1. a).

[16] *Id.*, paragraph 5.2.3.1. b).

[17] *Id.*, paragraph 3D.6.1.

The aerodrome certification process involves dealing with the expression of intent and interest by an applicant for the aerodrome certificate; assessment of the formal application, including evaluation of the aerodrome manual; assessment of the aerodrome facilities and equipment; issuance or refusal to issue an aerodrome certificate; and the promulgation of the certified status of an aerodrome so certified in an AIP.

Responsibility devolves upon the aerodrome operator to comply with the requirements of the certification regulations. However, the requirement is based on voluntary adherence. Aerodrome inspector's performing functions on behalf of the CAA or DAAS may be engineers or other relevant professionals as recognized by the CAA. The duties of such inspectors include verification of the aerodrome data in the Manual such as the location of the aerodrome; the name and address of the aerodrome operator; the movement area; the runway declared distances available; aeronautical ground lighting; ground services and notices of special conditions and procedures if any.[18] With regard to on-site inspections including verification and audits of aerodrome operating procedures include: the overall aerodrome safety management system; the aerodrome emergency plan and periodic aerodrome emergency exercise; rescue and fire fighting and various other factors that bear upon the safety of the aerodrome.[19] Appendix A to the Manual include particulars to be included in an aerodrome manual they are: general information that includes purpose and scope of the Aerodrome Manual; legal requirement for an aerodrome certificate; conditions for use of the aerodrome; the available aeronautical information system; the system for recording aircraft movements; and obligations of the aerodrome operator.

Particulars of the aerodrome site should also be included in the aerodrome manual additionally, aerodrome dimensions; details of aerodrome reporting; details of access to the aerodrome area; aerodrome emergency plan; rescue and fire fighting and other operational details are required to be placed in the aerodrome manual.

2.4 The Aerodrome Design Manual

2.4.1 Runways

The Aerodromes Manual is in six sections. This section deals with the design of runways and begins by stating that many factors affect the determination of the siting, orientation and number of runways. The more important factors are: weather, in particular the runway/aerodrome usability factor, as determined by wind distribution, and the occurrence of localized fogs; topography of the aerodrome site and

[18] *Id.*, paragraph 5.5.4. a).

[19] *Id.*, paragraph 5.5.4. b).

its surroundings; type and amount of air traffic to be served, including air traffic control aspects; aeroplane performance considerations; and environmental considerations, particularly noise. The primary runway, to the extent other factors permit, should be oriented in the direction of the prevailing wind. All runways should be oriented so that approach and departure areas are free of obstacles and, preferably, so that aircraft are not directed over populated areas.

An aerodrome should have runways that are sufficient to meet air traffic demands, which consist of the number of aircraft arrivals and departures, and the mixture of aircraft types, to be accommodated in 1 h during the busiest periods. The decision as to the total number of runways to be provided should also take into account the aerodrome usability factor and economic considerations. Particular attention is focused in the Manual as to whether the aerodrome is to be used in all meteorological conditions or only in visual meteorological conditions, and whether it is intended for use by day and night or only by day.

When a new instrument runway is being located, particular attention needs to be given to areas over which aeroplanes will be required to fly when following instrument approach and missed approach procedures, so as to ensure that obstacles in these areas or other factors will not restrict the operation of the aeroplanes for which the runway is intended.

Ecological and environmental considerations are noted in the Manual where it is said that the effect of a particular runway alignment on wild life, the general ecology of the area, and noise-sensitive areas of communities should be considered. The noise level produced by aircraft operations at and around the aerodrome is generally considered a primary environmental cost associated with the facility. Most noise exposure lies within the land area immediately beneath and adjacent to the aircraft approach and departure paths. Noise levels are generally measured through some formulation of decibel level, duration and number of occurrences. A large number of noise measuring techniques exist [see Annex 16—Environmental Protection and Recommended Method for Computing Noise Contours around Airports (Cir 205)]. Proper site selection and adjacent land use planning can serve to greatly reduce and possibly eliminate the noise problem associated with the aerodrome.

The rest of the Manual on runways has a variety of technical specifications on the length and breadth of the runway; the number of runways required and the positioning of runways in an aerodrome. There are four threats to runway safety: runway incursions; runway excursions; foreign objects and debris (FOD) and bird strikes. A bird strike is a collision between a bird and an aircraft which is in flight or on a takeoff or landing mode. However, this term is also used for aircraft collisions with other animals such as bats or other animals on ground. On 15 January 2009, US Airways Flight 1549 took off from La Guardia Airport in New York City at 3:03 P.M. Eastern time on its way to Charlotte, N.C., with 150 passengers and 5 crew members on board. As it gained altitude, it reportedly ran into a flock of geese, necessitating the ditching of the aircraft on the Hudson River.[20] On 3 October 2006,

[20] See Borrell (2009).

a Boeing 767-300, departing from Melbourne Australia on an internal flight, ran into a flock of gulls at rotation with evident ingestion and damage to the left engine. The flight crew considered the ingestion was not sufficiently serious to justify a return to land and the intended internal flight was completed. On March 4, 1999, a DC91 operated by USA Jet Airlines, at night and on final approach to land at Kansas City International Airport encountered a flock of large birds. The crew managed to regain sufficient thrust to continue the approach and land without further incident. On 6 December 1997, a British Airways Boeing 747-100, departing from London Heathrow airport, had an engine bird strike just after takeoff, causing substantial damage and falling debris.[21]

Like aircraft, migratory birds also follow well-defined flight paths in numbers and their close proximity to an airport could be hazardous to aircraft landing and taking off in the vicinity. In addition, birds are attracted to open areas of grass and water as well as shrubs and trees which provide food for birds.[22] The issue of bird strikes takes on an added dimension by affecting social and policy issues which are not strictly linked with air transport. The key area of environmental protection—particularly in the fields of wildlife policy and habitat management—brings to bear issues of State responsibility for national policy as well as a commitment towards maintaining the bio-diversity of the ecosystem. An example of dire consequences of a bird strike can be cited in the instance of a Boeing 747 aircraft departing Los Angeles Airport in late August 2000, which had to dump 83 tons of fuel to land safely after a bird strike.[23]

Annex 14 on Aerodromes, in Chapter 9, contains three Recommendations pertaining to bird strike reduction. The first Recommendation calls for a bird strike hazard on or in the vicinity of an aerodrome to be assessed through the establishment of a national procedure for recording and reporting bird strikes to aircraft and the collection of information from aircraft operators, airport personnel etc. on the presence of birds on or around an aerodrome.[24] The Annex also recommends that, when a bird strike hazard is identified at an aerodrome, the appropriate authority should take action to decrease the number of birds constituting a potential hazard to aircraft operators by adopting measures for discouraging their presence on, or in the vicinity of an aerodrome.[25] The final Recommendation of the Annex urges that garbage disposal dumps or any such other source attracting birds on or in the vicinity of an aerodrome be eliminated or their establishment prevented, unless studies indicate that such disposal units are unlikely to be conducing to bird activity and a bird hazard problem.[26]

---

[21] For more instances of bird strikes see http://www.skybrary.aero/index.php/Accident_and_Serious_Incident_Reports:_BS.

[22] For a detailed discussion on bird population trends and their impact on aviation see Maragakis (2009).

[23] See http://www.birdstrike.org/commlink/top_ten.htm at p. 3.

[24] Annex 14 *supra*, Recommandation 9.4.1 a).

[25] Annex 14, Recommendation 9.4.3.

[26] Recommendation 9.4.4.

Recommendation 9.4.5. which calls upon States to give due consideration to aviation safety concerns related to land developments in the vicinity of the aerodrome that might attract wildlife, encourages measures to be taken toward discouraging bird activity within the vicinity of an aerodrome. This is given effect to in guidance material formulated by ICAO in the form of provisions in the *Airport Services Manual*,[27] Part 3 of which is dedicated to bird control and reduction. The Manual gives detailed guidance to States on how to organize a National Committee and lays out the roles and responsibilities of a control programme. Chapter 4 of the Manual is particularly significant, in that it gives a detailed breakdown on how to organize an airport bird strike control programme. This calls for a very integrated approach to be evolved and developed to control bird activity at airports. Communications between field personnel and air traffic controllers, allocation of monies for bird control and assistance of aircraft operators in coordinating a concerted effort are some measures recommended. There is also a separate chapter on environment management and site modification, together with segments on dispersal methods, incompatible land use around airports, evaluation of wildlife control programmes and staffing airport bird control programmes being given special chapter treatment.

One commentator adds:

> The exercise of "due diligence" to manage wildlife hazards involves (in the USA) the assessment of wildlife hazards at the airport and, if needed based on the assessment, the implementation of a wildlife hazard management plan (FAA regulations in CFR 14 Part 139.337). An important component of the wildlife hazard management plan is the prevention of habitats and land uses on or in the vicinity of the airport that are attractive to hazardous wildlife. Wildlife hazard management at airports is a complex, public-sensitive, endeavor involving many species of wildlife and their habitats governed by various federal and state regulations. Airports need to employ professional biologists trained in wildlife damage control to assist in the development, implementation, and evaluation of wildlife hazard management plans. Such professionally developed and implemented management plans will minimize the likelihood of catastrophic or major-damage wildlife strikes on an airport and provide crucial support during litigation in the aftermath of any significant strike event that might occur.[28]

Annex 14, Volume I, requires the wildlife strike hazard on, or in the vicinity of, an aerodrome to be assessed through, among other things, the establishment of national procedures and an ongoing evaluation of wildlife hazards by competent personnel. The establishment of a national committee is ideally suited to addressing this task. Such committees have proven to be popular forums to gain and exchange information on research and development in airport wildlife control. Although the composition of a national committee may vary from State to State, it should include all stakeholders associated with or interested in the problem. It should be noted that national committees have very little authority in decision making and usually act as an information source for those in the aviation community.

[27] Airport Services Manual, Doc 9137 AN/598 Part 3, Third Edition, 1991.

[28] Dolbeer (2006), at 5.

Part 3 of the Airport Services Manual States that The State civil aviation authority (CAA) or national aviation administration (NAA) should ensure that any procedures in the airport certification manual relating to bird/wildlife control are developed and implemented as part of the aerodrome safety management system (SMS). Birds and other wildlife on, and in the vicinity of, the airport may represent a threat to aircraft safety. In some cases, this threat can be reduced by adapting the aircraft's schedule in favour of the wildlife, especially when the presence of wildlife is for a limited time. Reducing the presence of wildlife in aircraft flight paths can be achieved through ecological means such as habitat management or the dispersal or removal of hazardous wildlife. While the wildlife control programme will be airport-specific, the development of such nature and environmentally sensitive programmes should adhere to national environmental regulations.

States seeking assistance with the development of a wildlife control programme and the assessment of wildlife control issues may wish to contact the ICAO Secretariat as ICAO Technical Cooperation Programme experts are available to assist States in the development and implementation of bird/wildlife programmes and the assessment and identification of hazards and attractants associated with an airport.Because of the importance of bird/wildlife control, each airport operator has the responsibility to develop, implement and demonstrate an effective bird/wildlife strike and wildlife control programme at the airport, and this should be tailored to and commensurate with the size and level of complexity of the airport, taking account of the identification of the bird hazard and the risk assessment of that hazard. Airport operators, where practicable, should implement a programme tailored to local conditions, with assistance from the national committee or other outside agencies, as required. Where practicable, the airport operator should appoint an airport bird/wildlife control coordinator who is responsible and accountable for the airport's bird/wildlife hazard control policy and the personnel engaged in bird/wildlife hazard control. This may include the formation of a local airport bird/wildlife committee that will develop and implement the specific programme. It is imperative that personnel responsible for these tasks are able to demonstrate competence, are trained by qualified personnel and are provided with the appropriate resources and equipment to carry out their tasks.

With regard to runway incursions, ICAO defines a runway incursion as *any occurrence at an aerodrome involving the incorrect presence of an aircraft, vehicle or person on the protected area of a surface designated for the landing and take-off of aircraft.*[29] The Canadian Aviation Safety Board [now the Transportation Safety Board of Canada (TSB)] issued a report in 1987entitled *Report on a Special Investigation into the Risk of Collisions Involving Aircraft on or Near the Ground*

[29] *Ibid*. Transport Canada defines a runway incursion as *any occurrence at an aerodrome involving the unauthorized or unplanned presence of an aircraft, vehicle or person on the protected area of a surface designed for aircraft landings and departures*. See http://www.tc.gc.ca/eng/civilaviation/publications/tp185-1-02-292-536.htm.

at Canadian Civil Airports. The report stated that both the Canadian and U.S. experience would suggest an extremely wide range of cause-related factors for the occurrences which involve actual or potential ground conflicts, and identified u*nexpected human behaviors by far the most common causative factors in such occurrences.*

ICAO considers that information pertaining to the proximity of aircraft and/or the vehicle; geometry of the encounter; evasive or corrective action; available reaction time; environmental conditions, weather, visibility and surface condition; and factors that affect system performance are all necessary to properly classify the severity of a runway incursion.[30] The official definition of the Federal Aviation Administration of the United States is that a runway incursion is *any occurrence at an airport involving an aircraft, vehicle, person or object on the ground that creates a collision hazard or results in a loss of separation with an aircraft taking off, intending to take off, or intending to land.*[31] The FAA definition envisions various types of occurrences such as a pilot deviation—which is any action on the part of the pilot that results in violation of a Federal Aviation Regulation—an operational error, which is an occurrence attributable to an element of the air traffic control (ATC) system which has two results, the first being two or more aircraft coming within less than the minimum separation minima or between an aircraft and obstacles (vehicles, personnel and equipment on runways) and the second being an aircraft landing or departing on a runway closed to aircraft after receiving air traffic authorization; and a vehicle or pedestrian deviation—an occurrence resulting from a vehicle operator, non-pilot operator of an aircraft or pedestrian deviating onto the movement area including the runway without ATC authorization.

The world's worst airline disaster occurred on a runway when in 1977 582 persons were killed as a KLM Boeing 747 which was taking off slammed into a PAN AM 747 in the Canary Islands. There have been numerous incidents and accidents relating to runway incursions both before and after that fateful event. One of the more significant was the Comair accident which sent flight 5191 onto a wrong runway sending 49 people to their deaths. A similar incident occurred in 1993 where a pilot who was cleared for take off on a particular runway, accidentally chose a shorter one. In March 2006, the Federal Aviation Administration investigated three close calls at Chicago's O'Hare Airport. The first involved a Lufthansa jet and Delta Airlines plane that came within 100 ft of each other after both were cleared for take off from intersecting runways. The second incursion involved a United Airlines plane 2 days after the Lufthansa—Delta incident, which was instructed to take off from a runway already assigned to another carrier. The third incursion took place in mid March 2006 when a regional jet was cleared for takeoff on a runway moments before an Airbus A320 was cleared for takeoff on a runway that would have connected to the one to be used by the regional jet.

---

[30] *Manual for Prevention of Runway Incursions*, Doc 9870 First Edition, 2007 in Chap. 1 at 6-3.

[31] Dean Chamberlain (1999), pp. 9–12, continued at 25, at 9.

ICAO does not have a definition for a runway excursion. According to Skybrary, a runway excursion occurs when an aircraft departs the runway in use during the take-off or landing run and that such an excursion may be intentional or unintentional.[32] A runway excursion may occur when a departing aircraft fails to become airborne or successfully reject the take off before reaching the end of the designated runway. Another instance would be when a landing aircraft is unable to stop before the end of the designated runway is reached.

There are a couple of instances on runway excursions worth noting. On 14 October 2004, an MK Airlines Boeing 747 collided with terrain at Halifax International Airport, Nova Scotia due to reduced power at take off. The Aviation Investigation Report issued by Transport Canada revealed *inter alia* that at the time of the accident, MK Airlines was using the Boeing Laptop Tool (BLT) for determining performance calculations. The BLT is a Microsoft Windows based software application used to calculate take-off performance data, landing performance data, and weight and balance information. The Report also revealed that the company did not have a formal training and testing program on the BLT, and it was likely that the user of the BLT in this occurrence was not fully conversant with the software.[33]

On 2 August 2005, an Airbus A 340-313 aircraft (Flight AFR 358) overran Toronto's Pearson International Airport through heavy rain and caught fire. All passengers were safely evacuated. The Aviation Investigation Report issued by the Transportation Safety Board of Canada discusses four causative factors put forward by the National Aeronautics and Space Administration (NASA) of the United States as likely to contribute to decision errors of the flight crew: ambiguity of information; dynamically changing risks; goal conflicts (organizational or social pressures; and unanticipated circumstances.[34] The Accident Investigative Report discusses that low ceiling and poor visibility due to thunderstorms; rapid changes in surface pressure; lightning, hail, both within and outside a cloud, icing, damaging wind gusts and down drafts due to microbursts can all contribute to the unsafe operation of an aircraft while landing or takeoff.[35] One of the decisions taken by Transport Canada after the accident was to build safety areas at the ends of runways at Canadian airports.[36]

The Transportation Safety Board of Canada, in its investigative report suggested that the Department of Transport establish clear standards limiting approaches and landings in convective weather for all air transport operators at Canadian airports; France's Direction Générale de l.AviationCivile and other civil aviation authorities

---

[32] http://www.skybrary.aero/index.php/Runway_Excursion.

[33] MK Airlines Crash B-747 Halifax Excerpts Final Report, Aviation Investigation Report A04H0004, Halifax International Airport, 14 October 2004 at 6. The Report is available at http://www.wiloo.be/mk_airlines_final_report_crash_halifax.htm.

[34] Aviation Investigation Report A05H0002, Runway Overrun and Fire; Air France Airbus A 340-313 F-GLZQ, Toronto Lester B. Pearson International Airport, Ontario, 02 August 2005 at 82.

[35] *Id.* p. 120.

[36] *Id.* p. 119.

establish clear standards limiting approaches and landings in convective weather; and the Department of Transport mandate training for all pilots involved in Canadian air transport operations to better enable them to make landing decisions in deteriorating weather.[37] The Board also recommended that France's Direction Générale de l.AviationCivile and other civil aviation authorities mandate training for air transport pilots to better enable them to make landing decisions in deteriorating weather.

There were four lawsuits as a result of the Air France runway excursion. Air France and its insurers claimed damages over $200 million against NAV Canada, various employees of NAV Canada, the Greater Toronto Airports Authority (GTAA) and the Attorney General of Canada, claiming damages for the loss of the aircraft and indemnity for all claims paid by Air France as a result of the accident.[38] The passengers of AFR flight 358 filed a class action suit claiming damages against Air France, NAV Canada, the pilot and first officer, and others for damages sustained by the passengers and their families as a result of the accident.[39] Air France cross claimed against NAV Canada. The GTAA claimed against Air France, NAV Canada, the captain and the first officer for damages relating to environmental costs involving the cleanup of the wreckage area and the related fuel and fire extinguisher chemical costs.[40] Air France in turn cross claimed against NAV Canada in relation to these damages. A passenger who opted out of the class action instituted a separate action against Air France, NAV Canada, the GTAA, the captain and first officer and others, for damages caused to her and her family as a result of the accident.[41]

It is very clear that there are several actors involved in an accident pertaining to a breach of runway safety. They are mainly: the State and its relevant instrumentalities; the flight crew; the air navigation service provider; and the airport.

Foreign object debris is any object that does not belong in or near airplanes. Damage occurs when a FOD injures airport or airline personnel and damage airplanes. These debris may include any object found in an inappropriate location that—as a result of being in that location—can damage equipment or injure airplane or airport personnel.[42] FOD is known to include a wide range of material, including loose hardware, pavement fragments, catering supplies, building materials, rocks, sand, pieces of luggage, and even wildlife. FOD is found at terminal gates, cargo aprons, taxiways, runways, and run-up pads. It causes damage through direct contact with airplanes, such as by cutting airplane tires or being ingested into

---

[37] *Id.* pp. 121–123.

[38] *Socíeté Air France et al.* v. *GTAA et al.* Court File No 07-337564 PD3.

[39] *Hussain Abdulrahim et al.* v. *Air France et al.* Court File No. 05-CV-294746 CP.

[40] *Greater Toronto Airport Authority* v. *Air France et al.* Court File No. 07-CV-337545 PD2.

[41] *Strugarova et al.* v. *Air France et al.* Court File No. 07-CV-336943 PD2.

[42] http://www.boeing.com/commercial/aeromagazine/aero_01/textonly/s01txt.html. The resulting damage is estimated to cost the aerospace industry $4 billion a year. Airports, airlines, and airport tenants can reduce this cost by taking steps to prevent airport FOD.

engines, or as a result of being thrown by jet blast and damaging airplanes or injuring people.

On 25 July 2000 the Concorde (registered F-BTSC) operated by Air France took off from Paris Charles de Gaulle on a charter flight to New York with 9 crew and 100 passengers on board. On takeoff, one of its tires went over a FOD left behind by a departing aircraft that had used the runway on which the Concorde was taking off. This caused the Concorde's tyre to burst and parts of the tyre to be ingested into one of its engines, causing a fire. The aircraft crashed into a hotel at La Patted'Oie in Gonesse. All 109 persons in the aircraft perished and 4 others on the ground also died as a result of the collision.

The Final Report of the Investigation identified the following causes as probable in the context of the accident:

a) High-speed passage of a tyre over a part lost by an aircraft that had taken off 5 min earlier and the destruction of the tyre;
b) The ripping out of a large piece of tank in a complex process of transmission of the energy produced by the impact of a piece of tyre at another point on the tank, this transmission associating deformation of the tank skin and the movement of the fuel, with perhaps the contributory effect of other more minor shocks and/or a hydrodynamic pressure surge.
c) Ignition of the leaking fuel by an electric arc in the landing gear bay or through contact with the hot parts of the engine with forward propagation of the flame causing a very large fire under the aircraft's wing and severe loss of thrust on engine 2 then engine 1; and
d) In addition, the impossibility of retracting the landing gear probably contributing to the retention and stabilisation of the flame throughout the flight.[43]

It is worthy of note that, from a regulatory perspective, Annex 14 to the Chicago Convention requires that surfaces of all movement areas including pavements (runways, taxiways and aprons) and adjacent areas be inspected and their conditions monitored regularly as part of an aerodrome preventive and corrective maintenance programme with the objective of avoiding and eliminating any loose objects/debris that might cause damage to aircraft or impair the operation of aircraft systems.[44] Furthermore, the Annex prescribes that the surface of a paved runway shall be maintained in such a condition as to provide good friction characteristics and low rolling resistance. It also calls for the rapid and complete removal of snow, ice, slush, standing water, mud, dust, sand, oil, rubber deposits and other contaminants with a view to minimizing accumulation.[45]

---

[43] Accident on 25 July 2000 at La Patted'Oie in Gonesse (95) to the Concorde Registered F-BTSC Operated by Air France, Report Translation f-SC000725a.

[44] Annex 14 Aerodromes Volume 1, Aerodrome Design and Operations, Fifth Edition, July 2009, Standard 10.2.1.

[45] *Id.* Standard 10.2.8.

Part 9 of the ICAO Airport Services Manual,[46] which focuses on airport maintenance practices, recommends that, for safety reasons, the surfaces of runways, taxiways and aprons have to be clean of sand, debris, stones or other loose objects[47] and reference is made in the Manual to Standard 9.4 of Annex 14 which has been discussed above. The Manual; identifies the types of objects that could be found on runways and taxiways[48] and provides, in paragraph 4.6.1 for the cleaning of contaminants such as fuel, lubricants, hydraulic oils, marking paint or rubber. There are also provisions for removal of snow and ice.[49]

2.4.2 *Taxiways, Aprons and Holding Bays*

The Aerodrome Design Manual in its section addresses the subject of taxiways, aprons and holding bays. The Manual starts off by stating that optimal capacity and efficiency of an aerodrome are realized only by obtaining the proper balance between the need for runways, passenger and cargo terminals, and aircraft storage and servicing areas. These separate and distinct aerodrome functional elements are linked by the taxiway system. The components of the taxiway system therefore serve to link the aerodrome functions and are necessary to develop optimum aerodrome utilization.

The first recommendation is that the taxiway system should be designed to minimize the restriction of aircraft movement to and from the runways and apron areas. A properly designed system should be capable of maintaining a smooth, continuous flow of aircraft ground traffic at the maximum practical speed with a minimum of acceleration or deceleration. This requirement ensures that the taxiway system will operate at the highest levels of both safety and efficiency.

Irrespective of the nature of business that is carried out in the aerodrome or its varied functions, for any given aerodrome, the taxiway system should be able to accommodate (without significant delay) the demands of aircraft arrivals and departures on the runway system. At low levels of runway utilization the taxiway system can accomplish this with a minimum number of components. However, as the runway acceptance rate increases, the taxiway system capacity must be sufficiently expanded to avoid becoming a factor which limits aerodrome capacity. In the extreme case of runway capacity saturation, when aircraft are arriving and departing at the minimum separation distances, the taxiway system should allow aircraft to exit the runway as soon as practical after landing and to enter the runway just before take-off. This enables aircraft movements on the runway to be maintained at the minimum separation distance.

---

[46] Airport Services Manual, First Edition, 1984, Part 9.

[47] *Id.*, paragraph 4.5.1.

[48] *Id.* Paragraph 4.5.2.

[49] *Id.* Paragraphs 4.7.1–4.7.33.

It is recommended in the Manual that there be a sufficient number of entrance and exit taxiways serving a specific runway to accommodate the current demand peaks for take-offs and landings. Additional entrances and exits should be designed and developed ahead of expected growth in runway utilization. The following principles apply to the planning of these taxiway system components: the function of exit taxiways is to minimize the run-way occupancy time of landing aircraft. In theory, exit taxiways can be located to best serve each type of aircraft expected to use the runway.

Taxiway accidents, although not too frequent, nevertheless occur, calling for the installation in the wingtips of aircraft of cameras and other visual aids that could prevent such accidents. On November 13 2013, two aircraft belonging to Air India and Jet Airways taxiing at New York's John F. Kennedy Airport were involved in a low-speed ground collision. The taxiway accident, which did not cause any injuries, was the second time a bigger jet has clipped the tail of a smaller plane near gates at this particular airport. With the advent of larger jets such as the A 380 the problem may get worse. Reacting to this potential threat The National Transportation Safety Board urged United States and regulators in Europe in March 2013 to approve the installation of ground-collision prevention devices, such as wingtip cameras, on larger jetliners to help pilots avoid such problems. At the time of writing, there had been no response, positive or negative from the regulators concerned. There had been two other serious U.S. taxiway accidents earlier, in Chicago[50] and Boston,[51] which occurred since 2011. Some experts on runway safety maintain the compelling need for cameras since pilots of most wide-body jets are precluded from seeing the wing tips of their planes unless they open a cockpit window and strain their necks to look for obstructions.

In April 2007, a Boeing 747-400 aircraft operated by El Al had a hit a tug on a taxiway at Charles de Gaulle Airport (CDG) in Paris. The accident did substantial damage to the aircraft, and presumably to the tug. No people were injured, although those working in the ramp operating the tug had a very close call.[52]

The *Comair* crash report of 2006 gives the following interesting details of taxiway and runway incidents and accidents. "On October 31, 2000, Singapore Airlines flight 006, a Boeing 747, crashed during an attempted takeoff from a partially closed runway at Chiang Kai-Shek International Airport, Taoyuan, Taiwan 136. Of the 179 occupants aboard the airplane, 83 were killed". The report by

[50] The control tower manager at Chicago O'Hare International Airport (KORD) published an airport notice effective August 19 that reminds pilots of locations where tower controllers are unable to see their aircraft after a "line up and wait" instruction is issued.

[51] In July 2011, Delta Flight 266, a Boeing 767, was taxiing for departure at about 7:40 p.m., when the left wing hit the Canadair Regional Jet 900, which had 74 passengers and 3 crew members aboard. There were 204 passengers and 11 crew on the flight to Amsterdam. The planes were on taxiways that run nearly perpendicular to each other. The larger plane was moving; the Atlantic Southeast flight was stationary. The Atlantic Southeast flight was operated by Delta. No one was injured.

[52] El Al Flight 324 was preparing to depart from CDG for a scheduled flight to Tel Aviv.

Taiwan's Aviation Safety Council found that the pilots did not adequately review the taxi route to ensure that they understood that the route to runway 5L (the correct departure runway) required passing runway 5R (a parallel runway that was under construction and open only for taxi operations). The report also stated that the pilots did not verify the airplane's position with the taxi route as they were turning onto the runway and that the company's operations manual did not include a procedure to confirm an airplane's position on the active runway before initiating takeoff. The report concluded that the flight crew lost situational awareness and took off from the wrong runway despite numerous available cues that provided information about the airplane's position on the airport 137. The Aviation Safety Council recommended that Singapore Airlines "include in all company pre-takeoff checklists an item formally requiring positive visual identification and confirmation of the correct takeoff runway."

On January 25, 2002, China Airlines flight 011, an Airbus A340, departed from a taxiway at Ted Stevens Anchorage International Airport, Anchorage, Alaska, instead of the assigned runway. The available distance on the taxiway was 6,800 ft, but the airplane's calculated takeoff distance was 7,746 ft. The airplane took off, but its main landing gear left impressions in a snow berm at the end of the taxiway. The airplane proceeded to its destination and landed without further incident. The Safety Board determined that the probable cause of this incident was the captain's selection of a taxiway instead of a runway for takeoff and the flight crew's inadequate coordination of the departure, which resulted in a departure from a taxiway. The Board determined that a contributing factor to the incident was the lack of an operator requirement for the flight crew to verbalize and verify the runway in use before takeoff 138. As a result of this incident, China Airlines modified its Airbus A340 operating manual to include verbalization and verification of the runway in use.

Another flight that is relevant to this discussion is Alaska Airlines flight 61, a Boeing 737, took off from runway 34R instead of runway 34C (center), which was the assigned runway, at Seattle-Tacoma International Airport (SEA), Seattle, Washington. The airplane continued uneventfully to its destination of Juneau International Airport, Juneau, Alaska. According to the captain of the flight, the ATIS that was current at the time indicated that departing aircraft were taking off either with the full length of runway 34R or at the point where the runway intersected taxiway Q. The first officer of the flight stated that the takeoff briefing included a departure from runway 34R.

The captain stated that the controller instructed the flight crew to follow a Boeing 757 to runway 34R and that the 757 departed from runway 34R where the runway intersected taxiway Q. The captain also stated that the controller instructed the crew to taxi the airplane into position and hold on runway 34C. Further, even though he repeated this information to the controller, the captain was still thinking that the airplane would be taking off from runway 34R. During this time, the first officer was completing flight paperwork and conducting other pre-flight activities.

After receiving takeoff clearance from runway 34C from the controller, the captain stated that he lined up the airplane on runway 34R and transferred control of the airplane to the first officer. The airplane departed uneventfully from runway 34R.

According to the controller, he was scanning the runways and noticed that the airplane was rolling on runway 34R abeam the tower instead of runway 34C. Because there were no potential air traffic conflicts at the time, the controller thought that it would be safer to let the airplane depart from runway 34R than to have the pilots abort the takeoff. After the airplane had taken off, the controller informed the flight crew that the airplane had departed from the wrong runway.

On April 18, 2007, about 0625, United Airlines flight 1404, an Airbus A320, taxied onto a closed runway at Miami International Airport (MIA), Miami, Florida, and began its takeoff roll. Night VMC prevailed at the time. A NOTAM indicated that runway 9/27 was closed from 2300 on April 17 to 1000 on April 18; the NOTAM was included in the flight release paperwork. The runway closure was also included in the ATIS information broadcast.

The flight crewmembers reported that they had the airport charts out and available. The controller told the flight crew to taxi the airplane to runway 30. The captain stated that he observed taxiway S almost directly opposite from the airplane's position and chose to make a left turn from taxiway S onto taxiway Q. This parallel taxi route placed the airplane adjacent to runway 30, the assigned runway for takeoff. The captain stated that, as the airplane passed the intersection with taxiway T, he verified that the runway sign was for runway 30. The first officer stated that, during this time, he was busy with flight paperwork and was accomplishing flight control checks.

Taxiway Q made a slight bend to the left after the intersection with taxiway T so that the taxiway was parallel with runway 27. The captain stated that he saw a runway, which he believed to be runway 30, when he looked to the right.

The first officer called the tower and advised that the airplane was ready to depart on runway 30. The controller cleared the airplane for takeoff from runway 30 while the airplane was still on taxiway Q. The first officer acknowledged the clearance for takeoff but did not state the runway number for the departure. The captain stated that, as the airplane neared the end of taxiway Q, he observed the hold short line and that, because the airplane was cleared for takeoff, he chose to turn directly onto the runway without stopping and transfer control of the airplane to the first officer. The first officer stated that his heading display was rotating to the right and in the correct direction to line up with the runway, which was still located to the right.

The first officer stated that he advanced the throttles, and, just before they reached the cruise thrust position, the airplane's nose wheel light illuminated a truck flashing its lights on the right side of the runway. The captain and the first officer stated that they observed the truck at the same time. Simultaneously, the controller was querying the flight crew to determine whether the airplane was on runway 30. The first officer rejected the takeoff, and the captain assumed control of the airplane.

Ramp personnel called the tower to advise that an airplane was on a closed runway, and the controller acknowledged this information. The controller subsequently advised the crew to use caution for workers and equipment on runway

27 and instructed the flight crew to taxi the airplane to runway 30. The airplane then took off to its destination airport—Dulles International Airport, Chantilly, Virginia—"without further incident".[53]

To minimize current construction costs, an aerodrome's taxiway system should be only as complex as needed to support the near-term capacity needs of the runway. With careful planning, additional taxiway components can be added to the system in stages to keep pace with the growth in aerodrome demand. The layout of an aerodrome, its dimensions and/or the extension of its runway/taxiway system may require taxiways to bridge over surface transport modes (roads, railways, canals) or open water (rivers, sea bays). Taxiway bridges should be designed so as not to impose any difficulties for taxiing aircraft and to permit easy access to emergency vehicles responding to an emergency involving an aircraft on the bridge. Strength, dimensions, grades and clearances should allow unconstrained aircraft operations day and night as well as under varying seasonal conditions, i.e. heavy rain, periods of snow and ice coverage, low visibility or gusty winds. The requirements of taxiway maintenance, cleaning and snow removal, as well as emergency evacuation of the aircraft occupants, should be taken into account when bridges are being designed.

With regard to holding bays, the Manual states that the space required for a holding bay depends on the number of aircraft positions to be provided, the size of the aircraft to be accommodated and the frequency of their utilization. The dimensions must allow for sufficient space between aircraft to enable them to manoeuvre independently. In general, the wing tip clearance (increment) between a parked aircraft and one moving along the taxiway or apron taxiway should conform to certain specifications.[54]

2.4.3 Pavements

In this section the Aerodrome Design Manual addresses technical specifications of pavements. There is general concern over the adequacy of the available friction between the aeroplane tires and the runway surface under certain operating conditions, such as when there is snow, slush, ice or water on the runway and, particularly, when aeroplane take-off or landing speeds are high. This concern is more acute for jet transport aero-planes since the stopping performance of these aeroplanes is, to a greater degree, dependent on the available friction between the aeroplane tires and the runway surface, their landing and take-off speeds are high, and in some cases the runway length required for landing or take-off tends to be critical in relation to the runway length available. In addition, aeroplane directional

[53] *Infra*, note 59 at 50–52.

[54] These specifications are identified and laid out in Sect. 2.4.1 of the Aerodrome Design Manual, Sect. 2.4.2.

control may become impaired in the presence of cross-wind under such operating conditions.

A measure of the seriousness of the situation is indicated by the action of national airworthiness authorities in recommending that the landing distance requirement on a wet runway be greater than that on the same runway when it is dry. Further problems associated with the take-off of jet aeroplanes from slush- or water-covered runways include performance deterioration due to the contaminant drag effect, as well as the airframe damage and engine ingestion problem. Information on ways of dealing with the problem of taking off from slush- or water-covered run-ways is contained in the Airworthiness Technical Manual (Doc 9051).

Further, it is essential that adequate information on the runway surface friction characteristics/aero-plane braking performance be available to the pilot and operations personnel in order to allow them to adjust operating technique and apply performance corrections. If the runway is contaminated with snow or ice, the condition of the runway should be assessed, the friction coefficient measured and the results provided to the pilot. If the runway is contaminated with water and the runway becomes slippery when wet, the pilot should be made aware of the potentially hazardous conditions.

Before giving detailed consideration to the need for, and methods of, assessing runway surface friction, or to the drag effect due to the presence of meteorological contaminants such as snow, slush, ice or water, it cannot be overemphasized that the goal of the airport authority should be the removal of all contaminants as rapidly and completely as possible and elimination of any other conditions on the runway surface that would adversely affect aero-plane performance.

Evidence from aeroplane overrun and run-off incidents and accidents indicates that in many cases in-adequate runway friction characteristics/aeroplane braking performance was the primary cause or at least a contributory factor. Aside from this safety-related aspect, the regularity and efficiency of aeroplane operations can become significantly impaired as a result of poor friction characteristics. It is essential that the surface of a paved runway be so constructed as to provide good friction characteristics when the runway is wet.

With respect to either aeroplane braking or directional control capability, it is to be noted that an aero-plane, even though operating on the ground, is still subject to considerable aerodynamic or other forces which can affect aeroplane braking performance or create moments about the yaw axis. Such moments can also be induced by asymmetric engine power (e.g. engine failure on take-off), asymmetric wheel brake application or by cross-wind. The result may critically affect directional stability. In each case, runway surface friction plays a vital role in counteracting these forces or moments.

There are specific requirements regarding the inspection of pavements. Attention should be paid to the following points:

a) General cleanliness with particular attention to material which could cause engine ingestion damage. This may include debris from runway maintenance operations or excessive grit remaining after runway gritting. Any build-up of tire rubber deposits should be noted;

b) Signs of damage to the pavement surface including cracking and spilling of concrete, condition of joint sealing, cracking and looseness of aggregate in asphalt surfaces or break-up of friction courses. Damage or deterioration which could cause aircraft damage should be reported immediately for, inspection by the Airport Maintenance Department and, if the damage is sufficiently serious, the area closed to aircraft pending the results of such an inspection;
c) After rain, flooded areas should be identified and marked, if possible, to facilitate later resurfacing;
d) Damage of light fittings;
e) Cleanliness of runway markings.[55]

2.4.4 Visual Aids

In this section the Manual concerns visual aids, the proper design and installation of which are prerequisites for the safety and regularity of civil aviation. These aids are critical in establishing communications and contact between engineering staff and the technical crew on the flight deck. Visual aids provide engineering personnel with a general appreciation of the task of the pilot-in-command in relation to the use of and reliance upon visual aids and visual cues in approaching, landing and operating on the airport surface.

It is essential that aircraft cross the runway threshold with a safe margin of both height and speed. In order to effect a smooth touchdown, both the speed and the rate of descent must be simultaneously reduced in the manoeuvre known as the landing flare, so that the wheels touch the runway just prior to or as the wing stalls. After touchdown, the pilot has a continuing requirement for directional guidance to keep the aircraft along or near the middle of the runway (at touchdown speeds generally within a range of 100–160 kt or 185–296 km/h). The pilot also needs information from which an assessment can be made of the length of runway remaining and, once the aircraft has slowed sufficiently, advance warning of a suitable runway exit, its width clearly delineated where taxiway centre line lighting is not provided. Once clear of the runway, the pilot has to taxi the decidedly unwieldy vehicle along an often complicated layout of taxiways to the correct parking/docking position on an apron which may well be congested. The pilot must be given a clear indication of the route to follow and be prevented from crossing any runway in use, as well as being protected from conflicting taxiing aircraft and vehicles.

In the case of long-bodied jets, the taxiing pilot has to control one of the largest, heaviest and most inefficiently powered tricycles ever made. The pilot is seated at least 6 m above the ground, and the nearest point ahead which can be seen is more

[55] *Airport Services Manual*, Part 8—Airport Operational Services, First Edition: 1983, Chapter 3.

than 12 m. The steerable nose wheel is several metres behind the pilot's seat on the flight deck (this brings its own special problems when negotiating a curve), while the main wheel bogies are at least 27 m behind. There is, of course, no "direct drive" to these wheels, and thrust from the jet engines, notoriously inefficient at low forward speeds, must be used. As with many modern swept-wing jets (irrespective of size), it is often impossible for the pilot to see the wing tips from the flight deck.

Visual aids inspections are addressed in the Airport Services Manual. The integrity and reliability of lighting aids should be comparable with those of non-visual aids. The integrity of the lighting system will depend upon the design of both the internal airport circuits and the external power supply. The reliability of the system will depend upon the programme of preventive maintenance employed and the degree of inspection carried out.

The operational checking of lighting is normally carried out by the Movement Area Safety Unit but rectification is the responsibility of Airport Maintenance. At some smaller airports the checking may be delegated to Airport Maintenance.

Faults in the lighting systems will be detected by monitoring. Monitoring by visual display on the Control Panel will ensure detection of circuit failures and verification that brilliancy selection by air traffic control provides the desired light output. Monitoring by visual inspection will, however, be necessary to detect failed lamps, contamination of fittings by dirt and rubber.

The Manual prescribes that on a daily basis all inset and elevated approach lighting systems and runway and taxiway lights should be checked for lamp failures, breakage or gross misalignment, also stop bars and illuminated Category I1 or I11 holding position signs. Lamp failures on runway centre line lights of precision approach runways Category I1 and I11 should be repaired as soon as possible; and major deficiencies in electrical circuits affecting the integrity of visual aids, e.g. breaks in the distribution network or un-serviceability of the standby power generators, should be reported to airport operations, maintenance and air traffic control, and NOTAM action taken.

On a weekly basis the checks involve all approach lighting systems for burnt out lamps. Also obstacle lights in the vicinity of the airport should be checked which are the responsibility of the airport operator. The airport operator must also that ensure that grass cutting, etc., has been carried out and approach lighting systems are not becoming obscured. The frequency and detail of inspections will depend to some extent on the complexity of the visual aids provided. In the case of precision approach runways, both flight checks and ground inspections of visual aids should be more frequent and detailed than those carried out on other runways.

Airport runway lighting is critical to the pilot[56] as a visual aid. Chapter 14 of Part 4 of the Manual on visual aids details the characteristics of airport lighting, both with regard to illuminating obstacles and lighting up the runway. Although these provisions are highly technical in nature and are specific in terms of requirements,

[56] A professional pilot is a person who engages in such flying as makes it necessary that he or she holds a valid airline transport pilot's license (ATPL).

they have a bearing on the performance of the pilot and bring to bear his liabilities from a legal and regulatory perspective. A Report released by the Federal Aviation Administration of the United States observes:

> Today's commercial and military aircraft have sophisticated avionics and computer-based systems to assist aviators with many common flight operations. Aviation safety, however, is still largely dependent on the pilot's ability to efficiently process the visual scene, both inside and outside the cockpit, while controlling the aircraft in the aviation environment. Even the most technologically advanced aircraft require pilots to make quick decisions in response to air traffic control (ATC) instructions, changing weather conditions, and during "see-and-avoid" traffic situations.[57]

The study also found that flight crewmembers were more susceptible to night vision problems during the approach and landing phases of flight, possibly due to prolonged exposure to low-light levels prior to being illuminated by airport lighting systems or other bright light sources.[58]

The Report of the controversial Comair crash in 2006 said: "On August 27, 2006, about 0606:35 eastern daylight time, Comair flight 5191, a Bombardier CL-600-2B19, N431CA, crashed during takeoff from Blue Grass Airport, Lexington, Kentucky. The flight crew was instructed to take off from runway 22 but instead lined up the airplane on runway 26 and began the takeoff roll. The airplane ran off the end of the runway and impacted the airport perimeter fence, trees, and terrain. The captain, flight attendant, and 47 passengers were killed, and the first officer received serious injuries. The airplane was destroyed by impact forces and post crash fire. The flight was operating under the provisions of 14 Code of Federal Regulations Part 121 and was en route to Hartsfield-Jackson Atlanta International Airport, Atlanta, Georgia. Night visual meteorological conditions prevailed at the time of the accident.

The National Transportation Safety Board determines that the probable cause of this accident was the flight crewmembers' failure to use available cues and aids to identify the airplane's location on the airport surface during taxi and their failure to cross-check and verify that the airplane was on the correct runway before takeoff. Contributing to the accident were the flight crew's non pertinent conversation during taxi, which resulted in a loss of positional awareness, and the Federal Aviation Administration's (FAA) failure to require that all runway crossings be authorized only by specific air traffic control (ATC) clearances".[59]

These factors bring to bear the impact of poor and inadequate lighting on the runway, inadequate signage or even over bright lighting would have on the

---

[57] Van Nakagawara et al. (2006a), at 1. Pilots often need sunglasses when flying during daylight hours. Tinted lenses can reduce glare, visual fatigue, and dark adaptation problems later in the flight. However, sunglasses can compromise the read-ability of aircraft instruments and other aviation materials, such as charts and maps, inside the cock-pit. A 2001 study by the FAA found that improper use or not using sunglasses contributed to one aviation accident and six incidents. See by the same authors Van Nakagawara et al. (2006b), at p. 4.

[58] Van Nakagawara et al. (2006a), at 3.

[59] National Transportation Safety Board (2006), at Executive Summary.

responsibility cast on a pilot's performance. Assessments carried out from 1977 up-to-date reveal that pilot decision-making is a significant factor in aircraft accidents. In 1977, Jensen and Benel[60] reported that 35 % of all non-fateful and 52 % of all fateful general aviation accidents in the United States during the period from 1970 to 1974 could be attributed to faulty pilot decision-making. In 1991 Diehl[61]—another researcher—using the methodology of Jensen and Benel, concluded that 56 and 50 % of aircraft accidents in commercial aviation and the tree aviation respectively were attributable to pilot era all told decision-making on art of the pilot.

Commercial airline pilots operate in a highly complex environment, particularly in single pilot operations. The difficulties faced by pilots in the work environment are compounded by the fact that often inadequate information aggravates the problem. Pilots rely heavily on their visual and auditory senses while flying, and it is of paramount importance that accurate information be available to the pilot at all times. Most importantly, pilots have usually the predilection to complete their given schedule no matter what, such as competing a flight as planned, meeting schedules, impressing their employees and pleasing the people they carry. Therefore negligent issues concerning the professional conduct of a pilot are quintessential elements for a highly esoteric legal debate.

The tenets of international aviation law attribute to the pilot (hereafter also referred to as the commander) of an aircraft absolute responsibility for the safe operation of his aircraft. Often, this principle is seen to defeat its purpose in the determination of a single instance of professional conduct of the pilot when such is considered to have endangered the safety of the aircraft, its passengers and property. The main reason for this confusion is the clear dichotomy which exists between statutory provisions and international conventions on the one hand which unequivocally lay down the fact of absolute responsibility of the pilot and the treatment of single instances of negligent professional conduct of the pilot in their isolation, on the other. So far, no attempt has been made either by international law and local statute or by judicial decisions to recognize that the conduct of the pilot in the aircraft should be viewed in its entirety, due regard being given to fundamental principles of law, the conduct of the pilot as a professional in whose hands lie the lives of hundreds of passengers and who takes on his job assuring his employer that his special skills and expertise would transport the passengers and their property safely under normal circumstances and any special circumstance which would render the effect of that assurance nugatory.

The law as it exists lays down a presumption of absolute responsibility of the pilot. In sharp contrast, the adjudication of instances of professional conduct of the pilot shows a clear demarcation between good airmanship and bad airmanship. Of these, the latter shows clear evidence of having been decided on individual merits and not on a general criterion or principle of recognizing the elements of law,

[60] Jensen and Benel (1977). See also, Murray (1997), at 83–100, at p. 84.

[61] Diehl (1990).

special circumstances and the human factor as a composite whole. Therein lies the problem.

The following analysis would examine the question of bad airmanship of the pilot in its entirety thereby seeking to introduce certain general principles based on the presumption of responsibility that the law imposes. Such general principles could then be applied to response special circumstances which would thus give rise to special rules pertaining to the professional conduct of the pilot. To achieve this end, an examination and analysis of legal principles, judicial decisions and special circumstances is necessary.

According to accepted principles of law as laid down by international convention, it is incontrovertible that the final responsibility for the safe operation of an aircraft lies with the pilot. The Chicago Convention provides that:

> The pilot-in-command shall be responsible for the operation and safety of the aeroplane and for the safety of all persons on board, during flight time.[62]

This presumption of responsibility has influenced most States which have signed or ratified the Convention and is reflected clearly in their air navigation laws.[63] These laws have been observed to list requirements which any pilot with a sense of good airmanship would naturally comply with. Failure to comply with such regulations has been clearly interpreted to be bad airmanship which renders the pilot liable for prosecution on a criminal charge.[64] In any event, the fundamental postulate which imposes *prima facie* responsibility on the pilot has been accepted as a general principle of liability of the pilot which sets the base for determining his legal status and responsibility.[65]

The legal responsibility placed on the commander of the aircraft is therefore inextricably linked with the expectation of good airmanship. Airmanship has been regarded as an indefinable quality and has been used to describe the intuitive faculty

---

[62] See Annex 6 to the Convention on International Civil Aviation signed in Chicago on 7 December 1944 Para 4.5.1. Popularly called the Chicago Convention, this Convention sets out universal principles governing international civil aviation and came into effect on 4 April 1947.

[63] *See The British Air Navigation* Order (1985) Article 32, which states, *inter alia:*

> The Commander of an aircraft registered in the United Kingdom shall satisfy himself before the aircraft takes off -
>
> a) that the flight can safely be made, taking into account the latest information available as to the route and aerodromes to be used, the weather reports and forecasts available and any alternative course of action which can be adopted in case the flight cannot be completed as planned;

See also generally, *U.S. Federal Aviation Regulations* FAR 91.3 (a), Australian Air Navigation Regulations, Regulation 219 and New Zealand Civil Aviation Regulations (1953), Regulation 59.

[64] See Price (1976a) at pp. 238–239. See also generally the findings of the *New Zealand Royal Commission of Inquiry into the 1979 Aft. Erebus DCIO Disaster*.

[65] See Matte (1975) at 34. See also Escalada (1979) at 210–211, Speiser and Krause (1978), p. 473.

of the pilot where he concerns himself with what is right or wrong in the operation of an aircraft which is acquired by sustained experience in flying.[66] Whilst it is:

> the proper conduct of the normal flight to avoid creating hazard, it is also the ability to overcome potential hazard where failure has occurred. With procedures laid down, drills to cover eventualities and the installation of duplicated equipment it is not surprising that crew error is seen as an element in so many accidents.[67]

The above analysis seems to suggest that the pilot should be held absolutely responsible for the safety of his flight not only as he lays claim to special expertise but also as he has been given the benefit of sophisticated duplicate equipment which makes his job easier. Thus, the stringent legal responsibility placed upon the pilot is seen to be further justified.

The absolute responsibility cast upon the pilot inevitably carries with it absolute and final authority from take off to landing.[68] The status of the pilot therefore entails far reaching consequences making an instance of his negligent act open to be interpreted as a dangerous and unlawful act which could justify a charge of manslaughter in the least.[69] Criminality of the act of the pilot lies quite independently of the incontrovertible liability in negligence[70] which would follow from such act.

Yet another consequence that the pilot would face is loss of employment. The pilot who holds a valid licence is considered to be responsible both to the State and to his employer. The employer of the pilot has been recognized to demand of his employee the right to decide whether to continue the employment of a pilot if he constitutes a threat to air safety in the course of his employment.[71] This principle is obviously followed on the basis that the product that the aircraft operator offers the passenger would lose its value totally if his credibility as a safe operator is lost by the negligent act of his pilot. In this perspective, no reputation, however glamorous, would obviate adverse publicity regarding the safety standards of an airline. Further, the pilot naturally hinges his entire capability and eligibility for employment on his ability to transport his passengers and cargo safely from one point to another. To achieve at least minimum standards of safety the employer should ascertain the competence of the pilot on his record at the point of employment and the pilot should justify his employment by the professional conduct that is expected of him and not regard his employer as one who suspiciously watches the performance of his duties. The ideal relationship between the pilot and his employer has been expressed by Captain A. J. Burridge when he said:

---

[66] Burridge (1977), p. 206.

[67] See Hopkins (1977) at 203. See also generally, Escalada (1979) *op.cit.* at 210; Van Wijk (1975–1976), 301 at 302.

[68] See Matte (1975), *Supra note 38*, at 34.

[69] Price (1976b), 67 at 72–73. See also generally, Kolczvnski (1985), 1 at 4.

[70] See generally Shawcross and Beaumont, *Air Law* (4 ed. reissue) at V/86–V/90. The concept of negligence will be discussed at some length later in this Chapter.

[71] See Edwards (1977), 209 at 211.

> If the suspicions of pilots can be allayed, and if an atmosphere of mutual trust between pilots and airline managements can be created, I think that responsible pilots could be persuaded to accept that the standard of flight safety we all want requires that Draconian remedies must be applied to cases of really bad airmanship in order to prevent their recurrence.[72]

The basis of liability in negligence is founded on the principle that when a person owes a duty of care to another, a breach of such duty grounds an action in negligence against the offender.[73] The elements of negligence relevant in the case of a pilot is the duty or standard of care he owes and whether that duty has been breached. While the law imposes an objective test of how the "reasonable man" would execute that duty of care in ordinary circumstances which do not require of him some special skill, in the case of a pilot the standard applicable would be that of the reasonable professional pilot. In the words of Mc Nair J.:

> Where you get a situation which involves the use of some special skill or competence then the test as to whether there has been negligence or not is not the test of the reasonable man because he has not this special skill; a man need not possess the highest of expert skill; it is well established law that it is sufficient if he exercises the ordinary skill of an ordinary competent man exercising that particular art.[74]

The degree of negligent conduct required of a person in charge of transporting passengers and cargo has been set out in clear terms both in cases concerned with the responsibility of a captain at sea and a pilot in command of an aircraft. Brett L. J. delivering judgment on a captain of a ship said:

> Captains of ships are bound to shew such skills as persons of their position with ordinary nerve ought to shew under the circumstances.[75]

Perhaps the most significant case involving the negligence of a pilot is the decision in *Taylor* v. *Alidair Limited*[76] which related to an unfair dismissal action in which a pilot appealed against his dismissal following a heavy landing leading to an uncorrected bounce and the collapse of the nosewheel assembly of the Viscount aircraft he was flying. The aircraft made a heavy touchdown, bouncing 10 ft into the air and touching down heavily again on all three wheels on the runway. There was considerable damage to the engines and air-frame. Bristow J. held that:

> there are activities in which the degree of professional skill which must be required is so high and the potential consequences of the smallest departure from that high standard are so serious that one failure to perform in accordance with those standards is enough to justify dismissal. The passenger-carrying airline pilot, the scientist operating the nuclear reactor, the chemist in charge of research into possible effect of, for example, thalidomide, the driver of the Manchester to London express, the driver of an articulated lorry full of

---

[72] Burridge (1977), *supra note 39*, *at* 208.

[73] See *M'Allister(Donoghue) v. Stevenson* 1932 AC 562.

[74] *Bolam v. Friern Hospital Management Committee* (1957) 2 All.E.R. 118 at 121. See also *Phillips v. Whiteley* (1938) 1 K.B. 566. at 570.

[75] *The Bywell Castle* (1879) 4 P.D. 219 at 226.

[76] (1976) IRLR 420.

sulphuric acid, are all in the situation in which one failure to maintain the proper standard of professional skill can bring about a major disaster.[77]

This decision, which was upheld in appeal in the Court of Appeal[78] stems largely from the approach that fundamental principles of tortious liability relating to the duty of care are extended to expect a greater degree of care from a person who undertakes a profession which not only requires special skill but also involves the fact that resultant damage caused by a breach of duty on the part of the professional would be so great as to reasonably expect him to exercise more care than that exercised by the ordinary employee who performs less responsible functions. This rationale has so far been virtually unanimous that one single instance of irresponsible conduct which could cause serious damage would justify stringent legal measures being imposed on the professional.

The position of the pilot in command of an aircraft therefore seems to be governed by the application of three presumptions. They are:

a) The special skill and expertise the pilot is presumed to possess,
b) The enhanced duty of care expected of the pilot in view of such special skill and expertise, and
c) The magnitude of the damage that may be caused in the eventuality of a breach of the duty by the care by the pilot.

These three principles are no doubt inextricably connected to one another in that in a high risk profession such as that of the pilot of an aircraft the risks of flying are significant and require the special skills and expertise that a pilot not only possesses but should also use to preclude any eventuality of danger. Indeed, there is strong opinion that it is arguable that a duty would be cast on the employer to remove the pilot at the first clear sign of inefficiency of the pilot.[79]

In interpreting the rudiments of liability for negligence, judicial decisions have maintained that there is no liability for negligence unless in a particular instance a legal duty is owed by the defendant to the plaintiff, such duty to be one which is owed to the plaintiff himself and to no other.[80] The standard of conduct of the defendant which is required by the common law is that of the reasonable man.[81] However, courts have recognized that in exceptional circumstances a person may

---

[77] Id. 423. See also generally, *Australian National Airlines Commission v. The Commonwealth of Australia and Canadian Pacific, Airlines* (*I* 974–975) 132 CLR 582.

[78] See (1978@) IRLR 82 CA; *Air Law*, 1978, p. 49.

[79] See Shawcross and Beaumont, *Air Law*, *supra note 52*, at v/84.

[80] See *Palsgraf v. Long Island R.R. Co* (1928) 284 N.Y. 339. See also, *Le Lievre v. Gould* (1893) 1 Q.B. 491, *Bourhill v. Young* (1943) A.C. 92.

[81] See *Vaugban v. Menlove* (1837) 3 Bing. N.C. 468.

hold himself out as possessing a special skill or believing on reasonable grounds that he possesses the required skill to perform his duties.[82]

If such person, having held himself out to claim such special skills does not possess such or if he exhibits conduct showing lack of such skills he would be subjected to the application of the maxim *imperitia culpae adnumeratur*. The maxim requires professional conduct of a higher degree than that is expected of the reasonable man. Mc Nair J. states:

> [T]he test is the standard of the ordinary skilled man exercising and professing to have that special skill. A man need not possess the highest expert skill at the risk of being found negligent. It is well established law that it is sufficient if he exercises the ordinary skill of an ordinary competent man exercising that particular art.[83]

The "ordinary skill" approach adopted in instances where such professionals as doctors, surgeons, chemists and other similar categories have appeared as defendants has not been accepted in its entirety by the courts in cases concerning negligence of the pilot. While the degree of care required of the pilot has been interpreted to be more a question of fact to be decided by the jury[84] the courts have gone so far as to hold that to establish negligence of the pilot the plaintiff would have to present clear evidence of what exactly happened in the aircraft at the time of the alleged negligence of the pilot.[85] However, if facts are clear and need no elucidation, the plaintiff need not further enlighten court on the circumstance of the case[86] as it can be judged:

> What was done by the pilot that he ought not to have done, what was left undone by him that he ought to have done.[87]

However, if the plaintiff is unable to lead clear evidence in instances of ambiguity, even persuasive circumstantial evidence would suffice.[88]

Taylor v. Alidair Ltd[89] is perhaps the most important decision which sets out the principles of liability for negligence of the pilot. In this case, an employment appeal tribunal which examined the appeal of a company which suspended a pilot from flying who had successfully argued against his suspension at an industrial tribunal held that one failure to maintain the proper standard of professional expertise expected of an aircraft commander could bring about a major disaster. Such risk,

---

[82] See *Daly v. Liverpool Corporation* (1939) 2 All.E.R. 142 at 144, *Whiteford v. Hunter* (1950) W.N. 533, *Randall v. Tarrant* (1955) 1 W.L.R. 255 at 259, *Bolam v. Friern Hospital Management Committee* (1957) 2 All E.R. 118 at 120, *and Wells v. Cooper* (1958) 2.Q.B. 265.

[83] See *Bolam v. Friern Hospital Management Committee* (1957) 2 All E.R. 118 at 121. See also generally, *Phillips v. William Whiteley Ltd* (I 938) 1 K.B. 566 at 569.

[84] *Steinbock v. Schiewe* 330 F. 2d 510 (1964) at 512.

[85] *United States v. Vigderman* 194 F. 2d 977, affirmed in appeal in *Vigderman v United States* 175. F. Supp. 802 at 807.

[86] *Vigderman v. United States id.* 807–808.

[87] *Id.* 810.

[88] *Ibid.*

[89] *Supra* note. 76.

it was held, was so great that a pilot had to exercise the highest standards of care and skill to ensure the safety of his aircraft its passengers and property.

Taylor's case, which concerned the hard landing of an aircraft by the pilot was one which the appeal tribunal found to contain clear facts which enabled the tribunal to assess the conduct of the pilot. The pilot had, due to unskilled handling, hit the runway in a way that it bounced off and could, at that moment, have landed in the proper manner had the pilot exercised his skill as expected of him. There was indeed no evidence to show that after the bounce the situation was irretrievably hopeless.

It would not be incorrect to conclude that the findings of the appeal tribunal in *Taylor's* case clearly lay down the principles that:

a) In the instance of an error of omission or commission by a pilot which results in some damage, negligence can be imputed to the pilot.
b) If clear facts unequivocally demonstrate the commission of the error, negligence is presumed and,
c) Such negligence would incontrovertibly justify the suspension *in limine* of the pilot.

There have been many cases where, on objective criteria, negligence of the pilot has been established. Such instances as the omission to check quantities of fuel carried,[90] failure to comply with established proper procedure in pre-flight checks[91] and rules of air in flight,[92] improper handling of the controls[93] and negligence during take off[94] have all been decided on the basis that the professional ability and skill professed by the pilot would pre-suppose the justifiable expectation of the pilot to exercise due standards of care. At the least, negligence would be imputed to the pilot and at the most when facts are clear *in limine*, negligence would be presumed, which may result in the most drastic measures being taken against the pilot.

It is clear that *Taylor's* case and others of similar circumstances have taken up where provisions of conventions and local laws have left off. The stringent presumption of responsibility placed upon the pilot by written laws has been extended by the *cursus curiae* to impose a presumption of liability. So far the uniformity of this trend has been undisturbed. Perhaps the only other factor which competes with this proclivity towards uniformity is the immutable objectivity with which the pilot's actions are viewed in determining his liability.

---

[90] *Steinbock v. Scbiewe, note 36* in Chap. 1, *also, Keenan v. Martin*, 13 *Avi* 18,037 (N.Y. 1975).

[91] *Union Trust Co v. Eastern Airlines* 211 F. 2d. 62.

[92] *Herrick and Olsen v. Curtiss Flving Service Inc.* (I 932) US Av 110 (NY).

[93] See *Nichols v. Jones* 260 So 2d 748 (La. 1972). See also *Israel v. U.S.* 247 F 2d 426 (2nd Circ., 1957), *Robart v. Brehmer* 207 P 2d 898 (Cal. 19491).

[94] *Hovden v. Boyle* 254 P 2d 813 (Kan., 1953).

With regard to Articles 55 and 56 of the Air Navigation Order, one can notice that implicit in these provisions is a need for reasonable care or due diligence on the part of the pilot. In the 1994 case of *R. v. Adomako*[95] Lord McKay seemingly followed the earlier rationale of Lord Diplock in *R. v. Caldwell*[96] where His lordship observed as follows:

> "Reckless" as used in the new statutory definition of the mens rea of these offences is an ordinary English word. It had not, by 1971 become a term of legal art with some limited esoteric meaning than which it bore in ordinary speech, a meaning which surely includes not only deciding to ignore a risk of harmful consequences resulting from one's acts that one has recognized as existing, but also failing to give any thought to whether or not there is any such risk in circumstances where, if any thought were given to the matter, it would be obvious if there was.[97]

Although the interpretation given by Lord Diplock in the *Caldwell* case has been followed in later cases, to the effect that recklessness would cover both an attendant disregard of the reasonable and probable consequences of one's act by a person who professes special skill such as a pilot, and a negligent act by a "reasonable man", the offenses envisioned in Articles 55 and 56 of the Air Navigation Act do not necessarily need "recklessness" as an element for culpability of the pilot. Mere negligence is sufficient, on the ground that the pilot does not always have to be grossly negligent or reckless to be held liable under the Act. To support this premise, there is scholarly opinion[98] that both recklessness and negligence involve a common inability or failure on the part of the miscreant to comply with objective conduct. The following definition, which brings negligence on par with recklessness for the purpose of finding a person liable, is relevant to ascertaining possible future judicial attitudes towards the determination of negligence of the airline pilot:

> Negligence is conduct which departs from the standard to be expected of a reasonable man. This is not to say that a person's state of mind is always irrelevant when negligence is in issue. He may, for example, have special knowledge which an ordinary person would not possess. The question then is, whether a reasonable man, with that knowledge, would have acted as he did.[99]

It would appear from this emergent trend that the contentious *November Oscar* case of 1991,[100] which was decided on the recklessness of the pilot, may now be viewed within the parameters of negligence as well. The case involved the conduct of a pilot who, while attempting to make a category II landing in diminished visibility at London Heathrow Airport, made a deviation from the center line of landing, necessitating a turn around which took the plane just 5 ft higher than the top of a nearby hotel. The reasoning of the jury involved the decision making of the

95 (1994) 3 All E.R. 79.

96 (1981) 1 All E.R. 961.

97 *Ibid.* at 966.

98 See Smith and Hogan (1992), at 92.

99 *Ibid.*

100 For a detailed account of the case, see, Bennun (1995–1996), 331 at 341.

captain, and whether the decision taken was timely and appropriate and whether the captain had acted in an appropriate manner in taking the plane around for a second landing attempt.

2.4.5 Electrical Systems

In this section the Manual addresses electrical systems for aerodrome lighting and radio navigation aids and includes features which are not usually involved in other electrical installations. The manual therefore discusses not only the general features of electrical practices and installations but also those features which are of special significance for aerodrome installations. To ensure the regularity and safety of aviation, it is necessary that aerodrome lighting and radio navigational aids have high integrity and reliability. It is considered that the probability of failure of well designed and maintained lighting and radio aids at a critical moment is extremely low.

The Manual prescribes that the primary sources of power for aerodromes should be determined before the designs of the aerodrome lighting installations and the radio navigation aids are initiated. The electrical power for these installations is usually only a small part of the electrical power used by the aerodrome. Whether the visual and radio navigation aids being installed are for a new aerodrome or for modernization and expansion of an existing aerodrome, the sources of power should be analyzed for availability, capacity, reliability, practicality for the proposed installation, and for future expansion. This analysis should include both the primary power source and the secondary power source required by Annex 10, Volume I, 2.9 and Annex 14, 8.1 for use in cases of failure or malfunction of the primary power source.

Primary Power Sources

The primary sources of power for most aerodromes are feeders from a widely interconnected electricity network outside the aerodrome, usually from either a commercial or a public mains supply. In some cases the power may come from a local generating plant or from a limited distribution system. Two independent incoming power sources are desirable for major aerodromes, instead of a single primary power source. They should come from widely separated sections of the electricity network beyond the aerodrome with each supplying separate circuits that would provide integrity of facilities if one failed. Preferably, these sources will have separate feeders from separate substations and will also be from different generators.

On 8 February 2013 an electrical power failure *at Indira Gandhi International Airport*, New Delhi—the Indian capital's main airport—disrupted the radar system on Friday, delaying some flights. The airport had a three-tier system for electricity and when the power went out, the airport switched from the main supply to one of its two standby sources. Although the power supply switched over from 12:21 p.m. to 12:31 p.m., travelers reported experiencing much longer delays. The power failure affected the servers that control the radar system.

2.4.6 *Frangibility*

At airports, various visual and non-visual aids (e.g. approach lighting towers, meteorological equipment, radio navigational aids) are located near runways, taxiways and aprons, where they may present a hazard to aircraft in the event of accidental impact during landing, take-off or ground maneuvering. All such equipment and their supports should be frangible and mounted as low as possible to ensure that impact does not result in loss of control of the aircraft. This frangibility is achieved by use of lightweight materials and/or the introduction of break-away or failure mechanisms that enable the object to break, distort or yield under impact.

In this section the aerodrome Design Manual addresses obstacles at airports. Obstacles are defined as all fixed objects, or parts thereof, that are located on an area intended for the surface movement of aircraft or that extend above a surface intended to protect an aircraft in flight. The first objective should be to site objects so that they are not obstacles. Nevertheless, certain airport equipment and installations, because of their function, must be located in an operational area. All such equipment and installations as well as their supports should be of minimum mass and frangible in order to ensure that impact does not result in loss of control of the aircraft.

Annex 14—Aerodromes, Volume I—Aerodrome Design and Operations, Chapter 5, specifies that elevated approach lights and their supporting structures should be frangible except that, in that portion of the approach lighting system beyond 300 m from the threshold: where the height of a supporting structure exceeds 12 m, the frangibility requirement should apply to the top 12 m only; and where a supporting structure is surrounded by non-frangible objects, only that part of the structure that extends above the surrounding objects should be frangible.

Most city planning take into account obstacles which are outside the airport premises but could be a threat to aviation. An example is Sydney where the town centre is within the inner horizontal surface at 51 m AHD for the Sydney Airport Obstacle Limitation Surface. The planning therefore seeks to ensure that airport operations are not compromised by proposed development that penetrates the obstacle limitation surface. The provision requires that before granting development consent the consent authority must consult with Sydney Airport. Due to the proximity of the Town Centre to Sydney Airport, requirements for consideration of the noise impact of aircraft on development have been included in the Local Environmental Plan. The provision requires the consent authority, before granting consent, to consider whether the development is within and designed to appropriate standards, including interior noise levels.[101]

National governments gene sally have the basic authority and primary responsibility to establish criteria for the elimination of obstacles and to provide guidance and assistance to those directly concerned with elimination of obstacles.

Ultimate responsibility for limitation and control of obstacles must, in practice, rest with the airport operator. This includes the responsibility for controlling obstacles on airport property and for arranging the removal or lowering of existing obstacles outside the airport boundaries. The latter obligation can be met by negotiations leading to purchase or condemnation (where authorized) of air easements or title to the properly.[102]

Each airport manager should designate a member of his staff to be responsible for the continuing process of making sure that airport approach, departure and maneuvering areas remain clear of obstacles which may jeopardize safety. The airport manager, or his designee, should work closely with government agencies at all levels, national and local to ensure that all possible steps have been taken to prevent erection of obstacles, including providing information to zoning authorities on the location, length, orientation and elevation of runways on which obstacle limitation surfaces are based. The airport manager must maintain constant vigilance to prevent erection of obstacles around his airport and he should alert other agencies of potential problems which may arise under their jurisdiction. In order to fulfill these obligations, the airport manager should establish a programme of regular and frequent visual inspections of all areas around the airport in order to ensure that any construction activity or natural growth (i.e. trees) likely to infringe any of the obstacle limitation surfaces is discovered before it may become a problem. This inspection programme should also include a dally observation of all obstacle lights, both on and off the airport, and corrective action in the case of light failure.

In summary, once the national government sets forth the necessary criteria, he principal methods of controlling obstacles available to community authorities and airport operators are height zoning purchase of easements and purchase property. Each of them issues is dealt with in greater detail in the following paragraphs.

Enactment of zoning regulations incorporating height limits related to airport obstacle limitation surfaces is a difficult and complex process but a necessary one. As a general rule, any community desiring to adopt such an ordinance will need legal authority to do so from a higher level d government. Even when so authorized, the effectiveness of height zoning as a means of protecting airports may be severely limited.

---

[101] *City of Sydney Planning Proposal, Sydney Local Environmental Plan 2010* produced in March 2012 at 26.

[102] See Airport Services Manual, Part 6—Control of Obstacles, Doc 9137—AN/898, at 2.2.4.

It has become a well-established principle of law that warning cannot be so restrictive as to deprive a property owner of his right to the use of his property without adequate compensation. Many height zoning ordinances have been ruled invalid by the courts when property owners have claimed invasion of their property rights.

Such considerations limit the effectiveness of height zoning, particularly in the most critical areas close to runway ends, where obstacle limitation surfaces may require very low heights. Any height zoning must recognize this fact and provide for a minimum allowable height which is reasonable in terms of existing land use in the vicinity. Even so, local opposition to aircraft operations and to any form of restrictions on use of property may give rise to legal challenges leading to possible invalidation of any but the most carefully drafted zoning ordinance.

Height zoning, and indeed any form of zoning, cannot be made retroactive. Existing structures and trees which do not conform to the zoning limits are generally permitted to continue as non-conforming uses. Obstacles of this nature must be dealt with by other methods, such as purchase of easements or property rights.

The fact that obstacle limitation surfaces for n single airport may overlie the property of several independent communities or legal jurisdictions further complicates the problem of adopting effective zoning. Airport operators have no zoning powers, and must rely on the co-operation of neighboring communities. This may involve as many as 30 or 40 separate jurisdictions, some of which may be uncooperative. In some cases, higher governmental bodies have authority.

References

Bennun ME (1995–1996) Prosecuting professional pilots in the United Kingdom after November Oscar: reflections in the law and policy. J Air Law Commer 331

Borrell B (2009) What is a bird strike? How can we keep planes safe from them in the future? The Scientific Monitor, 15 January 2009. http://www.scientificamerican.com/article.cfm?id=what-is-a-bird-strike

Burridge J (1977) The dismissal of a pilot for poor airmanship – the employer's point of view. Aeronaut J 206

Dean Chamberlain H (1999) Runway incursion is no accident. FAA Aviat News 38(7):9–12

Diehl A (1990) The effectiveness of aeronautical decision making training. In: Proceedings of the 34th meeting of the human factors society, The Human Factors Society, Santa Monica

Dolbeer RA (2006) Bird and other wildlife hazards at airports: liability issues for Airport Managers. University of Nebraska, Lincoln DigitalCommons@University of Nebraska, Lincoln, p 5

Edwards M (1977) The continued employment of pilots involved in incidents or accidents: the operator's responsibilities and liabilities. Aeronaut J 209

Escalada V (1979) Aeronautical law, pp 210–211

Hopkins HA (1977) The dismissal of a pilot for poor airmanship. Aeronaut J 203

International Civil Aviation (2013) Aerodrome design and operations, vol 1, 6th edn

Jensen RS, Benel RA (1977) Judgment evaluation and instruction in civil pilot training (Tech. Rep. No. FAA-RD-78-24). National Technical Information Service, Springfield

Kolczvnski PJ (1985) The criminal liability of aviators and related issues of mixed criminal – civil litigation: a venture in the twilight zone. J Air Law Commer 51(1):1

Maragakis I (2009) Bird population trends and their impact on Aviation Safety 1999–2008. European Aviation Safety Agency, Safety Analysis and Research Department (09 January 2009)

Matte NM (1975) The international legal status of aircraft commander, p 34

Murray SR (1997) Deliberate decision making by aircraft pilots: a simple reminder to avoid decision making under panic. Int J Aviat Psychol 7(1):83–100

National Transportation Safety Board (2006) Aircraft accident report – attempted takeoff from wrong runway. Comair Flight 5191, Bombardier CL-600-2B19, N431CA, Lexington, 27 August 2006, NTSB/AAR-07/05

Price N (1976a) Pilot error, pp 238–239

Price ND (1976b) Essential law for pilots and their crew, p 67

Smith JC, Hogan B (1992) Criminal law, 7th edn, p 92

Speiser SM, Krause CF (1978) Aviat Tort Law 1:473

Van Nakagawara B, Montgomery RW, Wood K (2006a) Aircraft accidents and incidents associated with visual disturbances from bright lights during nighttime flight operations. Civil Aerospace Medical Institute, Federal Aviation Administration, Oklahoma City, p 1

Van Nakagawara B, Montgomery RW, Wood K (2006b) Aviation accidents and incidents associated with the use of ophthalmic devices by civilian pilots DOT/FAA/AM-01/14. Office of Aerospace Medicine, Washington, p 4

Van Wijk A (1975–1976) Responsibilities of airline pilots. Air Law 1:301

Chapter 3
Airport Planning

3.1 Introduction

The Council of ICAO on 10 March 1967 approved a proposal of the Secretary General that guidance material be prepared to assist States in planning the expansion of existing international airports and the construction of new ones.

This project was conceived in the realization of the major impact that expansion of air transport was having and would continue to have on facilities throughout the world, it being recognized that, in addition to the major problems of great expansion in absolute volume of passengers, cargo and air traffic, the introduction of very large-capacity aircraft was likely to cause special problems at an increasing number of airports. Existing programmes of ICAO did not provide airport authorities with guidance for the development of airport master plans in all their aspects, nor had it been intended that they should.

Both air transport and airports are growth industries which are heavily capital intensive. They are also inextricably intertwined, both in terms of planning and forecasting. Airports accommodate aircraft and therefore planning for the future of an airport is heavily reliant on the fortunes of the air transport industry. It follows that, prior to considering the technicalities of planning and building an airport, one has to consider the future of the air transport industry. Tourism stands in between the two as the catalyst.

The contagion effect as well as an economic downturn involving the major powers, particularly China and India, where the latter has an increasing population with disposable income could affect the way forward for air transport. Over 2010 and 2011, tourism showed an encouraging increase. According to the 2010 Annual Report of the United Nations World Tourism Organization (UNWTO)[1] 2010 will be remembered as the year of recovery for the global economy—following one of

[1] The World Tourism Organization (UNWTO) is the United Nations agency responsible for the promotion of responsible, sustainable and universally accessible tourism. As the leading international organization in the field of tourism, UNWTO promotes tourism as a driver of economic

R. Abeyratne, *Law and Regulation of Aerodromes*, DOI 10.1007/978-3-319-04780-5_3,

the most testing periods of recent history—but also the year of persistent uncertainties and challenges. This has also been true for international tourism. UNWTO further recorded that international tourist arrivals grew by 7 % in 2010 to a record 940 million, with positive growth reported in all world regions. Reflecting global economic trends, growth was driven largely by emerging economies, a development that looks set to continue over the coming years. The recovery of international tourism has confirmed the sector's extraordinary capacity to bounce back time and again from external shocks. Tourism is an extremely resilient sector and given its contribution to global economic growth, job creation and development, its faster-than-expected recovery in 2010 was welcome news. The global economic downturn in 2008–2009 has demonstrated more than ever the need for political recognition and support of the tourism sector. Throughout 2010, UNWTO worked to mainstream tourism in the global agenda by promoting its significant contribution to global prosperity, development and well-being. In 2010, UNWTO presented its Roadmap for Recovery—conveying the message that tourism means jobs, trade, economic growth and development—to leaders and decision.

UNWTO has reported that in 2011, international tourism receipts exceeded US $1 trillion for the first time, up from US$928 billion in 2010. In real terms, receipts grew by 3.8 %, following a 4.6 % increase in international tourist arrivals. An additional US$196 billion in receipts from international passenger transport brought total exports generated by international tourism in 2011 to US$1.2 trillion.[2]

According to the latest UNWTO World Tourism Barometer, international tourism receipts continued to recover from the losses of crisis year 2009 and hit new records in most destinations, reaching an estimated US$1,030 billion (euro 740 billion) worldwide, up from US$928 billion (euro 700 billion) in 2010. In real terms (adjusted for exchange rate fluctuations and inflation), international tourism receipts grew by 3.8 %, while international tourist arrivals increased by 4.6 % in 2011 to 982 million. This confirms the close correlation between both indicators, with growth of receipts tending to lag slightly behind growth of arrivals in times of economic constraints.

growth, inclusive development and environmental sustainability and offers leadership and support to the sector in advancing knowledge and tourism policies worldwide.

[2] International tourist arrivals grew by close to 5 % during the first months of 2011, consolidating the 7 % rebound registered in 2010. According to the April Interim Update of the UNWTO World Tourism Barometer, growth was positive in all world (sub)regions during January and February 2011, with the exception of the Middle East and North Africa. South America and South Asia led growth (both at +15 %), followed by Sub-Saharan Africa (+13 %) and Central and Eastern Europe (+12 %). Asia and the Pacific, the region with one of the fastest growth rates in 2010, saw its pace of growth slowdown (+6 %), although from a very strong performance the previous year. Results were better than expected for Europe (+6 %), boosted by the recovery of Central and Eastern Europe, and the temporary redistribution of travel to destinations in Southern and Mediterranean Europe due to developments in North Africa (−9 %) and the Middle East (−10 %). The Americas (+5 %) was in line with the world average, with strong results for South America and the Caribbean, but rather weaker growth in North and Central America.

If tourism is to continue its trend of the last 2 years economic restraints, both on air transport and tourism, should have to be removed, or in the least minimized. The most compelling restraint pertains to the environment. Tourism involves travel for predominantly recreational or leisure involving the provision of services to support this leisure travel. Tourists are generally defined as people who "travel to and stay in places outside their usual environment for not more than one consecutive year for leisure, business and other purposes not related to the exercise of an activity remunerated from within the place visited". Tourism has become a popular global leisure activity.

3.2 Tourism and Air Transport

UNWTO recorded in 2007 that the number of international tourist arrivals has risen from 25 million in 1950 to 840 million in 2006. The revenues generated by these arrivals—not including airline ticket sales and revenues from domestic tourism—have risen at an average rate of 11.2 % a year (adjusted for inflation) over the same span of time, which is nearly twice as fast as arrivals and a growth rate that far outstrips that of the world economy as a whole. International tourism receipts reached 735 billion dollars in 2006, almost 900 billion including air tickets, making tourism not only a socio-economic driver but one of the largest categories of international trade. Tourism represents one quarter of all exports of services—40 % with air transport revenues included. It is also noteworthy that the growth trend will continue, as according to a news release of 18 September 2007 issued by ICAO, total world airline scheduled passenger traffic in terms of passenger-kilometers is expected to grow at an average annual rate of 4.6 % up to the year 2025, half a percentage point lower than the growth rate achieved over the period 1985–2005, according to forecasts prepared by ICAO. Total freight traffic growth over the same period is forecast to be stronger, at 6.6 % per annum in terms of freight tonne-kilometers.

There can be particular benefits from tourism for the poorest economies, where international arrivals are growing at twice the rate in the industrialized States. Although they are still at a low level, the tourism receipts of the Least Developed Countries increased fivefold between 1990 and 2005, from 1 to 5 billion dollars. Tourism has become one of the largest sources of foreign exchange revenues for developing countries generally and for the 49 LDCs specifically, reducing their foreign debt and diversifying their economies. Tourism is often the principal service sector activity and it is a notably effective catalyst for gender equality, employment of young people, rural regeneration, cultural preservation and nature conservation.

Therefore WTO, which is the specialized agency of the United Nations with a central and decisive role in promoting the development of responsible, sustainable and universally accessible tourism, concludes that, for all these reasons, tourism can play a major role in improving the standard of living of disadvantaged populations and helping them lift themselves above the poverty threshold. Tourism can be a primary tool for achievement of the Millennium Development Goals of the United Nations, as long as a balance with climate change effects is maintained.

Tourism—business and leisure travel—is a significant global industry making positive contributions to growth, trade and development, with particular potential for poor countries. Tourism is both affected fundamentally by climate change and a contributor to the global emissions of greenhouse gases with air transport being a substantial contributor to total tourism emissions.

There is no doubt that tourism and air transport are symbiotic. Travel and tourism, the largest combination of industries and the largest creator of wealth, is estimated to generate $3.5 trillion a year in activity and potentially provides employment to 130 million people worldwide. This accounts for 10 % of the world's GDP, 10.3 % of the world's wages, 9.8 % of the profits and 11.7 % of indirect and direct taxes. WTO has recorded that about 40 % of the 840 million international tourist arrivals in 2006 were by air. In terms of long haul destinations, this figure could be even higher. Furthermore, the vast majority of the 931 million international passengers in 2006 were tourists.

In March 2010, Larry Elliott, writing to the Guardian said of the decade 2010–2020:

> Get ready for the austerity decade. Forget all thoughts that the economic storm of the past 30 months is about to blow over. We've had what Mervyn King once called the NICE period of non-inflationary constant expansion but now we face a long DRAG – deficit reduction, anaemic growth. The lessons of economic history, the current configuration of the economy, and inescapable long-term challenges that have to be faced provide the same message: it's payback time.[3]

Perhaps it is, and if there were to be anemic growth in the years ahead, indubitably the downturn would affect air transport adversely. The problem with air transport is that, while on the one hand it is a product, on the other hand regulations pertaining to this product may constrain its availability to the consumer by depriving him of the various choices of air travel he might have under a liberalized system. In other words, State policy and the protection of national interests take precedence over the interest of the user of air transport. The aviation industry offers only one product to the ultimate consumer and that is the air transport product. One might well ask why this product is precluded from attracting untrammeled foreign direct investment (FDI) like other products such as those in the agriculture, textile manufacture and energy industries.

Airports, particularly in Asia are planning ahead for the next two to three decades. A good example is Hong Kong International Airport (HKIA). Airports Authority of Hong Kong (AAHK) is preparing to connect HKIA to the new infrastructure that is being built nearby, including the Tuen Mun–Chek Lap Kok Link, the Hong Kong–Zhuhai–Macao Bridge and the Hong Kong Boundary Crossing Facilities. A government-led study on a proposed rail link connecting the airport

[3] http://www.guardian.co.uk/business/2010/mar/01/drag-deficit-reduction-anaemic-growth.

to Shenzhen International Airport is already under way. With these new facilities on or near the Airport Island, it is envisioned that HKIA will play an even more important role for Hong Kong and also for the Pearl River Delta.[4]

In Kuala Lumpur, plans for airport expansion were afoot in 2006 and matured in 2009. Kuala Lumpur International (KLIA) embarked on extensive property development, transforming the airport into a remarkable mixed-use of commercial, tourism and transportation hub called (tentatively) the "AEROPOLIS-KLIA". The mega-project will be developed around the existing airport on 2,730 acres of land. With this, KLIA will be transformed to be more than just an airport. The authorities claim that it will be an international meeting place which includes business parks, logistic parks, industrial estates and "free zones", retail centres and merchandise marts, ICT complexes, hotels, a theme park, tourism and entertainment centres and an airport residential neighbourhood.

Under the new Kuala Lumpur International Airport Masterplan, a new runway and a new satellite building will be constructed to accommodate the increasing number of passengers. The airport Phase 2 development plan was designed to handle 40 million passengers per year by 2008 with the expansion of low cost carrier terminal. For phase 3, the airport will expand to handle 75 million passengers per annum with the construction of a new satellite terminal and replacement of current low cost carrier terminal with a new low cost carrier terminal that will be capable of handling 30 million passengers alone. Under Phase 4, the airport will be capable to handle 130 million passengers per annum by 2020.

With the slight modification of the master plan, the future Terminal 2's satellite terminal will be combined into one satellite terminal. The expansion of Terminal 2's satellite terminal will be exactly the same as Terminal 1's satellite terminal, where initially the satellite terminal will have four arms, and another four arms when the terminal reached its capacity. There is sufficient land and capacity to develop facilities to handle up to 130 million passengers a year, five runways by the year 2020 and two mega-terminals, each linked with satellite terminals. The airport's vicinity will include hiking trails for jet-lagged travellers, golf courses, convention center, a theme park, a shopping center, hotels, and a wetlands nature preserve. Sepang International Circuit, which hosts Formula One, A1 Grand Prix, Super GT, IndyCar Series and MotoGP races, is also nearby. There has also been a proposal for a monorail link to the F1 circuit. KLIA is one of Asia's major aviation hubs and is a destination in itself. It is located at the top of the southern corridor of Peninsular Malaysia, bordering the states of Selangor and Negeri Sembilan. It is situated in the Sepang district, approximately 50 km from the capital city, Kuala Lumpur.

KLIA is a unique airport because it has within its boundaries all that is needed for business, entertainment and relaxation. The airport is part and parcel of the

[4] Airlines and Destinations as of 31 March 2011, more than 95 airlines operated from HKIA. These carriers serve about 160 destinations, including more than 45 cities on the Mainland.

Multimedia Super Corridor (MSC) where placement of high technology industries are being actively pursued.

Quite apart from the essential air side support given by airports to landing and departing aircraft, there are commercial facilities provided for both passengers and the public within the terminal building by concessionaires who are specialists in their own fields of business.

The airport authorities collect concession fees (non aeronautical revenues) from the concessionaires and in numerous airports around the world, the income derived from such resources are significant, often exceeding traditional income derived through the provision of landing fees and airport and air navigation services charges (aeronautical revenues) to incoming and outgoing aircraft.

More and more, airports are evolving from being basic aeronautical infrastructures into complex multi functional enterprises serving the travelling public while at the same time catering to their commercial needs and those of others who visit the airport. Such enterprises include duty free shops, specialty retail and brand name shops, restaurants, hotels and accommodation, banks, business and office complexes, leisure, recreation and fitness centres just to name a few.

In the present context, the major hubs are facing a non aeronautical boom in their commercial activities which are not directly related to air travel. For instance Chek Lap Kok, Hong Kong's international airport, has more than 50 high end designer shops\Singapore's Changi International pampers the human's physical fitness cravings and the continuing need for entertainment by hosting cinemas, saunas and even a swimming pool in the airport itself. Frankfurt has the world's largest airport clinic having the facilities to serve 36,000 patients annually while Detroit Metropolitan Wayne County has a 420 bedroom hotel in its main concourse. Munich airport has its own hospital while Amsterdam Schipol has a Dutch master's gallery. Beijing has quite a few banks carrying on business within the terminal building while Stockholm's Arlanda airport solemnized marriages and officiated over 450 weddings in 2005 in the vast chapel located within the terminal.

All this is of course due to the fact that the average air traveller is more affluent than the non traveller (they have higher income earners, typically three to five times the average) and a busy airport has scores of them continuously flowing through the airport. This has prompted airport managers to re-structure their operational management. For example, many airports have established separate real estate management and property units and divisions to capitalize on their landside commercial activities and enhance real estate values. One of the foremost in this area is Aeroports de Paris which established its real estate division in 2003 to manage landside commercial activities coming under the purview of the airport both in Paris and Orly.

Some others have aggressively put in place free trade zones, customs free zones, golf courses, child and day care centers, factory outlet stores and fitness centers. Amsterdam Schipol has also done the same and developed its real estate potential to build large office complexes, meeting and entertainment facilities logistics parks, shopping and other commercial activities. Beijing, which is one of the busiest airports, has gone ahead with building its Capital Airport City, which will provide shopping, entertainment, education, sports and leisure activities while accommodating activities related to commerce, finance trade and housing. Dallas Fort Worth (US) has concentrated its activities in the field of real estate development as a profitable adjunct to its traditional airport activities. Hong Kong airport's SkyCity is a colourful and fabulous project, which will contain a million square metres of retail, exhibition, business, office and hotel complex very near to the terminal. This complex will also accommodate cinemas and mini theme parks.

In Seoul, Incheon International Airport has its own mega complex in its "Winged City" which provides for large business areas, shopping and tourism districts, housing and medical services for airport workers and residents.

While still in Asia, Suvarnabhumi, the Bangkok International Airport has an entire airport city within the boundaries of the airport that houses an international business centre, international conference and exhibition complex, shopping malls, car parks, hospitals, restaurants and a large entertainment centre. It is clear that what these airports are doing is merely anchoring their strategically placed airport resources and potential on a metropolitan Commercial Business District (CBD) formula to create employment and generate revenue.

This is a highly lucrative and eminently strategic commercial practice among the major airports of the world who are aware of the trends with regard to passenger movements in their terminals. The aerotropolis is a natural corollary of the upturn of the economy in major cities as well as the contemporaneous advantages provided by airports in providing and promoting business in a fast moving globally networked economy. Advanced technology and high speed communication are essential for today's businesses and these are provided by these modern airport complexes and systems.

The success of an aerotropolis is smoothness and fluidity that would ensure a combination of high speed business, convenience and high quality products to the customer. Although this concept has attained fruition as a successful business model mostly in the Western world, Asia is not far behind and is gaining rapidly on a competitive level as the examples already given indicate.

ICAO has introduced a whole new area of thought into airport development. What was once a concern to merely provide easy facilities for the fluid movement of air traffic has now become in addition an ecological concern. By this process, airport development now falls into three main areas which are: the development of airport capacity and facilities; the balancing of airport development with necessary security measures; and, the balancing of airport development with ecology i.e. city planning, noise pollution avoidance etc. The ICAO Airport Planning Manual ensures a balance between airport development and ecological considerations.

Cooperation in technical and economic areas would have to be further expanded to include safety and ecological factors in the technical field and all economic research in city planning and infrastructural development in the economic field. These studies would have to be done in the form of committed and in depth country studies by individual States taking into consideration futuristic studies of a country's outlook and the financial outlay that the country would be prepared to make for an airport expansion programme. The outcome of these studies could then form legislation for the planning of airports in a State. Such legislation would present, for the first time, a cohesive and enforceable set of laws in that State that would meet the airport congestion problem.

Although the concept of airport planning laws can be summed up easily as above, the three broad areas of ecology, safety and infrastructural planning need a sustained approach of study before such are incorporated into laws. For a start, ICAO's Airport Planning Manual is geared to provide information and guidance to those responsible for airport planning, where information on a comprehensive list of planning subjects such as sizes and types of projects task identification, preparation of manpower and cost budgets, selection of consultants and standard contract provisions are given. With these guidelines each State can start its planning process.

3.3 The Airport Planning Manual

The ICAO The Airport Planning Manual[5] has been developed to assist airport authorities in the complex task of preparing master plans for the expansion of existing airports and construction of new ones. The manual outlines the planning system and the development of long-term forecasts covering aviation operations, economic factors and other considerations involved in master planning. It explains the need for consultation and co-operative planning by all the agencies concerned, including aircraft operators, national and local government planners, government control authorities customs, immigration, health, etc., national and local transport authorities, aircraft and equipment manufacturers and international aviation agencies.

Guidance is given on deciding the type of airport which may be required to meet the needs of a community or region and on the selection and evaluation of airport sites. Stress is laid on the importance of making an economic appraisal when deciding on the provision of an airport and assessing its worth to the community in comparison with other projects.

The need for a systems approach to preparation of the master plan is demonstrated together with the method of preparing the plan, the disciplines needed and the elements to be taken into account. The importance of balancing the respective capacities of the many elements and of ensuring flexibility and expansibility to meet changing needs is shown, together with methods of achieving these objectives. Guidance is provided on assessing the capacity of individual facilities and on planning runway, taxiway and apron configurations, passenger buildings, ground transport links and internal roads, car parks and cargo areas, to permit phased development of the master plan.

An airport master plan should be the most effective framework within which the individual facilities can operate their separate functions at the highest possible

[5] *Airport Planning Manual*, Part 1—Master Planning, Second Edition: 1987, Doc 9184-AN/902.

levels of efficiency. As explained above, it is not always possible for the best plans for individual facilities to be fitted together in a total plan for the airports without some modifications to make them compatible with each other. This often means some loss of perfection in the individual plans but good planning strikes an optimum balance so that a total plan is produced which is more effective in its operation, and therefore has a higher capacity and efficiency, than would be the case if there were no reconciliation between the plans of the individual facilities. Care must be taken, however, to ensure that compromises do not adversely affect safety.

The most efficient plan for the airport as a whole is that which provides the required capacity for aircraft, passenger, cargo and vehicle movements, with maximum passenger, operator and staff convenience and at lowest capital and operating costs. Flexibility and expansibility should be considered in conjunction and are fundamental to all aspects of planning. Particular features of some sites may make it necessary to decide that expansibility is not possible but that the plan should still proceed. This is a matter for local judgement relative to local conditions. However, it is never necessary to abandon the requirement for flexibility. Most airports can be planned with inherent flexibility, even though expansibility may not be possible.

Planning of airports is complicated by the diversity of facilities and services which are necessary for the movement of aircraft, passengers and cargo and the ground vehicles associated with them, and the necessity to integrate their planning. The manual is directed at authorities responsible for the planning and development of airports and particularly those which may not have experienced planning departments or staff. It is compiled in a manner intended to be suitable for use by these authorities and their planning staff in such matters as supporting requests to higher authorities for finance and in advising airport consultants, engineers, and planners of the airport authorities' requirements for development work.

Accordingly, if a master plan is to be useful to airport authorities certain preplanning requirements must be understood and followed. It is the purpose of this chapter to identify the most important of these preplanning considerations which, if followed, will provide the framework for an effective and implementable airport master plan. Preplanning considerations include: preplanning co-ordination; information sources; goals and schedules; land requirements; financing considerations; planning team; planning organization; planning procedure; and environmental considerations.

In the airport master planning process the roles of aviation interests as well as appropriate non-aviation interests must be considered. The airport master plan, with its recommended development projects, will be of interest to a diversity of people and organizations including, inter alia, private citizens, local and national organizations, aerodrome users, planning agencies, conservation groups, ground transportation officials, concessionaire interests, and airline and other aviation interests. If these groups are not consulted prior to and during the master planning programme there will be great risk of delay, or even stoppage, of future airport development. Therefore, it is essential that the master planning team co-ordinate its efforts and seek the advice of these interest groups prior to and during the critical stages of the master plan. This co ordination will help assure acceptance and permit import ant input from organized interests which will lead to a well integrated and implementable plan.

The preparation and collection of meaningful data on the usage of an airport and its components are basic to sound master planning, which also requires reliable forecasting techniques and meaningful statistical data on which future planning can be based. The nature of the data to be collected should not only cover the physical facilities of the airport but should also provide measures of utilization, volume and composition of traffic, the cost of transportation and related tariffs, the financial situation of the airlines using the airport, and government transportation policies and regulations.

The airport master planning process involves the preparation of both broad and specific policies, plans, and programmes needed to establish a viable airport. The goals of the airport master planning process should be to: provide for the orderly and timely development of an airport adequate to meet the present and future air transportation needs of an area or State; place aviation in its proper perspective relative to a balanced, regional or national multi-modal, transportation system plan or to an area-wide plan. Also to provide a basis for co-ordinating airport plans with other planning efforts—local, regional, and national another aim is to protect and enhance the environment through the location and expansion of aviation facilities in such a way that impairment of the ecology and the intrusion of unacceptable levels of noise and air pollution into the community are avoided. The Master Plan will also promote the establishment of an effective govern mental organization for implementing the master plan in a systematic fashion; ensure compatibility with the content, format, standards, and criteria of governmental aviation policy departments, ICAO and IATA, among others; co-ordinate the specific airport master plan with the state airport system and regional air transportation plans, when they exist.

It will also serve as a basis for co-ordinating plans for air navigation facilities, airspace use, and air traffic control procedures; inform public and private aviation interests, as well as the general public, of aviation requirements, and create a general awareness of the need for a system atic approach to planning and developing the airport; develop the aviation portion of long-range state plans and establish appropriate priorities for airport financing in short-term governmental budgeting for public facilities; optimize the use of land and airspace resources which are inherently limited in some areas.

Additionally the airport master plan will use air transportation facilities to help guide the growth pattern of the area and the state, according to comprehensive planning goals and objectives promulgated by local authorities. The planning process begins after the organization of the planning effort and financial arrangements are made arranged. The process starts with the development of general criteria and policy objectives sometimes called "policy formulation" and the study design. After these two steps are completed, the technical planning phase begins with an inventory of existing facilities. Next, a forecast of aviation demand is made in order to determine the future facility requirements. Alternative systems to meet the future facility requirements are then developed and evaluated. While this ends the initial planning process, a continuing planning process following these same general procedures is established while implementation of the long-range plan is underway.

The first step in the master planning process is the establishment of ground rules which may be termed policy objectives. For example, it is necessary to state at the outset the time frame, or planning horizons, for which planning is to be accomplished. The geographic limits of the planning area must also be established in order to guide such elements as data collection, forecasting, and potential site selection. Whether adherence to national or international airport design/dimensional standards will be required, should be determined.

Ideally, in the planning process, all attempts should be made to relate the communities' individual and sometimes unique objectives may take place at several points in the master planning process: during preparation, discussion, and initial adoption of an airport master plan; during major reconsideration of the entire plan; and during consideration of the day-to-day development matters which call for the review of general long-range policies. One of the major concerns in airport planning should involve aircraft noise in the vicinity of airports.

3.4 Aircraft Noise at Airports

There is definite medical evidence to prove that exposure to aerial noise causes deleterious psychological effects. For instance, a study made in relation to admissions to a psychiatric hospital in England draws a distinct relationship between the disturbed mental state of the admitted inmates of the hospital and high intermittent noise levels from Heathrow Airport, to which they were exposed.[6] One writer states that airport and industrial noise are the causes of mental stress and maladjustment, increases in chronic fatigue and neurotic complaints in some cases, although different personalities may underlie individual differences in noise effects.[7] A frequent factor that courts take into consideration in determining whether a particular activity is a nuisance is the locality of the alleged nuisance. For instance, in *Painter* v. *Reed*,[8] in determining whether the noises caused in the early morning by the movement and stamping of horses which disturbed the sleep of the plaintiff constituted an actionable nuisance and should be restrained by injunction, Richards J. considered carefully the locality in which the alleged nuisance occurred. His Honour was of the opinion that although the defendant's business was situated in a very suitable place in the city, yet the noise complained of was not as reasonable as the law would require. In *Dunstan* v. *King*,[9] in coming to the conclusion that the noise amounted to an actionable nuisance, the court considered the type of locality

[6] Abey-Wickrama et al. (1969), pp. 1275–1277.

[7] Cohen (1968), 25pp.

[8] [1930] S.A.S.R. 295.

[9] [1948] V.L.R. 269.

in question. Although it was adduced in evidence that there were other sawmills in the district, the court held that there was no other industrial undertaking within reasonable distance of the particular locality, which had the character of a quiet countryside.[10] In *Munro* v. *Southern Dairies Ltd.*[11] too, in considering whether the noise complained of was characteristic of the particular neighbourhood, Sholl J. held that it was not so.[12]

In another case[13] the defendant was a haulage contractor and the noise and the dust caused by his business constituted a substantial nuisance to the plaintiff. The court cited a great deal of judicial authority in this area of the law. After considering the pecuniary loss resulting to the defendant if the court granted a permanent injunction, the fact that no one else living in the neighbourhood supported the plaintiff and the fact that the plaintiff had a motive for complaining about the noise (there was ill-feeling between the two families) the court came to the conclusion that in a residential suburb a man is not at liberty habitually to start a noisy motor vehicle at very early hours of the morning when his neighbours are usually asleep. Upon the defendant undertaking to abate the nuisance, the action was dismissed. This case underscores the preoccupation of judges in considering the locality of the alleged nuisance important, even in circumstances where there is evidence in favour of the defendant.

The relevance of locality has been considered in situations where the defendant avers that the plaintiff came to the nuisance. However, "coming to the nuisance" is not a defence to an action in nuisance. Certain cases have discussed this non-defence. One of the earliest cases[14] which has done so held that the plaintiff's having come to the nuisance did not dis-entitle him to equitable relief. In *Barber* v. *Penley*[15] the offending noise came from the crowd at a theatre in the locality where the plaintiff lived. It was held that a person who deliberately goes next door to a theatre cannot expect to have precisely the same amenities that the lessee of a private house in a street occupied by private houses only in the West End would expect. However, the court held that such a lessee still has the right to expect that no nuisance shall be committed to the prejudice of such person.[16] In the recent case of *Miller* v. *Jackson*[17] Geoffrey Lane L. J. posed the question:

> ... can the defendants take advantage of the fact that the plaintiffs have put themselves in such a position by coming to occupy a house on the edge of a small cricket field, with the result that what was not a nuisance in the past now becomes a nuisance?[18]

---

[10] *Id.* 272.

[11] [1955] V.L.R. 332.

[12] *Id.* 337.

[13] *Kidman* v. *Page* [1959] Qd. R. 53.

[14] *Tipping* v. *St. Helen's Smelting Co.* [1865] 1 Ch. App. 66.

[15] [1893] 2 Ch. 447.

[16] *Id.* 449.

[17] [1977] Q.B. 966. (C.A.).

[18] *Id.* 986.

His Lordship held that although he was inclined to find for the defendants he could not do so as he was bound by judicial precedent. The case of *Sturges* v. *Bridgman*[19] was cited as authority for the proposition that it is no answer to a claim in nuisance for a defendant to show that the plaintiff brought the trouble upon himself by building and coming to live in a house so close to the defendant's premises that he would inevitably be affected by the defendant's activities.[20] Geoffrey Lane L. J. thought that this rule works injustice. He reluctantly held for the plaintiff. His Lordship seemed to have been much impressed by the fact that the locality was a country area in which cricket was an important activity. Therefore, courts throughout the ages have been influenced by the locality in question in considering whether the plaintiff came to the nuisance.

3.5 The Public Benefit Criterion

Certain cases have considered whether the benefit to the public by the defendant's activity would override the nuisance such activity would cause to the plaintiff. *Munro* v. *Southern Dairies Ltd.*[21] was such a case. In this case Sholl J. cited the early case of *Shelfer* v. *City of London Electric Lighting Company*[22] in support of his contention that the public benefit resulting from the defendant's activity was not sufficient to prevent the plaintiff from succeeding in the nuisance action. In the more recent English case of *Kennaway* v. *Thompson and another*[23] the Court of Appeal considered the jeopardy caused to the public interest in granting an injunction prohibiting the defendant, a boating club, from carrying on noisy activities which prevented the plaintiff from using and enjoying her land. Lawton L. J. held that although the plaintiff was not entitled to an injunction restraining all of the club's activities because there had to be a reasonable amount of give and take, those activities which caused a serious nuisance to her should be restrained by injunction.[24] His Lordship was of the opinion that the public benefit generated by the defendant's activities outweighed the inconvenience to the plaintiff who had to

[19] (1879) 11 Ch. D. 852. In this case the plaintiff who was a physician was hindered in his work by the noise and vibrations from the neighbouring confectionery shop.

[20] [1977] Q.B. 966 at 986, 987.

[21] [1955] V.L.R. 332.

[22] [1895] 1 Ch. 287. Lindley L. J. stated at 316:

> Neither has the circumstance that the wrongdoer is in some sense a public benefactor (e.g., a gas or water company or a sewer authority) ever been considered a sufficient reason for refusing to protect by injunction an individual whose rights are being persistently infringed. Cited at 337 in *Munro* v. *Southern Dairies Ltd.*

[23] [1980] 3 All. E. R. 329.

[24] *Id.* 333.

absent herself from her house for many days in order to avoid the noise.[25] In dismissing the case of *Miller* v. *Jackson*[26] as not binding on the present case, His Lordship held that the statement of Lord Denning M. R. in that case, that the public interest should prevail over the private interest, runs counter to the principles enunciated in the early case of *Shelfer* v. *City of London Electric Lighting Company.*[27] *Kennaway* v. *Thompson* reiterated the attitude of the courts in considering a person's right to use and enjoy his land as sacrosanct as opposed to the benefit to the public that may accrue from the defendant's activities.

The Chicago Convention is the fundamental source which grants regulatory powers to the international community on matters relating to international civil aviation. The Convention in its Preamble proclaims that the governments that are parties to it agree on certain principles and arrangements in order that international civil aviation may be developed in a safe and orderly manner. Public safety is a feature of major concern to the Convention which requires that:

> Each contracting State may, for reasons of military necessity or public safety, restrict or prohibit uniformly the aircraft of other States from flying over certain areas of its territory. . .Such prohibited areas shall be of reasonable extent and location so as not to interfere unnecessarily with air navigation. Descriptions of such prohibited areas in the territory of a contracting State, as well as any subsequent alterations therein, shall be communicated as soon as possible to the other contracting States and to ICAO.[28]

It must be remembered that it was the Convention which established ICAO which is required as one of its objectives to foster the planning and development of international air transport so as *inter alia* to ensure the safe and orderly growth of international civil aviation throughout the world,[29] meet the needs of the people of the world for safe, regular, efficient and economic air transport,[30] promote safety of flight in international air navigation,[31] and promote generally the development of all aspects of international civil aviation.[32] To this end, ICAO is mandated by the Convention to adopt and amend from time to time as may be necessary, international Standards and Recommended Practices and Procedures (SARPS) dealing *inter alia* with characteristics of airports and landing areas and such matters concerned with the safety, regularity and efficiency of air navigation as may from time to time be appropriate.[33] Each contracting State has undertaken to collaborate in securing the highest practicable degree of uniformity in the above regulations, standards and procedures of the Organization.

---

[25] *Ibid.*

[26] [1977] Q.B. 966. (C.A.).

[27] [1895] 1 Ch. 287.

[28] Article 9.

[29] Article 44(a).

[30] Article 44(d).

[31] Article 44(n).

[32] Article 44(i).

[33] Article 37(b).

In order to carry out its policies in environmental issues related to civil aviation, ICAO established the Committee on Environmental Protection (CAEP) in 1983.[34] CAEP is a technical committee reporting to the ICAO Council and consisting of 14 members nominated by their States. The members are experts in the field of aviation and the environment. The Committee is charged with addressing the main environmental problems affecting civil aviation, which are pollution caused by aircraft engine emissions and aircraft noise. The three main approaches adopted by CAEP in its work on aircraft noise concern reduction of noise at source; use of noise abatement operating measures; and land use planning.

Standards and Recommended Practices for aircraft noise were first adopted by ICAO on 2 April 1971 and designated as Annex 16 to the Convention. The development of the Annex originated in September 1968 at the 16th Session of the ICAO Assembly which adopted Resolution A 16-3 which recognized that the problem of aircraft noise was so serious in the vicinity of many of the world's airports that public reaction was mounting to a degree that gave cause for great concern and required urgent solution. The Assembly also noted that noise concerned the public and civil aviation and was becoming a matter for concern with the increase in air traffic and that the introduction of future aircraft types could increase and aggravate the problem further unless action was taken to alleviate the problem. Accordingly, the Assembly resolved to instruct the ICAO Council to call an international conference within the machinery of ICAO as soon as possible; establish international specifications and associated guidance material relating to aircraft noise; and, to include, in the appropriate Annexes and other relevant ICAO documents and possibly in a separate Annex on noise, such material as the description and methods of measurement of aircraft noise and suitable limitations on the noise caused by aircraft that was of concern to communities in the vicinity of airports.

In response to the Assembly Resolution, a Special Meeting on Aircraft Noise in the Vicinity of Aerodromes was convened in Montreal in November–December 1969 to examine the following aspects related to the problems of aircraft noise:

a) procedures for describing and measuring aircraft noise;
b) human tolerance to aircraft noise;
c) aircraft noise certification;
d) criteria for establishment of aircraft noise abatement operating procedures;
e) land use control; and,
f) ground run-up noise abatement procedures.

Based on the recommendations of the Special Meeting on Aircraft Noise in the Vicinity of Aerodromes, draft International Standards and Recommended Practices for Aircraft Noise were developed and, after amendment following the usual

[34] For more details on CAEP see Mortimer (1992), at 6. See also, Crayston and Hupe (1999), at p. 5.

consultation with the Contracting States of the Organization, were adopted by the Council to form the text of Annex 16.

With the development of Standards and Recommended Practices dealing with the control of aircraft engine emissions, it was felt that all provisions relating to environmental aspects of aviation should be included in a single document. Accordingly, Annex 16 was re-titled as "Environmental Protection". Volume I of the Annex contains the existing provisions relating to aircraft noise and Volume 11 contains the provisions related to aircraft engine emissions.[35] The much dreaded sonic boom[36] caused by supersonic aircraft was broadly discussed during the Second Meeting of ICAO's Sonic Boom Committee in Montreal in June 1973.[37] The Committee found that the sonic boom had no ill effects on the human eye and ear. As for psychological effects of the boom, it was noted by the Committee that it caused a startle reaction in the human being, in addition to a slight increase in heart rate which returned to normalcy within a very short period. It was also the Committee's view that the startle effects of the *Concorde* and *TU-144* aircraft did not give rise to any significant circulatory effects. With regard to the sociological effects of the sonic boom, the Committee considered a study of the *Concorde* aircraft over Australia in June 1972 and concluded that this aspect be best studied as both a public and private law issue by the Legal Committee of ICAO.

The ICAO Assembly has, in addition, adopted several Resolutions concerning aviation and the environment. At its 22nd Assembly held in September/October 1977 the ICAO Assembly adopted Resolution A 22-12 which recognized *inter alia* the following:

1) advancing technology has caused aviation to become a significant influence in the environment;
2) many of the adverse environmental effects of civil aviation activity can be reduced by, the application of integrated measures embracing technological improvements, appropriate noise abatement operating procedures, proper organization of air traffic and the appropriate use of airport planning and land use control mechanisms;

---

[35] See *Annex 16 to the Convention on International Civil Aviation*, Second Ed. 1988 Vol. 1 Foreword.

[36] See *ICAO Doc 8894*, SPB/11, at 1–5. Sonic boom was identified in 1970 as:

> . . . a phenomenon peculiar to supersonic flight. It is caused by the mach waves that an aircraft inevitably generates aerodynamically when it flies at a speed greater than that of sound. Roughly speaking these waves take the form of compression waves from the bow and the stern separated by expansion waves. . .these waves extend from the aircraft as an audible pattern of roughly conical shape, much as the water waves from a boat extend from it as a visible pattern of roughly v-shape, and just as the water waves from a boat cause a disturbance that often extends to and travels along a neighbouring shore as the boat passes by, so do these shock waves from an aircraft cause a disturbance that normally extends to and travels along the ground as the aircraft flies over., The passage of these shock waves is perceived as a sonic boom.

[37] See *ICAO Doc 9064*, SBC/2, at 4-1.

3) other international organizations are becoming involved in activities relating to noise abatement policies;
4) in fulfilling its role, ICAO strives to achieve a balance between the benefit of accruing to the world community through civil aviation and the harm caused to the human environment in certain areas through the progressive advancement of civil aviation;

The Assembly therefore declared:

1) that ICAO is conscious of the adverse environmental impacts that may be related to aircraft activity and of its responsibility and that of its Contracting States to achieve maximum compatibility between the safe and orderly development of civil aviation and the quality of the human environment;
2) that the Council Should maintain its vigilance in the pursuit of aviation interests related to the human environment and also maintain the initiative in developing policy guidance on all aviation matters related to the human environment, and not leave such initiatives to other organizations;

The Assembly also invited States to continue their active support for ICAO's Action Programme Regarding the Environment on all appropriate occasions as their participation in civil aviation's contribution to the United Nations Environment Programme (UNEP) and authorised the ICAO Council, if and when it deems this desirable, to enter into cooperative arrangements with the United Nations Environment Programme for the execution of environmental projects financed by the United Nations Environment Fund. The Assembly urged States to refrain from unilateral measures that would be harmful to the development of international civil aviation.

At the same Session, the Assembly adopted Resolution a 22-13 on airports and the environment, observing *inter alia*:

1) the compatibility between the airport and its environment was one of the elements to be taken into account in long-term systems planning;
2) the problem of aircraft noise in the vicinity of many of the world's airports continued to arouse public concern and required appropriate action;
3) the introduction of future aircraft types could increase and aggravate this noise unless action was taken to alleviate the situation.

The Assembly therefore requested the council to continue its work on establishing Standards and Recommended Practices relating to the alleviation of the problem and urged contracting States to adopt, where appropriate, the ICAO measures and procedures applicable.

In the following Session (September/October 1980), the Assembly adopted Resolution A 23-10 on aircraft noise and engine emissions from subsonic aircraft and requested contracting States not to allow the operation of foreign registered subsonic jet planes that did not conform to ICAO's specifications on noise certification standards as specified in Annex 16 until 1 January 1988.[38] At the 28th

[38] See *Assembly Resolutions in Force* (as of 6 October 1989), *ICAO Doc 9558* at 11–18.

Assembly Sessions held in October 1990, the ICAO Assembly observed that while certification standards for subsonic jet aircraft noise levels are specified in Volume 1, Chapter 2 and Chapter 3 of Annex 16 and that environmental problems due to aircraft noise continued to exist in the neighbourhood of many international airports, some States were consequently considering restrictions on the operations of aircraft which exceed the noise levels in Volume I, Chapter 3 of Annex 16. The Assembly also recognized that the noise standards in Annex 16 were not intended to introduce operating restrictions on aircraft and that operating restrictions on existing aircraft would increase the costs of airlines and would impose a heavy economic burden, particularly on those airlines which do not have the financial resources to re-equip their fleets. Therefore, considering that resolution of problems due to aircraft noise must be based on the mutual recognition of the difficulties encountered by States and a balance among their different concerns, the Assembly, by Resolution A 28-3, urged States not to introduce any new operating restrictions on aircraft which exceed the noise levels in Volume I, Chapter 3 of Annex 16 before considering:

a) whether the normal attrition of existing fleets of such aircraft will provide the necessary protection of noise climates around their airports;
b) whether the necessary protection can be achieved by regulations preventing their operators from adding such aircraft to their fleets through either purchase, or lease/charter/interchange, or alternatively by incentives to accelerate fleet modernization;
c) whether the necessary protection can be achieved through restrictions limited to airports and runways the use of which has been identified and declared by them as generating noise problems and limited to time periods when greater noise disturbance is caused; and,
d) the implications of any restrictions for other States concerned, consulting these States and giving them reasonable notice of intention

The Assembly further urged States:

a) to frame any restrictions so that Chapter 2 compliant aircraft of an individual operator which are presently operating to their territories may be withdrawn from these operations gradually over a period of not less than 7 years;
b) not to begin the above phase-in period for any restrictions before 1 April 1995;
c) not to restrict before the end of the phase-in period the operations of any aircraft less than 25 years after the date of issue of its first individual certificate of airworthiness;
d) not to restrict before the end of the phase-in period the operations of any presently existing wide-body aircraft or of any fitted with high by-pass ratio engines;
e) to apply any restrictions consistently with the non-discrimination principle in Article 15 of the Chicago Convention so as to give foreign operators at least as favourable treatment as their own operators at the same airports; and,

f) to inform ICAO, as well as the other States concerned, of all restrictions imposed.

The Assembly also strongly encouraged States to continue to cooperate bilaterally, regionally and inter-regionally with a view to:

a) alleviating the noise burden on communities around airports without imposing severe economic hardship on aircraft operators; and
b) taking into account the problems of operators of developing countries with regard to Chapter 2 aircraft presently on their register, where they cannot be replaced before the end of the phase-in period, provided that there is proof of a purchase order or leasing contract placed for a replacement Chapter 3 compliant aircraft and the first date of delivery of the aircraft has been accepted;

The Assembly, while urging States, if and when any new noise certification standards are introduced which are more stringent than those in Volume I, Chapter 3 of Annex 16, not to impose any operating restrictions on Chapter 3 compliant aircraft, urged the Council to promote and States to develop an integrated approach to the problem of aircraft noise, including land-use planning procedures around international airports, so that any residential, industrial or other land-use that might be adversely affected by aircraft noise is minimal. The Assembly further urged States to assist aircraft operators in their efforts to accelerate fleet modernization and thereby prevent obstacles and permit all States to have access to lease or purchase aircraft compliant with Chapter 3, including the provision of multilateral technical assistance where appropriate. This Resolution superseded Resolution A23-10, which was discussed above.

Resolution A 28-3 represented a cautious balance between the concerns of the aircraft manufacturers, the airline industry and developing States who do not wish to lose in the near future, the services of Chapter 2 aircraft which are already in use and service. Although aircraft manufactured prior to October 1977 that are included in Chapter 2 of Annex 16 and called "Chapter 2 aircraft" are required to be phased out, the compromise in Resolution A 28-3 allowed States that have noise problems at airports to start phasing out operations by Chapter 2 aircraft from the year 1995 and to have all of them withdrawn by the year 2002, with some exceptions. The Resolution envisaged that by the year 2002 only aircraft manufactured after October 1977 and described in Chapter 3 of Annex 16 (called "Chapter 3 aircraft") would be in operation. Following this resolution, a number of developed States started to phase out Chapter 2 aircraft, while giving due recognition to the compromise reached in Resolution A28-3.

At its 32nd Assembly, held in September 1998, Assembly Resolution A32-8[39] containing a consolidated statement of continuing ICAO policies and practices related to environmental protection was adopted, making current the regulatory policies relating to aviation and the environment. Appendix B to the Resolution

[39] *Assembly Resolutions in Force*, (As of 2 October 1998), *ICAO Doc 9730*, ICAO: Montreal, at 1–36.

cited Annex 16 Volume 1 as comprising, *inter alia,* noise certification standards for future subsonic aircraft and mentions that aircraft manufacturers and operators needed to note that future generations of aircraft had to be so designed as to operate efficiently and with the least possible environmental disturbance. Appendix C called upon Contracting States and international Organizations to recognize the leading role of ICAO in dealing with aircraft noise and requests the former to work closely together to ensure the greatest harmonization of work in the area of environmental protection as related to air transport. In Appendix G, which related to the problem of sonic boom, the Assembly reaffirmed the importance attached to ameliorating problems caused to the public by sonic boom as a result of supersonic flight, invites States involved in the manufacture of supersonic aircraft to furnish ICAO with proposals that would meet specifications established by ICAO on the subject.

The most topical issue addressed by Resolution A32-8, is in its Appendix D, which, whilst reiterating the time limits specified for the phasing out of Chapter 2 Aircraft and related dates, strongly encouraged States to continue to co-operate bilaterally, regionally and inter-regionally with a view to alleviating the noise burden on communities and also to take into account the problems that may be faced by some operators in phasing out their Chapter 2 aircraft before the end of the period specified. The Resolution also urged States, if and any noise certification standards are introduced new which are more stringent than those in Volume 1, Chapter 3 of Annex 16 not to impose any operating restrictions on Chapter 3 compliant aircraft. More importantly, States were urges to assist operators in their efforts of fleet modernization with a view to preventing obstacles and permit all States to have access to lease or purchase aircraft compliant with Chapter 3.

The qualification in Resolution A32-8 seemingly admitted of Chapter 2 aircraft which were converted to be compliant with Chapter 3 noise levels being considered for operation at least until 1 April 2002. The Resolution urged States to consider the difficulties faced by operators of Chapter 2 aircraft who are unable to make them Chapter 3 compliant by the given date, implying that it would be in the economic interests of such operators to be given additional time in order to make the necessary replacements. Chapter 2 aircraft could be made Chapter 3 compliant whereby the aircraft can be re-certified to Chapter 3 standards through re-engining or hush kitting. Chapter 2 aircraft which are likely to be re-engined or hush-kitted are Boeing 727s and 737s, DC-9s, BAC1-11s and some Boeing 747-100s that need hush-kitting.

There was an attempt on the part of the European Union to limit and eventually eliminate Chapter 3 compliant aircraft from operating within countries of the European Union. This ban would also be calculated to affect the importation of such aircraft into the region. Legislation passed by the Union in April 1999 was intended to bar Chapter 3 compliant aircraft from European registries from 4 May 2000 (originally 1 April 1999, which is 3 years before the date specified in Resolution A32-8, namely, 1 April 2002) and to prohibit their operation into the countries of the European Union after 1 April 2002. Such action was reportedly criticized by the Air Transport Association which claims that the inflexibility of such a deadline "will severely undercut, if not destroy entirely - ICAO's efforts to address environmental issues on a uniform international basis".[40]

The action of the European Union sought justification on the basis that the exponential air traffic growth in Europe will increase noise around European airports, requiring stringent noise standards. A related fear is reportedly that hush-kitted aircraft, which are rare in Europe, will find a new home in the Continent. Unlike in Europe, airlines in the United States were somewhat prolific in the use of hush-kits in aircraft[41] and many United States carriers operated Stage 2 hush-kitted aircraft into Europe and even have based equipment in the Continent. Although the U.S. State Department reacted forcefully to the European Union's hush-kitted aircraft ban, the application of which was extended by the Union until May 2000, it was then reported that both the United States and the European Union were working together on a possible new ICAO Standard (presumably to be called Chapter 4).[42]

The issue was a "double edged sword" involving two distinct disciplines. As discussed earlier, the European contention was based on the strictly legal issue of noise pollution and overtones of the tort of nuisance committed by operators whose aircraft were not compliant with Chapter 3 standards to the satisfaction of the European Union. Others who opposed what they claimed to be a premature enforcement of ICAO standards, as contained in Resolution A32-8, argued that the European hush-kit rule would cost the manufacturing industry significant losses. It was reported that the United States industry would lose $2 billion if the ban is enforced in Europe as scheduled.[43]

The aircraft noise issue entered a phase where trading and environmental issues were at a delicate balance. On the one hand, competition issues pertaining to the sale of hush-kits and other equipment calculated to reduce aircraft engine noise to levels prescribed by ICAO were quite significant from the perspective of international trade, and on the other hand, environmental issues that have been addressed by the ICAO Council through CAEP and also by the Assembly should also be given careful consideration. As discussed earlier, ICAO Assembly Resolution A32-8 urged States to give consideration to the economic difficulties that some States may have to face in phasing out Chapter 2 aircraft by the year 2002. However, the Resolution did not leave room for States to claim that pure economic factors would effectively preclude them from phasing out Chapter 2 aircraft by the date stipulated in the Resolution.

---

[40] Flint (1999), at p. 29.

[41] It was reported that American Airlines is installing the Raisbeck System on 52 B 727 aircraft and hush-kitting 20 more. United is installing hush-kits on 75 B 727 aircraft and 24 B 737-200s. Delta is hush-kitting 104 727s and 54 737-200s. Southwest, TWA, Alaska Airlines and US Airways are other carriers who plan to hush-kit their Chapter 2 aircraft. See Flint (1999), *Id.* at p. 34.

[42] Esler (1999), p. 52 at p. 53.

[43] Europe Considers Delaying Hushkit Ban, *Aviation Daily*, Thursday October 7 1999 at p. 1.

Fast forward to 2013, at the 38th Session of the ICAO Assembly in September/October, the Assembly adopted Resolution A 38-17 where States recognized that solutions to noise problems need to be tailored to the specific characteristics of the airport concerned, which calls for an airport-by-airport approach, and that similar solutions could be applied if similar noise problems are identified at airports; Recognizing that measures to address noise may have significant cost implications for operators and other stakeholders, particularly those from developing countries. States also recognized that States have relevant legal obligations, existing agreements, current laws and established policies which may influence their implementation of the ICAO "balanced approach"; and that some States may also have wider policies on noise management.

Considering that the improvements in the noise climate achieved at many airports through the replacement of Chapter 2 compliant aircraft (aircraft which comply with the noise certification standards in Volume I, Chapter 2 of Annex 16 but which exceed the noise levels in Volume I, Chapter 3 of Annex 16) by quieter aircraft should be safeguarded by taking account of the sustainability of future growth and should not be eroded by incompatible urban encroachment around airports, the Assembly called upon all ICAO Member States and international organizations to recognize the leading role of ICAO in dealing with the problems of aircraft noise and urged States to: (a) adopt a balanced approach to noise management, taking full account of ICAO guidance (Doc 9829), relevant legal obligations, existing agreements, current laws and established policies, when addressing noise problems at their international airports; (b) institute or oversee a transparent process when considering measures to alleviate noise, including: (1) assessment of the noise problem at the airport concerned based on objective, measurable criteria and other relevant factors; (2) evaluation of the likely costs and benefits of the various measures available and, based on that evaluation, selection of measures with the goal to achieve maximum environmental benefit most cost-effectively; and (3) provision for dissemination of the evaluation results, for consultation with stakeholders and for dispute resolution;

The Assembly, through Resolution A38-17 encouraged States to: (a) promote and support studies, research and technology programmes aimed at reducing noise at source or by other means taking into account interdependencies with other environmental concerns; (b) apply land-use planning and management policies to limit the encroachment of incompatible development into noise-sensitive areas and mitigation measures for areas affected by noise, consistent with Appendix F to this Resolution; (c) apply noise abatement operational procedures, to the extent possible without affecting safety and considering interdependencies with other environmental concerns; and (d) not apply operating restrictions as a first resort but only after consideration of the benefits to be gained from other elements of the balanced approach and in a manner which is consistent with Appendix E to this Resolution and taking into account the possible impact of such restrictions at other airports;

It also requested States to: (a) work closely together to ensure the harmonization of programmes, plans and policies to the extent possible; (b) ensure that the application of any measures to alleviate noise are consistent with the non-discrimination principle in Article 15 of the Chicago Convention; and (c) take into consideration the particular economic conditions of developing countries. States were invited to keep the Council informed of their policies and programmes to alleviate the problem of aircraft noise in international civil aviation. The Assembly requested the Council to: (a) assess continuously the evolution of the impact of aircraft noise; (b) ensure that the guidance on the balanced approach in Doc 9829 is current and responsive to the requirements of States; and (c) promote the use of the balanced approach, for example through workshops; and called upon States to provide appropriate support for this work on ICAO guidance and any additional work on methodologies, and for the assessment of the impact or effectiveness of measures under the balanced approach as necessary.

In Appendix E of Resolution A 38-17 pertaining to local noise restrictions at airports the Assembly recognized that at many airports, land-use planning and management and noise abatement operational procedures are already being used and other noise mitigation measures are in place, although urban encroachment continues in certain cases and whereas implementation of the phase-out of aircraft which comply with the noise certification standards in Volume I, Chapter 2 of Annex 16 but which exceed the noise levels in Volume I, Chapter 3 of Annex 16 (as provided for in Appendix D to this Resolution) has been completed in some States. Assuming continued growth in aviation activity, without further action the number of people exposed to aircraft noise at some airports in those States may increase, the Assembly observed that there are significant regional differences in the extent to which aircraft noise is expected to be a problem over the next two decades and some States have consequently been considering placing operating restrictions on certain aircraft which comply with the noise certification standards in Volume I, Chapter 3 of Annex 16.

Another consideration was that if operating restrictions on Chapter 3 aircraft are introduced at certain airports, this should be based on the balanced approach and relevant ICAO guidance (Doc 9829) and should be tailored to the specific requirements of the airport concerned, these restrictions could have a significant economic impact on fleet investments of aircraft operators from States other than those in which the restrictions are imposed. Recognizing that these restrictions go beyond the policy established the Resolution and other relevant policy guidance developed by ICAO, and recognizing that ICAO places no obligation on States to impose operating restrictions on Chapter 3 aircraft the Assembly recognized that the noise standards in Annex 16 were not intended to introduce operating restrictions on aircraft and, specifically, that the standard contained in Annex 16, Volume I, Chapter 4 and any further stringency levels adopted by the Council are based on the understanding that it is for certification purposes only.

An important consideration for the Assembly was that States have legal obligations, laws, existing arrangements and established policies which may govern the management of noise problems at their airports and could affect the implementation of the Appendix; The Assembly therefore urged States to ensure, wherever possible, that any operating restrictions be adopted only where such action is supported by a prior assessment of anticipated benefits and of possible adverse impacts while further urging States not to introduce any operating restrictions at any airport on aircraft which comply with Volume I, Chapter 3 of Annex 16 before: (a) completing the phase-out of aircraft which exceed the noise levels in Volume I, Chapter 3 of Annex 16, at the airport concerned; and (b) fully assessing available measures to address the noise problem at the airport concerned in accordance with the balanced approach.

States which, despite the considerations in Resolving Clause 2 above, permit the introduction of restrictions at an airport on the operations of aircraft which comply, either through original certification or recertification, with Volume I, Chapter 3 of Annex 16 were urged: (a) to base such restrictions on the noise performance of the aircraft, as determined by the certification procedure conducted consistent with Annex 16, Volume I; (b) to tailor such restrictions to the noise problem of the airport concerned in accordance with the balanced approach; (c) to limit such restrictions to those of a partial nature wherever possible, rather than the complete withdrawal of operations at an airport; (d) to take into account possible consequences for air transport services for which there are no suitable alternatives (for example, long-haul services); (e) to consider the special circumstances of operators from developing countries, in order to avoid undue hardship for such operators, by granting exemptions; (f) to introduce such restrictions gradually over time, where possible, in order to take into account the economic impact on operators of the affected aircraft; (g) to give operators a reasonable period of advance notice; (h) to take account of the economic and environmental impact on civil aviation; and (i) to inform ICAO, as well as the other States concerned, of all such restrictions imposed.

The Assembly further urged States not to permit the introduction of any operating restrictions aimed at the withdrawal of aircraft that comply, through either original certification or recertification, with the noise standards in Volume I, Chapter 4 of Annex 16 and any further stringency levels adopted by the Council.

3.6 Local Air Quality

The Airport Planning Manual, in Part 2 pertaining to land use and environmental control states that air quality in the vicinity of airports is affected by aircraft engine emissions, emissions from airport motor vehicle and access traffic, and emissions from other sources (e.g. heating/power plants and incinerators).[44] In Appendix H to Resolution A38-17 the Assembly recognized that ICAO has established technical Standards and fostered the development of operational procedures that have

[44] Paragraph 2.3.1. It further states that Air pollution refers to a condition of the air marked by the presence therein of one or more air contaminants that can: endanger the health, safety or welfare of persons; interfere with normal enjoyment of life or property; endanger the health of animal life; or cause damage to plant life or to property. See paragraph 2.3.2.

reduced significantly local air quality pollution from aircraft. Although many pollutants such as soot and unburned hydrocarbons from aircraft engines affecting local and regional air quality, have declined dramatically over the last few decades and progress in operational procedures such as continuous descent operations has resulted in further reduction of emissions from aircraft, an assessment of trends in aviation emissions of NOx, PM, and other gaseous emissions showed increasing global emissions values.

The Assembly noted that the impacts of aviation emissions of NOx, PM, and other gaseous emissions need to be further assessed and understood and recognized at the same time that robust progress had been made in understanding impacts of non-volatile components of PM emissions while the scientific and technical work continues on better assessment of volatile components of PM emissions. It was a fact that the impacts of aviation emissions on local and regional air quality was part of the total emissions in the affected area and should be considered in the broader context of all sources that contribute to the air quality concerns. It was also noted that the actual local air quality and health impacts of aviation emissions depend on a series of factors among which are the contribution to the total concentrations and the number of people exposed in the area being considered.

Focus was on policy and guidance material adopted by the ICAO Council related to the use of emissions-related charges to address the impact of aircraft engine emissions at or around airports and the fact that the ICAO Council has published information on environmental management systems (EMS) that are in use by aviation stakeholders as well as developing an Airport Air Quality Guidance Manual which has been subsequently updated. The Assembly requested the Council to monitor and develop its knowledge of, in cooperation with other relevant international organizations such as WHO, the effects of aviation emissions of PM, NOx and other gases on human welfare and health, and to disseminate information in this regard. It also requested the Council to continue its work to develop technologically feasible, environmentally beneficial and economically reasonable standards to further reduce the impact of local air pollution from aircraft and to continue to develop certification requirements for non-volatile PM emissions while continuing to monitor progress in scientific and technical understanding of volatile and non-volatile components of PM emissions.

The Assembly further encouraged action by Member States to aid the development of certification requirements for non-volatile PM emissions and requested the Council to ensure that the interdependencies between measures to reduce aircraft noise and engine emissions that affect local air quality as well as global climate are given due consideration. The Council was also requested to continue its work to develop long-term technology and operational goals with respect to aviation environmental issues, including NOx emissions from aircraft. Another task for the Council was that it continue to foster operational and air traffic improvements that reduce the impact of local air pollution from aircraft. Member States' action and that of other parties involved, limiting or reducing international aviation emissions affecting local air quality through voluntary measures and to keep ICAO informed was solicited. The Assembly welcomed the development and promotion of guidance material on issues related to the assessment of airport-related air quality and requested the Council to work with States and stakeholders in promoting and sharing best practices applied at airports in reducing the adverse effects of aviation emissions on local air quality. It also welcomed the development of the guidance on emissions charges related to local air quality and requests the Council to keep up-to-date such guidance and urges Member States to share information on the implementation of such charges; and urged Member States to ensure the highest practical level of consistency and take due account of ICAO policies and guidance on emissions charges related to local air quality.

References

Abey-Wickrama I et al (1969) Mental hospital admissions and aircraft noise. Lancet 2 (7633):1275–1277

Cohen A (1968) Noise and psychological state. National Centre for Urban and Industrial Health, United States Public Health Service, Cincinnati, 25 pp

Crayston J, Hupe J (1999) ICAO facing complex and evolving challenges in the environmental field. ICAO J 54:5

Esler D (1999) The latest noise about noise. Bus Commer Aviat 85:52

Flint P (1999) Breaking the sound barrier. Air Transp World 36(3):29

Mortimer LF (1992) Ambitious programme of future work to be undertaken by CAEP. ICAO J 47:6

Chapter 4
Regulation of Airport Financing and Economics

4.1 Investing in Airports

In the case of airports, as in any other investment undertaking, particularly by a foreign investment company, it must be noted that making a foreign investment is different in nature and scope from engaging in a trade transaction. A trade transaction is a one-off exchange of money, goods and services and investment involves a long term relationship between the investor and the host country. The investor plugs in resources to the project with the expectation of reaping returns on his investment without undue delay. The investor also bears the commercial and political risks involved such as the arrival of new competitors, market fluctuations and change of government and policies.

One f the key principles of the law of investment is good faith, which acts in favour of the investor. In a 1978 arbitration, the arbitration tribunal held that if subsequent action taken by a government is contrary to assurances given by that government to the investor at the time the investment contract was signed, the principles of public international law would protect that investor.[1] Thus, a foreign investor in an airport project would be protected when existing laws of a country which he relied upon as a basis for investing resources in a project act so as to ensure fair and equitable treatment.

In a 2006 case concerning an investment in Argentina the arbitration tribunal held:

> Argentina prepared with the investment banks an attractive framework of laws and regulations that addressed the specific concerns of foreign investors with respect to the country risks involved in Argentina. . .having created specific expectations among investors, Argentina was bound by its obligations concerning the investment guarantees *vis* a *vis* public utility licences.[2]

[1] *Revere Copper* v. *OPIC*, Award, 24 August 1978, 56 ILR (1980) 258, 271.

[2] *LG&E* v. *Argentina*, Award, 3 October 2006, at paragraph 133.

R. Abeyratne, *Law and Regulation of Aerodromes*, DOI 10.1007/978-3-319-04780-5_4,

In the context, investment treaties between States usually include what is called an "*umbrella clause*" which guarantees obligations originally undertaken by the host State to be discharged for the benefit of the investor. This is particularly so when a project involves both a foreign investor and a national company. In the 2001 Czech case of *CME* v. *Czech Republic*[3] where a local company partnering a foreign investor had terminated the investment contract under a legal situation created by a local regulatory authority, the tribunal hearing the case held that it was the legal duty and obligation of the host State to ensure that the situation which opened a window for the local company to renege on its obligations did not occur.[4] However, a contemporaneous case[5] in the same jurisdiction denied an investor this basic right, holding that the only right accorded to the investor was access to the courts to air his grievance.

Although the defence of necessity is usually a valid consideration, in investment scenarios it does not hold much water. Article 25 of the International Law Commissions Principles of State Responsibility states that:

> Necessity may not be invoked by a State as a ground for precluding the wrongfulness of an act not in conformity with the international obligations of that State unless the act a) is the only means for the State to safeguard an essential interest against a grave and imminent peril, and b) does not seriously impact an essential interest of the State or States towards which the obligation exists, or of the international community as a whole.
>
> In any case, necessity may not be invoked by a State as the ground for precluding wrongfulness if a) the international obligation in question excludes the possibility of invoking necessity or b) the State has contributed to the situation of necessity.

As discussed earlier, principles of customary international law recognize that there is no obligation on any State to admit foreign investment in its territory in whole or part thereof. However, if a State admits foreign investment, a host of legal principles come into play, mainly to protect the investor under minimum standards required of the host State.[6] Firstly, property of a foreign investor is protected by the principles of international law.[7] It has been argued that the extent of this protection is directly proportionate to the extent of guarantees afforded by the host state to the property of its own nationals.[8] Foreign investment is usually effected by treaty which often imposes more than minimum standards on the host State. Studies

---

[3] *CME* v. *Czech Republic*, Partial Award, 13 September 2001, 9 ICSID Reports 121, paragraph 613.

[4] *Ibid.*

[5] *Lauder* v. *Czech Republic*, Award, 3 September 2001, 9 ICSID Reports, paragraph 66, and paragraph 314.

[6] Root (1910) at 528.

[7] In the aftermath of signature of a Treaty on Friendship, Commerce and Navigation with France, in 1796, John Adams said: "there is no principle of the law of nations more firmly established than that which entitles the property of strangers within the jurisdiction of another country in friendship with their own to the protection of its sovereignty by all efforts in his power". Moore (1916), p. 5.

[8] Called the "Calvo Theory" this principle was established by Argentine Jurist John Calvo. See Dolzer and Schreuer (2008) at 12.

suggest that foreign investment treaties have positive effects on the economy of a host State by increasing foreign direct investments therein.[9]

Usually, unless agreed between the parties to a foreign investment treaty[10] or agreement, the investor has to be constituted under the laws of the country of registration.[11] The company of a foreign investor is a corporation, partnership or business association incorporated under the laws in force in the territory of any contracting party wherein the place of effective management is situated.[12] One of the fundamental requirements of investment is that investment regimes are required to define their respective jurisdictions *ratione materiae*. It has been judicially recognized that jurisdiction cannot be invoked by a claimant on the basis of an investment in the instance of a bank guarantee offered by him for performance of equipment on the basis that the guarantee was an ordinary feature of a sales contract.[13]

An investment is a complex transaction. A transaction which *per se* might not qualify for definition as an investment could be classified an investment if it were part of an overall operation that could be considered an investment.[14] However, a claimant cannot categorize as an investment expenses unilaterally incurred in preparation of an investment.[15] Investments need not be territorially entrenched in a physical sense. In the 1998 case of *Felix* v. *Venezuela*,[16] where the investor acquired promissory notes issued by the host country, the Court held that while usually an investment may involve a transfer of some kind of funds or other property to the host country, it was not an inflexible rule and that funds need not be physically transferred to a host country but could be put at its disposal elsewhere.

In the instance of an investment which is governed by two instruments such as an international Convention and national agreement, usually the Convention has entrenched what is known as the "most favourable" principle, where the Convention would include a provision to the effect that nothing in the Convention will preclude a Party who holds property in the territory of another Party from benefitting from the provisions that are most favourable to him.[17]

---

[9] Neumayer and Spess (2005), p. 1567. Also, Elkins et al. (2006).

[10] The Vienna Convention on the Law of Treaties, while recognizing treaties as a source of law, accepts free consent, good faith and the *pacta sunt servanda* as universally recognized elements of a treaty. Article 11 of the Vienna Convention provides that the consent of a State to be bound by a treaty may be expressed by signature, exchange of instruments constituting a treaty, ratification, acceptance, approval or accession, or by any other means agreed upon. See *Vienna Convention on the Law of Treaties*, United Nations General Assembly Document *A/CONF.39/27*, 23 May 1969.

[11] *Saluka* v. *Czech Republic*, Partial Award, 17 March 2006.

[12] ASEAN Agreement for the Promotion and Protection of Investments, 15 December 1987 27 ILM 612 (1987). See also, *Yaung Chi Oo* v. *Myanmar* Award, 31 March 2003, 8 ICSID Reports 463.

[13] *Joe Mining* v. *Egypt*, 19 ICSID Review-FILJ (2004) 486 para. 63.

[14] *CSOB* v. *Slovakia*, 5 ICSID Reports 335.

[15] Mihaly v. Sri Lanka, 17 ICSID Review-FILJ (2002) 142, para. 61.

[16] 37 ILM (1998) 1378.

[17] OECD Draft Convention (1967) contained in ILM Vol. 29 (1990) at 565.

The investor cannot be treated arbitrarily or discriminatively. The word "arbitrary" has been associated with measures by the host State that affect the investments of foreign nationals where that State does not engage in a rational decision-making process. Such processes may include a consideration of the effect of a measure on foreign investments and a balance of the interests of the State with any burden imposed on such investments.[18] In the case of discrimination, a discriminatory measure need not necessary have to violate domestic law, particularly when such a law may contain discriminatory measures against foreign investors.[19]

The North American Free Trade Agreement (NAFTA), although not applicable to air transport, provides a good example of fair treatment of foreign investors. NAFTA provides that each Party shall accord national treatment to the goods of another Party in accordance with Article III of the General Agreement on Tariffs and Trade (GATT,[20] now WTO),[21] including its interpretative notes and to this end Article III of GATT and its interpretative provisions form an integral part of NAFTA.[22] Article 304 of NAFTA precludes any Party from setting arbitrary and self imposed standards and duties pertaining to customs. Furthermore, Article 1103 stipulates that a Party to the agreement shall grant investors of another Party treatment no less favourable than it accords, in like circumstances, to investors of any other Party or of a non Party with respect to the establishment, acquisition,

[18] *LG&E* v. *Argentina*, Decision on Liability 3 October 2006 at Para. 158.

[19] *Ronald S. Lauder* v. *The Czech Republic*, Award, 3 September 2001, 9 ICSID Reports 66.

[20] GATT (now World Trade Organization) is a multilateral body established in Geneva on 1 January 1948 on coming into force of the General Agreement on Tariff and Trade (GATT) negotiated and signed by 23 countries. GATT functions as the principal international body concerned with negotiating reduction of trade barriers and with international trade relations. While being an organization to which member States belong, where they could use it as a forum in which they can discuss and overcome their problems and negotiate to enlarge world trading opportunities, GATT is also a code of rules which is calculated to liberalize world trade. The Uruguay Round is the eighth round of multilateral trade negotiations held by GATT so far, and by far, one of the most complex. This round of negotiations is assisted by the Group of Negotiators on Services (GNS) which the GATT established in 1986 to follow the services negotiations. The GNS has drafted a detailed agreement comprising 35 articles and 5 annexes. See Abeyratne (1994a) at 2, for a discussion of the history of multilateral trade negotiations held by GATT.

[21] Article III of GATT stipulates that the contracting Parties to GATT recognize that internal taxes and other internal charges and laws, regulations and requirements affecting the internal sale, offering for sale, purchase, transportation, distribution or use of products, and internal quantitative regulations requiring the mixture, processing or use of products in specified amounts or proportions, should not be applied to imported or domestic products so as not to afford protection to domestic production. Furthermore, the provision also states that the products of a territory of any contracting Party imported into the territory of any other contracting Party shall not subject, directly or indirectly, to any taxes or other internal charges of any kind in excess of those applied, directly or indirectly, to like domestic products. Moreover, no contracting Party shall otherwise apply internal taxes or other internal charges to imported or domestic products in a manner contrary to the principles set forth in the Agreement.

[22] *NAFTA*, Article 301.

expansion, management, conduct, operation and sale or other disposition of investments.[23] NAFTA therefore creates duties upon its Parties in two areas: (a) protection and security by one Party of investments of investors of other Parties to the Agreement according to the principles of international law, and fair and equitable treatment; and (b) treatment by one Party, of investors, their investments, financial institutions and cross-border financial service providers of other Parties to the Agreement on a basis no less favourable than accorded to others, whether they are Parties to the Agreement or not.[24] This principle endorses and confirms the most-favoured-nation treatment principle of GATT.

Another significant provision in NAFTA is Article 1406 which requires each Party to accord to investors of another Party, financial institutions of another Party, investments of investors in financial institutions and cross-border financial service providers of another Party treatment no less favourable than that it accords to the investors, financial institutions, investments of investors in financial institutions and cross-border financial service providers of any other Party or of a non Party in like circumstances.

NAFTA therefore creates responsibility on the part of a Party to the Agreement towards investments, investors and financial institutions of other Parties. Brownlie remarks:

> Today, one can regard responsibility as a general principle of international law, a concomitant of substantive rules and of the supposition that acts and omissions may be categorized as illegal by reference to the rules establishing rights and duties. Shortly, the law of responsibility is concerned with the incidence and consequences of illegal acts, and particularly the payment of compensation for loss caused.[25]

Another effective protective tool is the "umbrella clause" that appears in many investment agreements that protect the interests of the investor. Such a clause guarantees the investor of obligations to be kept by the host State by covering all obligations contained in the treaty by the use of such words as "each contracting party shall observe any obligation it may have entered into with regard to investments of nationals or companies of the other Contracting Party".[26] A more useful text is found in the Investment Protection Treaty between France and Hong Kong of 1995 which states:

> Without prejudice to the provisions of this Agreement, each Contracting Party shall observe any particular obligation it may have entered into with regard to investments of investors of the other Contracting Party, including provisions more favourable than those of this Agreement.[27]

[23] See Article 1139 of NAFTA for a definition of investment.

[24] For an in depth study on the principles of NAFTA see Abeyratne (1994b), pp. 115–136.

[25] Brownlie (1990) at 433.

[26] British Model Treaty, quoted in Dolzer and Schreuer, *supra* note 8 at p. 153.

[27] Dolzer and Schreuer, *Id.* at 153–154.

A critical factor in the role of FDI in air transport is its importance to developing States. In the context of Africa, some of Asia and South America, there could be numerous obstacles that could preclude the optimization of host country policies unless external action is brought to bear that could maximize FDI and minimize costs. One commentator identifies international civil society, the corporate social responsibility community, international donors and multilateral lenders as critical elements in this equation.[28]

From the foregoing discussion it is clear that FDI offers considerable protection to the investor as well as increased opportunity to the air transport industry to serve its consumer better and more efficiently. However, for regulators to open up the restrictive national ownership and control practice would require a radical change of mindset and a miraculous realization that we have got everything about air transport economics upside down from the time the Chicago Convention was signed in 1944. The aim of the Conference in November–December 1944, which led to the adoption of the Chicago Convention, in the words of the letter to States from convener President Roosevelt of the United States was to use the abundance of aircraft left over from the war to connect cities and countries and provide air services to the people of the world. The letter stated:

> The approaching defeat of Germany, and the consequent liberation of great parts of Europe and Africa from military interruption of traffic, sets up the urgent need for establishing an international civil air service pattern on a provisional basis at least, so that all important trade and population areas of the world may obtain the benefits of air transportation as soon as possible, and so that the restorative processes of prompt communication may be available to assist in returning great areas to processes of peace.[29]

4.1.1 Foreign Direct Investment

Foreign investment in airport building and development is indeed a feature of globalization. FDI promotes economic growth and facilitates competition. As Michael Spence, Nobel Laureate and Professor of Economics at New York University observes in the example of India:

> India's earlier slow growth was partly attributable to a distrust of foreign investors and a relatively low level of foreign investment by multinational firms. If you look at the data for India and China for example, the differences are dramatic. Of course this is changing now with India's growing options.[30]

Commercially, if this view applies to the industrial world in general, there is no reason it should not apply to air transport. Niall Ferguson, Professor of Business

---

[28] Moran (2011), United Nations: New York, at 70.

[29] *Proceedings of the International Civil Aviation Conference*, Chicago, Vol. 1, US Department of State: 1948 at 11.

[30] Spence (2011) at 73.

Administration at Harvard University draws the interesting parallel of Marco Polo's visit to China in the 1270s when he was impressed by the volume of traffic in the Yangzi. Polo observed that the quantity of merchandize carried up and down made the Yangzi looked like a sea rather than a river. In comparison to this Ferguson argues that the Thames in the early fifteenth century was the backwater.[31] Ferguson goes on to suggest that one of the reasons for the success of European States in the sixteenth century onwards was its opening out to commerce and competition.[32]

4.1.2 Financial Management

In the financial management of airports, principles of best commercial practices should be applied, whenever considered appropriate by States and/or airport operators. States should apply best practices in the quality and timeliness of airport services; assessment of investment proposals; consultation process and dealing with users; accounting practices and transparency; subsidization; and development plans. These practices would involve the recognition by airport operators of air carriers, passengers and others doing business at airports, as customers who want to be satisfied that services are provided to an appropriate standard of quality, in a timely and cost-effective manner. They would also imply responsiveness to changing customer requirements and demands and no unreasonable difference in the treatment of users. A two-way exchange of information and an in-depth consultation process between the airport operators and the users should be documented on the airport development plan showing the relationship between the quality of service, the level of investment, and the level of charges.

Transparent accounts, published on a regular basis, should enable costs, revenues and (where appropriate) subsidies and cross-subsidies to be clearly identified. At airports where non-aeronautical revenues are generated, and are taken into account when calculating aeronautical charges, there should be no differentiation between the income and costs from the two sources. Subsidization of user charges should not be regarded as a substitute for bearing down on operating costs. Where it is necessary for wider public interest reasons to subsidize airport operations, from public funds or from revenues generated by other airports in a common system (an airport network), this should be clearly shown in the accounting system.

Proposals for investments should be objectively assessed against financial and broader cost-benefit analyses, including evaluation of social needs, impact on national or local economy, and environmental effects. Safety and security requirements should also be reflected. The possible role of government, at national and local level, in defining these criteria should be acknowledged.

---

[31] Ferguson, note 38 in Chap. 1 at 21–22.

[32] *Ibid.*

In addition, principles of best commercial practices could also be applied in many other areas, such as: budgeting, bank and cash management, presentation of financial statements, benchmarking and measuring performance and productivity, service level agreements, economic pricing, collection of charges and concessions and rentals.

A service level agreement (SLA) is a tool by which airports and airlines define the level of service and the terms of engagement or rules that will govern the airport/airline(s) relationship on the agreed services. Financial accounting refers to the system according to which revenues and expenses are recorded and summarized so as to present an aggregate financial picture of the provision of airport services. How elaborate and detailed the financial accounts are depends on the extent of detail required and the size of the airport concerned. It is, however, essential from the outset to ensure that all accounting procedures are applied in accordance with recognized accounting rules, standards or conventions. The importance of good internal controls as well as external auditing must also be emphasized.

Financial accounts may also be supplemented by management accounts which apply accounting techniques for the purpose of assisting all levels of management in planning and controlling all the different functions and services at an airport. The basic purpose of financial control is to ensure that the resources used to operate airports are spent in an effective, timely, reliable and accountable manner. This involves the monitoring and controlling of service provision in financial terms to ensure that the magnitude of expenses and revenues incurred in a particular year are in accordance with a previously approved budget.

Financial control and accounting are of course interrelated, since management cannot exercise financial control effectively without having at its disposal the data provided by a sound financial accounting system. It is therefore essential that any procedure being established to provide financial control be accompanied by a thorough examination of the accounting system to ensure that the latter can adequately provide the financial data necessary for this purpose.

An airport business plan has to be carefully thought through. The purpose of the business plan is to specify infrastructure requirements and the actions to be followed over the plan period by the airport to achieve its long-term strategies. The plan should therefore prescribe specific objectives through which the goals will be achieved. In so doing, the plan should outline the business environment in which the airport is forecast to operate and its implications. Consideration will need to be given to political, legal, economic, social and technical factors, as well as regional and global developments that may affect the airport; in addition the plan will need to highlight assumptions made which particularly affect the forecast plan outcome. Specific objectives can be broken down into the level and costs of services and the recovery of costs associated therewith, highlighting who is responsible and accountable for carrying them out. The plan will also identify key objectives against which an airport's performance will be monitored. Such planning will not only be financially orientated but will include goals concerning safety, security, the nature and level of services, the forecast demand for such services and the requirements of users.

The plan should identify capital investment projects to be carried out together with their financial implications. It is important that new projects included in the business plan meet an operational requirement and be accompanied by an appraisal, setting out the economic and financial justification of the project. A compromise between the cost of technical solutions to meet operational requirements and the financial implications for users may need to be made. Forecast changes in numbers and type of staff over the plan period should also be included. The business plan should demonstrate that the airport is well managed by reference to relevant performance indicators, including unit costs and quality of service (as described in Part C). These should cover the recent past and show future projections based on the outcomes in the plan being achieved.

Typically a successful airport business plan should take into consideration forecasts (short, long and medium term) of air traffic; external economic assumptions (e.g. exchange rates, inflation, GNP and interest rates); staff numbers and changing qualifications, training and work skills required of staff; limits on expenditure and/or airport charges; changing institutional arrangements; changes in costs (salaries, operating expenses); income; and operating result (as measured by the difference between forecast revenues and costs).

Planning is a continuous process and the business plan needs to be updated annually to reflect substantial amendments. In order that these plans maintain continuity and do not become simply a series of "wish statements", it is recommended that a comparison of the previous year's plan be made against the current year's plan and any changes be identified and explained. Some flexibility should, however, be provided in order to keep the plan from being too rigid. The main uncertainties affecting the results, particularly in the later years, should be discussed (e.g. the effects on capital investment of lower than forecast traffic) and contingencies in the event of different outcomes could be indicated (e.g. prioritizing investment projects in the event of a constraint on borrowing for capital investment). The effect of different cost assumptions (e.g. higher staff costs) might also be assessed.

4.2 Airport Economics

International regulation of airport economics is governed by the ICAO Airport Economics Manual.[33] In June 1986, the ICAO Air Transport Committee decided that a manual on airport economics should be developed; consequently, the first edition of the *Airport Economics Manual* (Doc 9562) was released in 1991. In April 2001, the Air Transport Committee decided that the *Airport Economics Manual* should be revised as a follow-up to the Conference on the Economics of Airports and Air Navigation Services (ANSConf 2000). In view of developments that have

[33] Doc 9562, Third Edition: 2013.

taken place since then, which were emphasized at the Conference on the Economics of Airports and Air Navigation Services (CEANS 2008), the Air Transport Committee decided, in May 2009, that the *Airport Economics Manual* should be revised and updated.

Economic oversight of airports devolves ultimately upon the State in order to ensure its obligations under the Chicago Convention. States may perform their economic oversight function through legislation or rule-making, establishment of a regulatory mechanism, etc. The mechanism by which economic oversight takes place can be key to its success in achieving its objectives in an efficient and cost-effective manner. It is important for States to consider carefully the roles, rights and responsibilities of the different parties involved—governments, airports and users—and to exercise their economic oversight function, in particular concerning economic performance management and consultation with users, in an internally consistent manner.

Where the operation of one or more airports is performed by a government entity, the economic oversight function should be functionally separated from the operation and provision of airport services within the administration, and roles and powers should be clearly defined for each function. Taking account of local circumstances, a State may wish to establish an independent economic oversight entity with the responsibility of reviewing and sanctioning any action on pricing, investments and service quality. An appropriate balance between independence and accountability is required for the economic oversight entity as well as for the airport (s) that it would regulate. In order to hold the regulating entity accountable, the government would need to give it clear objectives, preferably through statute, coupled with sufficient operating autonomy. Without such a balance, there will be a risk to regulatory commitment and credibility.

A State can also use a third party advisory commission as a less formal tool to help perform its economic oversight function. The advisory commission is often considered appropriate when parties concerned do not form cohesive groups and thus have little or no means by which to organize for class action. The advisory commission might be composed of air carriers, general aviation, the military, representatives of end-users, and other principal parties concerned. A strong advisory commission would be equipped to engage in meaningful dialogue with the airport management on an ongoing basis and to review specific pricing, investments and service levels proposals.

Another important aspect to be considered is the possible need for additional resources to perform an economic oversight function. Some States may lack the capacity to adequately fulfil their economic oversight responsibilities, given competing priorities on safety, security, environment and liberalization of air transport. For those States, the adoption of a region-wide regulatory framework could be a useful option to pull their resources together in performing their economic oversight function.

The objective of the manual, the attest edition of which was released in 2013 by ICAO, is to provide practical guidance to States, airport managing and operating entities, and designated charging and regulatory authorities, to assist in the efficient management of airports and in implementing *ICAO's Policies on Charges for Airports and Air Navigation Services* (Doc 9082). The guidance in the manual takes into account the wide range of different circumstances faced by airport operators. It is based on international policies and principles on airport cost-recovery that States have developed through ICAO, and describes procedures and practices that are in conformity with these policies and principles. The basis for these policies and principles is set out in Article 15 of the Chicago Convention, which has been discussed earlier. Charges to be levied by airports for services rendered are related to ICAO guidelines which are in Doc 9082[34] pertaining to ICAOs policies on airports and Air navigation services charges.

An important consideration of Doc 9082 is that there should be a balance between the respective interests of airports and ANSPs on one hand and of aircraft operators on the other, particularly in view of the importance of an air transport system to States and its influence in fostering economic, cultural and social interchanges between States. This especially applies during periods of economic difficulty; therefore, it is recommended that States encourage increased cooperation between airports/ANSPs and aircraft operators to ensure that economic difficulties facing them are shared in a reasonable manner[35] Section I of Doc 9082 addresses some issues that are common to airports and air navigation services: scope and proliferation of charges; organizational and managerial issues; economic oversight; economic performance; consultation with users; prefunding of projects; and currency issues.

The ICAO Manual states that experience gained worldwide indicates that where airports and air navigation services have been operated by autonomous entities, their overall financial situation and managerial efficiency have generally tended to improve.[36] Therefore, it is recommended that, where this is economically viable and in the best interests of providers and users, States consider establishing autonomous entities to operate their airports and air navigation services (Doc 9082, Section I, paragraph 5). When considering the commercialization or privatization of airports, States should bear in mind that they are ultimately responsible for safety, security and economic oversight of these entities (Doc 9082, Section I, paragraph 6). Whenever an autonomous entity is established to operate an airport (s) and/or provide air navigation services, the State should ensure that all relevant obligations of the State specified in the Convention on International Civil Aviation, its Annexes and in air services agreements are complied with, and that ICAO's policies on charges are observed (Doc 9082, Section I, paragraph 7). Furthermore, States should ensure the use of best practices of good corporate governance for airports. In order to promote transparency, efficiency and cost-effectiveness in the provision of an appropriate quality of facilities and services, ICAO's policy

[34] ICAO's Policies on Charges for Airports and Air Navigation Services Doc 9082/7 Seventh Edition-2004.

[35] Doc 9082, Foreword, paragraphs 4 and 8.

[36] *Id.* Section I, paragraph 4.

suggests that airports should apply management best practices in all areas of their business.

The vexed issue of the need to reach consensus on a just and equitable basis for the imposition of charges levied on airlines by airports for services rendered has been the subject of discussion at many ICAO conferences. Part of the problem has been that airports have, over the years, been privatized and commercialized, necessitating them to be operated in a businesslike manner. However, some core issues have remained unchanged; the first being that, after everything is said and done, there is only one product in the air transport business and that is air transport which is provided by the airlines. The second is that it is an immutable principle that the State is ultimately responsible for meeting the needs of the people of the world for safe, regular, economic and efficient air transport services, working through ICAO, as per the Convention on international Civil Aviation. The blurring of concepts that has arisen in meshing these fundamental principles brings to bear the need to critically appraise one area that exemplifies the confusion—airports charges for services provided to airlines.

At the very core of the rationale for charging airlines for services rendered to them by airports is the Universal Declaration of Human Rights of the United Nations.[37] Article 7 of the Declaration states that all are equal before the law and are entitled without any discrimination to equal protection of the law. The provision goes on to say that all are entitled to equal protection against any discrimination in violation of the Declaration and against any incitement to such discrimination. Article 17 provides that everyone has the right to own property alone as well as in association with others[38] and that no one shall be arbitrarily deprived of his property.[39] Since property includes money[40] and charges levied on airlines by airports comprise money, the Declaration could be legally construed as prohibiting arbitrary charging in excess of amounts that correspond to the services rendered.

It has to be noted that the Declaration is not a treaty and therefore not a binding source of formal law. Therefore it is not a self-executing document and persons relying on the enforcement of these principles would have to rely on the justiciability of treaties that implement the Declaration.[41] However, the Declaration remains a statement of moral principles that is calculated to have a coercive influence on the community of nations. With this in mind, the starting point, as the moral denominator for charging, would be to recognize that to impose charges which are not commensurate with the services rendered would be tantamount to the

---

[37] Adopted and proclaimed by General Assembly Resolution 217 A (III) of 10 December 1948.

[38] Article 17(1).

[39] Article 17(2).

[40] See Qureshi (1994) at 295.

[41] For example, on 4 November 1950 the Council of Europe member States signed the Convention for the Protection of Human Rights and Fundamental Freedoms, also known as the Rome Convention, which implemented the principles of the Universal Declaration of Human Rights and, in Article 25 accorded an individual the right to complain if his rights enshrined in the Declaration were eroded.

levy of a tax that unjustly enriches the airport and the State concerned. In this context, it is worthy of note that ICAO, for the purpose of its policy objectives, makes a distinction between a charge and a tax, in that charges are levies to defray the costs of providing facilities and services for civil aviation while taxes are levies to raise general national and local government revenues that are applied for non-aviation purposes.[42]

Specific regulatory provisions applicable to charges levied by airports have their genesis in ICAO and are contained in Doc 9082 which, in the Foreword has the curious opening: "ICAO's policies on charges for airports and air navigation services which follow contain the recommendations and conclusions of the Council". It must be mentioned that the earlier version of this document used the words "statements" instead of "recommendations and conclusions". The former is seemingly more appropriate since the Convention on International Civil Aviation[43] does not empower the Council to arrive at recommendations and conclusions either in Article 54—which contain the mandatory functions of the Council—and Article 55—which lays down the permissive functions of the Council. These two provisions do not require the Council to issue guidance to States on any matter pertaining to air transport. However, Article 54 b) makes it a mandatory function of the Council to carry out the directions of the Assembly, although there is no clear definition of the word "directions". If this word were to be interpreted to include a request of the Assembly, one could apply resolving clause 5 of Assembly Resolution A36-15[44] which requests the Council to ensure that the guidance and advice (not conclusions and recommendations) contained in Doc 9082 are current and responsive to the requirements of Contracting States. In this context, one can only laud the ICAO Council for taking a leadership role and for taking the initiative to publish its recommendations and conclusions, however inconsistent the words may be between the Assembly Resolution and those used in Doc 9082.

The inconsistency of wording does not stop there. Paragraph 8 i) of Doc 9082 states that the Council recommends that States permit the imposition of charges only for services and functions which are provided for, directly related to or ultimately beneficial for, civil aviation operations. The anomaly lies in the word "functions" which is not defined or elaborated anywhere in the document. Does this give airports the licence to levy charges on airlines for "functions" as defined or determined by them? Or, could one take the wording of Doc 8632[45] and apply the word "facilities" which is used therein as being meant by the word "functions" in this context?

---

[42] ICAO's Policies on Taxation in the Field of Air Transport, Doc 8632, Third Edition: 2000, at 3.

[43] Convention on International Civil Aviation, signed at Chicago on 7 December 1944. See Doc 7300/9 Ninth Edition: 2006. This treaty will hereafter be cited as the Chicago Convention.

[44] Resolution A36-15, Consolidated Statement of Continuing ICAO Policies in the Air Transport Field, *Assembly Resolutions in Force* (as of 28 September 2007) Doc. 9902, III-1 at III-I3.

[45] *Supra* note 42.

Recent trends in regulatory control of the levy of airports charges dictate that a close look should be taken with view to evaluating whether there exists an environment for the imposition on airlines of airports charges on a just and equitable basis. This article will discuss this issue with emphasis on currently applicable regulatory provisions. Although the ensuing discussions will focus only on airports charges, it must be noted that the applicable ICAO regulatory policy also applies *ex aequo* to air navigation services.

4.2.1 Current Regulatory Provisions

The current policies of ICAO on charges for airports and air navigation services stemmed from the recommendations of the Conference on the Economics of Airports and Air Navigation Services (ANSConf 2000) which were endorsed by the Council of ICAO.[46] ANSConf 2000, which was held in Montreal on 19–28 June 2000, came to the conclusion that the profile of basic cost recovery policy may need to be raised.[47] It was recommended by the Conference that this measure could be adopted within the parameters of existing policy calling for revenues from charges levied on international civil aviation and it would only be applied towards defraying the costs of facilities and services provided for international civil aviation. It was also recommended that revenues from other sources than charges on air traffic shall be taken into account before the cost basis for charges on air traffic is determined. ICAO advised the Conference that airports and air navigation services may produce sufficient revenues to exceed all operating costs and so provide for a reasonable return on assets to contribute towards necessary capital improvements. Of course, the governing principle would be that consultation with users shall take place before significant changes in charging systems or levels of charges are introduced.[48]

The baseline of ICAO's policies on charges lies in Article 15 of the Chicago Convention, the basic philosophy of which is that every airport in a Contracting State which is open to public use by its national aircraft shall likewise be open under uniform conditions to the aircraft of all the other Contracting States. It also requires

---

[46] See Report of the conference on the economics of airports and air navigation services: air transport infrastructure for the twenty-first century. Montreal, 19–28 June 2000. Doc 9764, ANSConf 2000. ICAO: Montreal, 2000. For a discussion on ANSConf 2000 see Abeyratne (2001), pp. 217–230.

[47] *ANSConf-WP/4* at para. 5.1.

[48] *Id.* para. 5.3. ICAO's recommendations to ANSConf 2000 were both timely and practical, given the evolving fabric of economic forces which now govern airports and air navigation services. The recommendations also stimulate some reflection on the complexities of financing principles now applicable to the services provided by airports and air navigation services providers. In substance, the issue of costing and pricing of services would be dependent upon underlying practices and economic factors as the bunching of aviation and non-aviation revenues and their effect on the overall pricing policy relating to airports and air navigation services and a significant paradigm shift from Article 15 of the Chicago Convention.

that uniform conditions shall apply to the use, by aircraft of every Contracting State, of all air navigation facilities, including radio and meteorological services,[49] which may be provided for public use for the safety and expedition of air navigation.[50] Article 15 subsumes three fundamental postulates:

a) uniform conditions should apply in the use of facilities provided by airports and air navigation services;
b) aircraft operators should be charged on a non-discriminatory basis; and
c) no charges should be levied for the mere transit over, entry into or exit from the territory of a Contracting State.

Current ICAO policy also recognizes that the financial situation of airports and air navigation services are in a constant state of evolution and that the financial situation of the primary users, the scheduled airlines, generally fluctuates with the performance of national, regional and global economies.[51] Accordingly, the ICAO Council recommends that States permit the imposition of charges only for services and functions which are provided for, directly related to, or ultimately beneficial for, civil aviation operations. States are therefore encouraged to refrain from imposing charges which discriminate against international civil aviation in relation to other modes of transport.[52]

ICAO's policies are at best only authoritative in practice and, from a legal perspective, are rendered destitute of effect by the acknowledged lack of enforcement power afflicting them. In this context it is curious that, six decades after the establishment of ICAO some still refer to its powers and functions.[53] There are some others who allude to ICAO's mandate. The fact is that ICAO has only aims and objectives, recognized by the Chicago Convention which established the Organization.[54] Broadly, those aims and objectives are to develop the principles and techniques of international air navigation and to foster the planning and

[49] Article 28 of the Chicago Convention calls on each Contracting State, so far as it may find practicable, to provide airport and air navigation facilities, in accordance with the standards and practices recommended or established in pursuance of the Convention.

[50] Article 15 also provides that any charges that may be imposed or permitted to be imposed by a Contracting State for the use of such airports and air navigation facilities by the aircraft of any other Contracting State shall not be higher: as to aircraft not engaged in scheduled international air services, than those that would be paid by its national aircraft of the same class engaged in similar operations; and as to aircraft engaged in scheduled international air services, than those that would be paid by its national aircraft engaged in similar international air services.

[51] *ICAO's Policies on Charges for Airports and Air Navigation Services*, *supra* note 34, paragraph 7.

[52] *Id.* Paragraph 8. Paragraph 9 that follows states that the Council is concerned over the proliferation of charges on air traffic and notes that the imposition of charges in one jurisdiction can lead to the introduction of charges in another jurisdiction.

[53] MacKenzie (2008), Preface at 1.

[54] *Id.* Article 43. This article provides that an organization to be named the International Civil Aviation Organization is formed by the Convention. It is made of an Assembly, a Council, and such other bodies as may be necessary.

development of international air transport. In effect, this bifurcation implicitly reflects the agreement of the international community of States which signed the Chicago Convention that ICAO could adopt Standards in the technical fields of air navigation and could only offer guidelines in the economic field.

In its basic documentation, the ICAO Council notes that with the rapidly growing autonomy in the provision of airports and air navigation services, many States may wish to establish an independent mechanism for the economic regulation of airports and air navigation services[55] To this end the Council recommends *inter alia* that States should ensure there is no overcharging or other anti-competitive practice or abuse of dominant position.[56] The Council further states that for the successful collection of charges for airports and air navigation services entities, it is essential that a collection policy be established by an airport or air navigation services entity, or where applicable by a State.[57] In this regard the cost basis for airport charges is an important issue and the Council considers that, as a general principle it is desirable, where an airport is provided for international use, that the users shall ultimately bear their full and final share of the cost of providing the airport. It is therefore considered important that airports maintain accounts which provide information adequate for the needs of both airports and users and that the facilities and services related to airport charges be identified as precisely as possible.[58] It is interesting, once again to note that the term "facilities" has been used and that there is no mention of the word "functions". The cost to be shared is the full cost of providing the airport and its essential ancillary services, including appropriate amounts for cost of capital and depreciation of assets, as well as the cost of maintenance, operation, management and administration. However, there is a caveat that the costs to be shared must allow for all aeronautical revenues plus contributions from non-aeronautical revenues accruing from the operation of the airport to its operators.[59] The Council also states that the proportion of costs allocable to various categories of users, including State aircraft, should be determined on an equitable basis, so that no users shall be burdened with costs not properly allocable to them according to sound economic principles.

The aforesaid provisions have the underlying requirement of economic oversight if the regulators were to ensure that charges are being levied in a just and equitable manner.

---

[55] Doc 9082, *supra* note 34. at paragraph 15 ii).

[56] *Id.* paragraph 15 ii).

[57] *Id.* paragraph 18.

[58] Doc 9082, *supra* note 34 paragraph 21.

[59] *Id.* paragraph 22 i).

4.2.2 *Current Trends in Airports Charges*

A Conference of ICAO on the Economics of Airports and Air Navigation Services (CEANS), which was held in Montreal from 15 to 20 September 2008,[60] agreed to submit to the Council of ICAO crucial recommendations for international civil aviation which will take cooperation between the air transport, airport and air navigation services industries to a higher level and increase the efficiency and cost-effectiveness in the provision and operation of airports and air navigation services around the world. These recommendations are calculated to serve the aviation industry expeditiously in coping with the current challenges that air transport faces.

a) **Cost basis for charges**: On the basis that the cost basis of an airport for charging purposes has usually been established by taking into account the costs of operation and maintenance, cost of capital and depreciation of assets (based on historical value in most cases), and a "reasonable" return on assets, CEANS approached the issue by attempting to build a consensus on possible ways to assess what would constitute a "reasonable" rate of return, and explore the possibility of consolidating several airport cost bases into one cost base for charging purposes.
b) **Cost allocation and charging systems**: It was recognized that ICAO's current policies and guidance material on airport charges have provisions dealing with how the costs of the various airport facilities and services should be allocated to different categories of users. However, the Conference took note of the fact that some new trends have emerged such as the allocation of costs on a per passenger basis, which includes all or most cost bases of the aeronautical activities. The Conference's discussions revolved around the issue as to whether such new approaches are consistent with ICAO's policies, and consideration was given to appropriate amendments to the policies and guidance material on cost allocation.
c) **Non-discrimination aspects**: On the subject of non-discrimination, CEANS recognized that, in recent years, airport operators have developed certain differential charges to attract and retain new airline services, for example, discounts on passenger service charges and incentive schemes for particular airlines, including low-cost carriers. It was also noted that some of these differential charges might be non-transparent, discriminatory and anti-competitive, especially when they constitute a form of State aid. The Conference addressed the issue as to how to deal with the measures taken by airport operators that have the potential to create unfair treatment, as well as the issue of access to airport facilities.
d) **Financing and cost recovery of security measures**: According to ICAO's policies on security charges, the costs of security functions performed by States

[60] CEANS was attended by 520 delegates from 104 States and 19 international organizations.

such as general policing, intelligence gathering and national security should not be passed on to the airport users. However, it was noted that practices differ between regions and States, which have financial implications on users. The Conference reviewed the current policies and discussed how to achieve a more harmonized implementation of ICAO's policies regarding airport security charges.

4.2.3 Recommendations of CEANS

CEANS recommended that ICAO should amend Doc 9082 with a view to allowing more flexibility in setting airport charges. This calls for airports to maintain cost data in adequate detail which ensures transparency and oversight and the avoidance of discrimination in setting charges.

On rate of returns for airports and air navigation services it was recommended that within their economic oversight responsibilities, States should, where necessary and in the light of national circumstances, clearly define the methodology for determining what is a reasonable rate of return on assets for their service providers. ICAO was called upon to develop additional guidance material regarding possible methodologies to assess the risk element involved in cost recovery and the value of assets in the context of the determination of a reasonable rate of return.

On differential charges CEANS recommended that within their economic oversight responsibilities States should, where necessary, assess the positive and negative effects associated with specific forms of differential charges applied by airports on a case-by-case basis according to national circumstances. Furthermore, States were called upon to ensure that differential charges are offered on a non-discriminatory basis; that they are transparent in terms of their creation, purpose and the criteria on which they are offered; that, without prejudice to modulated charging schemes, costs associated with differential charges are not allocated, either directly or indirectly, to those other users not benefiting from them; and that, if the purpose is to attract and/or retain new air services, they are offered only on a temporary basis. ICAO was called upon to amend Doc 9082 to reflect the principles of transparency and time limitation for start-up aids in the application of differential charges.

It was the view of CEANS that the recommendations will make ICAO's policies on charges, which regulate the relationship between airports and air navigation services providers (ANSPs) on the one hand, and airlines and other airport and airspace users on the other, more authoritative in practice. The enhanced cooperation suggested by these recommendations would strengthen policies on States' economic oversight responsibility, requirements on implementation of performance management systems by all airports and ANSPs, and the establishment of a clearly defined, regular consultation process by all airports and ANSPs. At the same time, they recommend that States enshrine the main principles of non-discrimination, cost-relatedness, transparency and consultation with users in their national legislation, regulations or policies as well as all air services agreements between States.[61]

One of the fundamental premises addressed by CEANS is that the protection of users against the potential abuse of dominant position by airports and air navigation services providers is the primary responsibility of the State and could be discharged by the exercise of economic oversight. It was suggested during the discussions that such oversight could be effectively carried out by diligent monitoring by a State of the commercial and operational practices of these service providers.

There was discussion during CEANS where some delegations suggested that, in order to "give teeth" to ICAO policy, there be a recommendation in Doc 9082 to the effect that amendment to Doc 9082 should be incorporated by States in their national legislation. It is submitted that such a measure would be tantamount to treading uncharted and dangerous ground. While it is one thing to assert that the only way that ICAO policies could be implemented is for States to opt for incorporating such principles in their legislation, it is something quite different to recommend that States go ahead and do so.

As a necessary compromise and in order to reach a balance, the Conference broadly recognized the need for economic oversight in the increasingly commercialized and privatized environment for airports and air navigation services. It considered a number of suggestions that were made by the delegates for improving the proposed new text for Doc 9082. The following conclusions were reached by the Conference:

a) States should bear in mind that economic oversight is the responsibility of States with the objectives, *inter alia*, to prevent the risk that a service provider could abuse its dominant position, to ensure non-discrimination and transparency in the application of charges, to encourage consultation with users, to ensure the development of appropriate performance management systems, and to ascertain that capacity meets current and future demand, in balance with the efforts of the autonomous/private entities to obtain the optimal effects of commercialization or privatization;
b) States should select the appropriate form of economic oversight according to their specific circumstances, while keeping regulatory interventions at a minimum and as required. When deciding an appropriate form of economic oversight, the degree of competition, the costs and benefits related to alternative oversight forms, as well as the legal, institutional and governance frameworks should be taken into consideration;
c) States should consider adoption of a regional approach to economic oversight where individual States lack the capacity to adequately perform economic oversight functions; and

[61] Other essential features of the recommendations of the Conference are: more flexibility for commercialized airports and ANSPs in setting charges; support for separation of regulation from service provision; the application of good governance through best practices; and the efficient and cost-effective implementation of the global Air Traffic Management (ATM) concept.

d) ICAO should amend Doc 9082 to clarify the purpose and scope of economic oversight for airports and air navigation services with reference to its different forms and the selection of the most appropriate form of oversight.[62]

4.2.4 The Legal Status of ICAO Policy

Although there was much discussion at CEANS on "giving teeth" to ICAO policy in order to ensure economic oversight by States of their airports and air navigation services providers, the Conference failed to arrive at a consensus on including text in the recommendations to the effect that States should incorporate the principles enunciated in ICAO document 9082 in their legislation or rules. The end result was a somewhat watered down recommendation that States should select the appropriate form of economic oversight according to their specific circumstances, while keeping regulatory interventions at a minimum and as required. Most delegations were, quite rightly, reluctant to agree to a recommendation that would impose upon States an obligation to incorporate policy guidelines into national legislation. Furthermore, the Conference correctly noted that States differed considerably in their economic circumstances and demand for services rendered by airports and air navigation services in their territories and therefore should be left to decide the best course of economic oversight to be taken in their territories.

ICAO's economic policies emanate from the States. However, these policies are no more than consensual principles that offer policy guidance and are at best left to the discretion of the States to follow. To require or recommend that States incorporate such policy in their national legislation or regulations is a reversal of the empowerment of ICAO by States upon which ICAO is founded, whereby ICAO is enabled by States to pursue its aims and objectives under Article 44 of the Chicago Convention.[63]

No international body or institution can legitimately expect a sovereign State to incorporate, as national legislation, policies that the former adopts. In this case, such a policy directive would come from the ICAO Council, the mandatory functions of which are stipulated in Article 54 of the Chicago Convention.[64] Nowhere in either the mandatory or permissive functions (contained in Article

[62] Draft Report on Agenda Item 1.1., Economic Oversight, CEANS-WP/73, 16/9/08, Draft Report on Agenda Item 1.1.

[63] The overarching aims and objectives of ICAO, as contained in Article 44 of the Convention is to develop the principles and techniques of international air navigation and to foster the planning and development of international air transport so as to meet the needs of the peoples for safe, regular, efficient and economical air transport.

[64] The closest the Council comes in this respect is to adopt morally binding Standards and Recommended Practices, where, as per Article 54 l) of the Chicago Convention the Council may adopt international standards and recommended practices and for convenience, designate them as Annexes to the Convention and notify all Contracting States of the action taken.

55) is the Council given authority to act as legislator or regulator.[65] Even if such a function were to be elevated to the level of the ICAO Assembly, a resolution of the Assembly cannot require or even recommend that its principles be incorporated into national law or regulation. *Brownlie* has expressed the view that decisions by international conferences and organizations can in principle only bind those States accepting them.[66] Shaw, referring to the binding force of United Nations General; Assembly Resolutions states:

> ...one must be alive to the dangers in ascribing legal value to everything that emanates from the Assembly. Resolutions are often the results of political compromises and arrangements and, comprehended in that sense, never intended to constitute binding norms. Great care must be taken in moving from a plethora of practice to the identification of legal norms.[67]

With regard to the practice of other international organizations, a little more caution might be required, as a resolution might create a custom. Non binding instruments form a special category that is sometimes referred to as "soft law" which is definitely not law in the sense of enforceability.[68]

The above discussion brings to bear some anomalies that exist in the field of airports charges. The first is that, according to ICAO policy, four elements are critical for prudent charges policy: non discrimination (as enshrined in Article 15 of the Chicago Convention); transparency; cost relatedness; and consultation. The first two elements are self explanatory. However, cost relatedness and consultation are open to interpretation. One could argue that cost related charges need not necessarily be restricted to actual costs but could be geared to earn profits for the airports as long as such costs are calculated in relation to the cost of services provided. With regard to consultation, there have been instances where the service provider has met with users and other stakeholders and merely informed them that certain charges were to be increased.

The second anomaly is that, the statement in Doc 9082—that autonomy and privatization of airports are preferred modes of operating airports[69]—has inadvertently resulted in the obfuscation of the fundamental principle that the ultimate responsibility for the setting and levying of charges rests with the State concerned. Although by and large States have been observed to follow ICAO policy in this area, there are many airports today which set charges and impose them, with a cursory and *pro forma* notice to the State concerned which invariably approves it. The Chicago Conference of 1944, which resulted in the adoption of the Chicago Convention, in its consideration of draft Article 15 of the Convention at that time,

---

[65] For a discussion on the role of the Council in this context see Abeyratne (1992), pp. 387–394. Also by the same author, see The Settlement of Commercial Aviation Disputes Under the General Agreement on Trade in Services and the ICAO Council (1997), pp. 395–412.

[66] Brownlie (1990), p. 691.

[67] Shaw (2003), p. 110.

[68] *Id.* 111. See also Tammes (1958) at 265.

[69] Doc 9082 note 8 in Chap. 1 at paragraph 10.

has explicitly recorded that "[E]ach contracting State shall establish scales of charges for the use of such airports and air navigation facilities which shall be uniformly applicable to the aircraft of all other States..."[70] Article 15 of the Chicago Convention follows this approach when it states: "Any charges that may be imposed or permitted to be imposed by a contracting State..."clearly implying that it is the State which is responsible for the imposition of charges.

The third anomaly is that Doc 9082 which sets policy at a high level, is open to interpretation as some of its key provisions, as pointed out in the Introduction to this article, may open the possibility for interpretation and subjective treatment of critical principles concerned with ICAO's charging policy. This notwithstanding, there is no room for doubt that Doc 9082 is a generally clear policy statement which has served ICAO contracting States well and provided guidance over the years.

Finally, this discussion brings one to the conclusion that, ultimately, the responsibility clearly lies with the States, which not only have to oversee airport charges but to provide the necessary economic oversight to ensure that charges are levied justly, equitably and in a prudent manner. One effective way of ensuring this is for States to include the four elements of transparency; non-discrimination; cost relatedness and consultation in their bilateral air services agreements.

References

Abeyratne RIR (1992) Law making and decision making powers of the ICAO council – a critical analysis. Zeitschrift Luft Weltraumrecht 41(4):387–394

Abeyratne RIR (1994a) The liberalization of air transport services within GATT – some legal issues. Trading Law Trading Law Rep 13(1)

Abeyratne RIR (1994b) The legal and economic effects of NAFTA on Canada, Mexico and the United States. World Compet 18(2):115–136

Abeyratne RIR (2001) Revenue and investment management of privatized airports and air navigation services: a regulatory perspective. J Air Transport Manag 7:217–230

Brownlie I (1990) Principles of public international law, 4th edn. Clarendon Press, Oxford

Dolzer R, Schreuer C (2008) Principles of international investment law. Oxford University Press, New York

Elkins Z, Guzman A, Simmonds B (2006) Competing for capital: the diffusion of bilateral investment treaties 1960–2000. Berkeley Programme in Law and Economics, Annual Papers

ICAO Council (1997) A comparative analysis. International trade law and the GATT/WTO dispute settlement system. Kluwer Law International, London, pp 395–412

MacKenzie D (2008) ICAO, a history of ICAO. University of Toronto Press, Toronto

Moore JB (1916) A digest of international law, 4:5

Moran TH (April 2011) Enhancing the contribution of FDI to development: a new agenda for the Corporate Social Responsibility Community, International Labour and Civil Society, Aid Donors and Multilateral Financial Institutions. Transnational Corporations 20(1)

Neumayer E, Spess L (2005) Do bilateral investment treaties increase foreign direct investment to developing countries? World Dev 33:1567

[70] *Proceedings of the International Civil Aviation Conference*, Chicago: Illinois November 1-December 7, 1944, Vol. 1, at 663.

Qureshi AH (ed) (1994) The public international law of taxation, text, cases and materials. Graham & Trotman Ltd
Root E (1910) The basis of protecting citizens residing abroad. AJIL 4:517
Shaw MN (2003) International law, 5th edn. Cambridge University Press, Cambridge, p 110
Spence M (2011) The next convergence. Farrar, Straus and Giroux, New York
Tammes AJP (1958) Decisions of international organs as a source of international law. HR 94

Chapter 5
The Airport Business

The airline and airport business are interlinked and inter-connected and, since air transport is a growth industry, so is the airport industry. According to the global market forecast of Airbus Industrie forecasts that from 2009 to 2028, some 25,000 new passenger and freighter aircraft valued at US$3.1 trillion will be delivered.[1] This rapidly evolving demand is driven by emerging economies, evolving airline networks, expansion of low cost carriers and the increasing number of mega-cities as well as traffic growth and the replacement of older less efficient aircraft with more eco-efficient airliners. These are factors driving demand for new aircraft.

The forecast also attributes the demand for larger aircraft to the compelling need to ease aircraft congestion and to accommodate growth on existing routes and to achieve more with less. Needless to say, this exponential growth in air traffic[2] will place a burden on airport capacity and consequent demands upon the airport industry.

Airports are a complex, big business. The first element in the airport business equation is the customer and it is therefore a good starting point to determine who the customers of the airport are. It is incontrovertible that airline passengers generate the bulk of the concession revenue and that the airlines who bring them would normally generate most of the rental or lease income. However other market groups are by no means inconsequential.

---

[1] http://www.airbus.com/en/gmf2009/appli.htm?onglet=&page=. The forecast anticipates that in the next 20 years, passenger traffic RPK's will remain resilient to the cyclical effects of the sector and increase by 4.7 % per year or double in the next 15 years. This will require a demand for almost 24,100 new passenger aircraft valued at US$2.9 trillion. With the replacement of some 10,000 older passenger aircraft, the world's passenger aircraft fleet of 100 seats or more will double from some 14,000 in 2009.

[2] *Id.* The forecast states that the greatest demand for passenger aircraft will be from airlines in Asia-Pacific and emerging markets. The region that includes the People's Republic of China and India accounts for 31 % of the total, followed by Europe (25 %) and North America (23 %). In terms of domestic passenger markets, India (10 %) and China (7.9 %) will have the fastest growth over the next 20 years. The largest by volume of traffic, will remain domestic US.

R. Abeyratne, *Law and Regulation of Aerodromes*, DOI 10.1007/978-3-319-04780-5_5,

Airport employees who work for airlines, the airport authority, the concessionaires and other enterprises within the airport premises form a substantial customer category although their *modus vivendi* in purchasing goods and services, particularly from the concessionaire stores could be different from those of the passenger. While the former would look for convenience in buying goods in house during their work breaks without having to travel to the local stores and supermarkets in their neighbourhoods, the latter would buy gifts to take home. A good example of an airport which caters to the airport employee is Frankfurt Airport which has released the statistic that employees working at the airport spend approximately 15 % of their net household income at the airport's shops and service facilities.

Airline crews are another category of customer, particularly at larger airports where crew movement is prolific. Their needs are mostly work related and they may look primarily for clothes stores, dry cleaning, shoe repairs, hair-dressing salons and tailors in addition to some goods that are in demand for airport employees. Another category of customer is the person who goes to meet and greet an arriving passenger or one who goes to drop off a passenger. The meeter who comes in early and finds himself with time on his hands until the arrival of the flight in which the passenger whom he meets is travelling, could well stroll around and purchase goods that he needs or is attracted by. The same goes for the person who accompanies a departing passenger and hangs about until the passenger is admitted to security clearance. A prime attraction in this regard is the restaurant as well as other catering outlets.

Airport shops would usually have much longer opening hours than other shops offering goods and services to local residential areas, which could in turn attract visitors to the airport who would come in for the convenience of shopping after hours. Although not as significant as the ones already mentioned, this category of customer could include local residents who are attracted to the airport by the convenience of late shopping hours at airport shops, unlike those of their neighbouring supermarkets and shops. Today's airport, in its typical form, is primarily a commercial entity and operates as a business oriented entity. Most airports provide retail shops and parking facilities not only for airline passengers and their visitors but also to residents of the area. They are, in this sense, as much profit centres as are such retail outlets as K-Mart and Walmart. In addition, there are also airport free zones which are bonded areas, adjacent to the airport premises which, as the name suggests, are duty free areas promoting industry and other commercial activity.

The airport, like any other autonomous business enterprise, has to exploit inherent resources optionally; compete with other businesses of the area on quality of services offered; and reinvest funds in developing its business interests. The Council of ICAO recognizes the continuing importance to airports of income derived from such sources as concessions, rental of premises and "free zones". The Council recommends that, with the exception of concessions that are directly associated with the operation of air transport services, such as fuel, in-flight catering and ground handling, the full development of revenues of this kind be encouraged having regard to the need for moderation in prices to the public, the requirements of passengers and the need for terminal efficiency.[3] The fact that the general public are recognized as customers of airports by ICAO policy leaves room to attribute to the wisdom of the policy statement the acknowledgment that airports do not only cater to airline passengers and their visitors, but to shoppers who may wish to pick up a bargain at the airport.

The ICAO Council Statements (Doc 9802/5) leave it wide open for airports to optimize their revenue to exceed all direct and indirect operating costs, including general administration etc., and so provide for a reasonable return on assets (before tax and cost of capital) to contribute toward necessary capital improvements.[4] This policy statement encourages commercial autonomy of airports and the practice of deviating from being instrumentalities of the State. *A fortiori*, it urges airports to optimize revenues in order to boost capital investment toward improvement, which would not necessarily mean such revenues should subsidize airport and air navigation service charges. The *Airport Economics Manual*, which was first produced and issued by ICAO in 1991 stated:

> It should be noted that revenues from non-aeronautical activities are in fact the principal means by which a growing number of airports are able to recover their total costs because their profits from these activities more than cover the losses most of them incur on their air side operations[5] .. . . and in so far as ICAO cost recovery policies are concerned, not subject to the same limitations that it is recommended apply to charges on air traffic.[6]

It is arguable in the context of the above mentioned policy that, if two different criteria are applied, one strictly on the basis of recovery of costs of services provided which would essentially be a non-profit operation, as in the case of charges levied for the provision of airport and air navigation services, and another strictly on a profit making business basis, whether the latter, applicable to non-aeronautical revenues, is mutually exclusive from the former. If this argument were to prevail, one could maintain that charges for airport and air navigation services need not as of necessity be minimized as a result of capital injection towards facilities providing such services if such capital were to be derived from the non-aeronautical activities of the airport. Of course, this does not mean that an airport which wishes to inject some capital derived from one source to another should be precluded from doing so in the best interests of aviation.

Airports, like any other business enterprises, are compelled to compete with each other to attract air traffic and business flowing therefrom and from the general public. To this end, many airports are now privatized and operate as autonomous

---

[3] *ICAO's Policies on Charges for Airports and Air Navigation Services,* Doc 9082/6, note 34 in Chap. 4, at paragraph 24.

[4] Doc 9082/6 Id. paragraph 14 vii).

[5] *Airport Economics Manual*, supra, Chapter 6, para 6.3 at p. 50.

[6] *Id.* paragraph 4.60 at p. 40. It should also be noted that certain concession type facilities are established at an airport to provide services considered necessary for passengers, visitors and/or persons working at the airport. Such facilities may include cafeterias, post offices and tourist information counters. See *Airport Economics Manual*, note 44 in Chap. 4 at paragraph 6.11.

entities. Privatization brings not only fiscal benefits, but also legal liability (as the discussion below will show) which is a possible cost factor that should be taken into account. More importantly, privatization connotes a businesslike approach that requires a certain involvement with market forces and competition that would necessitate reinvestment in the airport business for the commercial sustainability of the airport.

The attractiveness of airports to the average shopper is largely due to the range of shops and services available in the airport premises. In this regard, local residents and airport employees share common interests and many airports have expanded the range of their shops to meet the demand posed by these categories. It has been known that those items which do not fall into the category of daily purchases, such as furniture, electrical goods, hardware are popular consumer items at some airports.

The local business community, which would find it more cost effective and productive from a sales perspective to conduct their business at the airport, could be another important customer of the airport. They could require office space, conference and meeting facilities which can enable them to take advantage of the airport's strategic location, inter-connectivity and diversity of nationalities which an airport attracts. Businesses may also need large storage and warehouse space for freight and therefore may seek space close to the passenger terminal. There needs may extend to land, warehouses, hangars or office buildings from which the airport can generate substantial rental income.

Rigas Doganis, whose analysis of the two airport models represented by Frankfurt and Athens airports respectively states:

> Frankfurt airport has had both the space and the commercial acumen to try to meet the needs of all these target groups in and around its main terminal. An analysis of concession revenues earned by the airport authority has shown that 76 per cent comes from passengers, 13 per cent from airport employees and the remaining 11 per cent from visitors of various kinds including meeters and greeters and local residents. This excludes rents from office space, land, etc. As a result of its strategy, Frankfurt had developed the extensive and very wide-ranging shopping, leisure, business and service facilities which were summarized earlier. Athens in contrast targets only two groups at its two terminals, the airlines and the passengers, and provides only the very minimum of facilities for both.
>
> Airports world-wide fall somewhere in the range represented by the two extremes of Athens and Frankfurt. Whether they have followed the traditional model or the commercial model will depend partly on the strategic options adopted by the management and in particular on which of the above customer groups they have decided to target. But the model adopted will also be dependent on the volume and composition of the traffic handled by each airport, by the terminal space and land available and the degree to which the management has been given the freedom to adopt commercially oriented policies.[7]

In view of the current trends in the airport business model, airports have to make strategic decisions to be financially self sufficient and be run like businesses. There should therefore be a commercial airport model which maximizes revenue, whether such is generated through aeronautical revenues (such as airport charges from

[7] Doganis (1992) at 117.

airlines) or non-aeronautical revenues (such as from concessionaires). They should also have a reasoned view on who their target clients are and who their most attractive customers are.

Airports are subject to both external and internal factors with regard to revenue generation and their cost–benefit equation. The most significant external factors are current and projected traffic levels, global and local economic fluctuations and currency exchange rates, taxes and charges imposed on airports by governments and authorities as well as charges that can be exercised by airports on their users. A large number of factors will influence an airport's ability to maximize its commercial revenues. There are first of all certain external factors, which are crucially important in affecting revenue generation or strategic options but which are largely outside the control of individual airport managements. These include the airport's traffic levels and its proportion of international traffic, exchange rates and the level of taxes or duties imposed on alcohol or tobacco. Then there are a variety of factors which can be influenced directly by management. These are the area and the location of terminal space allocated to commercial activities, the nature of the contracts negotiated with the concessionaires and the quality of the concessionaires themselves.

Airports have a range of goods, services and facilities to offer. Their income comes from rents and concession fees. Rental income is earned primarily from the renting or leasing of space and the customers are direct users of what airports have to offer, such as users airlines, freight forwarders and handling agents. The indirect users are hotels, catering firms, manufacturing companies and other similar business enterprises. Concession fees are earned from, payments made to the airport by the providers of various services for the right to offer their services in the airport premises. These fees are generally based on the volume of business generated by the concessionaires and not usually on the dimensions of space occupied, although it is not uncommon for some concession agreements to include a straightforward ground-rent criterion.

Duty- and tax-free shops are arguably the most attractive to airports in terms of non-aeronautical revenue. These shops are ready to pay competitive rents since consumers find them more attractive than city centre shops as the prices in the former are substantially low. An added attraction for concessionaires to pay high rents is that since the profit margins earned by the concessionaires are considerably high, airports can negotiate a contract that is advantageous in obtaining for the airport a large share of the profits earned by such shops.

Airports also recognize the need to provide duty and tax free shopping in the landside areas of the passenger terminal since duty-free shopping is only accessible to passengers who have entered the departure or transit lounges. A wide range of duty- and tax-free shopping needs to be provided in the public landside areas of airport terminals. These shops could sell goods such as travel goods, tobacco, books sweets, drugs and toiletries, food, flower, shops, fashion goods souvenirs, glassware, clothing, videos and records. As I any place where humanity gathers, the airport also needs food and drink outlets. The provision of these services would depend on market demand as determined by the type of passenger who frequents the area in question. Another revenue generating source is through bill board advertising and other types of promotional sources business enterprises might wish to have in the premises of an airport.

Another important element in the airport business caters to the financial transactions a passenger or visitor to the airport might need and his transport needs when he leaves the airport on arrival. These services are essentially related to those provided by banks, post offices, travel agents, car hire and hotel reservations. While car rentals produce most of the revenue, banks are the most popular. Car parks are clearly another source of revenue generation for airports, particularly where there are no regular public transport services. Finally, leisure facilities, which is a growing need for a generation acutely aware of the travails of air travel and the need to stay in shape, has proved popular. This category begins with health spas and health clubs but extends to swimming pools and entertainment facilities such as cinemas, discotheques, night clubs and billiard rooms.

It is an incontrovertible fact that there are many airports around the world that are run as commercially oriented profitable enterprises. Most of these airports initially started off as public utilities or instrumentalities of States with public service obligations. They have now transcended from their public role to an essentially private role of providing quality service and value for money. As discussed earlier, this is mostly because modern day airports not only serve airline passengers who use the airport for egress or ingress but also those who visit the airport to see these passengers off or meet them as well as members of the local community. Although there are still some States which regard their airports as public utilities, this approach is fast being relegated to the background and is being replaced by the profit making business model based on service.

Government or public ownership may take the form of direct control and management, for example through a civil aviation administration, or through another ministerial department, or through regional or municipal levels of governments. Government control can also be exerted through bodies benefiting from a certain degree of autonomy, such as a government body with financial and operational autonomy, an autonomous corporation established under the provisions of a special statute (a statutory body), or a company established under company law. Under this type of management, airports remain under the overall ownership and control of the government and the organizations operating them are expected to act with public interest in mind rather than primarily governed by profit considerations, although this should not preclude the setting of clear objectives and adoption of best commercial practices. This option may provide flexibility to States in ensuring that the development of airports will suit their national political, social and economic requirements. It has to be noted that in some cases the government may keep the ownership of airports (land and/or facilities), while the operation (i.e. the control) is vested to other interests.

On the other hand, an autonomous airport entity is essentially an independent body established for the purpose of operating and managing one or more airports, one objective of which is to permit local and user needs to be better met. In some instances, the scope of such autonomous airport entities has extended to the operation and management of air navigation services as well, although autonomous entities have also been established exclusively to operate and manage air navigation services, particularly with regard to the en-route (and approach) phase(s) of flights.

The number of autonomous airport entities is growing in all regions. They are particularly common in Europe and the United States. For example, in a majority of the States in Europe, the major international airports are operated by autonomous airport entities. While the establishment of an autonomous airport entity would not necessarily result in an unprofitable airport becoming profitable, experience gained worldwide from these developments indicates that where airports have been operated by autonomous entities their overall financial situation has generally tended to improve. Consequently, it is recommended that, where this is in the best interest of providers and users, States consider establishing autonomous entities to operate their airports.

Since the main purpose of establishing autonomous airport entities has been to improve efficiency and financial results, the tendency in some States has been to limit the area of their responsibility to those major international airports with sufficient traffic volumes to warrant expectations of attaining financial self-sufficiency. The establishment of autonomous airport entities can frequently be beneficial even where these conditions do not exist and subsidies continue to be required. As a consequence, new entities created in some States encompass both profitable and unprofitable airports.

5.1 The Airport Charter and Management Structure of Airports

Before an airport entity becomes operational, its charter, or a document of a similar character, needs to be drawn up. The charter should clearly describe the scope of the services and areas the airport entity is to be responsible for providing and operating. Because of different national practices, these tend to differ between airport entities. The areas or services concerned normally include most or all of the following: aircraft movement areas, passenger terminal facilities, cargo facilities, aircraft parking areas, hangar facilities, air traffic control including communications, and sometimes, meteorological services.

Where airport facilities already exist, the charter should make clear whether or not they are to become the property of the entities and, if so, what value is to be placed on these assets and whether or not a corresponding debt is to be charged to the entity? Also, on the financial side, the charter needs to make clear that the entity will be empowered to retain the revenues it generates for the purpose of defraying airport expenses and building up possible capital reserves. Where it is foreseen to be unlikely that the entity will be profitable in the short-term future, the charter may need to specify how shortfalls in revenues are to be covered. These objectives could be achieved by the drawing up of an annual financial plan to be agreed by the government, which would cover a specified period—5 years, for example.

The charter should state how the airport is to be governed—for example, whether a board of directors should be established (a normal practice) or whether the general manager or chief executive alone would be the most senior in the governing structure of the entity. It should also specify to whom the board of directors or management would ultimately report: for example, whether it is to a minister (at the state or provincial level), a director of civil aviation or a mayor (if a city established the entity). The charter may be subject to review as required.

With regard to personnel, it should be noted that an autonomous airport entity need not be required to use the civil service charter and the salary structure applied by the government for civil servants, but could offer more advantageous terms to personnel and thereby increase motivation and productivity. This may be relevant in circumstances where qualified personnel might otherwise be attracted to work for private industry because of higher salaries offered.

Airport entities may be looked upon as corporation-type entities and would be organized along similar lines. They would usually be governed by a board of directors reflecting expertise in such areas as commercial and technical operations and engineering as well as financial management and would also include representatives of the community at large. The board would be responsible for such aspects as policy development, final decisions on major investments and other matters having major implications for the overall operations of the entity.

A general manager, usually but not necessarily recruited by the board, and reporting to it, would be responsible for the day-to-day operations of the entity; normally, deputies responsible for such major areas as technical operations, finance, administration and commercial development would assist the general manager. However, organizational structure would vary between entities and would depend largely on the scope and functions of the airport entity concerned, as well as local circumstances.

A main objective of establishing an autonomous airport entity is to improve the efficiency and finances of the airport(s) concerned. This means turning losses into profits or at least reducing the level of losses. It should be noted in this context, however, that profitable operations may not be achievable for reasons beyond the control of the entity or State concerned, such as low traffic volumes.

It should be emphasized that many significant financial advantages may be achieved by vesting an airport entity with the necessary financial autonomy, including management and use of airport-generated revenues to defray airport expenses. Airport-generated revenues include landing, parking, passenger service and other charges on air traffic operations as well as rentals, concession fees and other non-aeronautical revenues. Financial independence permits and encourages airport management to exercise closer control over revenues and costs. It also offers the possibility of negotiating loans best suited to meeting the airport's needs (provided the entity is empowered to negotiate its own loans). Moreover, it places the airport in a stronger position regarding other financial matters, such as in the negotiation of concession contracts, and in industrial relations, for example when negotiating labour contracts or establishing the remuneration of staff. It also permits management to act swiftly and avail itself of special offers or quantity discounts for equipment and supplies which may only be available for a relatively short period.

In some instances, airport entities have been established without being given the necessary financial autonomy. Thus, all the revenues they generate from charges, rentals and concession fees are deposited directly to the account of the national treasury, a ministry or the civil aviation administration, resulting in the airport entity then having to apply for all funds required to cover airport expenses. The airport entities concerned nevertheless remain responsible for the levying and collection of charges on air traffic as well as for the promotion and development of non-aeronautical activities. Arrangements of this nature tend to substantially reduce the potential benefits offered by the airport entity. As experience has shown, they tend to significantly reduce the incentive of airport management to develop new revenue sources or increase income from existing sources when it cannot make use of revenues it generates to defray expenses for which it is held responsible.

Regular airport operation and maintenance as well as investments in new or expanded facilities usually require outlays of varying, but sometimes substantial, amounts to be made in convertible currency. To provide airport facilities and services in the most cost-efficient manner, it would be advisable for an airport entity to be given access to such convertible currency as it might generate, for example from charges on air traffic, in order to meet expenses it would need to incur in such currency. This may be particularly relevant when, for example, spare parts must be imported to enable essential equipment or facilities to remain operational or to be returned to service.

Whatever the form of ownership and control that the State has selected, the management of airports can be done either on an individual airport basis, on an airport system[8] basis, on an airport network[9] basis, or on a combination of these, since an airport network can encompass either an addition of individual airports or a combination of individual airports and one airport system (or more).

There are arguments in favour of operating and managing a group of airports within an airport network, a form of organization that has become more and more common at a national level. Smaller airports may derive some benefit within a common ownership which could include cross-subsidization. Other arguments point to, *inter alia*: the advantages for a State having a national air transport system in achieving its national development objectives; the advantages in terms of economies of scale and synergies; the easier access of all airports to capital markets;

[8] An airport system is composed of two or more airports serving the same major metropolitan area and operated under a single ownership and control structure.

[9] An airport network is a group of airports within a State operated under a single ownership and control structure; it can include all airports serving the territory of this State or only some of these airports. Cross ownership of airports in different States or management contracts obtained in different States by an international airport management company can also lead to a form of cooperation sometimes referred to as airport networks, or as airport alliances, but these forms of international cooperation are of a different nature than a network at a national level.

and the better management of capacity and use of resources throughout the network. In summary, an airport network can be a valuable method of collectively managing airports which, taken individually, would not be viable. Arguments against cross-subsidization are based on the fact that charges have to be cost-related; that users should not be charged for facilities they do not use; and that only those facilities used for international air services should be included in the cost basis for charges. In that sense, cross-subsidization between international airports and domestic airports is questionable, although it is recognized that in some States it may be the only way to maintain airports that serve, for example, landlocked regions. Opponents to the network approach also point out that if subsidies are to be provided for national planning purposes, these should rather come from the State than from users of other airports.

Another aspect is related to the operation and management of airports at an international, or multinational, level, including alliances between airports or airport groups. This is made possible by the operation and management of airports in different States by globalized airport companies. The main advantage of such a form of organization lies in the potential economies of scale, while the drawbacks may be found in a possible diversion of revenue and cross-subsidies between airports in different States (a form of cooperation that may be acceptable to some developing States).

One conclusion that may be drawn from this controversial issue is that equilibrium should be sought between the interests of airports and users; and that in cases where cross-subsidization within a national network is applied, full transparency is necessary. In the final analysis, it is for States to decide on what is in their best interest, taking the above advantages and disadvantages and their particular circumstances into account. In this respect, consideration should be given to paragraph 22 viii) of Doc 9082/7 where the possibility for States or charging authorities to recover less than their full costs is recognized, as well as to the possibility of cross-subsidization through revenues from commercial activities. With regard to international operation and management of airports, this form of organization should be exerted with caution and could be considered as acceptable as long as it brings lower charges through economies of scale.

When establishing the internal organizational structure of an airport (or group of airports), the principal aim should be to create a structure that enables the airport to meet its objectives and carry out its functions in the most efficient and cost-effective manner while maintaining a high standard of service.

Before defining or revising its internal organizational structure, particular attention should first be directed to the various functions and areas of responsibility of the airport (or group of airports). These functions and areas of responsibility are often described in the charter of the airport(s) or in documents of a similar character. Where these functions or areas of responsibility are not defined clearly or where the descriptions are considered incomplete or out of date, they should be redefined or updated.

The functions and responsibilities of an airport will vary according to its size, type of traffic and areas of responsibility. For example, some airports are responsible for air traffic control as well as for meteorological services, while at most other airports such services are provided by separate government entities. Many airports are involved in security functions in varying degrees and in providing facilities for customs, immigration and health authorities. Ground-handling services for the airlines, including terminal handling or ramp handling, or both, are provided by some airports, while at others they are provided by the airlines or by specialized agents or companies. Certain airports also perform functions that exceed the scope of conventional airport activities, such as consultancy services, public works, construction, and real estate development.

5.2 Privatization of Airports

Privatization of airports is yet another commercial tool which is sweeping the globe clear of modern challenges faced by the aviation industry. The almost uncontrollable growth in demand for air transport services has prompted countries across the world, from Australia to Zimbabwe, to consider seriously the selling of their airports to private entrepreneurs. In the past decade it was considered distinctly possible that, in keeping with this trend, hundreds of airports may be sold between 2000 and 2010 in order that airport infrastructures would be broad based to accommodate the overall passenger growth of 5.7 % between 1999 and 2000[10] and of 6 % thereafter, until the year 2005.[11]

Another reason which impels airports to go in for privatization and optimize their services is the impact of airline alliances on airport facilities. A good example is Miami International Airport which has made changes to a capital improvement programme, adding $500 million to an already buffered $5.4 billion programme in order to accommodate the alignment of airlines under One world, Star and North West-Continental alliances.[12]

Privatization involves a whole spectrum of economic activities which affect infrastructural services and could extend to such facilities as power generation and clearing services. Two of the main advantages of privatization are of course maximizing profit and improving efficiency of the services at airports.[13] Public enterprises, in sharp contrast, tend to focus on job creation, supporting national identity and pride and stimulating tourism, all of which could have a stultifying effect on profit making and efficiency. Be that as it may, public enterprise has largely lost its appeal, not only due to the cumbersome bureaucracy involved but also because of the evolution of globalization which has changed economic reality

---

[10] *The World of Civil Aviation* 1998–2001, at Tables 5–6.

[11] Outlook for Air Transport to the Year 2005, ICAO Circular 270-AT/111 p. 37. See also ICAO Assembly Working Paper A32-WP/105 at p. 4.

[12] Ott (1999) at p. 53.

[13] Pilarski (1993) at p. 207.

and made enterprises move toward markets and efficiency from being mere non-profit making services and facilities.

There are various forms in which airports could be privatized. Called Public-Private Partnerships (PPP), these arrangements are based on a contract or concession agreement between a government or statutory entity on one side and a private sector company on the other side, for delivering an infrastructure service on payment of user charges. The goal is to combine the best capabilities of the public and private sectors for mutual benefit. PPPs are used to build new and upgrade existing public facilities. Compared with traditional procurement models, in PPP the private sector assumes a greater role in the planning, financing, design, construction, operation, and maintenance of these facilities. A short description of each mode of privatization may be of interest at this juncture.

5.3 Build Operate Transfer (BOT)

Arguably, the most common form of a privatization agreement, BOT is an arrangement where the governmental hands over the constructing and operating rights of a project for a pre determined period to a private sector entity and has these rights transferred back to the government and after that period a flexibility in the BOT agreement is that the planning and designing can also be implemented by the private sector according to the agreement. The BOT modality has given rise to various corollaries and variations such as BOOT (Build Own Operate Transfer), DBOT (Design Build Operate Transfer), DBOM (Design Build Operate Maintain), BOO (Build Own Operate) *etc.*

5.4 Build Own Operate Transfer (BOOT)

The title speaks for itself. A BOOT occurs when a government grants a private entity or private sector organization a concession to build an aerodrome, own it and operate it for a specified period of time and finally transfer it to the government. A BOOT should not be confused with a Build Operate Transfer (BOT) where in the latter ownership does not take place. A good definition is: "Financing arrangement in which a developer (1) designs and builds a complete project or facility (such as an airport, power plant, seaport) at little or no cost to the government or a joint venture partner, (2) owns and operates the facility as a business for a specified period (usually 10 to 30 years) after which (3) transfers it to the government or partner at a previously agreed-upon or market-price".[14]

[14] http://www.businessdictionary.com/definition/build-own-operate-transfer-BOOT.html.

5.5 Build Own Operate (BOO)

In a BOO the group that builds takes on the responsibility of financing, constructing and operating the project with the ultimate view of syndicating all or part of its equity after the completion of the project. In this situation the company retains ownership and operates it indefinitely, deriving revenue from the project. The owners have the incentive of maintaining the project as well. In view of its vast potential for the operator to derive revenue and benefits from the project indefinitely, most governments may be reluctant to enter into a BOO agreement. In the large facilities construction industry such as in large airports there is a high risk of failure in a BOO type arrangement, due to the inability of the operator to come to terms with and control uncertainty. In a BOO mega-project organizations use their internal resources since funding is usually limited for outsourcing all phases of designing, building, and operating a large facility. Risk management in the BOO scenario also poses difficulties unlike in a BOT where the project sponsors transfer the risk to a private company to operate once the facilities are completed. However, in a BOT project the company still integrates all phases up until the facility is ready for business, to speed up the construction.

5.6 Design Build Finance Operate (DBFO)

The DBFO is similar in essence to a BOT except that in the former the promoter's remuneration is paid by the government based on traffic flow and income potential of the airport. An example is the Canadian Iqaluit International Airport Improvement project includes a new airport building; expanded aprons for planes to park; new lighting systems; an upgraded runway; and a new combined services building that will house the fire-fighting vehicles, support equipment and the heavy equipment that maintain the runways. The project will mean significant job creation, direct and indirect, as well as training and economic development opportunities for Iqaluit and Nunavut as a whole.

A private partner will be chosen by the Government of Nunavut through a competitive selection process to design, build, finance, operate and maintain the facility through a long term agreement. The project will have numerous social and economic benefits for the City of Iqaluit and Nunavut. It will support the objectives of the Nunavummi Nangminiqaqtunik Ikajuuti (NNI) Policy by: providing Inuit employment, education and training; improving the safety and services of the airport; improving transportation between northern communities; and facilitating the development of mineral resources in Nunavut to create more business and investment opportunities.

5.7 Build Lease Transfer (BLT)

In BLT private entities finance, design, build and retain ownership of the airport facility for an agreed period of time subject to a lease back agreement where the host government leases it from the investor. Under BLT a private entity builds a complete project and leases it to the government. On this way the control over the project is transferred from the project owner to a lessee. In other words the ownership remains by the shareholders but operation purposes are leased. After the expiry of the leasing the ownership of the asset and the operational responsibility are transferred to the government at a previously agreed price. For foreign investors taking into account the country risk BLT provides good conditions because the project company maintains the property rights while avoiding operational risk.

5.8 Lease Renovate Operate Transfer (LROP)

LROT can be identified as a contractual arrangement whereby an existing infrastructure facility is handed over to private, parties on lease, for a particular period of time for the specific purpose of renovating the facility and operating it for a specific period of time; on such terms and conditions as may be agreed to with the government for recovering the costs with an agreed return and thereafter, transferring the facility to the government.

5.9 Build Transfer Operate (BTO)

In a typical BTO public facilities are financed by the government whereas responsibility for maintenance and operation devolves upon the private sector operator.

PPPs became popular with the trend where the liberalization and globalization of markets were a necessary corollary to the shift in perception of world leaders from the evils of monopoly to the advantages and virtues of competition. This change in attitude was mainly due to the realization that with liberalization comes more entrepreneurs and companies who in turn, with their market entry, make larger markets potentially available. Furthermore, with liberalization and globalization come better opportunities for entrepreneurs to enter markets, thus intensifying competition. The result is of course more quality service at more competitive prices. In the case of airports this effect can immediately be seen in the typical reduction of consumer goods in some airport shops immediately after they are privatized.

From an economic perspective, it is incontrovertible that most States which have privatized their infrastructure have stood to gain financially, particularly when the revenue from privatization is injected to the government coffers. Cases in point are the British Airports Authority—which is the largest group of privatized airports in the United Kingdom—and Australia. In the case of the latter, several airports were subject to long term leases for upfront payments over the past decade (1990–2000).[15] The role of government at the post-privatization stage is substantially different from the role played when an airport was under government control. After privatization, governments are no longer responsible for management and development of airports. Management of facilities of the airport is transferred to the new administration as well as the collection of airport charges and other revenues.

Usually, apart from the basic advantage of attracting more finances to the government treasury, there are three reasons that impel a government to open an airport for public issue: lack of government funds to expand airport capacity to meet the demands of air transport; increase of efficiency of the airport and its services through private sector involvement; and he opening of a wider choice for airlines operating into the airport in terms of hub operations.

The United Nations introduced a global perspective to privatization by endorsing the practice, particularly by a General Assembly Resolution in 1992,[16] which, while recognizing the sovereign right of each State to decide on the development of its private and public sectors, notes that the private sector plays a positive role in mobilizing resources and promoting economic growth and sustainable developments. The Resolution goes on to urge all concerned to support national efforts of countries in implementing privatization, demonopolization, administrative deregulation and other relevant policies in the context of their economic regions and the opening of their economies.

Privatization of an airport brings to bear a certain focus on the changed status of the airport, particularly in terms of ownership and management and the inevitable corollaries of legal liabilities and fiscal responsibility which changes hands. Privatization, when essentially related to the change of ownership and management in the provision of airports services, is rather loosely associated with any deviation or movement away from government ownership and management of facilities and services.[17] Although this is generally the case and privatization has been generically defined as the shifting of governmental functions and responsibilities to the private sector, partially or wholly. It has been claimed that privatization can involve various scenarios. These range from change of ownership from public to private sector; change of ownership from central to local government; change of legal status from an autonomous governmental authority to a body corporate that is traded in public; involvement of private sector participation without the legal benefit of ownership; and financing by the private sector.[18] In the context of the

[15] Kesharwani (2002), at p. 160.

[16] A/RES/47/171, 22 December 1992.

[17] *Privatization in the Provision of Airports and Air Navigation Services*, ICAO Circular 284-AT/120, March 2002, at p. 3.

[18] Hong and Yoo (2000) at p. 3.

HKIA, this may prove too dismissive an interpretation as privatization should mean either full ownership or majority ownership of facilities and services.

In 1994, the World Bank reported that privatization provides countless examples of dramatic improvements in efficiency as a result of the alleged superiority of the private enterprise system and pointed out that, in developing countries in which utilities were largely run by instrumentalities of State, 40 % of power generating capacity was out of commission.[19] Harry P. Hatry contradicts the World Bank's thesis by stating:

> ... the major advantage of the privatization movement is not that the private sector can reduce costs or improve service to a great extent, but that consideration of privatization encourages public officials and public employees to innovate and to breakdown obstacles to improving public employee efficiency ...[20]

Hatry continues with the argument—that privatization would not necessarily lower costs—by showing the inherent disadvantages of privatization as encouraging corruption; reducing quality of service; and reducing access to service by disadvantaged citizens.[21] Concern has also been raised elsewhere with regard to disadvantages which may accompany privatization of airports with the possibility of private airport owners taking on projects or opening new businesses within the umbrella of airport activity which are not related to the core airport business.[22] There is also the apprehension that the sale of equity shares may lead new owners of airports to hasten towards quick profit making and a short term mentality that would effectively preclude the essential act of reinvesting of profits for infrastructure development.[23] Another negative throwback of airport privatization could well be related to public accountability or lack thereof where privatization may lead to cutbacks in expansion programmes and a reluctance to invest in infrastructure expansion.

On the balance, however, it could be argued *a fortiori* that the advantages of airport privatization outweigh the disadvantages. For instance, privatization usually results in improved operational efficiency and aggressive market related business practice such as opening up new non traditional capital sources calculated to contribute towards financing airport infrastructure and service development. Privatization remains a part of an overall strategy to replace the public sector culture with a private sector culture by more efficient use of resources and modernization of the economy concerned.[24]

Perhaps the most important feature of privatization is that it is essentially a political process involving a change in the role of the State with the sale of State or publicly owned property, or with transfer of management from State to private

[19] Pilarski (1999) at 204. See also Boycko et al. (1993), p. 1.

[20] Hatry (1999) at p. 263.

[21] *Ibid.*

[22] Update, *Airport Privatization*, Airports Council International, No. 6 September 1998 at p. 4.

[23] *Ibid* at p. 3.

[24] See UN (1993) at p. 12.

sources. This inevitably leads to issues of responsibility and legal liability. For instance, an airport previously publicly owned may not be under the same rules of legal liability as it would once privatized. This article addresses legal liability issues which necessarily follow privatization.

For the reasons given above, it is necessary, when considering a change in the management and ownership of an airport, to involve the existing management personnel in every stage of the transition process. The involvement of users of the airport facilities and other interested parties, at least on a consultancy basis, would also be desirable. Foremost in the transition process would be the undertaking of a thorough and meticulous study of existing infrastructure and a forecast, both short and long term (at least for a 10 year period) of the air traffic at the airport.

Privatization would usually make it easier to access private sector capital. The profile of the airport, particularly as one of the most prolific revenue generating airports in the world, would bring to bear the need for recognition by private sector investors of the enormous stability and promise held by the airport. Secondly, with privatization and the enormous trading potential of Hong Kong, airport operators could have the opportunity of exploiting other organizational opportunities adjacent to the airport. Thirdly privatization of an airport could introduce an efficient marketing oriented management.

The United Nations General Assembly, at its 93rd Plenary Session in December 1992 endorsed privatization in the context of economic restructuring, economic growth and sustainable development. By Assembly Resolution A 47/171 the General Assembly, while noting *inter alia* that many countries were attaching growing importance, in the context of their economic restructuring policies, to the privatization of enterprises, urged member States to support when requested the national efforts of States in implementing privatization. In 1993 the General Assembly followed up on its stance on privatization by adopting Resolution A 48/180 which *inter alia* requested the Secretary General to strengthen the activities of the United Nations System related to the promotion of entrepreneurship and to the implementation of privatization programmes.

On the specific issue of airport privatization, the Latin American Civil Aviation Commission (LACAC), at its 13th Ordinary Assembly held in Chile in July 1998 adopted Recommendation A 13-4 which recognized *inter alia* that airport privatization was becoming more prevalent in the Latin American Region and that the process of privatization involves a detailed analysis of different factors. Accordingly, the Assembly recommended that the LACAC member States consider the following issues in order to obtain the best results from the privatization process:

a) Define the role of the State and the responsibilities it must fulfil in order to guarantee the rights of users, as well as airport security and operational safety, in accordance with international standards in force.
b) Consider the convenience of maintaining public ownership of airports, granting concessions for suitable periods of time in keeping with investments made.

c) Clearly establish the required infrastructure, whose costs the State and/or the users will be willing to recognize, avoiding surpluses or deficiencies which may be detrimental to them.
d) Determine the services to be transferred to the private sector and those which will remain in the hands of the State, describing the standards to be used in defining the quality of the services provided.
e) As much as possible, aim at establishing a competitive environment for providers of the various services, seeking mechanisms such as public tenders. Maximum allowable rates should be established for monopolistic services.
f) Define the financing of the air transport sector, deciding whether higher-income airports should economically support the less profitable ones or those working at a loss, in order to maintain a self financed airport network compatible with national civil aviation needs.
g) The contract between the State and private airport service operators must be the result of an open public tender where the required conditions, evaluation formulae and criteria to be used to award the contract must be clearly established and made known to all interested parties, in an absolutely transparent way.
h) Reserve the right to implement the relevant measures to follow up on, and maintain operational control over the concession contract.
i) Pay special attention to the contract termination clause for its timely enforcement in case of non compliance and recovery of the relevant value.
j) The Civil Aviation Administrations should actively participate in all privatization processes.

5.10 Forms of Private Participation

It must be emphasized that "privatization" is commonly used in regard to the changes taking place in the ownership and management in the provision of airports and air navigation services. Significantly, the word is often loosely interpreted as any movement away from government ownership and management of facilities and services. This is too broad and over-encompassing an interpretation. In the strictest sense, privatization must necessarily involve either full ownership or majority ownership of facilities and services. Therefore, the elements of private participation, discussed below should not be described as privatization but rather as private participation or private involvement since the ownership control rests with the government.

There are various forms of privatized arrangements with regard to the running of airports. The first is a management contract. Under this option, the management of an airport or a group of airports is transferred to a private entity[25] for a limited

[25] Which can be a local/national concern, or an international airport managing group, or a consortium associating various interests of which the former two may be part.

period of time for a fee or predetermined payment terms. The airport(s) benefits from professional management, but development of the airport(s) is not included in the contract. The next is a lease or concession. Leases/concessions can be short-, medium-, or long-term. Under this option, an airport or a group of airports is transferred for management and development to a private entity for a fixed period. In almost all cases, the responsibility for expansion and development of airports rests with the lessee or concessionaire, under conditions that are either listed in the contract or depending on traffic growth. The payment terms of leases or concessions vary widely. In some cases, it is all down payment while in other cases it is partly down payment and partly annual payment or only annual payment. One of the most common forms is the BOT (Build-Operate-Transfer) scheme, an ownership and management system under which a private entity obtains the right to finance, build and operate a certain facility, including land and/or buildings, over a long period of time and on expiry of the right returns it to the owner. A transfer of minority ownership is another option under which ownership of an airport or a group of airports is partially transferred to the private sector, through outright sale of shares to a strategic partner, or an IPO (Initial Public Offer) on the stock exchange market. The advantage of this system is that the transfer of ownership can be carried out in stages, depending upon local circumstances and needs.

Under Private sector ownership and control, majority or full ownership of the airport is transferred to a private entity including non-profit corporations or trusts. In the event that a State would wish to regain ownership, it would have to buy back the shares, with the risk that their price may be higher than the original sale price. Private sector ownership and/or operation of parts of the activities of an airport involves the ownership and operation of certain facilities or services at an airport, For example a passenger terminal, or a cargo warehouse, or security services. The activities of the operator are regulated by a contract which, from a legal point of view, is similar to a commercial concession agreement.

In general terms of ownership and management of airports, States have various options to select from, such as government ownership; management contract; lease or concession; transfer of minority ownership; and private sector ownership and control. However, of these options, private participation in predominantly State owned airports can take three forms: management contracts; leases (which are otherwise called concessions); and transfer of minority ownership.[26] The first—management contracts—could involve a private company managing an airport.[27] A lease would involve management by a lessor, and is a common form of private participation. Australia is a significant contributor to the lease/concession concept and has leased at leased 17 major airports.[28] The last category—private

[26] *Privatization in the Provision of Airports and Air Navigation Services*, ICAO Cir. 284, AT/120, March 2002, at 8.

[27] An example of a management contract is Indianapolis International Airport in the United States which is managed by a private company with multiple partnerships. *Ibid.*

[28] Other countries are Canada, India and various countries in South America and Western Africa.

participation through transfer of minority ownership—usually takes place either through the sale of shares to a strategic partner or through share floatation. Some airports in Europe, in particular those in Austria, Denmark, Italy and Switzerland, airports in South Africa as well as Kansai in Japan are examples of minority owned airports.

Management of airports and their changing styles have largely been determined by economic, political and social factors. As a result, there exist in the world numerous ownership and management models for airports. A change in the ownership and management structure in the provision of airport services may not necessarily solve all the problems that an airport or a group of airports may be facing. The change may be harmful in the long run if poorly planned. The objectives of any change should be clearly defined.

States have to consider a number of major issues before embarking on privatization or private participation. The preeminent need would be to conduct an in-depth analysis of the current present state of the aviation infrastructure in the State, including a detailed profit and loss account. Such an analysis should also take into account growth forecasts. Consideration should be given to how the remaining airports and other services are to be managed and financed. Consideration should be given to the issue as to how the remaining airports and other services are to be managed and financed simultaneously and a decision has to be taken as to the most expeditious and profitable manner in which profitable airports could be identified as a distinct category in a different category. Moe importantly, the existing regulatory body should be suitably strengthened to absorb increasing responsibility that private management brings with it.

Careful planning is a pre requisite for privatization or private participation to be successful. The most important aspect of a successful privatization or private participation project is transparency. Tender documents should be well prepared and include all information necessary for taking a decision. Careful consideration should be given to the short-listing of suitable bidders. Moreover, the contract document should provide, *inter alia*, for the termination of the contract and the resumption of control of facilities and services in grave situations without paying undue compensation to the private sector. Since private participation and privatization in the provision of airport services is a complex process in which many States may not have sufficient expertise, it may be desirable and advantageous to obtain the advice of external consultants.

Privatization should essentially be driven by the fundamental determinants of aviation—safety, security and efficiency. These should not only form the primary objectives of the privatization process but should adapt to the model selected by States for their individual airports. It is incontrovertible that, regardless of the organizational form or legal status, the State remains ultimately responsible for safety and security.

There are two other terms which are used in relation to private involvement, particularly in the context of airports and they are corporatization and autonomy. In the context of airports and air navigation services corporatization means creating a legal entity outside the government to manage airports and/or air navigation services, either through a specific statute or under an existing general statute such as company law. The functions and powers of the corporatized body are defined in the specific statute of the Memorandum of Association or in a similar document if it is established under company law.

Usually, ownership of the corporation remains with the government. However, in a corporatized body, private sector participation is possible. Much depends upon the provisions of the statute under which it is established and the policy of the government. Corporatization is a legal organizational structure in which airports and/or air navigation services are vested for operation and management. It does not refer to any specific approach to management, which depends upon the provisions of the statute under which it is established and the policy of the government.

Autonomy on the other hand refers to the powers of the managers of airports and air navigation services in regard to utilizing revenues generated from the operation of various services and taking independent managerial decisions on issues falling within the charter of the organization. Autonomy does not refer to any specific organizational format, such as private participation, privatization, corporatization or leases. However, in the context of the provision of airports and air navigation services, the word is used in relation to government-owned facilities and services. Thus, autonomy can be related to a unit within the government, such as a civil aviation authority, a corporate authority or a company wholly owned by the government.

It is worthwhile examining the concept of autonomous management, in order to evaluate its desirability as a management option. A suitable and analogous case study in point would be the British Airports Authority, a government-owned corporate authority established in 1966, which was the first major public corporation to manage airports. The objective of the United Kingdom Government in establishing this authority was to establish managerial and financial autonomy for the airports and provide access to capital markets without foregoing ownership.[29] Many States followed the example of the United Kingdom and established autonomous airport authorities and the number of airports managed by autonomous authorities has gradually grown. It must be noted that, while the establishment of an autonomous airport authority would not necessarily result in an unprofitable airport becoming profitable, experience gained worldwide from these developments indicates that where airports have been operated by autonomous authorities their over-all financial situation has generally tended to improve. This finding provided further support for the movement to establish autonomous authorities. Nevertheless, for various reasons a large number of airports are still managed directly by governments.

The advantages of establishing autonomous authorities are multifarious. From a management perspective they can be seen as bodies empowering service providers through financial and operational autonomy; encouraging the growth of a business culture; lowering expenses per traffic unit relative to other airports of comparable

[29] The British Airports Authority was privatized in 1987 as BAA plc.

size; recycling various aviation user charges into aviation. Autonomous bodies also reduce the financing burden on governments and generally improve the quality of services, while establishing a clear distinction between the regulator and the provider of services.

Within the fringes of specific terminology lies the generic term "commercialization". Commercialization is an approach to the management of facilities and services in which business principles are applied or special emphasis is placed on developing commercial activities. In the context of airports, commercialization generally refers to a change in the approach to management of facilities and services. It can be achieved by establishing a corporation or a company under company law, normally without involving the private sector in the ownership or management. Sometimes a unit within the government can also be commercialized. Commercialization should not be equated to private participation or privatization. While the former connotes an approach to management, the latter refers to change in the ownership or control of management. Commercialization is often considered an alternative to private participation and privatization in the provision of airports and air navigation services for improving the delivery and financial performance of services.

A noteworthy feature of privatization, one which could be considered in the case of Hong Kong International Airport, is that in most States, private participation and privatization in the provision of airport services has taken place in stages. For example, in the United Kingdom, major airports were initially transferred to a government corporation. Several years later they were transferred to a government-owned company. Soon thereafter, the shares of this company were sold to the private sector. In some European countries, the airports were first transferred to separate companies owned by the State and the divestiture of shares was gradual. However, in almost all European airports where private participation has taken place, the government presently holds majority shares in the equity. China, Malaysia and South Africa are following the European model and the divestiture is gradual.

Another example for consideration is New Zealand, where airports were first transferred to companies owned by the government and a few years later, a major portion of the shares was sold to private entities. Local bodies continue to hold some shares. In Australia, major airports were first transferred to the Federal Airports Corporation, a government-owned corporation. A few years later, these same airports were divided into groups and were offered separately for lease in stages.

In Latin America, private participation is mainly taking place directly from government ownership, primarily through leases either for groups of airports or for individual airports. For example, airports in Mexico have been divided into four groups, while Argentina decided to lease most of its airports as a group. The limited evidence available suggests that States have generally benefited from a gradual change in ownership and management structure.

The final consideration in an airport's privatization process would be whether it should be wholly privately owned and managed. A fundamental premise in this regard is that, apart from airports originally owned by private entities, fully privatized airports or airports with majority private ownership are few. These primarily include some airports managed by BAA plc and certain other airports in the United Kingdom that are wholly owned by the private sector. In Canada, smaller airports have been sold to local communities. Airports with majority ownership in the private sector include Auckland and Wellington airports in New Zealand and a new international airport built in Macau a few years ago.

References

Boycko M, Shleifer A, Vishney R (1993) A theory of privatization. Howard University Press, Boston, p 1

Doganis R (1992) The airport business. Routledge, London

Hatry HP (1999) Privatization: the provision of public services by the private sector. McFarland & Company Inc., Jefferson, p 263

Hong S-K, Yoo KE (2000) A study on airport privatization in Korea: policy and legal aspects of corporation and localization over airport management. J Air L Com 66:3

Kesharwani T (2002) Privatization of aviation infrastructure. Asian Institute of Transport Development, New Delhi

Ott J (1999) Alliances spawn a web of global networks. Aviat Week Space Technol 151:53

Pilarski AM (1993) Columnist bureaucrats and the transition to the market economy. In: Garston N (ed) Bureaucracy: three paradigms. Kluwer Academic, Boston, pp 205–221

Pilarski AM (1999) Airline privatization: as a response to globalization. In: Jenkins D (ed) The handbook of airline economics, 1st edn. Aviation Weekly Group, Washington, p 201

UN (1993) Report of the ad hoc working group on comparative experiences with privatization on its second session. United Nations Conference on Trade and Development, Geneva

Chapter 6
Aerodrome Security

The airport is the frontier between the outside world and the State in which the airline passenger lands. It is also the final point at which a person can be checked before embarking on a flight. Moreover, the aerodrome is where cargo is loaded into an aircraft before takeoff. Therefore, security at the airport carries multiple dimensions, from border control to body scanning; from cargo security to security of the aircraft and its passengers.

Encouragingly, information technology assists in ensuring aerodrome security and overall airport operations. Facilities such as online check-in where airlines can check in passengers through their mobile services, ease congestion at the terminal check in counters; mobile devices and hand held terminals with Wi-Fi connections; biometric technology and passenger tracking technologies all go to ensure a more efficient and secure airport operation. Pilots and aircrew have *i*Pads and other tablets to deliver critical information and data; and passengers have smart phone apps top report any suspicious behaviour in their vicinity.

6.1 Border Security

Article 22 of the Chicago Convention states that each contracting State agrees to adopt all practicable measures, through the issuance of special regulations or otherwise, to facilitate and expedite navigation by aircraft between the territories of contracting States, and to prevent unnecessary delays to aircraft, crews, passengers and cargo, especially in the administration of the laws relating to immigration, quarantine, customs and clearance. This provision is followed by Article 23 which provides that each contracting State undertakes, so far as it may find practicable, to establish customs and immigration procedures affecting international air navigation in accordance with the practices which may be established or recommended from time to time, pursuant to this Convention.

The fundamental requirement in the immigration process is the passport. One of the key aspects of facilitation involves speedy, efficient and secure border crossing.

R. Abeyratne, *Law and Regulation of Aerodromes*, DOI 10.1007/978-3-319-04780-5_6,

The primary tool for this process is a valid travel document. A discussion of passports and visas has already take place in this book under Article 13. However, there remains one aspect to be discussed and that is State responsibility in protecting the integrity of the passport and the prevention of passport fraud.

The passport is a basic document in the transport by air of persons. Its use therefore is of fundamental importance as a travel document, not only because it reflects the importance of the sovereignty of a State and the nationality of its citizens but also because it stands for the inviolability of relations between States that are linked through air transport. The assassination of a leader of Hamas on 19 January 2010 by a group of individuals in Dubai who used forged passports belonging to various nations, raised a diplomatic outcry and brought to bear an important facet of air transport that is vulnerable to abuse and contention among States.

The fundamental issue that emerges is one that is critical to air law in the context of the integrity and ownership of the passport and its abuse in the course of criminal activity. There is also the issue, from a legal and diplomatic perspective as to whether a State or instrumentality of State, can, with impunity, use forged passports for travel of its staff on missions of espionage or assassination. *A fortiori*, an additional issue is whether a State could be complicit or condone or be seen to condone (in the absence of any action taken by the State to punish the miscreants) such abuse of travel documents belonging to other nations. In order to determine these issues, this article addresses two basic discussions: the first on complicity and condonation of a State and the second on the nature and integrity of the passport. Finally, it discusses issues of State responsibility, diplomacy and criminality.

On 19 January 2010, Mahmoud al-Mabhouh, considered to be a senior commander of Hamas, a radical Palestinian group, was assassinated at a hotel in Dubai in a manner usually employed by professionally trained military and secret service agencies. The killing was attributed to Mossad[1] The European Union, which considers Hamas a terrorist organization, nonetheless condemned the assassination of the Hamas leader and showed particular concern over the fact that the killers had used passports from Ireland, France, Germany and the UK—to coordinate their travel into Dubai from various parts of the world, synchronizing their arrival time from various flights into Dubai International Airport and checking into the hotel of the victim contemporaneously. The EU strongly condemned the fact that those involved in this action used fraudulent EU member states' passports and credit cards acquired through the theft of EU citizens' identities.[2]

Australia was another complainant who warned Israel that its friendly relations with Israel would be jeopardised if it were found to have condoned the suspected

[1] Mossad is responsible for the collection of intelligence and other covert activities including military operations. It is one of the most integral parts of the Israeli intelligence community and reports directly to the Prime Minister of Israel. See http://en.wikipedia.org/wiki/Mossad.

[2] Toby Vogel, EU Condemns Use of False Passports inn Hamas Killing, http://www.europeanvoice.com/article/2010/02/eu-condemns-use-of-false-passports-in-hamas-killing/67225.aspx.

theft of three Australian citizens' identities which Mossad used to carry out its political assassination. The diplomatic impasse occurred when three Australians from Victoria living in Israel at the time were confirmed among 26 people from four nations whose tampered passports were allegedly used by a team of suspected Israeli Mossad agents who assassinated al-Mabhouh. Australian Prime Minister Kevin Rudd is reported to have stated that Australia would be vocal in its contempt of any State if it were found that it "... has been complicit in the use or abuse of the Australian passport system, let alone for the conduct of an assassination, and has treated Australia with contempt and there will therefore be action by the Australian government in response".[3] Dubai authorities are reported to have said that they were virtually certain Israeli agents carried out the killing and had released the identities of 11 people who travelled on forged British, Irish, French and German passports to kill al-Mabhouh in a hotel.[4]

There is seemingly a history behind alleged Mossad involvement in the use of fake foreign passports in its activities. Reportedly, in 2004 New Zealand's prime minister imposed diplomatic sanctions—restricting visas and cancelling high level visits—after two Mossad agents were caught trying to acquire passports fraudulently—one in the name of a tetraplegic man. Seven years earlier, Mossad assassins carrying Canadian passports with assumed names attempted to murder the Hamas leader Khaled Meshaal by spraying nerve agent into his ear as he entered his office in Amman.[5]

The fundamental issue that emerges is one that is critical to air law in the context of the integrity and ownership of the passport and its abuse in criminal activity. There is also the issue, from a legal and diplomatic perspective is whether a State or instrumentality of State such as Mossad, can, with impunity, use forged passports for travel of its staff on missions of espionage or assassination. *A fortiori*, an additional issue is whether a State could be complicit or condone or be seen to

[3] http://www.theaustralian.com.au/news/world/australians-caught-in-hit-on-hamas/story-e6frg6so-1225834538825. It is reported that in 1997, Mossad bungled the assassination of top Hamas leader Khalid Mishal, who was injected while in Jordan with a poison by Israeli agents travelling on Canadian documents. He survived after his assailants were captured by his bodyguards and Israel provided the antidote. In 2004, two Mossad agents were jailed in New Zealand after trying to obtain fake passports, one in the name of a cerebral palsy sufferer. *Ibid.*

[4] http://www.euractiv.com/en/foreign-affairs/eu-unhappy-israel-over-fake-passports-james-bond-killings-news-278602.

[5] David Sapsted, and Loveday Morris, Israel in the Dock Over Fake Passports, http://www.thenational.ae/apps/pbcs.dll/article?AID=/20100218/NATIONAL/702179796/1133/sport.
Hamas, which won 2006 legislative elections in the Palestinian territories, is shunned by the West for rejecting its calls to recognise Israel and renounce violence. Hit squads dispatched by Mossad have used foreign passports in the past, notably in 1997 when agents entered Jordan on Canadian passports and bungled an attempt to kill Meshaal with poison. In 1987, Britain protested to Israel about what London called the misuse by Israeli authorities of forged British passports and said it received assurances steps had been taken to prevent future occurrences. In 2003, the offices of several EU member countries in the Council's Justus Lipsius building, including France, Germany and the UK, were found to be bugged. Although the Union has been discrete over the incident, many consider Mossad to have been responsible for the wiretapping. *Ibid.*

condone (in the absence of any action taken by the State to punish the miscreants) such abuse of travel documents belonging to other nations.

6.1.1 The e-Passport

Starting from the premise that the passport is primarily a document which establishes the identity of the holder,[6] the various approaches[7] taken by ICAO in advancing technologies that facilitate this task at borders have evolved into the use of biometric identification of the passport holder as the ultimate frontier in the identification process. The techniques of biometrics employed in a machine readable travel document (MRTD), be it a visa or passport,[8] enable the user to uniquely encode a particular physical characteristic of a person into a biometric identifier or biometric template which can be verified by machine to confirm or deny a claim regarding a person's identity. Accordingly, biometric identification of a person either correctly establishes his identity as being consistent with what is claimed in the passport he is holding or brings to bear the possibility that the person carrying a particular passport is an imposter. A biometric is a measurable, physical

---

[6] See *Naziranbai* v. *the State*, 1957 *Madhya Bharat Law Reporter*, at 1, where the court recognized the passport as essentially being a document of identity and nationality issued to citizens or subjects of a state who intend to travel overseas. See also, Turack (1972) at 20–21. Also, Abeyratne (1992) at 10.

[7] ICAO has been working on the development of passports since 1968. The Seventh Session of the ICAO Facilitation Division in 1968 recommended that a small panel of qualified experts including representatives of the passports and/or other border control authorities, be established: to determine the establishment of an appropriate document such as a passport card, a normal passport or an identity document with electronically or mechanically readable inscriptions that meet the requirements of document control; the best type of procedures, systems (electronic or mechanical) and equipment for use with the above documents that are within the resources and ability of Member States; the feasibility of standardizing the requisite control information and methods of providing this information through automated processes, provided that these processes would meet the requirements of security, speed of handling and economy of operation. See Facilitation Division, Report of the Seventh Session, 14–30 May 1968, ICAO Doc 8750-FAL/564, Agenda Item 2.3, at 2.3-4. See also *AT-WP/1079, 1/12/70*, Attachment A, which sets out the Terms of Reference of the Panel.

[8] A passport asserts that the person holding the passport is a citizen of the issuing State while a visa confirms that the State issuing the visa has granted the visa holder the non-citizen privilege of entering and remaining in the territory of the issuing State for a specified time and purpose. The machine readable passport (MRP) is a passport that has both a machine readable zone and a visual zone in the page that has descriptive details of the owner. The machine readable zone enables rapid machine clearance, quick verification and instantaneous recording of personal data. Besides these advantages, the MRP also has decided security benefits, such as the possibility of matching very quickly the identity of the MRP owner against the identities of undesirable persons, whilst at the same time offering strong safeguards against alteration, counterfeit or forgery. Abeyratne (1992), pp. 1–31.

characteristic or personal behavioral trait used to recognize the identity, or verify[9] the claimed identity of a person. In the modern context, biometrics are usually incorporated in an MRTD with a view to achieving five goals, the first of which is global interoperability[10] enabling the specifications of biometrics deployed in travel documents across the world to be applied and used in a universally operable manner. This is a critical need if the smooth application of biometric technology were to be ensured across borders. The second goal is to ensure uniformity within States in specific standard setting by States authorities who deploy biometrics in travel documents issued by them. The third is technical reliability, where States are required to ensure that technologies used in deploying biometrics are largely failure-proof and of sufficient quality and standard to ensure a State immigration authority reading documents issued by other States them that the details in the document do provide accurate verification of facts. Fourthly, the technology used has to be practical and not give rise to the need for applying disparate types of support technology at unnecessary cost and inconvenience to the user. The final goal is to ensure that the technology used will be sufficiently up to date for at least 10 years and also be backwardly compatible with new techniques to be introduced in the future.

Biometrics target the distinguishing physiological or behavioral traits of the individual by measuring them and placing them in an automated repository such as machine encoded representations created by computer software algorithms that could make comparisons with the actual features. Physiological biometrics that have been found to successfully accommodate this scientific process are facial recognition, fingerprinting and iris-recognition which have been selected by ICAO as being the most appropriate. The biometric identification process is four-fold: firstly involving the capture or acquisition of the biometric sample; secondly extracting or converting the raw biometric sample obtained into an intermediate form; and thirdly creating templates of the intermediate data is converted into a template for storage; and finally the comparison stage where the information offered by the travel document with that which is stored in the reference template.

Biometric identification gets into gear each time an MRTD holder (traveler) enters or exists the territory[11] of a State and when the State verifies his identity against the images or templates created at the time his travel document was issued.

---

[9] To "verify" means to perform a one-to-one match between proffered biometric data obtained from the holder of the travel document at the time of inquiry with the details of a biometric template created when the holder enrolled in the system.

[10] "Global interoperability" means the capability of inspection systems (either manual or automated) in different States throughout the world to exchange data, to process data received from systems in other States, and to utilize that data in inspection operations in their respective states. Global interoperability is a major objective of the standardized specifications for placement of both eye-readable and machine-readable data in all MRTDs.

[11] The Chicago Convention, *supra*, defines, in Article 2, "territory of a State" as the land areas and territorial waters adjacent to the State under the sovereignty, suzerainty, protection and mandate of such State.

This measure not only ensures that the holder of the document is the legitimate claimant to that document and to whom it was issued, but also enhances the efficacy of any advance passenger information (API)[12] system used by the State to pre-determine the arrivals to its territory. Furthermore, matching biometric data presented in the form of the traveler with the data contained in the template accurately ascertains as to whether the travel document has been tampered with or not. A three way check, which matches the traveler's biometrics with those stored in the template carried in the document and a central database, is an even more efficacious way of determining the genuineness of a travel document. The final and most efficient biometric check is when a four way determine is effected, were the digitized photograph is visually matched (non electronically) with the three way check described above.[13] In this context, it is always recommended that the traveler's facial image (conventional photograph) should be incorporated in the travel document along with the biometric templates in order to ensure that his identity could be verified at locations where there is no direct access to a central database or where the biometric identification process has not entered into the legal process of that location.

In May 2003, The New Technologies Working Group (NTWG) of the Technical Advisory group on Machine Readable Travel Documents (TAG/MTRTD) of ICAO, endorsed its *New Orleans Principle* of March 2003, which resolved that member States will continue to use the facial image as the primary identifier for MRTDs and as such the utilization of standardized digitally-stored facial images should be the globally interoperable biometric to support facial recognition technologies for machine assisted identity verification with MRTDs. Furthermore, the NTWG recognized that in addition to digitally stored facial images, member States of ICAO could also use digitally stored iris images or fingerprints as additional globally interoperable biometrics for purposes of identifying persons through MRTDs.

The challenges facing biometric technology are few, but significant. Biometric technology is evolving so rapidly that it is difficult to maintain consistent standards. The standards themselves are not regularly tested. Some technologies are not

[12] API involves exchange of data information between airlines and customs authorities, where an incoming passenger's essential details are notified electronically by the airline carrying that passenger prior to his arrival. The data for API would be stored in the passenger's machine readable passport, in its machine readable zone. This process enables customs authorities to process passengers quickly, thus ensuring a smoother and faster clearance at the customs barriers at airports. One of the drawbacks of this system, which generally works well and has proven to be effective, is that it is quite demanding in terms of the high level of accuracy required. One of the major advantages, on the other hand, is the potential carried by the API process in enhancing aviation security at airports and during flight. See Abeyratne (2002a), pp. 631–650.

[13] Issuing States must ensure the accuracy of the biometric matching technology used and functions of the systems employed if the integrity of the conducted checks are to be maintained. They must also have realistic and efficient criteria regarding the number of travel documents checked per minute in a border control situation and follow a regular biometric identification approach such as facial recognition, fingerprint examination or iris identification system.

adequately established so as to lend themselves to easy decoding and interpretation, particularly when confirming identity on a one-to-one basis with a large central database. More importantly, from a legal perspective, biometric technology brings to bear the compelling need to be aware of privacy issues[14] and data protection legislation of various jurisdictions, as well as liability of the database manager that might emerge pursuant to a breakdown of the database or inaccuracy of information produced as a result of data-matching, which in turn might lead to inconsistencies in the identification process.

The ePassport is the culmination of a sustained process of development of technical specifications for machine readable travel documents (MRTD). It introduces a new dimension to aviation security in that, within the conventional machine readable passport with its machine readable zone, an additional layer of verification of information contained in an electronic chip is placed, which verifies the information in the passport's machine readable zone by the use of a special reader. Much research has gone into the areas of the technology and verification in the development of the ePassport. At a Symposium held at ICAO in early October 2012, the ePassport was subjected to much discussion by the various experts gathered from across the globe.

It is important to note that the operative terms in the definition of the ePassport are "biometric identification" and "public key infrastructure (PKI) cryptographic technology". Biometric technology involves a measurable, physical characteristic or personal behavioral trait used to recognize the identity, or verify the claimed identity of a person. Biometric identification has been defined as "a generic term used to describe automated means of recognizing a living person through the measurement of distinguishing physiological or behavioural traits". Biometrics target the distinguishing physiological or behavioral traits of the individual by measuring them and placing them in an automated repository such as machine encoded representations created by computer software algorithms that could make comparisons with the actual features. Physiological biometrics that have been found to successfully accommodate this scientific process are facial recognition, fingerprinting and iris recognition which have been selected by ICAO as being the most appropriate.

The biometric identification process is fourfold: firstly involving the capture or acquisition of the biometric sample; secondly extracting or converting the raw biometric sample obtained into an intermediate form; and thirdly creating templates of the intermediate data is converted into a template for storage; and finally the comparison stage where the information offered by the travel document with that which is stored in the reference template. Biometric identification gets into gear each time an MRTD holder (traveler) enters or exists the territory of a State and when the State verifies his identity against the images or templates created at the time his travel document was issued. This measure not only ensures that the holder

---

[14] Abeyratne (2001), pp. 153–162. Abeyratne (2002b), pp. 83–115. Also Abeyratne (2002a), pp. 631–650.

of the document is the legitimate claimant to that document and to whom it was issued, but also enhances the efficacy of any advance passenger information (API) system used by the State to pre-determine the arrivals to its territory.

Furthermore, matching biometric data presented in the form of the traveler with the data contained in the template accurately ascertains as to whether the travel document has been tampered with or not. A three way check, which matches the traveler's biometrics with those stored in the template carried in the document and a central database, is an even more efficacious way of determining the genuineness of a travel document. The final and most efficient biometric check is when a four way determination is effected, where the digitized photograph is visually matched (non electronically) with the three way check described above. In this context, it is always recommended that the traveler's facial image (conventional photograph) should be incorporated in the travel document along with the biometric templates in order to ensure that his identity could be verified at locations where there is no direct access to a central database or where the biometric identification process has not entered into the legal process of that location.

6.1.2 Passenger Name Record

One of the most dramatic events pertaining to aviation security occurred in July 2005 when United States air traffic controllers turned back a KLM flight en route to Mexico City from Amsterdam, which was flying over US airspace. The action was grounded on the basis that two of the passengers in the passenger list earlier provided to the US authorities were on a "no fly" list. The importance of this drama to modern day aviation is that the aircraft was merely over-flying the territory of a State. Even more important is the fact that at the time of the incident, there was no US legislation covering the act of refusal to grant over-flying permission to an aircraft in that situation.[15] However, within days, The US Transportation Security Administration (TSA) announced that rules will be adopted to require that

[15] Consequent upon the events of 2001, President George Bush signed a new *American Transportation & Security Act* on November 25th 2002 making mandatory API transmission and the provision of PNR data pertaining to all passengers arriving in the United States. Such information, required prior to departure and arrival in the United States should include in the passenger and crew manifest for each flight, in accordance with, Section 115 of the *Transportation & Security Act* is

(a) The full name of each passenger and crew member;
(b) The date of birth and citizenship of each passenger and crew member;
(c) The sex of each passenger and crew member;
(d) The passport number and country of issuance of each passenger and crew member if required for travel;
(e) The United States visa number or resident alien card number of each passenger and crew member, as applicable;
(f) Such other information as the under Secretary, in consultation with the Commissioner of Customs, determines is reasonably necessary to ensure aviation safety.

passengers on all flights landing in and overflying US territory will be screened against a "no fly" list.[16]

The Passenger Name Record (PNR) is a subject that has been under intense scrutiny by the Council of ICAO which has developed PNR Data Guidelines that have been transmitted to Contracting States for their comments[17] This exercise was carried out on the understanding that, in the present context of the compelling need for the enhancement of aviation security, the global aviation community has shown an increased interest[18] in adding the PNR data as a security measure in addition to the already existing Advanced Passenger Information (API)[19] and the Machine Readable Travel Document (MRTD), which, although primarily are facilitation tools, greatly assist States authorities in ensuring border security.

One of the issues that emerge from PNR data collection is extraterritoriality and the question as to whether at law a State can require information held by other States relating to flights that originate and end in the latter States. An example is Canada, which may be required by the US to divulge information pertaining to passengers on domestic flights operating within the territorial limits of Canada but over-fly United States' territory for reasons of expediency and fuel efficiency. While there is no room for doubt that usually, requirements for safety and security of a State are based on sound legal justification with a view to protecting A State's integrity and internal security, a requirement for information by a particular State of those that do not enter the territory of that State might open itself to question, as to whether such would impinge upon another sovereign State's right to privacy[20] and dignity.

A Recommended Practice for inclusion in Annex 9 to the Chicago Convention (Facilitation) was adopted by the ICAO Council in March 2005. This Recommended Practice, which supplements an already existing Recommended

---

[16] Crossing the Line, *Airline Business*, August 2005, at 9.

[17] Attachment to State Letter EC 6/2-05/70, Passenger Name Record (PNR) data, 9 June 2005.

[18] The advantage of collection by States of PNR Data was first discussed by the global aviation community at the 12th Session of the ICAO Facilitation Division that was held in Cairo, Egypt from 22 March to 1 April 2004. Consequently, the Division adopted Recommendation B/5, that reads as follows:

> It is recommended that ICAO develop guidance material for those States that may require access to Passenger Name Record (PNR) data to supplement identification data received through an API system, including guidelines for distribution, use and storage of data and a composite list of data elements [that] may be transferred between the operator and the receiving State.

Pursuant to this recommendation, In June 2004, the Air Transport Committee of the ICAO Council requested the Secretary General to establish a Secretariat Study Group to develop Guidelines on PNR data transfer. The Council, in endorsing Recommendation B/5, directed that these Guidelines were to be submitted early in 2005.

[19] See Abeyratne (2002a), pp. 631–650. Also Abeyratne (2001), pp. 153–162, and also by Abeyratne (2003), pp. 297–311.

[20] See Abeyratne (2001).

Practice, provides that Contracting States requiring Passenger Name Record (PNR) access should conform their data requirements and their handling of such data to guidelines developed by ICAO. It is worthy of note that Article 13 of the Chicago Convention provides that the laws and regulations of a Contracting State as to the admission to or departure from its territory of passengers, crew or cargo of aircraft, such as regulations relating to entry, clearance, immigration, passports, customs, and quarantine shall be complied with, by or on behalf of such passengers, crew or cargo upon entrance into or departure from, or while within the territory of that State. This provision gives a State the discretion to specify the information it requires relating to persons wishing to gain entry into its territory. Accordingly, a State may require aircraft operators operating flights to, from or in transit through airports within its territory to provide its public authorities, upon request, with information on passengers such as PNR data.

The philosophy underlying the importance of PNR data and their efficient use by States for enhanced expediency in border crossing by persons is embodied in, the General Principles set out in Chapter 1 of Annex 9 which require Contracting States to take necessary measures to ensure that: the time required for the accomplishment of border controls in respect of persons is kept to the minimum[21]; the application of administrative and control requirements causes minimum inconvenience; exchange of relevant information between Contracting States, operators and airports is fostered and promoted to the greatest extent possible; and, optimal levels of security, and compliance with the law, are attained.

Contracting States are also required to develop effective information technology to increase the efficiency and effectiveness of their procedures at airports[22]

6.1.3 Definition and Application of PNR

The air transport industry regards a Passenger *Name Record* (PNR), as a, generic term applicable to records created by aircraft operators or their authorized agents for each journey booked by or on behalf of any passenger. The data is used by operators for their own commercial and operational purposes in providing air

[21] There is an abiding symbiosis between security and facilitation in the field of air transport. While security is of paramount interest to the global aviation community, it must not unduly disrupt or in any adversely affect the expediency of air transport. To this end, Recommended Practice 2.2 of Annex 9—Facilitation—to the Chicago Convention suggests that Each Contracting State should whenever possible arrange for security controls and procedures to cause a minimum of interference with, or delay to the activities of civil aviation provided the effectiveness of these controls and procedures is not compromised. See McMunn (1996) at 7.

[22] It must be noted that Annex 9 specifies that the provisions of the Annex shall not preclude the application of national legislation with regard to aviation security measures or other necessary controls.

transportation services.[23] The definition applicable in the United States identifies a PNR as a repository of information that air carriers would need to make available upon request under existing regulations and refers to reservation information contained in a carrier's electronic computer reservation system[24]

The above definitions and identifiers go to show that a PNR is developed and constructed from data that has been provided by or on behalf of the passenger concerning all the flight segments of a journey.[25] This data may be added to by the operator or his authorized agent, for example, changes to requested seating, special meals, additional services requested, *etc*. PNR data could be obtained in many ways. For example, information captured through reservations created by international sales organizations (global distribution systems "GDS" or computer reservation systems "CRS") with pertinent details of the PNR could be transmitted to the operating carrier(s). When reservations are made directly by the aircraft operator and the complete PNR is stored within the operator's automated reservations systems, the information therein could be a useful repository of PNR data. Information contained in records of some operators who may hold sub-sets of the PNR data within their own automated departure control systems (DCS), for their information or for onward transmittal to contracted ground handling service providers, calculated to support airport check-in functions would be another way in which PNR data could be provided. However, it must be noted that in each case, operators (or their authorized agents) will have access to, and be able to amend only that data that has been provided to their system(s). An important consideration in this regard is that some DCS systems are programmed such that details emerging from check-in (i.e. seat and/or baggage information) can be overlaid into the existing PNR for each passenger. However, that capability is limited—covering less than 50 % of operating systems today.

The time element, with regard to the capture and relevance of PNR data, is relevant to the use of such data. For instance, Data could be entered into a reservation system many days or weeks in advance of a flight. This could extend to as long as 345 days in advance of departure. Under such circumstances, both the provider and the receiver of PNR data must bear in mind that Information in reservation systems is dynamic and may change continuously from the time when the flight is open for booking. On the other hand, passenger and flight information in the DCS, becomes available only from the time the flight is "open" for check-in

[23] The Industry Standards related to PNR creation are detailed in IATA's *Passenger Services Conference Resolutions* and in the ATA/IATA *Reservations Interline Message Procedures (AIRIMP) Manual.*

[24] Passenger Name Record Information Required for Passengers on Flight in Foreign Air Transportation to or from the United States of 2001, 66 *Fed. Reg.* 67482 (2002).

[25] There are two possible methods of PNR data transfer currently available: (a) the "pull" method, under which the public authorities from the State requiring the data can reach into the aircraft operator's system and extract ("pull") a copy of the required data into their database; and (b) the "push" method, under which aircraft operators transmit ("push") the required PNR data elements into the database of the authority requesting them.

(up to 48 h prior to departure). In such an instance, departure control information for a flight will be finalized only upon flight closure, and may remain available 12–24 h after arrival of a flight at its final destination.

In the case of aircraft operators specializing in charter air services, who often do not hold PNR data in an electronic form, but still use a DCS which will only enable them to have a limited PNR record after the flight has closed, they would still be required to provide any captured data to States requesting it regardless of the process by which they receive PNR data. States could also require supplemental or "requested service" information which may be contained in the PNR, such as information relating to special dietary and medical requirements, "unaccompanied minor" information, requests for assistance etc.

Operators should take particular care in refraining from incorporating in PNR data any information that is not essential to facilitate the passenger's travel. Such information would include, but not be necessarily restricted to details of the passenger's racial or ethnic origin, political opinions, religious or political beliefs, trade-union membership, marital status or data relating to a person's sexual orientation. The ICAO guidelines make specific mention of the fact that Contracting States should not require aircraft operators to collect such data in their PNRs.

The above notwithstanding, any information which would legitimately facilitate the carriage of the passenger, such as details of meal preferences and health issues as well as free text and general remarks, could comprise the PNR. Sensitive data contained in the PNR and is submitted in compliance with a regulation of a State should not be used as the primary source for assessment of risk that the passenger might present to the State concerned.

6.1.4 The Importance of PNR Data to States

From a regulatory perspective, the two main areas to which PNR data make a contribution are expedition of customs and immigration processing at airports; and facilitation of passenger traffic and the safeguard of the legitimate rights of the passenger. The Chicago Convention provides a sound basis for States to require PNR data in the current context. The Convention, in Article 22, recognizes the importance of facilitating the passage of a person through borders by requiring each contracting State to adopt all practicable measures, through the issuance of special regulations or otherwise, to facilitate and expedite navigation by aircraft between the territories of contracting States, and to prevent unnecessary delays to aircraft, crews, passengers and cargo, especially the administration of the laws relating to immigration, quarantine, customs and clearance.

The main reason for States to require the advance submission of PNR data is that such data could prove to be a valuable tool in ensuring aviation security. PNR data are critically important for the threat assessment value that can be derived from the analysis of such data, not only in possible instances of unlawful interference with civil aviation but also in relation to the fight against terrorism. This critical value of

PNR data has prompted some States to enact legislation or develop draft legislation for approval by their Legislatures requiring that aircraft operators provide their public authorities with PNR data.

PNR data primarily enable States, through the identification of potentially high-risk passengers through PNR data analysis, to improve aviation security; enhance national and border security; prevent and combat terrorist acts and related crimes and other serious crimes that are transnational in nature, including organized crime; and to enforce warrants and prevent flight from custody for such crimes. Such data could also protect the vital interests of passengers and the general public, including their health.

States are aware that, if the guidelines are implemented in a uniform manner, would provide a global framework enabling all States to benefit from the value-added analysis of PNR data for shared security/safety purposes. Air carriers would also benefit from having to comply with only one set of common requirements for PNR data transfer. As for the consumer of air transport, all passengers would o benefit from basic protection afforded to them by the exchange of PNR data between air carriers and State authorities.

The above notwithstanding, there are certain fundamental obligations that the State receiving the data has to fulfill. Firstly, States should require PNR data only of those passengers on flights that are scheduled to enter, depart or transit through airports situated in their territories. Secondly, a State obtaining PNR information should, as a minimum limit the use of data to the purpose for which it collects it. States must restrict access to such data, ensure that the data is adequately protected, and limit the period of data storage, consistent with the purposes for which data is transferred. States must also ensure that individuals are able to request disclosure of the data that is held on them, consistent with the guidelines, in order to request corrections or notations, if necessary. More importantly, they must ensure that individuals aggrieved by the PNR data collection and usage process have an opportunity for redress.

The responsibility of ensuring that their public authorities have the appropriate legal authority to process PNR data requested from aircraft operators, in a manner that observes the guidelines, devolves entirely upon the States. They have been requested by ICAO to forward the full texts of legislation pertaining to PNR data dissemination and use to ICAO for online dissemination to other States, for information. The State concerned will be responsible for responding to any queries arising from such legislation.

6.1.5 Advantages of Unified Guidelines

Through the PNR Data Guidelines ICAO has introduced uniform measures for PNR data transfer and the subsequent handling of that data by the States concerned. The guidelines are both durable and easy to follow, making them cost effective for the parties concerned. They would ensure accuracy of information, while at the same time protecting the data subject against encroachment of his privacy. The Guidelines call for completeness of data and the need for timely submissions and effective collection of data. They also ensure that data management will be efficient and efficacious. From a practical perspective, the guidelines also provide useful directions assisting States in designing data requirements and procedures, in order to minimize technical difficulties that might prove too onerous and may impair the implementation of the uniform measures suggested. The Guidelines also contain detailed instructions with a view to assisting both air carriers and States on PNR data transfer from an operator's system to a State and the management of the data including arrangements for storage and protection.

States are enabled, by the guidelines, to design systems and establish arrangements that are compatible with the guidelines while not impairing their ability to implement their laws and enforce them. The guidelines do not interfere with the preservation of national security and public safety of a State. Arguably, one of the most important features of the unified PNR data guidelines is that, by their very nature, they would effectively obviate the complexities that aircraft operators could face with regard to legal, technical and financial issues if they were to be required to respond to multiple, unilaterally imposed or bilaterally agreed PNR data transfer requirements that differ substantially from one another.

States also have the responsibility of enacting explicit legal provisions concerning data transfer. Such legislation should clearly elaborate on the reasons for requiring PNR data, or provide explanatory material accompanying such laws or regulations, as appropriate. Since an aircraft operator is obliged to comply with the laws of both the State from which it transports passengers (State of departure) and the State to which these passengers are transported (destination State), when a destination State legislates with regard to its PNR data transfer requirements, it should do so cognizant of the fact that *existing* laws of other States may affect operators' ability to comply with these requirements. Therefore, where there could be an inconsistency between two legal regimes of the departure State and the destination State, or where a conflict arises between any two States, or where an operator advises of a conflict, The ICAO guidelines suggest that the States involved should consult each other to determine what might be done to enable affected operators to continue to operate within the bounds of the laws in both States.

6.1.6 Extra Territoriality

Strictly interpreted, extra-territoriality at international law means the attempt of one State to apply its laws outside its territory[26] and there is a general presumption

[26] Shaw (2003) at pp. 611–612.

against the application of extra-territoriality.[27] In the 1979 case of *Mannington Mills* v. *Congoleum Corporation*[28] the United States Supreme Court extended the concept of extra territoriality by introducing a test of balance that ensured consideration by one State for the interests of another State.

The above principle of extra-territoriality might not sit comfortably in the instance of a State requiring PNR data from a flight over-flying its territory as there is no *stricto sensu* application of a requirement in a foreign territory. The most fundamental principle of public international law, that of State sovereignty, is embodied in Article 1 of the Chicago, thus importing the principle into the tenets of air law. This Article provides that Contracting States recognize that every State has complete and exclusive sovereignty over the air space above its territory. The territory of a State, for the purposes of the Convention, cover the land areas and territorial waters adjacent to and under the sovereign, suzerainty, protection and mandate of the State concerned.[29] Arguably, these provisions would give the United States the right *in limine* to prescribe requirements on aircraft flying over its territory. Article 12 of the Chicago Convention provides, *inter alia*, that each contracting State undertakes to adopt measures to insure that every aircraft flying over or manoeuvring within its territory and that every aircraft carrying its nationality mark, wherever that aircraft may be, shall comply with the rules and regulations relating to the flight and manoeuvre of aircraft there in force. This rule can apply to a foreign carrier who is over-flying the territory of any State having a regulation that certain data pertaining to a flight that over-flies its territory has to be submitted to that State. Also important is Article 9 of the Convention, which allows a Contracting State to restrict or prohibit an aircraft from flying over its territory for reasons of military necessity or public safety. The provision goes on to say that each contracting State could also reserve the right, in exceptional circumstances or during a period of emergency, or in the interest of public safety and with immediate effect, temporarily to restrict or prohibit flying over the whole or part of its territory, provided such action would apply without distinction of nationality to aircraft of all States.[30]

At the 28th Session of the International Law Association held in Madrid in 1913, the meeting drew up text which stated that it was the right of every State to enact prohibitions, restrictions and regulations as it may think proper in regard to passage of aircraft through the airspace above its territory and territorial waters.[31] However,

[27] *Holmes* v. *Bangladesh Biman Corporation* [1989] 1 AC 1112 at 1126. Also, *Air India* v. *Wiggins* [1980] 1 WLR 815 at 819. In the 1991 case of *EEOC* v. *Arabian American Oil Company and ARAMCO Services* 113 L E 2d 274, the US Supreme Court held that the practice of extra territoriality by one State against the other cannot in any way be justified under the principles of public international law.

[28] 595 F.2d 1287; 66 ILR at 487. See also *Timberlane Lumber Company* v. *Bank of America*, 549 F 2d 597 (1976); 66 ILR at 270.

[29] Chicago Convention, *supra*, Article 2.

[30] *Id.* Article 9 b).

[31] International Law Association, 28th Report, Madrid, 1913, 533–545 at 540.

the text contained a caveat that such restrictions should be subject to the rights of subjacent States and the liberty of passage of aircraft of every nation.[32] The balance advocated at the Madrid meeting of the ILA goes to show that even as early as the beginning of the last century, the thinking was that a State ought to allow other States free passage for their aircraft through the airspace above its territory. There is no doubt that the same position prevails even now, particularly through the currently applicable International Air Services Transit Agreement (IASTA) which was concluded at the same time as the Chicago Convention in December 1944 and has been ratified by many ICAO Contracting States. IASTA allows aircraft of foreign States freedom of peaceful transit (over the airspace of a State) and freedom of making non-traffic (non-revenue) stops for such purposes as refuelling and repair. It has been acknowledged that without these two freedoms, the air transport industry could not survive[33]

The above discussion brings one to the inexorable conclusion that there are two major issues at stake. The first is whether the OPNR is an acceptable tool which helps in enhancing facilitation and security measures in air transport. The answer to this question, as provided by the 12th ICAO Facilitation Division in March/April 2004 and subsequently by the ICAO Council[34] is a resounding "yes". This affirmation brings to bear the need to consider whether the PNR should be used strictly as intended, firstly to facilitate customs and immigration procedures regarding persons and secondly to advise States in advance of persons on board an aircraft approaching their territory for purposes of landing there, enabling States to determine appropriate security clearance measures. The security angle of the PNR brings one to the second issue, as to whether a State can use information contained in the PNR to disallow the right of passage to an aircraft flying over its territory, thereby denying that aircraft a fundamental right acknowledged by States through IASTA.

The second issue raises the question of extra territoriality, which can be answered by invoking Articles 9 and 12 of the Chicago Convention, as earlier discussed. These provisions clearly give a State the right to prohibit an aircraft from over-flying its territory if it believes that such over-flying could be a security hazard. The final issue would be to determine the extent to which a State could exercise its right without touching the sensitivities and dignity of a State in an instance where an aircraft plying domestic services within two points in its territory but passes through the airspace of the prohibiting State is disallowed from using the right of passage.

The entire issue of diversion of an aircraft which is exercising its fundamental right of passage, and the justification of a State for disallowing that aircraft from using that fundamental right hinges on the circumstances prevailing at the time. As was mentioned earlier, this is no legal issue as the question of extra-territoriality does not arise with regard to action taken by a State within its territory. The

[32] Madrid Report, *Id*, at 538.

[33] Honig (1956) at 29.

[34] *Ibid.*

fundamental postulate in the debate is that sovereignty should no longer mean the mere exercise by one State of rights over its territory but should also mean the right of that State to ensure the safety and security of its citizens as well as the integrity of the State.

Public international law is increasingly becoming different from what it was a few decades ago. It can be said with some justification that international law is the thread which runs through the fabric of international politics and provides the latter with its abiding moral and ethical flavour. Without principles and practices of international law, foreign policy would be rendered destitute of its sense of cooperation and become dependent on a nation's self interest. As President Woodrow Wilson once claimed:

> It is a very perilous thing to determine the foreign policy of a nation in the terms of material interests ... we dare not turn from the principle that morality and not expediency is the thing that must guide us, and that we will never condone equity because it is convenient to do so.[35]

This statement, made in 1950, has great relevance today, when continued progress is being made in technological and economic development and policy decisions of States have far reaching consequences on a trans-boundary basis. Nation States are becoming more interdependent, making decisions made by a particular State in its own interest have a significant negative impact on the interests of other States. Therefore ethics in foreign policy has largely become a construct which combines cultural, psychological and ideological value structures. Within this somewhat complex web of interests, decisions have to be made, which, as recent events in history have shown, require a certain spontaneity from the international community. For example, when Iraq invaded Kuwait in 1990, the members of the United Nations chose economic sanctions against Iraq, claiming that war was the last resort to be embarked upon against Iraq if economic sanctions did not prove to have any effect. In hindsight, one could argue one way or another, firstly, as did the United States, that the use of force bore quick results and, on the hand, as did many officials in Paris, Moscow, Ottawa and Washington, that the decision to wage war against Iraq was too precipitous as not enough time had been given to economic sanctions to compel Iraq to retreat from Kuwait. The precipitous but quick action taken in going to war with Iraq might be justified by some with the analogy of Britain appeasing Hitler in the 1930s without adopting a more aggressive and perhaps belligerent attitude toward German atrocities. This action, which was later labeled as folly by most political scientists, was applauded and endorsed at that time in the British Parliament. In the absence of extra territoriality the only balancing factor in favor of State which orders the diversion of an aircraft overflying its territory, on the basis that persons therein are unacceptable is to have sound justification for doing so in the interests of security and safety.

[35] Quoted in Morganthau and Thompson (1950) at p. 24.

6.1.7 Public Key Directory

Aviation has reached the stage where quantum physics not only assists in the aeronautical aspects of air transport but also contributes to the day to day activities involving passenger clearance, immigration and customs. A brand new technique known as quantum cryptography is on the way, calculated to eliminate the terrifying vulnerabilities that arise in the way digitally stored data are exposed to fraudulent use. This new technique uses polarized photons instead of electronic signals to transmit information along cables. Photons are tiny particles of light that are so sensitive that when intercepted, they immediately become corrupted. This renders the message unintelligible and alerts both the sender and recipient to the fraudulent or spying attempt. The public key directory—designed and proposed to be used by customs and immigration authorities who check biometric details in an electronic passport, is based on cryptography—and is already a viable tool being actively considered by the aviation community as a fail-safe method for ensuring the accuracy and integrity of passport information. This article examines the technical and legal consequences that might flow from the use of the public key directory.

In order to assure inspecting authorities (receiving States) that they would know when the authenticity and integrity of the biometric data stored in the MRTD, which they inspect, are compromised and tampered with, the Public Key Infrastructure (PKI) scheme was developed by the TAG/MRTD, which has been pioneering work on the MRTD for over a decade.[36] The scheme is not calculated to prescribe global implementation of public key encryption, but rather acts as a facilitator enabling States to make choices in areas such as active or passive authentication, anti skimming and access control and automated border crossing, among other facilitative methods. The establishment of a public key directory, through means of public key cryptology and in a PKI environment, is consistent with ICAO's ultimate aim and vision for the application of biometric technology on the fundamental postulate that there must be a primary interoperable form of biometric technology for use at border control with facilities for verification, as well as by carriers and the issuers of documents. This initial premise is inevitably followed by the assumption that biometric technologies used by document issuers must have certain specifications, particularly for purposes of identification, verification and the creation of watch lists. It is also ICAO's vision that States, to the extent possible, are protected against changing infrastructure and changing

---

[36] ICAO's terms of reference in the development of specifications for machine readable passports stem from the Chicago Convention which provides for ICAO's adoption of international Standards and Recommended Practices dealing, *inter alia,* with customs and immigration procedures. Chicago Convention, *Supra*, Article 37(j). It is interesting that, although passports apply to other modes of international travel as well, ICAO has been singly recognized as the appropriate body to adopt specifications for MRTDs. This alone speaks for the uniqueness of ICAO's facilitation programme. See Machine Readable Travel Documents, *ICAO Doc 9303/3* Third Edition 2005, 1-1 to 1-3.

suppliers, and that a technology, once put in place, must be operable or at least retrievable for a period of 10 years.

The Public Key Directory is a central repository for all public keys that are established individually by States. A key is a string of characters which is used to encrypt or decrypt critical information in a document. Therefore the PKI system ensures that digital signatures assigned to data (and not the data itself) in a MRTD are encrypted or decrypted using both a private key—which is used by the passport issuing authority to encrypt the digital signature—and a public key—to be used by the party reading the document to decrypt the signature. Both the private key and the public key play critical roles in the process of encryption and decryption, which is the essence of the public key directory. It is integral to the programme to have an efficient and commonly accepted means of sharing and updating the public keys in effect for all non-expired passports in existence for all participating countries at a given time. Each participating State will therefore install its own secure facilities to generate key pairs. In each case the private key, used to encrypt digital signatures, will be held secret by the State. The public key, on the other hand, can be released for circulation in the public domain. The reading authority at the point of entry would use the appropriate public key to decrypt the information in order to verify whether the data in the MRTD has been altered in any way.

Public key encryption is purely a mathematical process designed to scramble and unscramble messages using two keys (the public key and the private key) and numerical data which contain information the process scrambles the contents of a message. The keys are shared between the scrambler and the un-scrambler. When translated to the e-passport the process works in the following way. The State which issues the passport encrypts information that is placed in the passport using its private key. The State which examines the passport (on arrival of the passenger) obtains the issuing State's public key and uses it to decrypt the information in the passport.

Contrary to popular belief, the PKD is neither a database of e-passports nor a repository of passport information. It is also not a look-out list nor is it a list of persons. Above all, it is not a large database as it remains a database only of public keys. Public keys do not carry personal information but are decoders of information that have been encrypted. The encryption process entitles a reading State to decode the encrypted digital signature on the mandatory passport data which cannot readily be deciphered. Other mandatory data in the machine readable zone of the passport, such as the facial image (photograph) of the passport holder, which is readily visible, do not fall within the process of decryption.

Public keys contain information that can and should be released into the public domain in order to provide for a globally interoperable system that authenticates the contents of integrated circuit chips in passports. There is thus no security issue involved in any potential user's access to public keys, and distribution via the Internet is planned. However, access to the web site will effectively be limited to the users of the system, and specialized system protocols will be required in such transactions. The transmission of key certificates from e-passport issuing States to ICAO, however, will require protection to ensure that bogus keys are not inserted into the system. One of the requirements to be placed on the successful contractor is to demonstrate the capability and competence to build a system with the necessary security measures. The rules and regulations will require adherence to procedures necessary to implement these measures.

The operation of the PKD and the transactions between the PKD and the users will be relatively simple. The PKD will function as a sort of message board, containing "messages" (public key lists) posted by ICAO after ICAO has verified them as genuine. Contributing administrations will be required to send their key lists to ICAO for posting well in advance of their effective date. Accessing the PKD to verify individual passports is not contemplated. Entities using the system will periodically download the whole directory to update the lists in their own systems and use these lists to verify individual passports. This arrangement, together with the redundancy built into the system, is expected to mitigate the risks associated with any system failure. However, the expected level of system performance will be stipulated in the contract with the PKD operator.

6.1.8 ICAO's Role Regarding the Public Key Directory

In May 2003, the ICAO Council considered work[37] conducted by its Air Transport Committee[38] and the approval by the Committee of a "Blueprint" for incorporating biometric identification in passports and other MRTDs for the purpose of ascertaining and verifying identity. The Committee had taken into consideration a rigorous and sustained 6-year study of technology options for introducing the capability to link a document positively to the rightful holder and to verify the authenticity of the document. The study itself had resulted in a four-part recommendation of the TAG/MRTD. The Blueprint specifies that the primary biometric to be used worldwide will be the face and that the compressed image of the face will be stored, along with the data from the machine readable zone of the passport, in a contact-less Integrated circuit chip. The validity of the data in the chip has to be ensured and, in order to give the reader that assurance, the data in the chip, as well as the facial image, will be digitally "signed". The Committee was apprised that a specially tailored public key infrastructure (PKI) scheme had been specified in order to protect the signed data from counterfeiting or unauthorized alteration by ensuring that any overwriting of data on the chip does not go undetected. The basic

[37] See Establishment of A Public Key Directory (PKD), C-WP/12384, 19/11/04 Revised, 2/2/05, presented to the Council by the Secretary General.

[38] Article 54 d) of the Chicago Convention provides that it shall be a mandatory function of the ICAO Council to appoint and define the duties of an Air Transport Committee, which shall be chosen from among the representatives of the members of the Council and which shall be responsible to it. The Committee is therefore a subordinate body of the Council which largely considers work conducted by the Secretariat in the field of air transport prior to forwarding such work to the Council for final consideration.

premise underlying the study and the recommendation of the TAG/MRTD was that, in the absence of any PKI, the trustworthiness of data in a chip, and hence the global interoperability of the e-passport, cannot be assured.

Based on the above, the TAG-MRTD recommended to the Air Transport Committee that ICAO be the designated Organization to oversee the PKD. This recommendation was based on an interpretation provided to the Council, by the TAG/MRTD, that ICAO had a clear mandate under the Chicago Convention[39] to adopt standards dealing with customs and immigration procedures and to provide for compliance with, *inter alia*, passport laws and regulations, taking into consideration the Organization's sustained and long track record as the developer of MRTD standards, and its international stature as a UN agency. Furthermore, it was claimed that an oversight role in the PKD is deemed particularly appropriate for ICAO due to its substantial interest in document security as an essential component of the aviation security and facilitation programmes elaborated in Annexes 9 and 17. It was the view of the TAG/MRTD that a politically neutral site overseen by ICAO and funded by the e-passport issuing States would provide a trusted resource from which government inspection agencies, airlines, and other entities in all member States might download all public keys in circulation for the purpose of verifying the authenticity of passports as documents of identity, with full confidence that the keys were genuine. It was further contended that, in this regard, an important function of ICAO would be to receive the public keys sent in by issuing States by diplomatic means and perform a technical "due diligence" procedure to verify their authenticity before uploading them to the data base.

The Council was also advised that, in playing an oversight role, ICAO would not be authenticating individual passports or their content. Authentication of a passport remains the function and responsibility of the government agency or aircraft operator examining it.

The envisioned scheme involved the oversight of a central public key directory by ICAO, which was deemed essential for a cooperative, interoperable regime for passport security that will be accessible by all member States. Furthermore, it was contended that a central PKD would be accessible by aircraft operators, who are on the "front lines" as the first to examine the passports of travellers. As a deterrent to the fraudulent alteration or counterfeiting of passports, or the use of stolen passports by imposters to gain access to aircraft, PKI is potentially a most effective anti-terrorism and aviation security measure.

In terms of organizational matters, the proposal for ICAO's oversight role involves two components, *i.e.* maintaining and administering the PKD, both of which would be funded by the fees collected from States issuing e-passports and

[39] Chicago Convention, *Supra*, Articles 13, 23 and 37j. Although Article 37 (j) is directly in point, it is somewhat questionable as to whether Articles 13 and 33 bestow upon ICAO any special mandate to address the need to develop machine readable travel documents and technology related thereto. Article 13 merely states that the laws of States with regard to various aspects of entry and departure should be complied with. Article 23 provides that each Contracting State undertakes, *inter alia*, to establish customs and immigration procedures.

uploading their public keys. As the supervisory authority, ICAO would act on behalf of e-passport issuing States; be responsible for establishment of the PKD system, appointment of the PKD operator; and providing oversight of the system operation, financial matters and policies as decided or approved by the Council. In this regard ICAO's functions would include: receipt of new key certificates from e-passport issuing States, verification of their authenticity, and formal acceptance and uploading to the PKD; liaison with all country contributors and users, and with contractor operational staff, in administrative and operational matters such as new country sign-up and collection of fees; calculation of proposed fee schedules; distribution of revenue to the PKD operator and relevant ICAO units, and development of the regulations and procedures manuals; and periodic reporting to the Council on all of the above matters.

Separately, the contractor chosen or the PKD operator would have the responsibility to design, install and operate the PKD system in accordance with the contractual agreement made with ICAO. The PKD operator would provide data base services not only to contributing States but also to States and other entities using the keys to verify e-passports presented to them.

As for financial management and outlay, the proposal for ICAO involvement in the PKD as outlined above will be based and carried out on the principles of cost-recovery, whereby fees from the States that produce e-passports and send their public keys to ICAO for uploading to the Directory will support administrative and other expenses incurred. At the time of writing, ICAO had already received an advance contribution from one member State and had received letters of intent and requests for invoices from several others. The cost-income formula will be calculated on a schedule of country sign-up fees and annual user fees based on the total estimated cost of a 5-year operation and the number of countries expected to sign up in each year. A special account would be set up in ICAO for the receipt and distribution of contributions and assessments.

Essentially, there will be three main protagonists in the PKD process. Firstly there would be the "group" of e-passport issuing States, comprising a group that would be constituted as a legal body with its own governance structure. This body would be the owner of the PKD and determine independently its mode of operations—including membership, and financial operations. Secondly, there would be ICAO, duly authorized by the Council to act as an agent of the Group, with defined responsibility for providing advice to the Group and executing the work of the group based on agreed terms and conditions. It is envisioned that such an arrangement would cover ICAO against any financial liability arising either from contracting with a third party or a shortfall in the finances of the group. The Group, as a whole, should underwrite the financing of the activities undertaken by ICAO. The last person in the triangle is the contractor, who is appointed either by the group or by ICAO on authority granted by the Group. ICAO's responsibility for the management of the contractor's activity would be defined by the Group.

6.1.9 Legal Liability of ICAO

As stated above, ICAO's responsibility with regard to oversight of the PKD process would involve two areas, i.e. maintenance and administration. A host of functions are attached to these two supervisory functions, such as acting on behalf of e-passport issuing States, and being responsible for establishment of the PKD system, appointment of the PKD operator and providing oversight of the system operation, financial matters and policies as decided or approved by the Council. The first question that arises in regard to ICAO's legal status is whether the Organization has the legal capacity to perform the abovementioned functions and be responsible for them. In other words, if ICAO's legal liability were to be questioned in a court of law in any jurisdiction of an ICAO member State, would the courts recognize ICAO as having the legal capacity to assume these functions and be legally accountable for them?

6.2 Security of Aircraft and Passengers

Aviation is an important global business and a significant driver of the global economy. It is vital, therefore, that stringent measures are taken to counter acts of unlawful interference with civil aviation. The *Convention on International Civil Aviation* signed at Chicago on 7 December 1944, states in its *Preamble* that whereas the development of civil aviation may help preserve friendship and understanding among the people of the world, yet, its abuse could become a threat to general security.

The genealogy of the term "*Terrorism*" lies in Latin terminology meaning "to cause to tremble" (*terrere*). Since the catastrophic events of 11 September 2012, we have seen stringent legal measures taken by the United States to attack terrorism, not just curb it. The famous phrase "war on terror" denotes pre-emptive and preventive strikes carried out through applicable provisions of legitimately adopted provisions of legislation. The earliest example is the *Air Transportation Safety and System Stabilization Act* (ATSAA) enacted by President Bush less than 2 months after the 9/11 attacks. Then, 2 months after the attacks, in November 2001, Congress passed the *Aviation and Transportation Security Act* (ATSA) with a view to improving security and closing the security loopholes which existed on that fateful day in September 2001. The legislation paved the way for a huge federal body called the Transportation Security Administration (TSA) which was established within the Department of Transportation. The Homeland Security Act of 2002 which followed effected a significant reorganization of the Federal Government.

Since the events of 11 September 2001, there have been several attempts against the security of aircraft in flight. These threats have ranged from shoe bombs to dirty bombs to explosives that can be assembled in flight with liquids, aerosols and gels.

In every instance the global community has reacted with pre emptive and preventive measures which prohibit any material on board which might seemingly endanger the safety of flight. Some jurisdictions have even gone to extremes in prohibiting human breast milk and prescriptive medications on board.

New and emerging threats to civil aviation are a constant cause for concern to the aviation community. Grave threats such as those posed by the carriage of dangerous pathogens on board, the use of cyber technology calculated to interfere with air navigation systems, and the misuse of man portable air defence systems are real and have to be addressed with vigour and regularity. ICAO has been addressing these threats for some time and continues to do so on a global basis.

It is a platitude to say that aviation security is a largely reactive process. It will be recalled that after the spate of hijackings in the late 1960s and 1970s, States rushed to install detectors with X-Ray capability at the entrance to the aircraft gate. Then, as the *displacement theory*[40] demonstrated, terrorists moved their attention towards attacking airports, which prompted States to install screening equipment at centralized points in the terminal itself. In similar vein, in the aftermath of the attempted bombing of an aircraft on 25 December 2009 by a person who is alleged to have carried explosives in his undergarments, some States began to look seriously into tightening airport security, particularly through a more stringent body scanning process. While the United States toughened screening measures on US bound flights, particularly with regard to passengers arriving from 14 targeted nations,[41] airports in the United Kingdom began the use of full body scanners at both Heathrow and Manchester airports.[42] In Canada, Rob Merrifield, Minister of State for Transport is reported to have stated that 44 scanners have been ordered to be used on passengers selected for secondary screening at Canadian airports. The machines, which can scan through clothing, will be installed in Vancouver, Calgary, Edmonton, Winnipeg, Toronto, Ottawa, Montreal and Halifax.[43] This measure is partly due to the fact that the Christmas day incident was later classified as having occurred due to a serious lapse in security.

---

[40] The Displacement Theory suggests that removing opportunity for crime or seeking to prevent a crime by changing the situation in which it occurs (see Situational Crime Prevention) does not actually prevent crime but merely moves it around. There are five main ways in which this theory suggests crime is moved around: crime can be moved from one location to another (geographical displacement); crime can be moved from one time to another (temporal displacement); crime can be directed away from one target to another (target displacement); one method of committing crime can be substituted for another (tactical displacement); and one kind of crime can be substituted for another (crime type displacement).

[41] Afghanistan, Algeria, Cuba, Iran, Iraq, Lebanon, Libya, Nigeria, Pakistan, Saudi Arabia, Somalia, Sudan, Syria and Yemen. See US Toughens Screening for US-Bound Flights, *Air Letter*, No. 16896, Monday 04 January 2010, at 1.

[42] UK Airports Commence Use of Full Body Scanners, *Air Letter*, No. 16918, Wednesday 03 February 2010 at 2. According to this report, scanning equipment were scheduled to be installed in Birmingham in late February 2010. *Ibid.*

[43] CBC News, January 5, 2010. See: http://www.cbc.ca/canada/story/2010/01/05/security-canada-us-airport.html#ixzz0eVT3wBNY.

In response to the attempted sabotage of Northwest Airlines Flight 253 on 25 December 2009,[44] ICAO used the AVSEC Point of Contact (PoC) Network to communicate information and recommendations to participating States, numbering 99 as of 31 May 2010. States were encouraged to conduct risk assessments and implement appropriate screening measures in light of the incident, and were reminded of the need for cooperation in all matters related to aviation security. The 21st meeting of the AVSEC Panel was held at ICAO Headquarters from 22 to 26 March 2010. The Panel considered the threat and risk environment in light of the attempted sabotage of 25 December 2009 and issued a number of recommendations. Provisions in Annex 17 to the Chicago Convention on Security were updated and strengthened, and are expected to become applicable in 2011, following formal consultation with Member States and approval by the Council.

6.2.1 Body Scanners

Full body scanners, costing about $250,000 each and claimed by some security experts as an effective tool in detecting hidden explosives, show the contours of the human body as well as body parts in some detail, prompting some to question the legality and ethical justification of their use. In the United States, passengers handpicked for a full-body scan can opt out of the screening, but if they do, they must submit to full-body pat-downs by an officer of the Transport Security Administration (TSA).[45] The technology was introduced a couple of years ago, but U.S. airports have been slow to install the machines, partly because of privacy concerns raised by some members of Congress and civil liberties groups.

It must be noted that in the United States, the Fourth Amendments states:

> The right of the people to be secure in their persons, houses, papers and effects, against unreasonable searches and seizures, shall not be violated, and no Warrants shall issue, but upon probable cause, supported by Oath or affirmation, and particularly describing the place to be searched, and the persons or things to be seized.[46]

The significance of this provision lies in the fact that the prohibition is against unreasonable searches, and that too by agents of the governments, the latter fact being borne out by a strong *cursus curiae* in the United States.[47] It can therefore be assumed that the Fourth Amendment may not be applicable in instances where scanning is carried out by airport security officers who are not government agents.[48] If, however, the scanning at the airport is conducted by officers of the government,

[44] For a discussion of this incident, See Abeyratne (2010), pp. 167–181.

[45] Rucker (2010) at 1.

[46] *US Constitution*, Article 1 Sec. 4 Clause 6.

[47] See Sweet (2008) at 45.

[48] *Ibid.*

by law, the consent of the passenger has to be obtained before such scanning is carried out.[49]

States which are installing full body scanners are fully aware that their use could bring to bear issues of privacy. However, it should be noted that this is just one more reactive step—to ensure that no person enters an aircraft with explosives hidden in his underwear—and the only known way to respond to this new threat is to use full body scanner. The question then arises as to whether the responsibility of the State toward its constituents and those using aircraft for transport from and to their territory, to prevent private acts of terrorism overrides the right of privacy of the individual. This article will address the balance between the two interests.

6.2.2 Privacy Rights of the Person

The Chicago Convention, which established the regulatory framework for international civil aviation, underscores the fundamental aim of States in the context of civil aviation to exchange privileges which friendly nations have a right to expect from each other. In his message to the Conference in Chicago, President Roosevelt said: "the Conference is a great attempt to build enduring institutions of peace, which cannot be endangered by petty considerations or weakened by groundless fears".[50]

The Chicago Convention embodies in its *Preamble* the need to create and preserve friendship and understanding among the nations and peoples of the world, and cautions Contracting States that the abuse of this friendship and understanding can become a threat to general security. Article 13 of the Convention provides that the laws and regulations of a Contracting State as to the admission to and departure from its territory of passengers, crew or cargo of aircraft, such as regulations relating to entry, clearance, immigration, passports, customs and quarantine shall be complied with by or on behalf of such passengers, crew or cargo upon entrance into or departure from, or while within the territory of that State. This provision ensures that a Contracting State has the right to prescribe its own internal laws with regard to passenger clearance and leaves room for a State to enact laws, rules and regulations to ensure the security of that State and its people at the airport. However, this absolute right is qualified so as to preclude unfettered and arbitrary power of a State, by Article 22 which makes each Contracting State agree to adopt all practicable measures, through the issuance of special regulations or otherwise, to facilitate and expedite navigation of aircraft between the countries.

The above notwithstanding, there are three rights of privacy relating to the display and storage and use of personal data:

---

[49] See *US* v. *Favela* 247 F.3d.838, 2001 and *U.S.* v. *Eustaquio* 198 R.3d 1068 (8th Cir.1999).

[50] Proceedings of the International Civil Aviation Conference, Chicago, Illinois, November 1–December 7 1944, The Department of State, Vol. 1 at p. 43.

1. The right of an individual to determine what information about oneself to share with others, and to control the disclosure of personal data;
2. The right of an individual to know what data is disclosed, and what data is collected and where such is stored when the data in question pertains to that individual; the right to dispute incomplete or inaccurate data; and
3. the right of people who have a legitimate right to know in order to maintain the health and safety of society and to monitor and evaluate the activities of government.[51]

It is incontrovertible that the data subject has a right to decide what information about oneself to share with others and more importantly, to know what data is collected about him. This right is balanced by the right of a society to collect data about individuals that belong to it so that the orderly running of government is ensured.

The data subject, like any other person, has an inherent right to his privacy.[52] The subject of privacy has been identified as an intriguing and emotive one.[53] The right to privacy is inherent in the right to liberty, and is the most comprehensive of rights and the right most valued by civilized man.[54] This right is susceptible to being eroded, as modern technology is capable of easily recording and storing dossiers on every man, woman and child in the world.[55] The data subject's right to privacy, when applied to the context of the full body scanner is brought into focus by Alan Westin who says:

> Privacy is the claim of individuals, groups or institutions to determine for themselves when, how, and to what extent information is communicated to others.[56]

The role played by technology in modern day commercial transactions has affected a large number of activities pertaining to human interaction. The emergence of the information superhighway and the concomitant evolution of automation have inevitably transformed the social and personal life styles and value systems of individuals, created unexpected business opportunities, reduced operating costs, accelerated transaction times, facilitated accessibility to communications, shortened distances, and removed bureaucratic formalities.[57] Progress notwithstanding, technology has bestowed on humanity its corollaries in the nature of automated mechanisms, devices, features, and procedures which intrude into personal lives of individuals. For instance, when a credit card is used, it is possible to track purchases, discovering numerous aspects about that particular individual,

---

[51] Hoffman (1980), p. 142.

[52] Abeyratne (2001), pp. 153–162. Abeyratne (2002b), pp. 83–115.

[53] Young (1978) at 1.

[54] Warren and Brandies (1890–1891) at 193.

[55] As far back as in 1973 it was claimed that ten reels, each containing 1,500 m of tape 2.5 cm wide, could store a 20 page dossier on every man, woman, and child in the world. See Jones (1973).

[56] Westin (1970) at 124.

[57] Orwell (1978).

including, food inclination, leisure activities, and consumer credit behaviour.[58] In similar vein, computer records of an air carrier's reservation system may give out details of the passenger's travel preferences, *inter alia*, seat selection, destination fondness, ticket purchasing dossier, lodging keenness, temporary address and telephone contacts, attendance at theatres and sport activities, and whether the passenger travels alone or with someone else.[59] In similar vein, does it follow that a full body scanning exercise would reveal imperfections of the human body which person would desire to keep private? This scheme of things may well give the outward perception of surveillance attributable to computer devices monitoring individuals' most intimate activities, preferences and physical attributes, leading to the formation of a genuine "traceable society".[60]

The main feature of this complex web of technological activity is that an enormous amount of personal information handled by such varied players from the public and private sector, may bring about concerns of possible "data leaks" in the system, a risk that could have drastic legal consequences affecting an individual's rights to privacy.

At the international level, privacy was first recognized as a fundamental freedom in the *Universal Declaration of Human Rights*.[61] Thereafter, several other human rights conventions followed the same trend, granting to individuals the fundamental right of privacy.[62] The pre-eminent concern of these international instruments was

[58] For a detailed analysis of the implications of credit cards with respect to the right of privacy see Nock (1993) at 43.

[59] The paramount importance of airline computer reservation system records is reflected in the world-renowned cases *Libyan Arab Jamahiriya* v. *United Kingdom* and *Libyan Arab Jamahiriya* v. *United States of America* regarding the PANAM 103 accident at Lockerbie, Scotland in 1988, where the International Court of Justice requested air carriers to submit to the Court the defendants' flight information and reservation details. See International Court of Justice. News Release 99/36, "Questions of Interpretation and Application of the 1971 Montreal Convention arising from the Aerial Incident at Lockerbie" (1 July 1999), online: http://www.icj-cij.org/icjwww/idocket/iluk/iluk2frame.html (date accessed: 14 July 2000). In a similar vein, Arthur R. Miller describes the significance of airline computer reservation system records when dealing with federal, state, local, and other types of investigations where these dossiers could provide valuable information. See also Miller (1971) at 42.

[60] See Scott (1995) at 307; Burnham (1983) at 20. *A contrario* to the argument supported in this thesis that the advancement of technology directly affects the intimacy of individuals. U.S. Circuit Judge Richard Posner favours the idea that other factors, such as urbanisation, income, and mobility development have particularly weakened the information control that, for instance, the government has over individuals: this denotes that individuals' privacy has increased. See Posner (1978) at 409.

[61] The text reads: "No one shall be subjected to arbitrary interference with his privacy, family, home or correspondence, nor to attacks upon his honor and reputation. Everyone has the right to the protection of the law against such interference or attacks". See *Universal Declaration of Human Rights*. GA Res. 217(III), 10 December 1948, Art. 12.

[62] See *International Covenant on Civil and Political Rights,* GA Res. 2200 (XXI), 16 December 1966, Art. 17; *American Declaration on the Rights and Duties of the Man* (1948), Art. 5; *American Convention on Human Rights,* 22 November 1969, San Jose, Costa Rica, Art. 11; *Convention for the Protection of Human Nations Convention on Migrant Workers*, A/RES/45/158, 25 February 1991, Art. 14; *United Nations Convention on Protection of the Child,* GA Res. 44/25, 12 December 1989, Art. 16.

to establish a necessary legal framework to protect the individual and his rights inherent to the enjoyment of a private life.

Privacy represents different things for different people.[63] The concept *per se* has evolved throughout the history of mankind, from the original non-intrusion approach, which defended an individual's property and physical body against unwanted invasions and intrusions, then manifesting in whom to associate with, later enlarging its scope to include privacy as the individual's decision-making right,[64] and culminating in the control over one's personal information.[65] Thus, the conceptual evolution of privacy is directly related to the technological advancement of each particular period in history.

The right of privacy, as enunciated by the United States Judge Thomas M. Cooley, was the right "to be let alone" as a part of a more general right to one's personality. This idea was given further impetus by two prominent young lawyers, Samuel D. Warren and Louis D. Brandeis,[66] in 1890.[67] Before this idea was introduced, the concept of privacy reflected primarily a somewhat physical property or life. The foundations of "information privacy", whereby the individuals would determine when, how, and to what extent information about themselves would be communicated to others, inextricably drawing the right of control of information about oneself,[68] is a cornerstone of privacy. With the development of computer capabilities to handle large amounts of data, privacy has been enlarged to include the collection, storage, use, and disclosure of personal information.[69] The notion of informational privacy protection, a typically American usage, has been particularly popular both in the United States and Europe, where the term "data protection" is used.[70]

---

[63] See Regan (1995) at 33; Freund (1971) at 182.

[64] In this case, the US Supreme Court acknowledged the right of women to have abortions based on the grounds that the federal government could not interfere within her "decisional privacy" sphere. See *Roe* v. *Wade*, 410 U.S. 113 (1973). See also Cate (1997) at 49. See also Zelermyer (1959) at 16.

[65] In a remarkable case concerning the legality of a national census scheduled by the authorities, the German Constitutional court connected the individual's liberty and the personal data processing of the intended census, to rule that if the individuals do not know for what purposes and who is collecting the data, that situation will eventually create an abdication of the individual's rights to the processor's command, "which cannot be tolerated in a democratic society". See Simitis (1995), pp. 447–448. See also Hoffer (2000) at 8.1.; Gavison (1980), p. 421.

[66] See Cooley (1888), as cited in Warren and Brandeis (1980) at 195.

[67] The definition of privacy as the "Right to be Alone" is often erroneously attributed to Warren and Brandeis. See Warren and Brandeis (1980). See Cooley (1888) as cited in Warren and Brandeis (1980) at 195. Additionally the concept of privacy as "the right to be let alone", and "the right most valued by civilized man": was embraced by US courts in the landmark dissenting opinion of Justice Louis D. Brandeis in *Olmsted* v. *United States*. See *Olmsted* v. *United States*, 277 U.S. 438, 478 (1928) [hereinafter *Olmstead*].

[68] See Westin (1967) at 368. For a similar conceptualisation of privacy, see Fried (1978) at 425.

[69] See Reidenberg (1995) at 498.

[70] The former Privacy Commissioner of British Columbia, Canada, has asserted that privacy was originally a "non-legal concept". See Flaherty (1991) at 833–834. The term "data protection" has been translated from the German word *Datenschutz*, referring to a set of policies seeking to regulate the collection, storage, use, and transfer of personal information. See Bennet (1992) at 13.

Self-determination in the right to protect one's privacy was first judicially embraced by the German Bundesverfassungsgericht in 1983. The US Supreme court followed this trend by adopting the principle of privacy self-determination in *DOJ* v. *Reporters Comm. for Freedom of the Press.*[71]

It must be borne in mind that privacy is not an absolute, unlimited right that operates and applies in isolation.[72] It is not an absolute right, applied unreservedly, to the exclusion of other rights. Hence there is frequently the necessity to balance privacy rights with other conflictive rights, such as the freedom of speech and the right to access information when examining individuals' rights *vis-à-vis* the interest of society.[73] This multiplicity of interests will prompt courts to adopt a balanced approach when adjudicating on a person's rights, particularly whose interests of a State are involved.

Since the data contained in equipment such as body scanners may be subject to trans-border storage, there is a compelling need to consider the introduction of uniform privacy laws in order that the interests of the data subject and the data seeker are protected. Although complete uniformity in privacy legislation may be a difficult objective to attain[74] (as has been the attempt to make other aspects of legislation uniform), it will be well worth the while of the international community to at least formulate international Standards and Recommend Practices (in the lines of the various ICAO Annexes) to serve as guidelines of State conduct. After all, as Collin Mellors pointed out:

> Under international agreements... privacy is now well established as a universal, natural, moral and human right. Article 12 of the Universal Declaration of Human Rights, Article 17 of the United Nations Covenant on Civil and Political Rights and Article 8 of the European Convention for the Protection of Human Rights and Fundamental Freedoms, all specify this basic right to privacy. Man everywhere has occasion to seek temporary "seclusion or withdrawal from society" and such arrangements cannot define the precise area of the right to privacy.[75]

It is such a definition that is now needed so that the two requirements of ensuring respect for information about individuals and their privacy on the one hand, and the encouragement of free and open dissemination of trans-border data flows on the other, are reconciled.

As for the use of information resulting in a full body scan, such information is purely biological and should be used only for purposes of identifying weapons or dangerous objects on the person with an explicit undertaking by the authorities concerned who use the information that it will not be used for any purpose other

---

[71] See *DOJ* v. *Reporters Comm. for Freedom of the Press*, 489 U.S. 749 AT 763 (1988).

[72] See Simmel (1971) at 71.

[73] See Halpin (1997) at 111. See also Foschio (1990) at 35. For a comprehensive study on the conflictive interest on privacy and the mass media and the Freedom of Speech, see Pember (1972) at 227; Prowda (1995) at 769. See also Montgomery Curtis (1992) at 2.

[74] Hoffman (1980) at 146.

[75] Mellors, *Governments and the Individual – Their Secrecy and His Privacy*, cited in, *A Look at Privacy*, Young (1978) at 94.

than for purposes of scanning. Before a process for the collection of such information is formally put into practice, legal issues pertaining to privacy, cultural sensitivity and ethical justification should be carefully thought out, and given foremost consideration.

In the provision of biometric data, the provider of the information and the receiver thereof are both under obligation to ensure that the data is not used for any purpose other than clearance of the owner of the information through customs barriers. This information may not later be used for commercial or other gain for instance for advertising purposes (such as using the physical profile of a prominent actor or actress whose biometric information originally given for customs clearance).[76]

In the body scanning process, there is an implicit link between ownership rights and privacy. Data protection legislation, including data privacy laws have been enacted by many countries throughout the world for two main reasons: protection of privacy; and ensuring of access by the owner to his information stored in a computer. Although the exact nature can vary from State to State, there is a common thread that weaves itself into the fabric of legislation in general, to ensure that: data is obtained by lawful means and processed in a fair manner; data is stored for the legitimate purpose intended and not used for any purpose incompatible with the original purpose; the collection of data is done in a reasonable manner and not excessively in order to store data over and above what is necessary; the accuracy of the data should be ensured; and the time of preservation of data is limited to the period during which such data is used.

The protection of human rights is the most significant and important task for a modern State, particularly since multi ethnic States are the norm in today's world. Globalization and increased migration across borders is gradually putting an end to the concept of the nation State, although resistance to reality can be still seen in instances where majority or dominant cultures impose their identity and interests on groups with whom they share a territory. In such instances, minorities frequently intensify their efforts to preserve and protect their identity, in order to avoid marginalization. Polarization between the opposite forces of assimilation on the one hand and protection of minority identity on the other inevitably causes increased intolerance and eventual armed ethnic conflict. In such a scenario, the first duty of governance is to ensure that the rights of a minority society are protected.

6.2.3 Security of the State

The foregoing discussion addressed the right of privacy of the individual which is paramount over most legal considerations. The only factor that would override this

[76] See *Gould Estate* v. *Stoddart Publishing Company* (1996) O.J. No. 3288 (Gen. Div).

would be the security of State. Inherent to the concept of security of State is State responsibility to its citizens and others who are in its territory. The fundamental issue in the context of State responsibility for the purposes of this article is to consider whether a State should be considered responsible for its own failure or non-feasance to prevent a private act of terrorism against civil aviation or whether the conduct of the State itself can be impugned by identifying a nexus between the perpetrator's conduct and the State. One view is that an agency paradigm, which may in some circumstances impute to a state reprehensibility on the ground that a principal–agent relationship between the State and the perpetrator existed, can obfuscate the issue and preclude one from conducting a meaningful legal study of the State's conduct.[77]

At the core of the principal–agent dilemma is the theory of complicity, which attributes liability to a State that was complicit in a private act. Hugo Grotius (1583–1645), founder of the modern natural law theory, first formulated this theory based on State responsibility that was not absolute. Grotius' theory was that although a State did not have absolute responsibility for a private offence, it could be considered complicit through the notion of *patienta* or *receptus*.[78] While the concept of *patienta* refers to a State's inability to prevent a wrongdoing, *receptus* pertains to the refusal to punish the offender.

The eighteenth century philosopher Emerich de Vattel was of similar view as Grotius, holding that responsibility could only be attributed to the State if a sovereign refuses to repair the evil done by its subjects or punish an offender or deliver him to justice whether by subjecting him to local justice or by extraditing him.[79] This view was to be followed and extended by the British jurist Blackstone a few years later who went on to say that a sovereign who failed to punish an offender could be considered as abetting the offence or of being an accomplice.[80]

A different view was put forward in an instance of adjudication involving a seminal instance where the Theory of Complicity and the responsibility of states for private acts of violence was tested in 1925. The case[81] involved the Mexico–United States General Claims Commission which considered the claim of the United States on behalf of the family of a United States national who was killed in a Mexican mining company where the deceased was working. The United States argued that the Mexican authorities had failed to exercise due care and diligence in apprehending and prosecuting the offender. The decision handed down by the Commission distinguished between complicity and the responsibility to punish and the Commission was of the view that Mexico could not be considered an accomplice in this case.

[77] Caron (1998) at 153–154 cited in Becker (2006a) at 155.

[78] Grotius and Scott (1646), pp. 523–526.

[79] De Vattel and Fenwick (1916), p. 72.

[80] Blackstone and Morrison (2001) at 68.

[81] *Laura M.B. Janes (USA)* v. *United Mexican States* (1925) 4 R Intl Arb Awards 82.

The Complicity Theory, particularly from a Vattellian and Blackstonian point of view is merely assumptive unless put to the test through a judicial process of extradition. In this Context it becomes relevant to address the issue through a discussion of the remedy.

The emergence of the Condonation Theory was almost concurrent with the *Jane* case[82] decided in 1925 which emerged through the opinions of scholars who belonged to a school of thought that believed that States became responsible for private acts of violence not through complicity as such but more so because their refusal or failure to bring offenders to justice, which was tantamount to ratification of the acts in question or their condonation.[83] The theory was based on the fact that it is not illogical or arbitrary to suggest that a State must be held liable for its failure to take appropriate steps to punish persons who cause injury or harm to others for the reason that such States can be considered guilty of condoning the criminal acts and therefore become responsible for them.[84] Another reason attributed by scholars in support of the theory is that during that time, arbitral tribunals were ordering States to award pecuniary damages to claimants harmed by private offenders, on the basis that the States were being considered responsible for the offences.[85]

The responsibility of governments in acting against offences committed by private individuals may sometimes involve condonation or ineptitude in taking effective action against terrorist acts, in particular with regard to the financing of terrorist acts. The United Nations General Assembly, on 9 December 1999, adopted the International Convention for the Suppression of the Financing of Terrorism,[86] aimed at enhancing international co-operation among States in devising and adopting effective measures for the prevention of the financing of terrorism, as well as for its suppression through the prosecution and punishment of its perpetrators.

The Convention, in its Article 2 recognizes that any person who by any means directly or indirectly, unlawfully or wilfully, provides or collects funds with the intention that they should be used or in the knowledge that they are to be used, in full or in part, in order to carry out any act which constitutes an offence under certain named treaties, commits an offence. One of the treaties cited by the Convention is the International Convention for the Suppression of Terrorist Bombings, adopted by the General Assembly of the United Nations on 15 December 1997.[87]

The Convention for the Suppression of the Financing of Terrorism also provides that, over and above the acts mentioned, providing or collecting funds toward any

---

[82] *Ibid.*

[83] *Black's Law Dictionary* defines condonation as "pardon of offense, voluntary overlooking implied forgiveness by treating offender as if offense had not been committed."

[84] Jane's case, *Supra* note 82, at 92.

[85] Hyde (1928) at 140–142.

[86] International Convention for the Suppression of the Financing of Terrorism, adopted by the General Assembly of the United Nations in resolution 54/109 of 9 December 1999.

[87] A/52/653, 25 November 1997.

other act intended to cause death or serious bodily injury to a civilian, or to any other person not taking an active part in the hostilities in the situation of armed conflict, when the purpose of such act, by its nature or context, is to intimidate a population, or to compel a government or an international organization to do or to abstain from doing any act, would be deemed an offence under the Convention.

The United Nations has given effect to this principle in 1970 when it proclaimed that:

> Every State has the duty to refrain from organizing or encouraging the organization of irregular forces or armed bands, including mercenaries, for incursion into the territory of another State. Every State has the duty to refrain from organizing, instigating, assisting or participating in acts of civil strife or terrorist acts in another State or acquiescing in organized activities within its territory directed towards the commission of such acts, when the acts referred to in the present paragraph involve a threat or use of force.[88]

Here, the words *encouraging* and *acquiescing in organized activities within its territory directed towards the commission of such acts* have a direct bearing on the concept of condonation and would call for a discussion about how States could overtly or covertly encourage the commission of such acts. One commentator[89] identifies three categories of such support: *Category I* support entails protection, logistics, training, intelligence, or equipment provided terrorists as a part of national policy or strategy; *Category II* support is not backing terrorism as an element of national policy but is the toleration of it; *Category III* support provides some terrorists a hospitable environment, growing from the presence of legal protections on privacy and freedom of movement, limits on internal surveillance and security organizations, well-developed infrastructure, and émigré communities.

Another commentator[90] discusses what he calls the *separate delict theory*' in State responsibility, whereby the only direct responsibility of the State is when it is responsible for its own wrongful conduct in the context of private acts, and not for the private acts themselves. He also contends that indirect State responsibility is occasioned by the State's own wrongdoing in reference to the private terrorist conduct. The State is not held responsible for the act of terrorism itself, but rather for its failure to prevent and/or punish such acts, or for its active support for or acquiescence in terrorism.[91] Arguably the most provocative and plausible feature in this approach is the introduction by the commentator of the desirability of determining State liability on the theory of causation. He emphasizes that:

> The principal benefit of the causality based approach is that it avoids the automatic rejection of direct State responsibility merely because of the absence of an agency relationship. As a

---

[88] Declaration on Principles of International Law Concerning Friendly Relations and Co-operation Among States in Accordance with the Charter of the United Nations, UN General Assembly Resolution 2625 (XXV) 24 October 1970.

[89] Steven Metz, State Support for Terrorism, Defeating Terrorism, Strategic Issue Analysis, at http://www.911investigations.net/IMG/pdf/doc-140.pdf.

[90] Becker (2006b).

[91] *Id*. Chapter 2, 67.

> result, it potentially exposes the wrongdoing State to a greater range and intensity of remedies, as well as a higher degree of international attention and opprobrium for its contribution to the private terrorist activity.[92]

The causality principle is tied in with the rules of State Responsibility enunciated by the International Law Commission and Article 51 of the United Nations Charter which states that nothing in the Charter will impair the inherent right of individual or collective self-defense if an armed attack occurs against a Member of the United Nations, until the Security Council has taken measures necessary to maintain international peace and security. The provision goes on to say that measures taken by Members in the exercise of this right of self-defense will be immediately reported to the Security Council and will not in any way affect the authority and responsibility of the Security Council under the present Charter to take at any time such action as it deems necessary in order to maintain or restore international peace and security.

The conclusion to this discussion is inevitable, *i.e.* security of the State is paramount and the State can legislate to ensure that measures are taken to guarantee that security. However, as the case law cited in this article reflects, these measures have to conform to the constitutional guarantees given to citizens, one of which is the Fourth Amendment to the United States Constitution. In this context, the consent of the individual selected for a full body screen is essential and a full body scan taken by the State or an instrumentality of that State without a person's consent would tantamount to a breach of the Fourth Amendment. In the final analysis, however, the State is answerable to the public to show that it took every measure to avoid clear and present danger. The responsibility of a State for private acts of individuals which unlawfully interfere with civil aviation is determined by the quantum of proof available that could establish intent or negligence of the State, which in turn would establish complicity or condonation on the part of the State concerned. One way to determine complicity or condonation is to establish the extent to which the State adhered to the obligation imposed upon it by international law and whether it breached its duty to others. In order to exculpate itself, the State concerned will have to demonstrate that either it did not tolerate the offence (by using such measures as body scanners) or that it ensured the punishment of the offender. *Brownlie* is of the view that proof of such breach would lie in the causal connection between the private offender and the State.[93] In this context, the act or omission on the part of a State is a critical determinant particularly if there is no specific intent.[94] Generally, it is not the intent of the offender that is the determinant but the failure of a State to perform its legal duty in either preventing

---

[92] Becker (2006b) at 335.

[93] Brownlie (1983) at 39.

[94] Report of the International Law Commission to the United Nations General Assembly, UNGOAR 56th Session, Supp. No. 10, *UN DOC A/56/10*, 2001 at 73.

the offence (if such was within the purview of the State) or in taking necessary action with regard to punitive action or redress.[95]

A perceived inadequacy of the global framework of aviation security is the lack of an implementation arm. ICAO has taken extensive measures to introduce relevant international conventions as well as Standards and Recommended Practices (SARPs) in Annex 17 to the Chicago Convention. There is also a highly classified *Aviation Security Manual* developed by ICAO which is provided to States. Additionally, the Organization provides focused security training courses to its member States. However, ICAO's role is largely confined to rule making and the provision of guidance, bringing to bear the need for an aviation security crisis management team on a global scale that could work towards effectively precluding acts of terrorism.

Another measure that could proactively facilitate the arrest of terrorism is the global curbing of the financing of terrorism. The United Nations General Assembly, on 9 December 1999, adopted the International Convention for the Suppression of the Financing of Terrorism, aimed at enhancing international co-operation among States in devising and adopting effective measures for the prevention of the financing of terrorism, as well as for its suppression through the prosecution and punishment of its perpetrators.

The Convention, in its Article 2 recognizes that any person who by any means directly or indirectly, unlawfully or wilfully, provides or collects funds with the intention that they should be used or in the knowledge that they are to be used, in full or in part, in order to carry out any act which constitutes an offence under certain named treaties, commits an offence. The treaties listed are those that are already adopted and in force and which address acts of unlawful interference with such activities as deal with air transport and maritime transport. Also cited is the International Convention for the Suppression of Terrorist Bombings, adopted by the General Assembly of the United Nations on 15 December 1997.

The *Convention for the Suppression of the Financing of Terrorism* also provides that, over and above the acts mentioned, providing or collecting funds toward any other act intended to cause death or serious bodily injury to a civilian, or to any other person not taking an active part in the hostilities in the situation of armed conflict, when the purpose of such act, by its nature or context, is to intimidate a population, or to compel a government or an international organization to do or to abstain from doing any act, would be deemed an offence under the Convention.

The above notwithstanding, one cannot ignore the incontrovertible fact that security is a systemic process. The mere use of full body scanners by no means ensures total security against acts of unlawful interference with civil aviation. As the Christmas day incident showed, intelligence gathering, sharing of information, and more importantly, integration and analysis of such information[96] are critical to

---

95 de Arechaga (1968) at 535.

96 As stated by President Obama, "this was not a failure to collect intelligence. . .it was a failure to integrate and understand the intelligence that we already had. . ." Airline Bomber could Have Been Stopped, *The Air Letter*, Tuesday 05 January 2010, No. 16897, at 1.

the security chain. What is most important is to establish a global security culture that ensures the cooperation of the 190 ICAO member States by working in harmony. A perceived inadequacy of the global framework of aviation security is the lack of an implementation arm. ICAO has taken extensive measures to introduce relevant international conventions as well as Standards and Recommended Practices (SARPs) in Annex 17 to the Chicago Convention. There is also a highly classified *Aviation Security Manual* developed by ICAO which is provided to States. Additionally, the Organization provides focused security training courses to its member States. However, ICAO's role is largely confined to rule making and the provision of guidance, bringing to bear the need for an aviation security crisis management team on a global scale that could work towards effectively precluding acts of terrorism.

6.3 Cargo Security and Handling

Many aviation disasters, including the PANAM disaster over Lockerbie, Scotland in 1988 and the Air India disaster off the coast of Ireland in 1985 have been due to explosives packed in cargo containers. Such acts are committed within the premises of the aerodrome. The 37th Session of the ICAO Assembly in 2010 adopted a Declaration unanimously adopted by participants, which reaffirmed international commitment to enhance aviation security collaboratively and proactively through screening technologies to detect prohibited articles, strengthening international standards, improving security information-sharing and providing capacity-building assistance to States in need. The Assembly also put its full support behind a comprehensive, new ICAO aviation security strategy.

At a high level Conference held in ICAO from 12 to 14 September 2012 on aviation security the conference recognized that air cargo advanced information for security risk assessment is a developing area that enhances air cargo security, particularly in the context of express delivery carriers such as FEDEX, UPS, DHL Express and TNT Express who carry around 30 million shipments daily, which typically contain high-value added, time-sensitive cargo. These carriers guarantee the timely delivery of these vast volumes of shipments, ranging from same-day delivery to 72 h after pick-up, virtually anywhere in the world. They operate in 220 countries and territories.

The conference noted that a real risk in the area of cargo and mail security would arise when an express delivery carrier experiences a technical problem in an aircraft and is forced to transfer cargo to a passenger carrier, in which instance strict supply chain standards should be adhered so that the risk in the transfer of cargo could be obviated.

Participants agreed that it was essential that solid standards and mutual recognition programmes be in place in order to make sure that States all along an air cargo supply chain satisfy themselves that air cargo is secure, and so let it flow unimpeded. Such standards and recommended practices should allow for the speedy transit and transhipment of legitimate air cargo worldwide, through any combination of air routes and transit or transhipment points.

One of the threats to aerodrome security is what is known as the "insider threat" where informants from within the aerodrome (in many instances who are working as staff) alert their accomplices outside with critical security information. In February, a security breach in Antwerp, Belgium led to one of the biggest diamond heists in recent history. Under the cover of darkness, eight gunmen in hooded police clothing gained access through an airport perimeter fence and drove onto the tarmac in two black vehicles with flashing blue police lights. With great speed and precision, the heavily armed thieves sorted through and removed packages from the cargo hold of a parked Helvetic Airways aircraft, loaded them in their vehicles and made a high speed getaway.

Preliminary speculation is that the thieves had inside information or assistance, much like the infamous Lufthansa Heist of 1978 at John F. Kennedy Airport in New York. Aided by the knowledge of an airport employee, members of the Lucchese crime family were able to steal in excess of 6 million dollars in untraceable U.S. currency and jewels from a temporary holding vault on the airport property. Insider knowledge and assistance was central to that crime's success. Ajay Jain, in an article published in January 2013 states:

> Various airline employees, vendors and multiple tenants need to be authenticated every day. Their physical access rights need to be controlled and managed dynamically based upon their role and policies affecting their access. In fact, airports present one of the most complicated scenarios when administering restricted-area access control, identity verification and issuance of an access credential. Many airports have siloed systems and processes used to manage employees' access credentials.
>
> Physical identity and access management operations are handled manually, leading to potentially dangerous errors, a higher cost of operations, enrollment and termination delays and a lower level of security. A multi-layer balance between security, costs and practicality is required to address this issue. Leveraging technologies to achieve security goals can also improve efficiencies and customer service.[97]

Jain states that physical identity and access management software can solve these and related problems by unifying identity management airport-wide, integrating physical security systems, automating processes and simplifying control of employees, vendors and other identities. He states further that software allows airports to manage the lifecycle of identities as they relate to physical access, including synchronized on/off-boarding across all systems harboring an identity record, access profile, zone management and role-based physical access. Comprehensive background check of all personnel selected for hire/employment at an airport needs to be carried out by the relevant State's security agencies based on risk assessment. In addition, re-vetting of airport workers such as cleaners, duty free

[97] Ajay Jain, *Addressing the Insider Threat*, at http://security-today.com/Articles/2013/01/01/Addressing-The-Insider-Threat.aspx.

shop personnel, catering staff and concessionaires must be carried out frequently in order to mitigate collusion to commit acts of unlawful interference.[98]

What has been suggested by experts is a 100 % screening process for all aerodrome employees. One study states:

> Ground crews are largely unseen by the general public. But in much the same way as flight crews, they have intimate knowledge about their work environment. They also have unrestricted access to the exterior and interior of aircraft. Despite this access, these employees are not subject to the same security screenings as passengers and most flight crews.
>
> Ground-crew employees usually access the inner workings of the airport through an employee entrance. This entrance should have a guard present and is accessed by a key, coded lock, biometric device, or other door-locking mechanism. It is not considered a screening checkpoint because its only purpose is to restrict access to unauthorized personnel—not to inspect employees or their belongings. Once inside, however, these individuals are given largely unfettered access to the airport property. They, like flight crews, know the inner workings of the airport and its security weaknesses.[99]

Britain has a programme which vets applicants for sensitive 'airside' jobs to see if they have committed offences abroad. However, those who already hold security passes—including pilots and baggage-handlers—will not be checked. Be that as it may, to effectively respond to insider threat at airports requires predictive risk analytics and utilization of cutting-edge security convergence technology.

6.3.1 Human Remains

Although the carriage of human remains comes within the purview and responsibility of the airline, the aerodrome is the place of loading and adequate facilities have to b provided with sensitivity and understanding. If a person dies in a country other than his own, there are no global rules or guidance that dictates the manner in which his remains could be transported back to his country, with dignity and care. This matter was highlighted in 2003 before the European Parliament with a real example of a British national who died while on holiday in Greece. The Greek authorities had carried out an autopsy which concluded that the deceased tourist had died of a heart attack. When the body was transported back home the deceased's family had requested a second autopsy, only to find that most of the deceased's organs had been removed in Greece after the autopsy and destroyed, according to Greek law. This had caused severe mental distress to the deceased's kin.

The inevitable fact is that there are two dimensions to this subject: the health and sanitation aspects of carrying human remains by air; and the rights of close relatives of the deceased to bring his remains back home with speedy dispatch. It also

[98] The Reality of Mitigating the Insider Threat, *ATCM—WP/11*, 12th Meeting of the AFCAC Air Transport Committee Dakar, Senegal, 30–31 October 2012, at 1.

[99] Goff (2013).

highlights the serious lacuna in regulatory consistency in the carriage by air of human remains and traces attempts by the international community to address the subject. The discussions lead to the conclusion that, although several attempts have been made at international level in the past—some clear and some unclear—they lack unification and stand fragmented and ambivalent. To their credit, airlines, under the guidance of the International Air Transport Association (IATA), have adopted their own principles in carrying human remains with compassion and dedication. The conclusion suggests a way forward in binding the threads of this issue in a harmonious manner.

Human dignity is an international concept which is extended both to the living and the dead. The 1948 *Universal Declaration of Human Rights* of the United Nations—the cornerstone of human dignity—declares that the inherent dignity and the equal and inalienable rights of all members of the human family are the foundations of freedom, justice and peace in the world and that all human beings are born free and equal in dignity and rights. This statement establishes human dignity as the conceptual basis for human rights. Seventy-five percent of the constitutions of ICAO's 191 member States use the concepts of "human dignity" or "personal dignity" explicitly.[100] It follows therefore that if the remains of a human being are not given equal respect and dignity, the moral imperative of the doctrine of human dignity[101] would be rendered destitute of meaning and purpose.

From an aviation perspective, most airlines in the world offer services for the transportation of human remains and cremated remains. These services are varied according to the policies of each airline, but all share a common thread of dedication and compassion in offering the service in the transportation of funeral shipments. Usually, airlines employ specially trained staff to address all the travel-related issues that may arise when shipping such very sensitive cargo. The tasks assigned to these staff include providing advice to those seeking the airlines' services on applicable regulations, taking into account the delicateness of the responsibility that devolves upon the carrier.

In terms of property rights pertaining to a cadaver or other remains, such rights do not exist at common law. However, for the purpose of transportation—whether it be for embalming, cremation or internment—the corpse or cremated remains of a human being is considered to be property or quasi-property, the rights to which are held by the surviving spouse or next of kin. This right cannot be transferred and does not exist while the deceased is living. A corpse or urn carrying cremated remains may not be retained by either an undertaker or a carrier as security for unpaid funeral expenses, particularly if such were kept without authorization and payment was demanded as a condition precedent to its release. Upon burial the

---

[100] http://www.constitution.org; http://www.oefre.unibe.ch/law/icl; http://www.psr.keele.ac.uk.

[101] Human dignity has not been comprehensively defined and has remained a somewhat squishy subject, often explained theologically. However, the dictionary definition of dignity is that it is *inter alia* "the quality or state of being worthy of esteem or respect". See http://www.thefreedictionary.com/dignity.

body accrues to the ground and any appurtenant property such as jewelry which was on the corpse on burial accrue to their rightful owner as determined by applicable principles of property laws and wills and testaments as they might exist.

The purpose of this article is to discuss *de legelata* the fragmented regime applicable to the carriage by air of human remains. Two antiquated multilateral agreements, one Resolution and one Regulation all in Europe; some maundering by the ICAO Council decades ago; two Annexes to the Chicago Convention which may have applicability to this subject; some proactive guidelines by the International Air Transport Association and the World Health Organization and procedures and policy of individual air carriers comprise the history of this subject. Against this backdrop, this article will inquire into the need for a global regulatory process that would properly address this esoteric but important area of carriage by air.

6.3.2 International Agreements

The Berlin Agreement of 1937

The *International Arrangement Concerning the Conveyance of Corpses*[102] (Berlin Agreement), signed at Berlin on 10 February 1937 was the first recorded attempt at the unification of rules relating to the carriage of human remains. The agreement, which applied to the international transport of corpses immediately after decease or exhumation, was designed to avoid the difficulties resulting from differences in the regulations concerning the conveyance of corpses, and recognized the necessity and the convenience of laying down uniform regulations in this area of transportation. Accordingly, the signatory States[103] undertook to accept the entry into their territory, or the passage in transit through their territory, of the corpses of persons deceased in the territory of any one of the other contracting countries upon certain conditions, which were incorporated in the Agreement.

The initial condition, as laid out in Article 1 of the Agreement was that, for the conveyance of any corpse by any means and under any conditions, a special laissez-passer be issued for a corpse which would state the surname, first name and age of the deceased person, and the place, date and cause of decease. The competent authority for the place of decease or the place of burial in the case of corpses exhumed had to issue the laissez-passer and it was recommended that the laissez-passer should be made out, not only in the language of the country issuing it, but also in at least one of the languages most frequently used in international relations.

[102] League of Nations, Treaty Series 1938, No. 439r at 315–325.

[103] Germany, Belgium, Chile Denmark, Egypt, France, Italy, the Netherlands, Switzerland, Czechoslovakia and Turkey.

The Berlin Agreement further stated that neither the country of destination nor the countries of transit shall require, over and above such papers as are required under international conventions for the purpose of transports in general, any document other than the laissez-passer referred to in Article 1. The following had to be presented to the competent authority for the issuance of laissez-passer: a certified true copy of the death certificate; and official certificates to the effect that conveyance of the corpse is not open to objection from the point of view of health or from the medico-legal point of view, and evidence that the corpse has been placed in a coffin in accordance with the regulations laid down in the Agreement.[104]

As for packaging the human remains, the Agreement, in Article 3 provided that corpses must be placed in a metal coffin, the bottom of which has been covered with a layer approximately 5 cm. of absorbent matter such as peat, sawdust, powdered charcoal or the like with the addition of an antiseptic substance. Where the cause of decease was a contagious disease, the corpse itself was required to be wrapped in a shroud soaked in an antiseptic solution. A further requirement was that the metal coffin must thereupon be hermetically closed (soldered) and fitted into a wooden coffin in such a manner as to preclude movement. The wooden coffin was required to be of a thickness of not less than 3 cm. and its joints must be completely watertight. It was also required that the coffin be closed by means of screws not more than 20 cm. distant from one another, and strengthened by metal hoops. In the case of transport by air, The Agreement, in Article 7, required that coffins must be conveyed either in an aircraft specially and solely used for the purpose or in a special compartment solely reserved for the purpose in an ordinary aircraft.

The Agreement precluded bodies of persons who had died as a cause of plague, cholera, small-pox or typhus from being conveyed between the territories of the contracting parties until the lapse of at least 1 year after the demise. No articles were permitted to be transported along with the coffin in the same aircraft or in the same compartment, other than wreaths, bunches of flowers and the like.[105]

Agreement on the Transfer of Corpses (Strasbourg—1973)

The second international agreement was in 1973 called the *Agreement on the Transfer of Corpses*, and it was drawn up within the Council of Europe by the European Public Health Committee. The Strasbourg Agreement was opened for signature by the member States of the Council of Europe on 26 October 1973. This agreement was designed to adapt the provisions of the Berlin Agreement concerning the conveyance of corpses, to the new situation arising from developments in the field of communications systems, international relations and commercial and tourist activities. A proposal to examine anew the problem of the transfer of corpses with a view to drawing up a new instrument was approved by the

[104] Berlin Agreement, *supra* note 102, Article 2.

[105] *Id.* Article 4.

Committee of Ministers of the Council of Europe in 1967 and this task was entrusted to the European Public Health Committee which, in the course of its work, gave due consideration to the observations, among others, of the European Federation of Funeral Directors (Brussels) and the European Funeral Directors Association (Vienna). The text of the draft Agreement was submitted to the European Committee on Legal Co-operation (CCJ) before its final adoption by the Committee of Ministers of the Council of Europe in April 1973. It was opened for signature by member States of the Council of Europe on 26 October 1973.

The Strasbourg Agreement defines the transfer of corpses as the international transport of human remains from the State of departure to the State of destination. Accordingly, the State of departure is that in which the transfer began; in the case of exhumed remains, it is that in which burial had taken place; the State of destination is that in which the corpse is to be buried or cremated after the transport. The Agreement does not apply to the international transport of ashes. Article 3 of the Agreement states that during the transfer, any corpse is required to be accompanied by a special document (laissez-passer for a corpse) issued by the competent authority of the State of departure. The laissez-passer has to include at least the information set out in the model annexed to the Agreement; and be made out in the official language or one of the official languages of the State in which it was issued and in one of the official languages of the Council of Europe.

Article 4 provides that, with the exception of the documents required under international conventions and agreements relating to transport in general, or future conventions or arrangements on the transfer of corpses, neither the State of destination nor the transit State shall require any documents other than the laissez-passer for a corpse. The laissez-passer is issued by the competent authority referred to in Article 8 of the Agreement,[106] after it has been ascertained that: all the medical, health, administrative and legal requirements of the regulations in force in the State of departure relating to the transfer of corpses and, where appropriate, burial and exhumation have been complied with; the remains have been placed in a coffin which complies with the requirements laid down in Articles 6 and 7 of the Agreement; and that the coffin only contains the remains of the person named in the laissez-passer and such personal effects as are to be buried or cremated with the corpse.

Article 6 requires that the coffin must be impervious and that the inside must contain absorbent material. If the competent authority of the State of departure consider it necessary the coffin must be provided with a purifying device to balance the internal and external pressures. It may consist of: either an outer coffin in wood with sides at least 20 mm thick and an inner coffin of zinc carefully soldered or of any other material which is self-destroying; or a single coffin in wood with sides at least 30 mm thick lined with a sheet of zinc or of any other material which is self-

[106] Article 8 states that each Contracting Party shall communicate to the Secretary General of the Council of Europe the designation of the competent authority referred to in Article 3, paragraph 1, Article 5 and Article 6, paragraphs 1 and 3 of the Agreement.

destroying. If the cause of death is a contagious disease, the body itself is required to be wrapped in a shroud impregnated with an antiseptic solution.

Article 6 further provides that the coffin, if it is to be transferred by air, has to be provided with a purifying device or, failing this, present such guarantees of resistance as are recognised to be adequate by the competent authority of the State of departure. If the coffin is to be transported like an ordinary consignment, it has to be packaged so that it no longer resembles a coffin, and it shall be indicated that it be handled with care.[107]

Resolution 2003/2032 (INI)

The European Community was dissatisfied with both the Berlin Agreement and the Strasbourg Agreement (which only some member States had signed), claiming that these Agreements advocated indirect discrimination by providing for non-European Community residents. Also it was claimed that these two agreements imposed strict rules on the cross-border transfer of mortal remains, applied essentially to 'non-nationals' and hence ran counter to the Community scheme of things. Accordingly, and with a view to addressing the case where a Community citizen expired in a Community country other than his own and his remains had to be repatriated to his country, a Committee was appointed by the European Parliament to consider an instrument that addressed the conveyance of mortal remains suggested in 2003 Resolution 2003/2032 (INI). This Resolution noted that, on account of the above agreements, the death of a Community citizen in a Member State other than his country of origin results in more complex procedures, a longer period of time before burial or cremation takes place and higher costs than if the death had occurred in the deceased person's country of origin,

Another compelling reason for this Resolution was the recognition that, in view of the growth in intra-Community tourism, the increasing numbers of retired people who choose to live in a country other than their own and, more generally, greater intra-Community mobility which is actually encouraged, the number of Community citizens who die in a country other than their country of origin was bound to increase. This was considered against the backdrop that Community citizens should, *mutatis mutandis*, be able to move between and reside in Member States in similar conditions to nationals of a Member State moving around or changing their place of residence in their own country, and that exercising the right to freedom of movement and freedom of residence should be facilitated to the utmost by reducing administrative formalities to an absolute minimum.

The European Community was of the view that, at the time the Resolution was proposed, it was still far from true that a Community citizen who dies in a Member State other than his own is treated in the same way as a national who dies in his home country. For, example, the fact that a zinc coffin is required for the

[107] Article 7 of the Strasbourg Agreement.

repatriation of a corpse from Salzburg to Freilassing (a distance of 10 km) but not for the transfer of a body from Ivalo to Helsinki (a distance of 1,120 km) (2).

Therefore it was pointed out that the repatriation of mortal remains without excessive cost or bureaucracy in the event of the death of a European Community citizen in a country other than the one in which either burial or cremation was to take place may be regarded as a corollary of the right of each EU citizen to move and reside freely within the territory of the Member States.

The Resolution called upon the Commission to see that the standards and the procedures applied in the cross-border transportation of corpses were harmonized throughout the Community and to endeavor to ensure that, as far as possible, Community citizens were treated in the same way as nationals in their home country.

A Regulation, covering intra-community transport of bodies according to the European Standard CEN/BT/TF 139 on Funeral Services and approved on 27 July 2005 goes on to say in Article 1 that the identification of the deceased must be performed before the body is placed in the coffin by the funeral enterprise or operator of the country of departure. The elements of identification relate to the civil status of the deceased and are indicated on the laissez-passer for the body. For identification, the body must be provided with: an identification bracelet attached to the body part (wrist, ankle...,); and a non-removable and tamper-proof identification tag attached to the coffin and its wrapping, if any. The information required on the bracelet were: surname and first name(s); sex; date and place of birth; date and place of death; and nationality. The information required on the identification tag were to be: surname and family name(s); date of birth; and date of death.

Article 2 of the Regulation required that the coffin or casket that carried the remains must be made of solid material—the main material used in Europe being wood (excluding the use of carton or chipboard). The material used for the coffin must be biodegradable. It also required that the coffin must be impervious; the products used to make it impervious must be biodegradable and in conformity with the standards applicable to crematorium emissions. In particular, the coffin must be impervious to decomposition liquids and fitted with absorbent material. The out cover of the coffin/casket was required to meet necessary sanitary requirements.

The Regulation had chemical requirements that were not contained in the 1937 Berlin Agreement and the 1973 Strasbourg Agreement. For instance, Articles 2.3 and 2.5, specified conditions for international carriage of corpses by providing that if the cause of death was a contagious disease (as per the WHO official list), the outer container (usually wooden) used for the transport of the body may be lined with a hermetically sealed container. The hermetically sealed container must be provided with a purifying filter. If the consecutive treatments (thanatopraxy) have been performed within 36 h after the death the body must be encoffined within 6 days. The transport must be done not more than 48 h after encoffining and sealing. The conditions required for long distance international transport outside Europe under the Agreement were: hermetically sealed container; and/or embalming/thanatopractical treatment; and/or refrigeration. In the case of refrigeration at no time shall the temperature inside the container exceed 80 °C during transport.

The Regulation requires two types of documents for carriage of corpses: medical certificate upon death; and a laissez passer. The medical certificate is required to be drawn up, on the one hand, in the language of the country of departure in which the death had occurred and, on the other hand, in one of the following languages: English, German or French. It must contain information relating to the deceased such as: surname and maiden name in the case of a married woman; first name(s); date and place of birth; date and place of death; sex; and cause of death.

6.3.3 ICAO Initiatives

The Council

The Council of ICAO, at its 32nd Session in 1957 addressed the carriage under the heading "Carriage of Sick Persons, Pregnant Women, Live Animals and Coffins—Sanitation on Board Aircraft" at which IATA recommended that in addition to the prevailing requirement—that human remains be placed in hermetically-sealed coffins which are enclosed in outside cases—human remains should be embalmed prior to being placed in the coffin. IATA further suggested that acceptance of such coffins is dependent upon the type of aircraft, requirements of entry and clearance and prior approval of the countries of origin, transit and destination.[108] The Council noted that comments on the carriage of coffins had been received from 27 States (from a total of 72 member States at that time) and two overseas territories. Three of these States reported that they were bound by the provisions of the 1937 Berlin Agreement and Eight States advised ICAO that the carriage of corpses existed in their national legislations. Thirteen States commented that they had not, in their experience encountered serious difficulties in this area. The United States made the comment:

> Because of known effects of rare atmosphere at high altitude on sealed caskets, such caskets should not be carried by aircraft.[109]

The ICAO Secretariat responded in assent:

> Differences in atmospheric pressure are known to have caused bursting of coffins, particularly when sealed hermetically (by welding) according to provisions of Articles 5 and 7 of the Berlin Arrangement, or similar provisions in national legislation. Prompted by rapid decomposition in flight, such transports occasionally arrive in appalling conditions; in some States (Australia, Philippines, Venezuela, Netherlands Antilles), therefore, it is required that corpses be embalmed prior to air transport, thus eliminating at least certain difficulties. If some pressure-relief system were applied to sealed caskets, the difficulties caused by pressure differences might disappear, but international transport would not permitted by existing laws.

[108] C-WP/2448, 5/6/57, Addendum and Corrigendum, 21/11/576 at 3.

[109] *Id.* Paragraph 20.1 at p. 10.

It is noteworthy that during these discussions, cremated human remains were not mentioned, except by Belgium which said that "incinerated corpses are accepted without any restrictions and are carried on all types of aircraft".[110] The ICAO Council concluded that the difficulties reported by States were caused by variations of atmospheric pressure; a characteristic of transport by air, while for international transport coffins must be hermetically sealed.

ICAO has approached this subject from another dimension *i.e.* the carriage of human remains of an aircraft accident victim. In 2001 the Council released its *Guidance on Assistance to Aircraft Accident Victims and their Families*[111] where ICAO recognizes that in an accident context the identification, custody and return of human remains are very important forms of family assistance but remains are often difficult to recover and identification can be an arduous and time consuming process. The ICAO guidance goes on to say that legislation often requires a post mortem examination of those killed in an accident and in some instances there may be remains that cannot be identified.[112] ICAO also calls for personal effects of the deceased to be correctly handled and returned to their lawful owners.[113] The Guidance also calls for the State of occurrence to provide for the return of human remains[114] while also devolving that burden—of the carriage of such remains—upon the aircraft operator involved in the accident.[115]

Annexes 9 and 18 to the Chicago Convention

There are two Annexes to the Chicago Convention which bear some relevance to the carriage of human remains by air—Annex 9 (Facilitation) and Annex 18 (The Safe Transport of Dangerous Goods by Air). The Annex 9 definition of cargo implies that human remains could be categorized as cargo by giving the definition of cargo as "*any property carried on an aircraft other than mail, stores and accompanied or mishandled baggage*". This definition is slightly different from the one contained in another ICAO document—*Technical Instructions for the Safe Transport of Dangerous Goods by Air*[116] which defines "cargo" as "*any property carried on an aircraft other than mail and accompanied or mishandled baggage*". Annex 18 does not define the word "cargo" but defines "dangerous goods" as articles or substances which are capable of posing a risk to health, safety, property or the environment and which are shown in the list of dangerous goods in the

[110] C-WP/2448, 5/6/57, Appendix "A" at 25.

[111] *Guidance on Assistance to Aircraft Accident Victims and their Families, ICAO Circular 285 – AN/166.*

[112] *Id.* Paragraph 3.10.

[113] *Id.* Paragraph 3.11.

[114] *Id.* Paragraph 5.1.

[115] *Id.* Paragraph 5.7.

[116] ICAO Doc 9284, AN/905 (2011–2012 Edition).

Technical Instructions or which are classified according to those instructions. The Technical Instructions do not list human remains as being dangerous cargo. However, it behooves the international aviation community to inquire, along the lines of ICAO discussions in the Council, whether human remains could be ruled out as not posing a risk to health or the environment under any circumstances of carriage by air or whether human remains, depending on the way it is packed for transport, could be considered as dangerous goods.[117]

Getting back to Annex 9, there is a whole chapter in the Annex—Chapter 4—dedicated to the entry and departure of cargo and other articles. Surprisingly, there is no provision in the Annex for priority of clearance or transport of human remains over other cargo, despite the prominence given to the subject in *ICAO Circular 285 – AN/166*.[118] Another surprise is that, although there is a *Recommended Practice* in the Annex which suggests that electronic information systems for the release and clearance of "goods" (my emphasis) should cover their transfer between air and other modes of transport,[119] there is no definition of "goods" in the Annex. Do corpses or cremated human remains come under the purview of "goods"? This question is valid in the context of Appendix 3 to the Annex which has a template for a cargo manifest where there exists a column for "Nature of Goods". There is no mention of the word "cargo" in this template.

In view of the above discussion it might be worthwhile for a detailed discussion on the status of human remains in the global aviation context and a re-visit of the 1957 discussions in the ICAO Council. The added dimension of related ICAO documentation such as Circular 285 – AN/166 makes it all the more compelling.

IATA, WHO and UNITED STATES Guidelines

The International Air Transport Association has clear, cogent guidance on the carriage by air of human remains. In its *Airport Handling Manual* (AHM) IATA prescribes that for special cargo, such as valuable cargo, perishables, vulnerable cargo, human remains and shipments of special importance or urgency, particular points to be considered are: that all personnel concerned are made fully aware of the nature and handling requirements of all such shipments; suitable arrangements are made for the security of valuable and vulnerable cargo; perishables are handled in accordance with the requirements of the particular commodity and in particular the most recent edition of the Perishable Cargo Regulations Manual; that a check is made to ensure that the final load assembled for dispatch to the aircraft *does* include shipments of special importance or urgency; and that shipments considered as

[117] American Airlines requires that human remains packed in dry ice are subject to dangerous goods regulations. https://www.aacargo.com/shipping/humanremains.jhtml.

[118] *Supra* note 111.

[119] Annex 9 to the Convention on International Civil Aviation, 13th Edition: July 2011, *Recommended Practice* 4.18.

special cargo have "special consignment" labels visibly attached to each package.[120]

The *IATA Ground Operations Manual* (IGOM) provides that human remains should be carried in an aircraft only if accepted by the operating airline for transport. The IGOM requires the carrier to make sure that a Human Remains Acceptance Checklist has been used (if required by the operating airline). Carriers are required, according to the IGOM, not to accept any human remains that are consolidated with any cargo other than other human remains. With regard to cremated human remains the Manual requires that only urns or other suitable containers as cargo with no special restrictions are accepted for carriage and that the carrier should make sure that the urn or other container is packed in a neutral outer pack that will protect the urn from breakage and/spillage.[121] It also prescribes that human remains in coffins should not be stored next to food or live animals, adding that there appears to be no scientific or technical reason why live animals and human remains should be segregated in aircraft cargo compartments, except that it may be ethical for cultural reasons to segregate them.

IATA in AHM 333 states that, should a body fluid leakage occur while transporting dead bodies, the usual accepted guidelines endorsed by WHO for dealing with spilled body fluids should be followed and the handler is advised to: wear disposable gloves and, if available, a plastic apron. If the spillage has occurred on an aircraft, the AHM provision advises the handler to only use cleaning materials suitable for aircraft use. He should not try to clean the body fluids by hosing with water or air and should use material that will adsorb the body fluids and scrape the material into a biohazard bag. Afterwards, he should wash the area with water/ disinfectant after removal of the adsorbent material, dispose of gloves and apron in a biohazard bag and wash hands thoroughly with soap and water afterwards.

WHO has also some guidance pertaining to the handling of human remains, and recommends as a fundamental measure that the handling of human remains should be kept to a minimum. Additionally, WHO recommends, particularly in the case of deaths caused by infectious diseases that remains should not be sprayed, washed or embalmed and that only trained personnel should handle remains during the outbreak. Personnel handling remains should wear personal protective equipment (gloves, gowns, apron, surgical masks and eye protection) and closed shoes.[122]

In the United States, there are no requirements for importation into the country if human remains consist entirely of: clean, dry bones or bone fragments or human hair; teeth; fingernails or toenails; and human remains that are cremated before entry into the United States. Human remains intended for interment or subsequent cremation after entry into the United States must be accompanied by a death

[120] IATA Airport Handling Manual, AHM 310 at 149.

[121] IATA IGOM, Chapter 3.

[122] Interim Infection Control Recommendations for Care of Patients with Suspected or Confirmed Filovirus (Ebola, Marburg) Haemorrhagic Fever, BDP/EPR/WHO, Geneva, March 2008.

certificate stating the cause of death. If the death certificate is in a language other than English, then it should be accompanied by an English language translation.

If the cause of death was a quarantinable communicable disease (i.e., cholera, diphtheria, infectious tuberculosis, plague, smallpox, yellow fever, viral hemorrhagic fevers, SARS, or pandemic influenza), the remains must meet the applicable standards and may be cleared, released, and authorized for entry into the United States only if: the remains are cremated; or the remains are properly embalmed and placed in a hermetically sealed casket; or the remains are accompanied by a permit issued by the Director of the Centre for Disease Control and Prevention (CDC). The CDC permit (if applicable) must accompany the human remains at all times during shipment. If the cause of death was anything other than a quarantinable communicable disease, then the remains may be cleared, released, and authorized for entry into the United States if: the remains meet the standards for applicable or properly embalmed and placed in a hermetically sealed casket, or are accompanied by a permit issued by the CDC Director; or the remains are shipped in a leak-proof container.

Federal quarantine regulations (42 CFR Part 71) state that the remains of a person who is known or suspected to have died from a quarantinable communicable disease may not be brought into the United States unless the remains are; properly embalmed and placed in a hermetically sealed casket, cremated, or accompanied by a permit issued by the CDC Director. Quarantinable communicable diseases include cholera; diphtheria, infectious tuberculosis; plague; smallpox, yellow fever; viral hemorrhagic fevers (Lassa, Marburg, Ebola, Congo-Crimean, or others not yet isolated or named); severe acute respiratory syndrome (SARS); and influenza caused by novel or re-emergent influenza viruses that are causing or have the potential to cause a pandemic. A CDC permit may be required when the remains are not embalmed or cremated, especially if the person is suspected or known to have died from a communicable disease.

Persons wishing to import human remains, including cremated remains, into the United States must obtain clearance from CDC's Division of Global Migration and Quarantine (DGMQ). Clearance can be obtained by presenting copies of the foreign death certificate and if needed, a CDC/DGMQ permit to the CDC Quarantine Station with jurisdiction for the U.S. port of entry. A CDC/DGMQ permit may be needed to import human remains if the deceased is known or suspected to have died from a quarantinable communicable disease. A copy of the foreign death certificate and the CDC/DGMQ permit must accompany the human remains at all times during shipment. The foreign death certificate should state the cause of death and must be translated into English.

The basic principle that should apply to the handling of human remains must be consistent with the policy which currently applies in case of aircraft accident investigations, in that the country in which the death occurred must act contemporaneously and in close consultation with the country of nationality. This would obviate the case of the British tourist who died in Greece. The second principle should be that the principles of *ICAO Circular 285 – AN/166* should be incorporated into Annex 9 along with a Standard in Chapter 4 that human remains should be accorded priority and dignity and that specially reduced rates should be promulgated by States on their airlines for this purpose. This Standard should be adopted in accordance with the basic philosophy of Article 44 d) of the Chicago Convention which states that ICAO should strive to meet the needs of the people of the world for safe, regular, efficient and economical air transport.

Annex 9 should contain a separate Appendix for the carriage of human remains by air, which would lay down global principles for the handling, care and commitment that States could ensure. This Appendix should have a cross reference to Annex 18 and the *Technical Instructions* contained in Doc 9284[123] with appropriate linkages that ensure the harmonious application of both Annexes to this sensitive subject.

As for Annex 18, a study should be undertaken to determine as to when a cadaver or cremated remains would, if at all, become a dangerous good. The focus area would be both on the condition the human remains are at the point of acceptance for carriage, and the manner in which they are packaged. In the ultimate analysis, there has to be core global rules in place for this important area of air transportation. It cannot be left for individual States or airlines to decide.

Enhancing global civil aviation security and facilitation is one of ICAO's Strategic Objectives as adopted by the Council in May 2012. This is the first time facilitation has been mentioned in ICAO's strategic language and it should be a harbinger of new studies and new cooperation with the international community between ICAO and its member States o the carriage by air of human remains.

References

Abeyratne RIR (1992) The development of the machine readable passport and visa and the legal rights of the data subject (Part II). Ann Air Space Law (Annales de Droit Arien et Spatial) XVII:1–31

Abeyratne RIR (2001) The exchange of airline passenger information – issues of privacy. Commun Law 6(5):153–162

Abeyratne RIR (2002a) Intellectual property rights and privacy issues: the aviation experience in API and biometric identification. J World Intellect Property 5(4):631–650

Abeyratne RIR (2002b) Attacks on America – privacy implications of heightened security measures in the United States, Europe, and Canada. J Air Law Commerce 67(1):83–115

Abeyratne RIR (2003) Profiling of passengers at airports – imperatives and discretions. Eur Transport Law XXXVIII(3):297–311

Abeyratne RIR (2010) The NW 253 flight and the global framework of aviation security. Air Space Law 35(2):167–181

Becker T (2006a) Terrorism and the state, Hart monographs in transnational and international law. Hart, Portland, p 155

Becker T (2006b) Terrorism and the state; rethinking the rules of state responsibility. Hart, Portland

Bennet CJ (1992) Regulating privacy. Cornell University Press, Ithaca, p 13

[123] *Supra* note 116.

Blackstone W, Morrison W (eds) (2001) Commentaries on the laws of England (1765–1769), 4th edn. Cavendish, London, p 68

Brownlie I (1983) System of the law of nations: state responsibility, Part 1. Clarendon, Oxford, p 39

Burnham D (1983) The rise of the computer state. Random House, New York, p 20

Caron DD (1998) The basis of responsibility: attribution and other trans-substantive rules. In: Lillich RB, Magraw DB (eds) The Iran–United States claims tribunal: its conclusions to state responsibility. Transnational Publishers, Irvington-on-Hudson, p 109

Cate FH (1997) Privacy in the information age. Brookings Institution Press, Washington, p 49

Cooley TM (1888) A treatise on the law of torts, 2nd edn. Callaghan, Chicago

de Arechaga EJ (1968) International responsibility. In: Sorenson M (ed) Manual of public international law. St. Martin's Press, New York, p 531

De Vattel E, Fenwick CG (tr) (1916) The law of nations or, the principles of natural law: applied to the conduct and to the affairs of nations and sovereigns, 2nd edn. Legal Classics Library, New York, p 72

Flaherty DH (1991) On the utility of constitutional rights to privacy and data protection. Case W Res 41:831

Foschio LG (1990) Motor vehicle records: balancing individual privacy and the public's legitimate need to know. In: Kuferman TR (ed) Privacy and publicity. Meckler, London, p 35

Freund PA (1971) Privacy: one concept or many. In: Pennnock JR, Chapman JW (eds) Privacy. Atherton, New York, p 182

Fried C (1978) Privacy: economics and ethics a comment on Posner. Georgia Law Rev 12:423

Gavison R (1980) Privacy and the limits of the law. Yale Law J 89:421

Goff S (2013) The insider threat to airport security, 14 March 2013. http://strategicstudyindia.blogspot.ca/2013/03/the-insider-threat-to-airport-security.html

Grotius H, Scott JB (tr) (1646) De Jure Belli Ac Pacis 2: 523–526

Halpin A (1997) Rights & law analysis & theory. Hart, Oxford, p 111

Hoffer S (2000) World cyberspace law. Juris Publishing, Huntington

Hoffman LJ (ed) (1980) Computers and privacy in the next decade. Academic, New York, 142

Honig JP (1956) The legal status of aircraft. Martinus Nijhoff, The Hague, p 29

Hyde C (1928) Concerning damages arising from neglect to prosecute. Am J Int Law 22:140

Jones RV (1973) Some threats of technology to privacy, privacy and human rights. In: Robertson AH (ed) Presented at the third colloquy about the European Convention on human rights, Brussels, 30 September–3 October 1970, Manchester University Press, Manchester

McMunn MK (1996) Aviation security and facilitation programmes are distinct but closely intertwined. ICAO J 51:9

Miller AR (1971) The assault on privacy. The University of Michigan Press, Ann Arbor, p 42

Montgomery Curtis J (1992) Memorial seminar. The public, privacy and the press: have the media *gone too far?* American Press Institute, p. 2

Morganthau H, Thompson KW (1950) Principles and problems of international politics. Knopf, New York, p 24

Nock SL (1993) The costs of privacy. Aldine De Gruyter, New York, p 43

Orwell G (1978) Nineteen eighty-four. Clarendon, Oxford

Pember DR (1972) Privacy and the press. University of Washington Press, Seattle, p 227

Posner R (1978) The right of privacy. Georgia Law Rev 12(3):393

Prowda JB (1995) A layer's ramble down the information superhighway: privacy and security of data. Fordham Law Rev 64:738

Regan PM (1995) Legislating privacy. The University of North Caroline Press, Chapel Hill, p 33

Reidenberg JR (1995) Data protection law and the European Union's directive: the challenge for the United States: setting standards for fair information practice in the U.S. private sector. Iowa Law Rev 80:497

Rucker P (2010) TSA tries to assuage concerns about full body scans. Washington Post, Monday, 4 January 2010

Scott GG (1995) Mind your own business – the battle for personal privacy. Insight Books, New York, p 307

Shaw MN (2003) International law, 5th edn. Cambridge University Press, London, pp 611–612

Simitis S (1995) From the market to the polis: the EC directive on the protection for personal data. Iowa Law Rev 80:445

Simmel A (1971) Privacy is not an isolated freedom. In: Pennnock JR, Chapman JW (eds) Privacy. Atherton, New York, p 71

Sweet K (2008) Aviation security and passenger rights. In: Thomas AR (ed) Aviation security management, vol 2. Praeger Security International, Westport, p 45

Turack DC (1972) The passport in international law. D.C. Heath & Co., Lexington, pp 20–21

Warren SD, Brandeis LD (1980) The right of privacy. Harv Law Rev 4(5):193

Warren SD, Brandies LD (1980–1981) The right to privacy. Harv Law Rev 4:193

Westin A (1967) Privacy and freedom. Atheneum, New York, p 368

Westin AF (1970) Privacy and freedom. Bodley Head, London, p 124

Young JB (1978) A look at privacy. In: Young JB (ed) Privacy. Willey, New York, p 1

Zelermyer W (1959) Invasion of privacy. Syracuse University Press, Syracuse, p 16

Chapter 7
Joint Use of Military and Civil Airports

7.1 Introduction

The foregoing discussion pertained solely to civil airports. The Chicago Convention, by virtue of Article 3 asserts that the Convention applies only to civil aircraft, thus excluding State aircraft. This presumption extends to the Annexes to the Convention as well as the ICAO manuals that have so far been discussed in this book. However, there is no specific exclusion of military aircraft landing at civilian airports. Furthermore, in terms of domestic airports, this distinction between civil and military airports is blurred. For example, in the United States there are 23 military airfields that follow the joint use concept of having both military and civil aircraft landing at and taking off from them.

The inherent concern this joint use brings to bear is that civil aircraft operations may interfere with strategic military air operations and State security. Another concern is the possible difficulty of allocating space for a civil-military mixed operation within the premises of the airport as well as logistics involved in accommodating military installations and dwellings for personnel within a community. The increased noise that military aircraft might bring to a civilian population is another concern.

Civil-military cooperation and symbiosis at an airport generally occurs when resources owned by the State are limited and it becomes a necessity to utilize available resources in an efficient manner. An example can be found in the Republic of Korea which has a total of 15 airports used for civil aviation, 8 of which are operated by the military. This practice is supported by a joint programme between the Ministry of National Defence and the Ministry of Land, Infrastructure and Transportation.

Fundamentally, there is no known obstacle to the joint use of airports at public international law. It is a matter of State sovereignty, provided the State concerned does not flout accepted norms of international law. The distinction that would arise would be in the recognition that military aviation is distinct from civil aviation and must be treated as such by the airport administration. The priority one gets over the

R. Abeyratne, *Law and Regulation of Aerodromes*, DOI 10.1007/978-3-319-04780-5_7,

other at a joint use airport would entirely depend on the local norms set by the State authorities. The nature of military and civil aviation therefore plays a major role in this equation.

In recent times, both statesmen and members of the aviation community have been consciously aware of the dual role played by civil and military aviation, while sharing the same sky. This has called for delicate diplomacy and political compromise. When dealing with issues of aviation to which politics is applied, it is important to remember that from the distant past, it has been recognized that a nation's air power is the sum total of all its civil and military aviation resources.[1] Furthermore, the importance of aviation toward maintaining peace has been accepted since World War II and is aptly reflected in the Statement of the British at that time, that civil aviation holds the key to power and importance of a nation and therefore it must be regulated or controlled by international authority.[2] Lord Beaverbrook for the British Government of that time stated in Parliament:

> Our first concern will be to gain general acceptance of certain broad principles whereby civil aviation can be made into a benign influence for welding the nations of the world together into a closer cooperation. . .it will be our aim to make civil aviation a guarantee of international solidarity, a mainstay of world peace.[3]

The intensely political overtones that moulded the incipient civil aviation system of the world immediately after the War, thereby incontrovertibly establishing the relevance of diplomacy, international politics and international relations in civil aviation, is borne out by the statement of the first President of the ICAO Council when he said:

> It is well that we should be reminded. . .if the extent of the part which diplomatic and military considerations have played in international air transport, even in periods of undisturbed peace. We shall have a false idea of air transport's history, and a very false view of the problems of planning its future, if we think of it purely as a commercial enterprise, or neglect the extent to which political considerations have been controlling in shaping its course.[4]

In retrospect, it must be noted that this statement is a true reflection of what civil aviation stood for at that time, and, more importantly, that the statement has weathered the passage of time and is true even in the present context. A more recent commentator correctly observes that over the past decades, civil aviation has had to serve the political and economic interests of States and that, in this regard, ICAO has alternated between two positions, in its unobtrusive diplomatic role and its more pronounced regulatory role.[5]

---

[1] van Zandt (1944), pp. 28, 93.

[2] Wings for Peace—Labour's Post War Policy for Civil Flying, published by the Labour Party of England, April 1944, cited in van Zandt, *Id.* at 1.

[3] *Flight*, Vol. XLV, No. 1331, January 27, 1944, at pp. 97–98.

[4] Warner (1942), p. V.

[5] Sochor (1991), p. xvi.

An inherent characteristic of aviation is its ability to forge inroads into human affairs and promote international discourse. It also promotes international goodwill and develops "a feeling of brotherhood among the peoples of the world".[6] Therefore, it has been claimed that problems of international civil aviation constitute an integral part of the universal political problems of world organization and therefore aviation problems cannot be solved without involving the world political and diplomatic machinery.[7] It is at these crossroads that one encounters the profound involvement of the United Nations mechanism in general and ICAO in particular.

Military aviation and civil aviation are intrinsically different from each other in their nature and functions. However, both operate in the same air traffic management environment and therefore use common airspace which needs to be stringently managed, not only for safety reasons but also for reasons of efficiency. While military aviation is essential for national security and defence and therefore is a legitimate and indispensable activity, civil air transport is not only necessary for global interaction between nations but it also makes a significant contribution to the global economy.[8] These two equally important activities call for uncompromising cooperation between one another in the shared use of airspace and an enduring understanding of each other's needs. Military aviation not only includes the operation of conventional aircraft for military purposes but also involves the use of unmanned aerial systems (UAS)[9] and missile testing, all of which call for a close look at the use of airspace in the modern context.

A grave concern confronting the civil aviation community is that, with the proliferation of military activity will inevitably come the issue of endangerment of air routes. The consequences of the nuclear missile firings of 5 July 2006 by the Democratic Peoples' Republic of Korea (DPRK)[10] brought to bear the hazards and grave dangers such activities pose to civil aviation. In this instance, missiles launched by DPRK crossed several international air routes over the high seas. It was revealed that, when extrapolating the projected paths of some of the missiles, it appeared that they could have interfered with many more air routes, both over Japan and the air space of the North Pacific Ocean.

This is not the first instance of its kind. A similar incident took place on 31 August 1998 in the same vicinity in which the North Korean missiles were fired in July 2006. An object propelled by rockets was launched by North Korea and a part of the object hit the sea in the Pacific Ocean off the coast of Sanriku in north-

---

[6] Schenkman (1955) at p. 6.

[7] *Id.* vi.

[8] Abeyratne (2007) at 25–47.

[9] The potential explosion of unmanned aircraft Systems (commonly called UASs) in airspace also brings to bear the need to have a closer look at the civil-military aviation airspace demarcation. UASs are commonly associated with military operations in many parts of the world. The question that would arise in this context is how would a State feel about sharing airspace over contiguous States with a swarm of UASs operated by a mix of military/law enforcement and commercial enterprises? For more information see Abeyratne (2009), pp. 503–520.

[10] http://au.china-embassy.org/eng/xw/t261698.htm.

eastern Japan. The impact area of the object was in the vicinity of the international airway A590 which is known as composing NOPAC Composite Route System, a trunk route connecting Asia and North America where some 180 flights of various countries fly every day.

From an aeronautical perspective, Annex 11 to the Chicago Convention,[11] which deals with the subject of air traffic services, lays down requirements for coordination of activities that are potentially hazardous to civil aircraft. The International Standards and Recommended Practices in the Annex, Chapter 2 (2.17 and 2.18 in particular), contain provisions for co-ordination between military authorities and air traffic services and co-ordination of activities potentially hazardous to civil aircraft. These provisions specify that air traffic services authorities shall establish and maintain close co-operation with military authorities responsible for activities that may affect flights of civil aircraft. The provisions also prescribe that the arrangements for activities potentially hazardous to civil aircraft shall be co-ordinated with the appropriate air traffic services authorities and that the objective of this co-ordination shall be to achieve the best arrangements which will avoid hazards to civil aircraft and minimize interference with the normal operations of such aircraft. Standard 2.17.1 stipulates that arrangements for activities potentially hazardous to civil aircraft, whether over the territory of a State or over the high seas, shall be coordinated with the appropriate air traffic services authorities, such coordination to be effected early enough to permit timely promulgation of information regarding the activities in accordance with the provisions of Annex 15 to the Chicago Convention. Standard 2.17.2 of Annex 11 explains that the objective of the coordination referred to in the earlier provision shall be to achieve the best arrangements that are calculated to avoid hazards to civil aircraft and minimize interference with the normal operations of aircraft. One must of course hasten to add that Article 89 of the Convention stipulates that in case of war, the provisions of the Convention (and, by implication its Annexes) shall not affect the freedom of action of any of ICAO's member States affected, whether as belligerents or as neutrals.[12] The same principle would apply in the case of any member State which declares a state of national emergency and notifies the fact to the ICAO Council.

---

[11] Convention on International Civil Aviation, signed at Chicago on 7 December 1944. ICAO Doc 7300 9th edn, 2006.

[12] In October 1949, on the occasion of the adherence of Israel to the Chicago Convention, the Government of Egypt advised ICAO that, in view of considerations of fact and law which at that time affected Egypt's special position with regard to Israel and in pursuance of Article 89, Israeli aircraft may not claim the privilege of flying over Egyptian territory. See letter dated 16 October 1949 reproduced in Annex A to Doc 6922-C/803 at p. 125. It was Egypt's claim, as was later clarified by Egypt upon a query of the Secretary General of ICAO that a state of war existed between the two countries. The Government of Iraq also advised ICAO along similar lines, that a state of emergency had been declared on 14 May 1848 and therefore Article 89 was applicable and all Israeli aircraft were denied the privilege of flying over the territory of Iraq. On 28 November 1962 the Government of India informed ICAO that as a result of external aggression into Indian Territory by the People's Republic of China a state of grave emergency existed and the Government of India may not find it possible to comply with any or all of the provisions of the Chicago

The above considerations of safety notwithstanding, it are incontrovertible that cooperation in the activities of military and civil aviation is not only about sharing airspace. It is also about the efficient allocation of airspace to both categories of activity in separating such flights, particularly in the context of military flights which operate in special use airspace and those proceeding to special use airspace across civilian air routes. This brings to bear the inevitable conclusion that there must essentially be coordination between military authorities and air navigation service authorities.

At the Global Air Traffic Management Forum on Civil and Military Cooperation,[13] convened by the ICAO on 19 October 2009, the International Air Transport Association (IATA)[14] noted that, given the equal importance of civil and military aviation, it was imperative that airspace, which is an international and national resource, be managed as a whole, as a continuum and one common source and not a collection of segregated areas. This called for minimal restrictions on the use of airspace by both users, which in turn called for a structured and systematic management of the scope and duration of the use of airspace.

At the ICAO Forum, the Civil Air Navigation Services Organization (CANSO)[15] underscored the fact that increasing growth in civil air transport and

---

Convention. On 6 September 1965 the Government of Pakistan notified ICAO of the state of emergency under Article 89. In all instances, ICAO relayed the communications received to all its member States.

[13] The theme of the Forum was "*Time to take it global: Meeting each other's needs without compromising the Mission*". The event was held as a follow up to recommendations of the 11th Air Navigation Conference (Doc 9828, Rec. 1/2) concerning coordination with military authorities with a view to achieving enhanced airspace organization and management and as an integral supporting mechanism of the successful series of civil/military air traffic management summits instituted by the Air Traffic Control Association (ATCA). It was also a follow up to ICAO Assembly Resolution A36-13, Appendix O, *Coordination of civil and military air traffic* wherein States are asked to take appropriate action to coordinate with military authorities to implement a flexible and cooperative approach to airspace organization and management. The Forum was intended to create awareness among civil and military policy makers and regulators, civil and military air navigation service providers (ANSPs) and civil and military airspace users, on the need to improve civil/military cooperation and coordination in support of an optimum use of airspace by all users.

[14] The International Air Transport Association, an association of air carriers, was formed in 1919 as the International Air Traffic Association. Encapsulated in IATA's overall mission are seven core objectives: to promote safe, reliable and secure air services; to achieve recognition of the importance of a healthy air transport industry to worldwide social and economic development; to assist the air transport industry in achieving adequate levels of profitability; to provide high quality, value for money, industry-required products and services that meet the needs of the customer; to develop cost effective, environmentally-friendly standards and procedures to facilitate the operation of international air transport; to identify and articulate common industry positions and support the resolution of key industry issues; and to provide a working environment which attracts, retains and develops committed employees.

[15] CANSO is the global voice of the air traffic management profession. Its members comprise over 50 air navigation service providers who control more than 85 % of global air traffic movements. CANSO seeks to promote best practices within the industry.

traffic was putting pressure on limited airspace resources and that civil-military cooperation was becoming imperative. CANSO, while calling for a global platform of cooperation, emphasized that the key to successful cooperation is the establishment of trust, respect, transparency and flexibility on all key players and that States could play a lead role in developing a framework of cooperation. It also stated that a regional approach (as against a national approach) was essential, citing EUROCONTROL[16] as a true civil military agency which involved both civil and military offices at policy making level. In summing up, CANSO called for a fully integrated Civil-Military ATM, leading to the complete union of Civil-Military partners at national, regional and global level.[17]

A good example of the management system called for by IATA, and balanced cooperation as referred to by CANSO is the establishment of a Single European Sky (SES) legislation that is aimed at ensuring a harmonized regulatory framework for air traffic management and which uniformly and harmoniously applies in all 27 member States of the EU and 28 other associated States surrounding the Union. This legislation is accompanied by a technology programme called Single European Sky Air Traffic Management Research (SESAR) which modernizes and helps run the European air traffic control infrastructure modernization programme making SES and SESAR the essential components of the full air transport policy of Europe.

The outcome of this merger between policy and infrastructure technology has resulted in a robust civil-military aviation cooperation enabling all EU member States to be represented by a civilian and a military officer in the EU Single Sky Committee (which, *inter alia*, develops legislation) and military officers to be included in other bodies working on SES and SESAR.

The counterpart of SESAR in the United States is the Next Generation Air Transport System (NextGen). Next Gen, which is scheduled to be effective from 2012 to 2025, calls for a shift in airspace management to a trajectory-based system. It will have the following five attributes: Automatic dependent surveillance broadcast (ADS-B) which will use the Global Positioning System (GPS) satellite signals to provide air traffic controllers and pilots with much more accurate information that will help to keep aircraft safely separated both in the air and op runways; System-wide Information Management System (SWIM) which will provide a single infrastructure and information management system to deliver high quality, timely data to many users and applications; Next Generation Data Communications

[16] EUROCONTROL, the European Organisation for the Safety of Air Navigation, is an intergovernmental organisation made up of 38 Member States and the European Community. Its primary objective is the development of a seamless, pan-European air traffic management (ATM) system. EUROCONTROL contributes to making European aviation safer, performance-driven and environmentally sustainable. It was originally founded in 1960 as a civil-military organisation to deal with air traffic control for civil and military users in the upper airspace of its six founding European Member States. EUROCONTROL has developed into a vital European repository of ATM excellence, both leading and supporting ATM improvements across Europe.

[17] See Civil-Military Cooperation—The CANSO Perspective, October 2009.

which will provide an additional means of two-way communication for air traffic control clearances, instructions, advisories, flight crew requests and reports; Next Generation Network Enabled Weather (NNEW) which will cut weather-related delays at least in half; and NAS Voice Switch which will replace existing voice systems with a single air/ground and ground/ground voice communications system.

Both SESAR and NextGen, which are targeted for post 2020, would improve the performance of the air traffic management system by combining increased automation with new procedures that improve and achieve benefits related to safety, economic efficiency, capacity and environmental protection.

7.2 Legal and Regulatory Issues

7.2.1 Distinction Between Civil and Military Aviation

A simplistic but apt definition of civil aviation is "aviation activities carried out by civil aircraft". A civil aircraft has been defined as any aircraft, excluding government and military aircraft, used for the carriage of passengers, baggage, cargo and mail.[18] However, civil aviation comprises in general all aviation activities other than government and military air services which can be divided into three main categories: commercial air transport provided to the public by scheduled or non scheduled carriers; private flying for business or pleasure; and a wide range of specialized services commonly called aerial work, such as agriculture, construction, photography, surveying, observation and patrol, search and rescue, aerial advertisement *etc.*[19] By the same token, military aviation must be aviation activities carried out by military aircraft. Military aircraft have been defined as aircraft that are designed or modified for highly specialized use by the armed services of a nation.[20]

Military aviation therefore can be identified as the use of aircraft and other flying machines for the purposes of conducting or enabling warfare, which could include the carriage of military personnel and cargo used in military activities such as the logistical supply to forces stationed along a front. Usually these aircraft include bombers, fighters, fighter bombers and reconnaissance and unmanned attack aircraft such as drones.[21] These varied types of aircraft allow for the completion of a wide variety of objectives.

---

[18] Groenewege (1999) at 437. It must also be noted that an aircraft has been defined in Annexes 6–8 to the Chicago Convention as any machine which can derive support in the atmosphere from the reactions of air other than the reactions of air on the Earth's surface.

[19] *Ibid.*

[20] http://www.answers.com/topic/military-aircraft.

[21] In a report released on 21 December 2009, Venezuelan President Hugo Chavez is reported to have announced that, on Sunday 20 December, military drones had penetrated Venezuelan

Arguably, the most fundamental difference between the operation of civil and military aircraft lies in the fact that, although they are expected to share the same skies, the procedures by which they do this vary greatly. Civil aircraft depend entirely on predetermined flight paths and code of commercial conduct which vary depending on aircraft type and types of traffic carried, whereas military aircraft operate in line with the exigency of a situation and are not necessarily always guided by predetermined flight paths. This dichotomy led to the adoption, at the 10th Session of the ICAO Assembly (Caracas, 19 June to 16 July 1956) of Resolution A10-19 which, while recognizing that the skies (airspace) as well as many other facilities and services were commonly shared between civil and military aviation, focused on ICAO's mandate to promote the safety of flight.[22]

The preponderance of weight in prioritizing civil and military aviation seems therefore to be in favour of civil aviation, particularly when taking into consideration this Resolution and the earlier discussion on Annex 11 to the Chicago Convention, thus attenuating the principle that military aviation should, of necessity, consider the compelling need to protect civil aviation from the spontaneous risks that the former may carry with it.

The above notwithstanding, a glaring example of conflict in the civil and military aviation environment can be seen in the ongoing conflict between Greece and Turkey (Aegean crisis). According to reports,[23] the core of the conflict is the persistent abuse of "Flight Information Region" (FIR)[24] responsibility by Greece. FIR responsibility over the Aegean international airspace was assumed in 1952 by Greece. The report goes on to say that Greece considers the FIR as a national boundary line and a defence perimeter (i.e. Western boundary of Turkey and Eastern boundary of Greece, embracing all international airspace in the Aegean beyond Turkish territorial sea within Greek sovereignty area) and that consequently, Greece maintains the view that military aircraft entering into Athens FIR and flying in international airspace should submit flight plans and come under control of Greek air traffic control authorities.

Against Greece's alleged claim that non-submission of flight plans by Turkish military aircraft constitutes a violation of the Greek FIR, some have argued that there is no need for Turkish military aircraft to file flight plans under the Chicago Convention as the Convention explicitly states in Article 3 that it would not apply to

airspace along the North-western border with Colombia He had warned that Venezuela was prepared to defend itself if any State were to violate its sovereignty. See http://www.venezuelanalysis.com/news/5022. On 4 January 2010, it was reported that a US drone had fired two missiles in Pakistan, flattening an extremist hideout in Pakistan's lawless tribal belt on Sunday 3 January 2010, killing five militants in a recent spike in drone attacks. See http://www.channelnewsasia.com/stories/afp_asiapacific/view/1028351/1/.html.

[22] As per Article 44 of the Chicago Convention.

[23] http://www.aegeancrisis.org/category/air-space/.

[24] FIRs were devised by ICAO in the 1950s to provide facilities and services to the civilian aircraft in the international airspace. FIR arrangements solely entail technical responsibility. It does not change the free status of the airspace over the high seas under international law.

State aircraft (which includes military aircraft) and that there is no possibility of one violating an FIR which has nothing to do with the territorial sovereignty of a State, thus leading to the conclusion that Greek abuse of FIR responsibility is yet another manifestation of her claim of "de facto sovereignty" over the whole Aegean airspace.[25]

7.2.2 The Use of Civil Aircraft for Military Purposes

The distinction between civil and military aviation cannot be made without addressing the purpose for which an aircraft is employed. This is particularly significant in instances where civil aircraft are used for military purposes. The fact that military strategists have come to expect support services from civil aviation is becoming more evident with the increasing need for military operations both in war situations and in instances of human tragedy brought about by civil conflict or natural disasters. There have been many such instances, ranging from the use by British military of chartered commercial cargo aircraft in the Falklands in 1982 to earlier practices of India and Pakistan in 1971 when both countries used civilian passenger aircraft for the transportation of their troops during the Indo-Pakistan war.

The use of civil aircraft for military purposes brings to bear issues of identification of aircraft and the status of aircraft under article 3 of the Chicago Convention.[26] The question as to whether civil aviation and military aviation have demarcated operational regimes or whether they can still function in symbiosis has become an argumentative one in view of developments in the air transport industry which have occurred over the years. There are some determinants in this regard. Firstly, the nature of the cargo carried. Are they supplies or equipment for the military, customs or police services of a State? Article 35 of the Chicago Convention recognizes that the mere carriage "of munitions or implements of war" does not by itself make an aircraft a state aircraft. Then there is the question of ownership of the aircraft. Is it owned privately or by the State? The degree of control and supervision of the operation of the aircraft by the specified services are also factors to be considered in this equation. The nature of the passengers or personnel carried is also a consideration. Are they military, customs or police officials, or members of the public at large? Is the particular flight open for use by members of the public? Do aircraft registration and nationality markings become relevant? Will a usual civil (ICAO) flight plan be submitted and the usual air traffic clearances obtained? What is the

[25] *Supra*, note 23 *ibid*.

[26] Article 3 of the Chicago Convention states that the Convention applies only to civil aircraft and not to State aircraft, and goes on to explain that aircraft used in military, customs and police services shall be deemed to be State aircraft. Article 3 c) prohibits State aircraft of one State from flying over the territory of another State or landing thereon without special agreement or otherwise.

nature of crew? Are the crew civilian, or are they military, customs or police personnel, or employed by these services? Who is the operator? Is the operator a military, customs or police agent? What sort of documentation is carried in the aircraft? Are the documents required by the Chicago Convention and its Annexes to be carried on civil aircraft in fact being carried (e.g. certificate of registration, certificate of airworthiness, licences for the crew, journey log book, etc.)? What would the area of operations be? Will the aircraft fly to, or over, areas in a situation of on-going or imminent armed conflict? What about customs clearances? Will the normal clearances be obtained?

The broad answer to all these questions would lie in the fact that, in the ultimate analysis, the responsibility of using civil aircraft and crew for military purposes rests with the State concerned. The fundamental legal premise which applies in such situations is that, in international relations, the erosion of one's legal interests by another brings to bear the latter's responsibility. State responsibility is a recognized principle of international law in the current context. The law of international responsibility involves the incidence and consequence of acts which are irregular at international law, leading to the payment of compensation for the loss caused. It might therefore just be worthwhile to inquire as to whether Article 89 of the Chicago Convention should be reviewed so that the international community and ICAO could be given more flexibility in the determination of propriety in the use of civil aircraft for military purposes.

7.2.3 Some Recent Developments

At the Global Air Traffic Management Forum on Civil and Military Cooperation[27] ICAO subsumed its position by stating that airspace is a natural resource with finite capacity for which demand from all users is constantly expanding and that there has been an increased requirement on airspace use to meet a fast-growing aviation demand. States elected to be parties to the Chicago Convention in order that international civil aviation may be developed in a safe and orderly manner and that international air transport services may be established on the basis of equality of opportunity and operated soundly and economically. To achieve these objectives in recent years and to take due account of current and future needs in aviation, ICAO developed its vision of a seamless air traffic management (ATM) system.[28] ICAO further advised that, although the Chicago Convention governs international civil aviation and is not applicable to State aircraft (aircraft used in military, customs and police services)[29] State aircraft as well as military CNS/ATM systems

[27] *Supra*, note 13.

[28] Global Air Traffic Management Operational Concept, *ICAO Doc 9854*, AN/458, First Edition-2005, Chapter 1, Para 1.1.

[29] Chicago Convention, *Supra*, note 11 Article 3.

and services are an integral part of the aviation community. A much closer cooperation between civil and military organizations will contribute to the vision encapsulated in the preamble to the Chicago Convention, leading to the optimum use of the airspace and balancing State requirements for both civil and military aviation.

ICAO drew the attention of the Forum to Assembly Resolution A 36-13[30] adopted at the 36th ICAO Assembly (Montreal, 18–28 September 2007), Appendix O of which recognizes that the airspace as well as many facilities and services should be used in common by civil aviation and military aviation and that the ICAO Global ATB Operational Concept[31] states that all airspace should be a usable resource and that therefore any restriction on the use of any particular volume of airspace should be considered transitory, and all airspace should be managed flexibly. It was noted by the Forum that, through A36-13, the Assembly resolved that the common use by civil and military aviation of airspace and of certain facilities and services shall be arranged so as to ensure safety, regularity and efficiency of international civil air traffic and that the regulations established by ICAO member States to govern the operation of their State aircraft over the high seas shall ensure that these operations did not compromise the safety, regularity and efficiency of international civil air traffic and to the extent possible such operations conformed to the Rules of the Air contained in Annex 2 to the Chicago Convention. The resolution also requested the Council of ICAO to provide guidance and advice to States that wished to establish civil/military agreements.

Against this backdrop, ICAO advised the Forum of the need for a strengthened civil/military cooperation and coordination which called upon ICAO Member States to initiate as necessary or improve the coordination between their civil and military air traffic services. It was important that States, in view of the increasing need to cooperate with multiple airspace users, developed an integrated and cohesive civil-military coordination strategy with a roadmap indicating short, mid and long term objectives. ICAO further advised that the benefits of enhancing civil-military cooperation should be considered at the global level with a view to identifying best practices through dialogue and exchange of information. Effective civil/military cooperation and coordination is required not only to meet future civil and military air traffic requirements for increased safety, security, capacity, efficiency, environmental sustainability but also to achieve interoperability, seamlessness and harmonisation through sound policy, a structured framework, effective liaisons and management at working level.[32]

---

[30] Consolidated statement of continuing ICAO policies and associated practices related specifically to air navigation, Assembly Resolutions in Force (as of 28 September 2007), *Doc 9902*, II-2.

[31] *Supra*, note 30.

[32] In its briefing, ICAO emphasized that cooperation between civil and military authorities should be aimed at achieving optimal use of the airspace resulting in increased airspace capacity, operational flexibility, and savings in flying time, fuel and CO_2 emissions. The Forum noted that safety, economical impact, efficiency and interoperability are objectives shared by both civil and military aviation communities.

7.2.4 ICAO Initiatives

One of the recent initiatives is the ICAO global air traffic management operational concept[33] which visualizes an integrated, harmonized and global interoperable ATM[34] system. The broad vision of this concept is to achieve an interoperable global air traffic management system for all users during all phases of flight that meets agreed levels of safety, provides for optimum economic operations, is environmentally sustainable and meets national security requirements.[35] The ATM system is based on the provision of services, through a framework which involves airspace, aerodromes, aircraft and persons which are part of the ATM system. The benefits accruing to all members of the ATM community are greater equity in airspace activity; greater access to timely and meaningful information for decision support and more autonomy in decision making including conflict management, and the opportunity to better deliver business and individual outcomes within an appropriate safety framework.

ICAO has also issued guidelines on the coordination between military authorities and air traffic services (ATS) authorities which recognize *in limine* that coordination between the responsible military authorities and appropriate ATS authorities is essential to the safety of civil aircraft operations whenever activities potentially hazardous to such operations are planned and conducted by any military units.[36] These guidelines go on to state that in the event that a sudden outbreak of armed hostilities or any other factors preclude this normal coordination process, appropriate State and ATS authorities, civil aircraft operators and pilots-in-command of aircraft must assess the situation based on the information available and plan their actions so as not to jeopardize safety.[37]

The Guidelines recommend that, in the event that a military unit observes that a civil aircraft is entering, or is about to enter, a designated prohibited, restricted or danger area or any other area of activity which constitutes potential hazards, a warning to the aircraft should be issued through the responsible ATS unit. The warning should include advice on the change of heading required to leave, or

---

[33] An operational concept is a statement of what is envisioned.

[34] Air traffic management is the dynamic, integrated management of air traffic and airspace—safely, economically and efficiently—through the provision of facilities in collaboration with all parties. See *ICAO Doc 9854*, *supra* note 31 at 1-1.

[35] *Ibid.*

[36] Manual Concerning Safety Measures Relating to Military Activities Potentially Hazardous to Civil Aircraft Operations, *ICAO Doc 9554-AN/932* First Edition, 1990, paragraph 3.1.

[37] *Id.* Paragraph 3.1.1. Examples of military activities which may pose a threat to civil aircraft and which should be coordinated with ATS authorities include practice firings or testing of any weapons air-to air, air to surface, surface to air in an area or in a manner that could affect civil air traffic; certain military aircraft operations such as air displays, training exercises and the intentional dropping of objects and paratroopers; launch and recovery of space vehicles; and operations in areas of conflict, when such operations include a potential threat to civil air traffic. See Paragraph 3.2. of Doc 9554.

circumvent, the area.[38] If the military unit is unable to contact the responsible ATS unit immediately and the situation is deemed to be a genuine emergency, an appropriate warning to the aircraft may be transmitted on the VHF emergency channel 121.5 MHz. If the identity of the aircraft is not known, it is important that the warning include the SSR code, if observed, and describe the position of the aircraft in a form meaningful to the pilot, e.g. by reference to an ATS route and/or the direction and distance from an airport or an aeronautical radio navigation aid, an established waypoint or reporting point.[39] In the case where an unauthorized aircraft is observed visually to be flying in, or about to enter a prohibited, restricted or danger area, the following visual signal is prescribed by the International Standards in Annex 2 to the Chicago Convention — *Rules of the Air*, Appendix 1 to indicate that the aircraft is to take such remedial action as is necessary.[40] The Guidelines caution that the importance of co-ordinating with the responsible ATS unit(s), whenever possible, the issuance of any warnings and advice to civil aircraft regarding changes of flight path should be emphasized in any briefings or instructions given by military authorities to their units, since uncoordinated warnings and associated navigational advice, when followed, may result in a potential risk of collision with other aircraft in the area.[41]

The objective of the co-ordination between the military authorities planning activities potentially hazardous to civil aircraft and the responsible ATS authorities is to reach agreement on the best arrangements which will avoid hazards to civil aircraft and minimize interference with the normal operations of civil aircraft. Ideally, this means the selection of locations outside promulgated ATS routes and controlled airspace for the conduct of the potentially hazardous activities. If the selection of such locations is not possible due to the nature and scope of the planned activities, temporary restrictions imposed on civil air traffic should be kept to a minimum through close co-ordination between the military units and the ATS unit.[42]

The Guidelines are clear on the fact that although Article 89 of the Chicago Convention provides that in the event of armed conflict or the potential for armed conflict, the Convention does not affect the freedom of action of any Contracting State affected, whether as belligerents or as neutrals). Nonetheless, the need for close co-ordination between civil and military authorities and units is even more critical. The responsibility for initiating the co-ordination process rests with the States whose military forces are engaged in the conflict. The responsibility for instituting special measures to ensure the safety of international civil aircraft operations remains with the States responsible for providing air traffic services in the airspace affected by the conflict, even in cases where co-ordination is not

---

[38] *Id.* Paragraph 8.1.

[39] *Id.* Paragraph 8.2.

[40] *Id.* Paragraph 8.3.

[41] *Id.* Paragraph 8.4.

[42] *Id.* Paragraphs 9.1 and 9.2.

initiated or completed.[43] Based on the information which is available, the State responsible for providing air traffic services should identify the geographical area of the conflict, assess the hazards or potential hazards to international civil aircraft operations, and determine whether such operations in or through the area of conflict should be avoided or may be continued under specified conditions. An international NOTAM containing the necessary information, advice and safety measures to be taken should then be issued and subsequently updated in the light of developments. All those concerned with initiating and issuing of NOTAM should be aware of the provisions governing the duration of the published NOTAM. Annex 15, Standard 5.3.1.2 states that a NOTAM given Class I distribution shall be superseded by a NOTAM given Class II distribution when the duration of the circumstances notified is likely to exceed 3 months or the NOTAM has remained in force for 3 months. A copy of the NOTAM should be forwarded to the appropriate regional office of ICAO.[44] If the necessary information is not forthcoming from the States whose military authorities are engaged in the armed conflict, the State responsible for providing air traffic services should ascertain the nature and scope of the hazards or potential hazards from other sources, such as aircraft operators, the International Air Transport Association (IATA) and the International Federation of Air Line Pilots' Associations (IFALPA), adjacent States or in some cases the relevant ICAO regional office.[45]

Separate guidelines[46] issued by ICAO provide that aircraft shall not be flown in a prohibited area, or in a restricted area, the particulars of which have been duly published, except in accordance with the conditions of the restrictions or by permission of the State over whose territory the areas are established.[47] The same guidelines also provide that special procedures shall be established with a view to ensuring that air traffic units are notified if a military unit observes that an aircraft which is, or might be a civil aircraft is approaching, or has entered any area in which interception might be necessary. In such an event all possible efforts should be made to confirm the identity of the aircraft and to provide it with the navigational guidance necessary to avoid the need for interception.[48] There is also a requirement to the effect that air traffic services authorities establish and maintain close cooperation with military authorities responsible for activities that may affect flights of civil aircraft.[49] As soon as an air traffic services unit becomes aware of an unidentified aircraft in its area, it is required to establish the identity of the aircraft

[43] *Doc 9554*, Paragraph 10.2.

[44] *Id.* Paragraph 10.3.

[45] *Id.* Paragraph 10.4.

[46] See Manual Concerning Interception of Civil Aircraft, *ICAO Doc 9433-AN/926* Second Edition—1990.

[47] *Id.* Paragraph 3.2.4.1.

[48] *Id.* Paragraph 3.2.6.1.

[49] *Id.* Paragraph 3.1.7.1.

whenever this is necessary for the provision of air traffic services or required by the appropriate military authorities in accordance with locally agreed procedures.[50]

As the foregoing discussion indicates, there is ample regulatory guidance from a civil aviation perspective to ensure a seamless and interoperable sharing of airspace between civil and military aviation activities. However, there remain some weak spots, the first being the perceived inadequacy and lack of clarity of Article 89 of the Chicago Convention which renders the legal structure in this context destitute of certainty and effect. Another contentious area is missile testing involving airspace and air routes used by civil aircraft as was demonstrated by the DPRK issue of 2006. Many concerned parties voiced their perturbation over the incident, including ICAO which, through the President of the Council sent a letter to the DPRK authorities voicing the grave concern of the international aviation community that Standards 2.17 and 2.18 of Annex 11 to the Chicago Convention were not followed by the military authorities of DPRK. Concurrently, Chinese Foreign Minister Li Zhaoxing held phone talks with U.S. Secretary of State Condoleezza Rice, Japanese Foreign Minister Aso Taro, Minister of Foreign Affairs and Trade of the Republic of Korea Ban Ki-Moon and Australian Foreign Minister Alexander Downer respectively. Countries across the world joined in the protest, and the United Nations Security Council met for an emergency meeting to discuss the missile tests.

The United Nations Security Council condemned the test firing by DPRK of missiles and adopted Resolution 1695 which requested all Member States to prevent the transfer of missile and missile-related items, materials, goods and technology to the Democratic People's Republic of Korea's missile or weapons of mass destruction programmes, as well as procurement of such items and technology from that country. It also addressed the transfer of financial resources in relation to those programmes.

The resolution affirmed that such launches jeopardize peace, stability and security in the region and beyond, particularly in light of the country's claim that it has developed nuclear weapons. The Council underlined that DPRK needed to show restraint and refrain from any action that might aggravate tension, and continue to work on the resolution of non-proliferation concerns, through political and diplomatic efforts. In that connection, the Security Council strongly urged the country to return immediately to the six-party talks without precondition, to work towards expeditious implementation of the September 2005 joint statement and return to the Treaty on the Non-Proliferation of Nuclear Weapons (NPT) and International Atomic Energy Agency (IAEA) safeguards.[51]

In May 2009, DPRK test fired another short-range missile, apparently in clear violation of Resolution 1695 and, it is reported,[52] stated that it would take self defence action if the United Nations Security Council were to impose tougher sanctions. This missile, which was fired from the Masudan-ni site on DPRK's

[50] *Id.* Paragraph 3.1.9.1.

[51] http://www.un.org/News/Press/docs/2006/sc8778.doc.htm.

[52] http://www.chinadaily.com.cn/cndy/2009-05/30/content_7953420.htm.

east coast, was the latest in the series of missiles the DPRK test fired since conducting a major nuclear test a few days before the firing.

If the response of State authorities who fire missiles into the air without paying heed to applicable regulations and guidelines were to be that, since the State concerned has sovereignty over its airspace (as recognized by Article 1 of the Chicago Convention) and that it does over its airspace is its concern, it must be pointed out that air routes are used by airlines of various nationalities carrying persons of various nationalities and that there must be recognition that the concept of sovereignty, in its pristine purity and simplistic interpretation cannot be sustained in this instance. One commentator states very aptly:

> The role of the State in the modern world is a complex one. According to legal theory, each State is sovereign and equal. In reality, with the phenomenal growth in communications and consciousness, and with the constant reminder of global rivalries, not even the most powerful of States can be entirely sovereign. Interdependence and the close knit character of contemporary international commercial and political society ensures that virtually any action of a State could well have profound repercussions upon the system as a whole and the decisions under consideration by other States.[53]

Therefore, in the ultimate analysis, cooperation between civil and military authorities, in accordance with the existing regulations and guidelines is essential, with the underlying consideration that civil aviation, with 15,000 aircraft airborne at any given time carrying 2.2 billion passengers annually, should not under any circumstances be compromised.

7.3 Drones and State Responsibility

Another area in which, similar to missile testing, that the place of takeoff and landing brings to bear the responsibility and accountability of the State, and the demarcation between civil and military landing and takeoff points, is the realm of unmanned aircraft systems. In October 2013, CNN reported that 400 civilians had been killed in Pakistan by unmanned aircraft (UA)[54] since President Obama took office in 2009. Transnational legal theory suggests that such attacks are illegal and, in 2009, the United Nations special rapporteur on extra judicial killings suggested that the use of drones by the Obama administration in Afghanistan and Pakistan was untenable and contrary to international law. The underlying concerns with regard to legal issues are state sovereignty, responsibility, and liability. One of the contentious issues would be whether unmanned aircraft flying outside their permitted areas violate state sovereignty, and if so—what can be done to prevent future UA violations of sovereignty of the airspace. Another would be, as earlier mentioned, whether the killings carried out by drones amount to extra judicial killings. The

[53] Shaw (2003) at 120.

[54] Unmanned aircraft are sometimes referred to in this article as drones.

focus of this article is on legal challenges and whether military functions of UA can be brought under international regulation. Despite the inherent advantages of this relatively new mode of aviation—such as camouflage, low cost, and the avoidance of risk to the pilot on board in UA operations—serious concerns abound, which go to the heart of the law of humanity. This article addresses these concerns from a legal perspective.

The problem of drones[55] has indeed become contentious. A compelling argument is that killing of humans, whether they fall into the category of terrorists or not, is premeditated murder. In many jurisdictions around the world premeditated murder is a crime, as it is in all 50 States of the United States. Additionally, political killings, which drone attacks often accomplish, are outlawed in the United States.[56] The crime is made more heinous when it is committed in foreign lands without the consent of the State concerned, and with callous disregard to the sovereignty of that State. The only exception to the use of drones in a foreign land (and this does not extend to arbitrary attacks that might involve non combatants) is in authorized armed conflict such as in instances where the international community, through the United Nations Security Council, authorizes such use in battle zones.

From an international perspective, the operative law with regard to victims of war is international humanitarian law. This limb of law is also known as the law of war, the laws and customs of war or the law of armed conflict. Basically, international humanitarian law encompasses four limbs, the first being that persons who are not, or are no longer, taking part in hostilities shall be respected, protected and treated humanely. They should be given appropriate care, without any discrimination. Secondly, captured combatants and other persons whose freedom has been restricted are required to be treated humanely. They should be protected against all acts of violence, in particular against torture and if they are brought to trial they have the right to enjoy the fundamental guarantees of a regular judicial procedure. Thirdly, the right of parties to an armed conflict to choose methods or means of warfare is not unlimited. No superfluous injury or unnecessary suffering should be inflicted. Finally, in order to spare the civilian population, armed forces are required

[55] The UA is not a new strategy and has nearly a century-old history in aviation. First included in Jane's All the World's Aircraft in 1920, UAs were tested during World War II, but not used in combat during that war. Germany's use of the simple yet deadly V-1 "flying bomb" during World War II laid the groundwork for post-war UA programs in the United States. However, it was not until the Vietnam War in the late 1960s and early 1970s that UAs such as the AQM-34 Firebee were used in a surveillance role (by the United States). The Firebee exemplifies the versatility of UAs. Initially flown in the 1970s, it was modified to deliver payloads and flew its first flight test as an armed UA on December 20, 2002.

[56] Executive Order 11905 [in Section 5(g)] issued by President Ford in 1976 explicitly provides that no employee of the United States shall engage in, or conspire to engage in political assassination. Later, President Reagan issued Executive Order 12333 which, by Section 2.11 provides that no person employed by or acting on behalf of the United States Government shall engage in or conspire to engage in assassination. The Order goes on to state that no agency of the Intelligence Community shall participate in or request any person to undertake activities forbidden by the Order.

at all times to distinguish between the civilian population and civilian objects on the one hand, and military objectives on the other. Neither the civilian population as such nor individual civilians or civilian objects should be the target of military attacks.

Certain circumstances over the past decade have made the world more cautious, leading it to guide its philosophy of mutual trust along a path which is now called "the precautionary approach". The world would no longer sit and wait, reacting only when a crisis causes massive human suffering and loss of lives. A new doctrine, propounded by a group of scholars at the behest of the United Nations Secretary General Kofi Annan in 2001 has come into being. Called "the responsibility to protect", this doctrine embraces the principle that all member States of the United Nations have a responsibility to protect the lives, liberty and basic human rights of their citizens, and that if they fail or are unable to carry it out, the international community has a responsibility to step in.

7.3.1 *What Is an Unmanned Aircraft?*

Unmanned Aircraft [UA] is a pilotless aircraft capable of flying autonomously or semi-autonomously with some pilot assistance from a remote station and hence the term 'Remotely Piloted Aircraft' [RPA].[57] The United States Department of Defense defines UA as "a powered aerial vehicle that does not carry a human operator, uses aerodynamic forces to provide vehicle lift, can fly autonomously or be piloted remotely, can be expendable or recoverable, and carry a lethal or non-lethal payload."[58] In contrast, the ICAO circular has a simple definition of UA i.e. "An aircraft which is intended to operate with no pilot on board."[59] Unmanned Aircraft is one of the main components of the many sub-systems of Unmanned Aircraft system which includes an aircraft [unmanned air vehicle],

[57] An Unmanned aircraft is a self piloted or remotely piloted aircraft that can carry cameras, sensors, communications equipment or other payloads. Therefore in its ultimate definition, a UA is an aircraft, which is defined by Annex 2 to the Convention on International Civil Aviation (Chicago Convention) as "any machine that can derive support in the atmosphere from the reactions of the air other than reactions of the air against the earth's surface." In addition to this quality, a UA is also a powered, aerial vehicle that does not carry a human operator, uses aerodynamic forces to provide vehicle lift, and can fly autonomously or be piloted remotely. A UA can be expendable or recoverable, and can carry a lethal or non lethal payload. UAs have been used to conduct reconnaissance and intelligence-gathering for nearly 60 years (since the 1950s).

[58] Unmanned Aerial Vehicles: Background and Issues for Congress, Report for Congress written by Elizabeth Bone and Christopher Bolkcom, Congressional Research Service: The Library of Congress, 25 April 2003 CRS 1.

[59] ICAO, Secretary General, *Unmanned Aircraft Systems* (*UAS*), Circular Cir 328 AN/190 (Montreal: ICAO, 2011) at x.

payloads [dispensable or non-dispensable], communication and control systems, launching systems, transport systems etc.[60] Modern UA contain varying levels of autonomous decision making algorithms which enables UA to exchange data with its control base and to transfer thermal images along with its positioning, speed, altitude and other information it was designed for.[61] UA is also commonly known as 'Drone'. The leading aeronautical consultant Reg Austin reasons that UA is technically different than drone.[62] Another extension of UA is the Unmanned Combat Air Vehicles [UCAV] which is armed and specifically assigned to attack each target.[63] However, since the term drone has been popularized in the main-stream media, for the purposes of this paper the term UA will be interchangeably used with drones.

7.3.2 Evolution of the Unmanned Aircraft

From the humble beginnings of 'Aerial Torpedo', an unpiloted bomber plane made of wood, in the early twentieth century to the contemporary 'Predators' with the capability of high resolution video cameras and payload weapons guided by the precision lasers, the metamorphosis of UA has come a long way.[64] UA come in various shapes, sizes, and capabilities' ranging from High altitude long endurance [HALE] which can fly up to 24 h and over 15,000 m altitude to Mini UAV [MUAV] which weigh less than 20 kg and is capable of flying up to 30 km range when hand-launched.[65] The history of UA changed forever when Predator made it first successful flight in 1994. Richard Newman notes that "Predator became an instant hit because it could transmit live video footage of enemy actions to commanders on the ground and aircrews above the battlefield. It illuminated targets for precision weapons fired from afar. It even, on occasion, fired its own weapons, a rarity for a UAV."[66] At present, Global Hawk is widely regarded to have taken over the Predator and has been flown over the Afghanistan, Bosnia, Iraq, Kosovo, Pakistan and Yemen. As one writer put it "Global Hawk does much broader surveillance. It flies at elevations of 60,000 feet or more, like the U-2, and has higher resolution cameras than the Predator. Global Hawk can fly for nearly day and a half without

[60] Austin (2010) at 3.

[61] *Ibid.*

[62] *Ibid.*

[63] See generally, Friedman (2010) at 1.

[64] Austin (2010) at 304–314.

[65] *Ibid.* at 4.

[66] See generally Newman (2002) at 49.

being refueled, meaning it can take off from a base 1,200 miles away, loiter for 24 hours, then fly back."[67] Today, the sky is no longer the exclusive domain of the birds or jumbo jets as thousands of UA are hovering all over the skies.

7.3.3 Commercial Use of Unmanned Aircraft

UA are primarily used for military purposes but their commercial use in on the rise. UA's are often used for 3D's i.e. 'dull, dirty, and dangerous jobs.'[68] Besides, UA are used in research and development of the aeronautical areas such as airborne testing under the real conditions.[69] There are many advantages of UA as compared to its counterpart manned aircrafts. Less operating costs, low fuel and maintenance costs, cheaper insurance and low salaries for the ground based personnel all translate into a lucrative monetary benefits to pursue UA for commercial purposes. Due to financial benefits associated with the UA, it is likely that UA rental business will soon sell their services.[70] Manned helicopters have been used in South Africa and Australia to monitor herds during hot weather and difficult terrains but it may save time and money if UA are used to keep track of these herds.[71] UA could be in hands of news channels and broadcasting companies for covering emergency events, real-time sports events, monitoring traffic accidents and war zones.[72] For the first time, the United Nations has ordered surveillance drones from an Italian firm for its peacekeeping missions in Congo and diplomats hope that if successful the drones could be deployed for missions in Ivory Coast and South Sudan.[73]

The advertisement line for drones is catchy, who wants to buy an expensive three million police helicopter when a much cheaper drone can do the same job more effectively. UAs have the potential of hunting down the suspects, criminals, and law-offenders. With the Global Positioning System [GPS] auto-pilot and a live video feed, one cannot hide from these omnipresent drones.

[67] *Ibid.*

[68] *Ibid.* at 5.

[69] *Ibid.* at 6.

[70] Austin (2010) at 273.

[71] *Ibid.* at 274.

[72] *Ibid.*

[73] The U.N. spokesman Martin Nesirky told reporters that "Unarmed UAVs (unmanned aerial vehicles) will allow our peacekeepers in the Democratic Republic of Congo to monitor the movements of armed groups and protect the civilian population more efficiently. The selected vendor is the Italian company Selex ES. The UAV is known as the Falco and is designed to be a medium altitude, medium endurance surveillance platform capable of carrying a range of payloads including several types of high resolution sensors." See Michelle Nichols, 'Italian firm to provide surveillance drone for U.N. in Congo,' Reuters (1 August 2013) online at http://www.reuters.com/article/2013/08/01/us-congo-democratic-un-drones-idUSBRE97014720130801.

7.3.4 State Utilization of Unmanned Aircraft

Approximately 70 countries now possess the UA however, only few possess the armed UA notably the US, UK, Israel, Italy, and China.[74] Although, the US is the leader when it comes to armed UA, it no longer has the monopoly over the expansion of drones. The militaries of various nations are quickly learning to develop UA capable of delivering lethal blow to the enemy taking advantage of the loopholes in the current international legal framework on the legitimate use of drones.[75] In 2001, a Predator evolved into a UCAV from a reconnaissance UA when it fired a Hellfire-C laser guided missile at a tank.[76] Meanwhile, the Israeli Defense Forces [IDF] have been using the UA for multiple intelligence and data gathering programs from 1980s.[77] Japan has been developing the UA for dual purposes i.e. both civilian and military uses since World War II.[78] The South Korean government has developed a smart vertical take-off and landing UA and is on the verge of developing an upgraded version of the US Eagle Eye tiltrotor UA.[79] The Italian Air Force has its hands on a precision strike UA and Rome is negotiating a "black" medium-altitude, long-endurance [MALE] project that would be flying in 2017–2018 told the Air Force Lt. Gen. Claudio Debertolis, Italy's secretary general of defense and national armaments director.[80] The Russian military has long collaborated with France's Dassault for manufacturing UAVs and is now acquiring the so-called mini-class of the drones.[81] Germany is in negotiations with Israel over the Heron UAV and with the U.S. for the Reaper UAV. "A Government spokesman told AFP: 'The intention is that we acquire 16 such devices in future and that the armed forces have them at their disposal

[74] Roberts (2013).

[75] *Ibid.*

[76] Lazarski (2002).

[77] Bone and Bolkcom (2003).

[78] See generally Staff, Commercial use of UAVs—Widespread in Japan, in 2004 Yearbook: UAVs Global Perspective 138 (UVS International, Blyenburgh & CO.); Id. at 127.

[79] UAV Categorisation, in 2004 Yearbook: UAVs Global Perspective 156 (UVS International, Blyenburgh & Co.) at 156.

[80] Butler (2013).

[81] Denis Fedutinov, a UAV expert described these new state of the art UAVs, "These are the short-range systems, with a range measuring from 5 kilometres to 25 kilometres, Denis Fedutinov says. These are small devices that are comparable to a model aero-plane. But they are very effective in ensuring the transmission of video- and photo-images in real time, and they can also reconnoiter over by the hill, in the close-in zone. These devices make it possible for the lowest-echelon units to quickly obtain intelligence and operational information and depend in no way on higher-echelon air-reconnaissance systems." **See** Nekhai (2013).

from 2016, three years from now.'"[82] France made a $1.5 billion foreign military sales agreement with the US to buy 16 Reapers (UAVs) developed by General Atomics.[83] "Britain bought US Predator drones and rented Israeli drones for use in Britain's wars in Iraq and Afghanistan. . .the Watchkeeper system for surveillance, and two separate BAE armed drones."[84] Besides conventional reconnaissance and surveillance the UCAVs can perform multiple offensive and defensive tasks such as "suppression of enemy air defenses [SEAD], close air support [CAS], defensive counter air [DCA], offensive counter air [OCA], and air interdiction [AI]."[85]

UA are increasingly used from reconnaissance to surveillance to security to border patrolling to law and order operations and every possible imaginable task. It is only a matter of time that drones will become a modern military necessity for each state.[86] One better pay heed to the words of General Petraeus, former head of the US Central Command, "[w]e can't get enough drones".[87] UA importance resonated with former CIA Director Leon Panetta affirming that the unmanned aerial vehicles are "[t]he only game in town"[88] when it comes to tackling Al-Qaeda.

7.4 Legal Issues Related to Unmanned Aircraft

7.4.1 State Sovereignty

Sovereignty here refers to air-space autonomy of each independent state as per Article 1 of the Chicago Convention stating that "[t]he contracting states recognize that every State has complete and exclusive sovereignty over the airspace above its territory."[89] Article 8 of the Chicago Convention titled '*Pilotless aircraft*' explicitly prohibits all States to fly UA without the prior consent of the other state.

---

[82] Evans (2013).

[83] Harthy (2013).

[84] Cole and Wright (2010a).

[85] Peterson (2005) published at 18.

[86] See Friedman (2010) at 33, Friedman notes, "Militaries adopt revolutionary technology and tactics because they cannot go on the way they have been operating. In some cases, such as ours, circumstances make the existing way of war either literally impossible or unaffordable-or there are new requirements that existing forces cannot meet. In others the general adoption of some new technology makes it impossible to go on as before."

[87] See Capaccio (2010): "[t]he new aviation plan projects spending for all aircraft to increase to $29 billion by 2020 from about $22 billion in fiscal 2011, an average of 3 percent annual growth adjusted for inflation."

[88] Shachtman (2009).

[89] Convention on International Civil Aviation, 7 December 1944, 15 UNTS 295, 61 US Stat 1180 (entered into force 4 April 1947).

UA used for surveillance and reconnaissance are in danger of breaching Article 36 of the Chicago Convention which gives authority to the contracting states to prohibit or regulate the use of photographic apparatus in aircraft over its territory.[90] Peterson calls this "an operational limitation" to UA reconnaissance functions and notes that the underlying principle is state sovereignty over airspace.[91] "Drones will no doubt make possible the dramatic expansion of the surveillance state. With the convergence of other technologies it may even make possible machine recognition of faces, behaviors, and the monitoring of individual conversations."[92] At present, the increased surveillance and unbridled reconnaissance by the major super-powers is breaching the principle of sovereignty. This embodies a legitimate concern of states. Moreover, UA carrying dangerous payloads or war munitions without authorization breach Article 35 of the Chicago Convention. With the rapid emergence of military drones, these UA carrying payloads, missiles and arsenals must be flown with the permission of the host State or else they will the state sovereignty.

Another paramount concern is when the State totally neglects the principle of sovereignty or blatantly breaches the terms and conditions of the parties' agreement? What should be the consequences for those states which habitually penetrate the foreign airspace? Prof. Milde suggests that such an aircraft may be "intercepted for purposes of identification; directed to leave the violated air space by a determined route; directed to land for the purpose of further investigation/prosecution; forced to land for further investigation/persecution."[93] Should the UA be shot down without any warning? Article 3 of the Chicago Convention prohibits the use of weapons against civil aircrafts—with a caveat that the same protection is not extended to the State aircraft in international law. In this context, one can draw a conclusion that UA do not enjoy any special immunity in international law. In reality, most states do not possess the technology to detect the stealthy UA,[94] even if, they detect foreign UA the fear of repercussions of shooting down a drone would make them think twice. But recently in May 2013, the Al-Shabaab militants shot a US drone in Somalia and posted pictures on the Twitter. The US officials confirmed the incident but did not provide any specifications to drone model believed to be one of *Schiebel* UAVs.[95] In an another case, the Russians in collaborations with Iranians observed the US drone's routes and its surveillance of Iranian skies, hacked into the drone system and forced it to land in Iran on 4 December 2011.[96] The

---

[90] Article 36 of the Chicago Convention reads, "Each contracting State may prohibit or regulate the use of photographic apparatus in aircraft over its territory."

[91] Peterson (2005) at 47.

[92] *See* Cole and Wright (2010b).

[93] Micheal (2012) at 65.

[94] The fact that majority of the UAs like Predator, Global Hawk, and Reapers fly above 70,000 feet and are beyond the technological or military capacity of most States to detect them, let alone shoot them.

[95] Laing (2013).

[96] Kahlili (2013). "A Russian military team from its air and space division had secretly entered Iran days after a strategic agreement between the two countries in 2007 and was stationed at

Russians helped decode American drone RQ170s intercepted by the Iranians in exchange for anti-defense air system S300.[97] Despite the request by the US government to return it back, the Iranians have refused to comply and diplomatic tensions have escalated since then. Nonetheless, State reserves the right to regulate or prohibit the carriage in or above its territory in the interests of public order, safety, and above all its sovereignty.

7.4.2 Unmanned Aircrafts Operating Over High Seas

In accordance with Article 12 of the Chicago Convention, states cannot deviate from the rules of flight over the high seas which comprises for 70 % of airspace. Article 87 of the United Nations Convention on the Law of the Sea[98] of 1982 grants unrestricted freedom for the aircraft of all States to fly over the high seas. Dr. Abeyratne notes that "an important consideration in delineating territorial sovereignty lies in the expansion of Flight Information Regions [FIR] and the provision of air traffic management services by States particularly when such measures are influenced by the revenue generating capabilities."[99] Prof. Bin Cheng agrees that States must comply with the rules pertaining to the flight and maneuver of all aircrafts over the high seas as laid out in the Article 12 of the Chicago Convention.[100] Annex 2 of the Chicago Convention, further solidifies that State aircrafts over the high seas "[s]hall ensure that these operations do not compromise the safety, regularity and efficiency of international civil air traffic."[101]

Revolutionary Guard bases to help the Guards with its weapons program and access to modern U.S. technology. With this collaboration, all the information of the stealth drone is now in the hands of the Russians, and much has been given to Iran's Defense Ministry."

[97] *Ibid.*

[98] The Law of the Sea, Original Text of the United Nations Convention on the Law of the Sea, all Annexes and Index, United Nations: New York, 1983. Moreover Article 29 gives the definition of a warship i.e. "a ship belonging to the armed forces of a state bearing the external marks distinguishing such ship of its nationality, under the command of an officer duly commissioned by the government of the State and whose name appears in the appropriate service list or its equivalent, and manned by a crew which is under regular armed forces discipline."

[99] Abeyratne (2010) at 162.

[100] Cheng (1962) at 148.

[101] Annex 2 to the Convention on International Civil Aviation, "Rules of the Air", 2.1.1 Note.

7.4.3 *Are Unmanned Aircraft a State or Civil Aircraft?*

What is the status of UA under international air law? The Chicago Convention,[102] the *Magna Carta* for aviation and the primary bedrock source of the public international air law—in Article 3 distinguishes between civil and state aircraft. A distinct anomaly is observed in the question as to "how an international treaty, which on the one hand prescribes that it applies only to civil aircraft [Art. 3(a)], turns around and prescribes a rule for State aircraft [Art. 3(c)]."[103] However, Article 3 does not provide a definition but at best gives a rebuttable presumption as those aircrafts utilized in furtherance of state activities such as search and rescue, natural disasters, governmental transport, and other state related services can be categorized as State aircraft.[104] This is far from a comprehensive definition and unreliable since the same Unmanned aircraft can transform into 'civil' or 'state' aircraft depending on the course of function.[105]

Whether UA is a 'civil' or 'state' aircraft raises different set of obligations and liabilities. If UA is a state aircraft, then UA would not come within the purview of Chicago Convention. If UA is a civil aircraft, then it would fall under the jurisdiction of ICAO and national laws. Some distinguishable characteristic of the Unmanned Aircraft for the purposes of interception and regulation can be the i) design of UA, ii) registration marks, iii) ownership, and iv) type of operation.

i) Design: In 2010, CIA deployed micro UA in Pakistan, approximately the size of a pizza platter specially designed to survey targets with more precision in order to minimize civilian causalities.[106] The drone operators also changed tactics by targeting terrorists in vehicles rather than residences to reduce collateral

[102] Convention on International Civil Aviation also known as the Chicago Convention was signed at Chicago on December 7th, 1944. See ICAO doc 7300/9 Ninth Edition, 2006.

[103] Abeyratne (2010) at 168.

[104] In the absence of any definition of 'military services' the interpretation must be done in accordance with the Article 31 of the Vienna Convention on the Law of Treaties that "ordinary meaning to be given to the terms of the treaty in their context and in the light of its object and purpose."

[105] **See**, Accident Investigation Board Report, August 1996, at 4 when USAF CT-43 A, a military equivalent of B-737-200 carrying VIP Croatian officials crashed at Dubrovnik on 3 April 1996; the investigation report deemed the aircraft as civil aircraft per Article 3 of the Convention. **See also**, Resolution 1562 (2007) of the Parliamentary Assembly of the Council of Europe titled "Secret detention and illegal transfers of detainees involving Council of Europe member States" which was critical of countries involved with US authorities in transporting suspected terrorists in Gulfstream civilian aircrafts online at http://assembly.coe.int/main.asp?Link=/documents/adoptedtext/ta07/eres1562.htm. In the aftermath of 911, special rendition flights were performed to transport high-value terrorists for questioning in countries where they would not enjoy immunity against torture. The aircrafts identified were civilian B-737 and had US nationality marks but were used in a secret operative manner that would categorize them as State aircrafts. See also Milde (2008), pp. 477–486.

[106] Warrick and Finn (2010).

damage. However, the difficulty to distinguish UA lies in the fact when they can be easily re-modified for other purposes.

ii) Registration: The registration bearings can also distinguish an aircraft. However, the nationality and registration itself are insufficient proof that an aircraft is used solely for state or civil purpose. In a well-documented case of civil airplane B-737 MisrAir flight 2843 from Cairo to Tunis, suspected of carrying terrorists under Military Police escort was intercepted by US fighter planes and forced to land in Italy. The US explained its action stating that "it is our view that the aircraft was operating as a State aircraft at the time of interception. The relevant factors—including exclusive State purpose and function of the mission, the presence of armed military personnel on board and the secrecy under which the mission was attempted—compel this conclusion."[107]

iii) Ownership: The ownership may indicate that whether the aircraft is owned by the State or by a private entity. However, the problem arises where a state contracts out its military duties to private security contractors. For instance, the US State Department is operating surveillance drones to protect the US embassy in Iraq and is accepting bids from private security contractors to manage the drones program.[108] This has outraged the Iraqi officials who believe this program is an affront to Iraqi sovereignty.[109] Thus, ownership itself does not prove that the UA is used in state or a civil operation rather it further complicates the matter when the UA are contracted to private military security companies in the event liability arises.[110]

In an another case, the Elbit Systems which is a defense electronics manufacturer, trades on NASDAQ and sells Unmanned Aircraft systems to many countries around the world. Although, 45 % shares are owned by Micheal Federmann, due to its close connections with the Israeli Ministry of Defense, Elbit Systems has been a target of the pro-Palestinian BDS (boycott,

---

[107] ICAO document LC/29-WP/2-1 (1994) at pp. 11–12.

[108] As Schmitt and Schmidt reported, "American contractors say they have been told that the State Department is considering to field unarmed surveillance drones in the future in a handful of other potentially high-threat countries, including Indonesia and Pakistan, and in Afghanistan after the bulk of American troops leave in the next two years. . .The drones are the latest example of the State Department's efforts to take over functions in Iraq that the military used to perform. Some 5,000 private security contractors now protect the embassy's 11,000-person staff, for example, and typically drive around in heavily armored military vehicles." **See** Schmitt and Schmidt (2012).

[109] *Ibid.*

[110] 'The Montreux Document' is not legally binding however, it highlights the responsibilities of Contracting States that hire Private Military Security Companies (PMSCs) and emphasizes that States have an obligation to uphold international humanitarian law and have a duty to hold PMSCs accountable for criminal behavior. Both the US and Iraq have ratified 'The Montreux Document.' See "The Montreux Document on pertinent international legal obligations and good practices for States related to operations of private military and security companies during armed conflict" A/63/467-S/2008/636 (entered into force on 17 September 2008), online at www.icrc.org/eng/assets/files/other/icrc_002_0996.pdf.

divestment, sanctions) movement due to the use of its Hermes 450 drone in West Bank and Gaza.[111]

iv) Type of Operation: The type of operation can prove the nature of either the UA flight for civil or secret state purpose. The drone operations in Yemen planned to go after Al-Qaeda in a way that they cannot escape, qualifies these drones as state aircrafts. For example, the CIA drone operation killed Anwar al-Awlaki, an American-born leader of a Yemen Al-Qaeda network without affording him an opportunity for a trial. Besides, these drone strikes have increased resentment both against the Yemeni and the US government.[112]

In the absence of any other regulatory guidance, the term 'used' in Article 3 (b) of the Chicago convention can determine the actual status of the UA. This functionality is the dispositive factor in ascertaining whether UA is a state or a civil aircraft. The CIA's use of drones in Pakistan, Yemen and Somalia is raising controversial issues. The CIA is not a military agency rather it is an independent civilian agency of the U.S.[113] This begs the question of whether the CIA drones operators who are civilians engaged in armed conflict can be categorized as unlawful combatants and subject to prosecution.[114] And whether the drone used for extra-judicial killing violate the UN Charter and state sovereignty.

7.4.4 Pros and Cons

For reasons adduced earlier in this article, drones would remain the popular weapon of choice despite calls to reduce its reliance on them. This incontrovertible fact is brought to bear by the fact that the Obama administration has used more than 400 drone strikes so far as against 50 strikes sanctioned by President George W. Bush during his 8 years in office.[115] On the positive side, drones have effectively rid the world of terrorist leaders and decimated terrorist organizations in foreign countries that are infested with terrorist activity. One commentator unreservedly states that drones remain "a necessary instrument of counter-terrorism".[116]

---

[111] Cole and Wright (2010).

[112] Michael Smith (2012).

[113] Central Intelligence Agency, online: CIA https://www.cia.gov/about-cia/todays-cia/index.html.

[114] As Solis notes, "An unlawful combatant is one who takes an active and continuous part in armed conflict who therefore should be treated as a combatant in that he/she is a lawful target of attack, not enjoying the protections granted to civilians. Because unlawful combatants do not differentiate themselves from civilians and do not obey the laws of armed conflict they are not entitled to the privileges of combatants, for example, prisoner-of-war status." **See** Solis (2007) at 130.

[115] Byman (2013), pp. 32–43 at 32.

[116] *Id.* 32.

One of the effective achievements of drones is their ability to cut off communications of terrorist cells and destroy their training capabilities. However, a distinct danger is that along with the advantages to States fighting terrorism with drone attacks would be the tendencies to use such attacks at whim and indiscriminately on the tenuous justification that if it is good for the United States to use drones with impunity, they should also have the license to do so.

On the other side of the coin is a compelling argument against the use of drones, that the drone programme has taken a life of its own "to the point where tactics are driving strategy instead of the other way around"[117] resulting in "remote controlled repression".[118] Another grave disadvantage of drone attacks, particularly from a strategic point of view is that it kills individuals suspected of terrorism or proven terrorists without giving States the flexibility and advantage of questioning them. Therefore drone attacks are only good when a State decides that a terrorist would have to be eliminated rather than captured. However, the most compelling and indisputable argument against drone attacks is that drones have proved to be lethal to innocent civilians[119] whose killings go to the heart of the most important law of all brought to prominence in recent times with the growing instances of torture and killings of non-combatants in warfare and the solid grounding of international society—the law of humanity.

The use of drones brings to bear the age old maxim *Inter arma enim silent leges* attributed to Cicero, which translates as "In times of war, the laws are silent". In the twenty-first century, this maxim, which was purported to address the growing mob violence and thuggery of Cicero's time, has taken on a different and a more complex dimension, extending from the idealistic synergy between the executive and the judiciary in instances of civil strife, to the overall power, called "prerogative" or "discretion" of the sovereign, to act for the public good as the guardian of the rule of law.

One commentator has said:

> In recent years, international criminal lawyers have proclaimed the arrival of a new order where impunity for war criminals is extinguished or swept aside by crusading domestic prosecutors (e.g. Garzon in Spain), by national courts (e.g. the House of Lords in *Pinochet*), by bold legislators (e.g. the Belgian war crimes legislation in 1993 and 1999, notwithstanding subsequent amendments), and by proliferating . . .international tribunals.[120]

However, the good news is that the trend is shifting towards a preponderance of State responsibility. Dr. Rudi Teitel, Professor of Comparative Law at New York Law School and Visiting Professor, London School of Economics, Global Governance, says:

[117] Kurth Cronin (2013), pp. 44–54 at 44.

[118] *Id.* 47.

[119] The Bureau of Investigative Journalism has reported that in 2011 alone 900 non combatants including almost 200 children were killed by drone strikes. See Byman (2013), p. 64 at 37.

[120] Simpson (2007) at 133.

> Sovereignty is no longer a self-evident foundation for international law. This shift is driving the move from the State-centric normative discourse of global politics—which had prevailed until recently—to a far ranging, transnational discourse in which references to changed subjectivity have consequences. That new discourse is constructed more among humanity law lines.[121]

This statement is consistent with the pronouncement of the International Criminal Tribunal for the former Yugoslavia which in its adjudication of *Prosecutor* v. *Dusko Tadic* said: "a state-sovereignty oriented approach has been gradually supplanted by a human being oriented approach".[122]

There are two broad reasons for this shift: the natural historical progression of world affairs which shifted trends chronologically; and the growing instances of torture, rape and killings in circumstances of internal strife and military warfare. Let us take the chronological evolution first. After World War II, the world has, over the past 70 years or so, gone through three global political and economic stages. The first was the modernist era, where naturally, State sovereignty was considered paramount over any other consideration in the immediate and proximate aftermath of the War where nations and States were attacked. This lasted until the 1960s.

From then on the trend shifted to the post-modernist era where the focus veered from the interests of the State to the welfare of the citizen. Post modernism, which was a characteristic of the 1960s and 1970s, progressed steadily toward the twenty-first century. Post modernist thinking was geared to accepting that human culture, as we knew it from a social and economic perspective, was reaching an end. This school of thought associated itself with the momentum of industrial society, drawing on an image of pluralism of cultures and a multitude of groups. The interaction between political modernism, which brought to bear the globalization of nations and deconstruction of separatism of human society, while at the same time ascribing to the individual certain rights at international law that transcended natural legislation parameters, has been symbiotic and essentially economic. In the post modernist era, the fundamental modernist philosophy of state sovereignty and peace gave way to an industrial culture that emphasized economic coexistence for the betterment of the global citizen.

The neo post modernist era was signaled as an immediate consequence of the attacks of 11 September 2001 where close to 3,000 human beings were decimated by terrorist activities within a few minutes. The principle of State Responsibility with regard to world peace and security which lies primarily in Article 24 of the United Nations Charter which calls upon all members to refrain in their international relations from the threat or use of force against the territorial integrity or political independence of any state, or in any other manner inconsistent with the

---

121 Simpson (2011) at 35.

122 Decision of 2 October 1995, Case No. IT-94-1-T 14 July 1997, United Nations International Tribunal for the Prosecution of Persons Responsible for Serious Violations of International Humanitarian Law Committed in the Territory of former Yugoslavia since 1991.

purposes of the United Nations, was immediately resuscitated in the minds of the international community.

This principle is embodied in the work of the International Law Commission, through Article 2 of the Draft Articles on Responsibility of States for Internationally Wrongful Acts which provides that international responsibility of a State, which is referred to in Article 1, is attributable to that State if conduct of the State constitutes a breach of an international obligation of that State. The document also provides that the wrongfulness of an act of a State is precluded if the act constitutes a lawful measure of self defence taken in conformity with the Charter of the United Nations. The State responsible for an internationally wrongful act is under an obligation to compensate for damage caused, including reparation for financially assessable damage including loss of profits.

In addition to State responsibility for conduct attributable to that State, the International Law Commission has established that a crime against the peace and security of mankind entails individual responsibility, and is a crime of aggression. The Rome Statute of the International Criminal court, defines a war crime, *inter alia*, as intentionally directing attacks against civilian objects; attacking or bombarding, by whatever means, towns, villages, dwellings or buildings which are undefended and which are not military objects; employing weapons, projectiles, and material and methods of warfare that cause injury The Statute also defines as a war crime, any act which is intentionally directed at buildings, material, medical units and transport, and personnel using the distinctive emblems of the Geneva Conventions in conformity with international law.

The law of war categorizes justification for killing into four groups: military necessity; distinction; proportionality and humanity. The last is what applies to drone killings. Targeting of civilians and medical personnel by no means comes even close to any of these categories. That drones—which some call "assassination machines"—in their missions of targeted killings, are used contrary to Article 51 of the United Nations Charter[123] make them clearly contrary to the principles of public international law. Drones are precision instruments which rarely miss their targets but unfortunately lack the means to distinguish between the innocent and the guilty.

Killings by drones come within the new heading under international law called the "conscience of mankind". It is a universal law which goes as far back as 1949 when the International Court of Justice (ICJ) recognized:

> Certain well recognized principles, namely elementary considerations of humanity, even more existing in peace than in war.[124]

[123] Article 51 states: "Nothing in the present Charter shall impair the inherent right of individual or collective self-defence if an armed attack occurs against a Member of the United Nations, until the Security Council has taken measures necessary to maintain international peace and security. Measures taken by Members in the exercise of this right of self-defence shall be immediately reported to the Security Council and shall not in any way affect the authority and responsibility of the Security Council under the present Charter to take at any time such action as it deems necessary in order to maintain or restore international peace and security".

[124] *Corfu Channel Case* (*United Kingdom* v. *Albania*), ICJ Reports (1949) at 22.

Again in 1951 the ICJ made a similar pronouncement which appeared once again in 1976 in the Draft Articles of the International Law Commission which recognized the existence of "international crimes". The principle of humanity law was immutably established with no room for doubt in 1986 when the ICJ in the *Nicaragua Case* evolved "elementary considerations of humanity" which essentially devolved responsibility of ensuring the safety and security of humanity on the State even outside treaty law, such as the provisions contained in the 1949 *Geneva Conventions on International Humanitarian Law*.[125]

The future of UA will largely depend on how technology, regulators, and states can work in tandem. As already discussed, the status of an unmanned aircraft can be ascertained by the actual function it is performing at the given moment. Any UA on a particular journey would be considered military if it is surveying for a combat mission, other time the same UA can be considered civil if it is surveying for a humanitarian relief. Hence, the status of each flight must be pre-approved by the approved flight plan accepted by the States to be flown above and should beforehand specify the nature of the flight. As history unfolds and technology advances the future of UAVs will largely rely on the governmental funding of its research and development. The advances in technology will not only decrease the costs as the demand increases but their easy availability may raise the problems of UA getting in wrong hands. Thus, the legislatures and engineers should work hands in hands to make sure that the use of unmanned aircrafts is for the good of humanity not for its destruction. In view of this article, the future regulation of Unmanned Aircrafts remains a step-by-step process.

Drones are retaliation to mass murder and the unacceptable abuse and torture of humanity. More than 12 years have passed since the outrageous and catastrophic events of 11 September 2001. Yet, none of us can get over the outrage we felt at the dastardly terrorist acts which killed nearly 3,000 people in a day. Most of the world that day felt an amalgam of concern, fear, and anger that motivated us to take precautions. Overnight, we converted ourselves from a society that was both laid back and reactive to a society that took pre-emptive and preventive action to make sure such things never happened again. For purposes of definition, Preemption is when an act, which is potentially harmful to a State and is imminent, is effectively precluded by military or other action. Prevention is when an act, which is potentially harmful to a State and is inevitable, is effectively precluded by military or other action.

Alan Dershowitz, Professor of Law at Harvard University, asserts that "There is a desperate need in the world for a coherent and widely accepted jurisprudence of

---

[125] The Geneva Conventions and their Additional Protocols are at the core of international humanitarian law, the body of international law that regulates the conduct of armed conflict and seeks to limit its effects. They specifically protect people who are not taking part in the hostilities (civilians, health workers and aid workers) and those who are no longer participating in the hostilities, such as wounded, sick and shipwrecked soldiers and prisoners of war.

preemption and prevention, in the context of both self-defence and defense of others".[126] Preemption and prevention are necessary elements in today's political and military fabric, where legal legitimacy is ascribed to actions of States which act swiftly to avoid harm and protect its citizenry. These practices, however well meant from a strategic context, inevitably give rise to the law of outrage. Referring to the Holocaust during World War II President Roosevelt said on October 7, 1942: "It is our intention that just and sure punishment shall be meted out to the ringleaders responsible for the organized murder of thousands of innocent persons in the commission of atrocities which have violated every tenet of the Christian faith." The next year Roosevelt, Stalin and Churchill vowed, through the Moscow Declaration, to bring the perpetrators to justice. On 26 October 1943 the United Nations War Crimes commission composed of 15 allied nations met for the first time in London. On March 24, 1944 President Roosevelt again issued the warning: "None who participate in these acts of savagery will go unpunished. All who share in the guilt shall share the punishment". The last sentence was reiterated in a different way by Present George W. Bush in the aftermath of the events of 9/11: "Every nation has a choice to make. In this conflict, there is no neutral ground. If any government sponsors the outlaws and killers of innocence, they have become outlaws and murderers themselves. And they will take that lonely path at their own peril".[127]

Although this is the ultimate justification for the eradication of the vermin of terrorism that nature ever suffered to crawl upon the surface of the world, historic responses such as drone attacks are extreme measures resonating killings of both the innocent and the guilty summarily, without arraignment or judgment. There are some societies that are terrorized by drone attacks where they occur. In instances of hooliganism and vandalism as in the London riots of 2011 the statement in Parliament of Prime Minister David Cameron during: "We will not allow a culture of fear to exist on our streets. And we will do whatever it takes to restore law and order and to rebuild our communities... anyone charged with violent disorder and other serious offences should expect to be remanded in custody not let back on the streets and anyone convicted should expect to go to jail" might resonate.[128] But whether this philosophy can be extended to civilians of Afghanistan or Pakistan or Yemen who, while celebrating their relatives wedding at a party find a drone attack descending on them killing the bride and most of the happy relatives, is entirely another matter.

[126] Dershowitz (2006), p. 72.

[127] James Joyner, Was Afghanistan Worth It? *The National Interest*, http://nationalinterest.org/commentary/was-afghanistan-worth-it-8182.

[128] UK riots: text of David Cameron's address to Commons, *The Telegraph*, 11 August 2011, at http://www.telegraph.co.uk/news/uknews/crime/8695272/UK-riots-text-of-David-Camerons-address-to-Commons.html.

References

Abeyratne RIR (2007) Air law and policy. PublishAmerica, Baltimore, pp 25–47

Abeyratne RIR (2009) Regulating unmanned aerial vehicles – issues and challenges. Eur Transport Law XLIV(5):503–520

Abeyratne RIR (2010) Aviation security law. Springer, Heidelberg, p 162

Austin R (2010) Unmanned aircraft systems, UAVs design, development and deployment. Wiley, West Sussex, p 3

Bone E, Bolkcom C (2003) Unmanned aerial vehicles: background and issues for Congress. Congressional Research Service, Washington, RL31872, 25 April 2003, p 2. http://www.fas.org/irp/crs/RL31872.pdf

Butler A (2013) Italy looking to develop black MALE UAV. Aviation Week & Space Technology, 20 May 2013. http://www.aviationweek.com/Article.aspx?id=/article-xml/AW_05_20_2013_p26-578980.xml

Byman D (2013) Why drones work – the case for Washington's weapon of choice. Foreign Aff 92(4):32–43

Capaccio T (2010) Pentagon to increase stock of high-altitude drones. Bloomberg, 4 February 2010. http://www.bloomberg.com/apps/news?pid=newsarchive&sid=aUYvb_D1LBzM

Cheng B (1962) The law of international air transport. Oceania Publications, London, p 148

Cole C, Wright J (2010a) Campaign against military drones. Peace News, Issue 2519, March 2010. http://peacenews.info/node/3426/campaign-against-military-drones

Cole C, Wright J (2010b) What are drones? Drone Wars UK, January 2010. http://dronewars.net/aboutdrone/

Dershowitz A (2006) Preemption – a sword that cuts both ways. Norton, New York, 72

Evans B (2013) Terrifying video captures moment German drone missed Afghan plane carrying 100 passengers by just two meters. Mail Online, 3 June 2013. http://www.dailymail.co.uk/news/article-2335122/Terrifying-video-captures-moment-German-drone-missed-Afghan-plane-carrying-100-passengers-just-metre.html

Friedman N (2010) Unmanned combat air systems: a new kind of carrier aviation. Naval Institute Press, Maryland, p 1

Groenewege AD (1999) Compendium of international civil aviation, 2nd edn. International Aviation Development Corporation, Canada, p 437

Harthy C (2013) France requests $1.5B general atomics reaper UAV sale. 2 July 2013. http://www.suasnews.com/2013/07/23626/france-requests-1-5b-general-atomics-reaper-uav-sale/

Kahlili R (2013) Iran gives stealth drone secrets to Russia. WND, 10 February 2013. http://www.wnd.com/2013/02/iran-gives-stealth-drone-secrets-to-russia/

Kurth Cronin A (2013) Why drones fail. Foreign Aff 92(4):44–54

Laing A (2013) US drone 'shot down by al-Shabaab in Somalia'. The Telegraph, 29 May 2013. http://www.telegraph.co.uk/news/worldnews/al-qaeda/10086660/US-drone-shot-down-by-al-Shabaab-in-Somalia.html

Lazarski A Lt Col USAF (2002) Legal implications of the uninhabited combat aerial vehicle. Aerospace Power Journal, Summer 2002. http://www.airpower.maxwell.af.mil/airchronicles/apj/apj02/sum02/lazarski.html

Michael Smith J (2012) Drone 'blowback' is real: a new analysis finds five ways drone strikes in Yemen are hurting American interests. Salon, 5 September 2012. http://www.salon.com/2012/09/05/drone_blowback_is_real/

Micheal M (2012) International air law and ICAO, 2nd edn. Eleven International Publishing, Hague, p 65

Milde (2008) Rendition flights' and international law. pp 477–486. www.redress.org/downloads/publications/Prof_Dr_Micheal_Milde_for_REDRESS_June_2008_2_.pdf

Nekhai O (2013) State-of-the-art UAVs to enter service in the Russian Army. The Voice of Russia, 14 June 2013. http://voiceofrussia.com/2013_06_14/State-of-the-art-UAVs-to-enter-service-in-the-Russian-Army-0448/

Newman RJ (2002) The little predator that could. Air Force Magazine, March 2002, p 49. http://www.airforcemag.com/MagazineArchive/Pages/2002/March%202002/0302predator.aspx

Peterson ME (2005) The UAV and the current and future regulatory construct for integration into the national airspace system. LL.M. Thesis, McGill University Institute of Air and Space Law

Roberts K (2013) When the whole world has drones. National Journal, 21 March 2013. http://www.nationaljournal.com/magazine/when-the-whole-world-has-drones-20130321

Schenkman J (1955) International Civil Aviation Organization. Librairie E. Dross, Geneve, p 6

Schmitt E, Schmidt M (2012) U.S. drones patrolling its skies provoke outrage in Iraq. New York Times, 29 January 2012. http://www.nytimes.com/2012/01/30/world/middleeast/iraq-is-angered-by-us-drones-patrolling-its-skies.html?pagewanted=all&_r=0

Shachtman N (2009) CIA chief: drones 'Only Game in Town' for stopping Al-Qaeda. Wired, 19 May 2009. http://www.wired.com/dangerroom/2009/05/cia-chief-drones-only-game-in-town-for-stopping-al-qaeda/

Shaw MN (2003) International law, 5th edn. Cambridge University Press, Cambridge, p 120

Simpson G (2007) Law, war & crime – war crimes trials and the reinvention of international law. Polity, Cambridge, p 133

Simpson G (2011) Humanty's law. Oxford University Press, Oxford, p 35

Sochor E (1991) The politics of international aviation. Macmillan, London, p xvi

Solis G (2007) Targeted killing and the law of armed conflict. Naval War College Rev 60(2):130

van Zandt P (1944) Civil aviation and peace. The Brookings Institutions, Washington, pp 28, 93

Warner E (1942) Foreword to international air transport and national policy by Lissitzyn O.J. Oceana, New York, p V

Warrick J, Finn P (2010) Amid outrage over civilian deaths in Pakistan, CIA turns to smaller missiles. Washington Post, 26 April 2010. http://www.washingtonpost.com/wp-dyn/content/article/2010/04/25/AR2010042503114.html

Chapter 8
Conclusion

There are three critical factors affecting modern day airport law and regulation. They are foresight; the synergy between airports and airlines; and governance. With regard to foresight, the weather crisis at European airports in the winter of 2010 brought to bear the fundamental reality that airport planners have to be sensitive towards the three broad areas of ecology, safety and infrastructural planning when planning and running an airport. Mr. Siim Kallas, Vice President of the European Commission urged the aviation industry to introduce a set of quality standards to obviate any future disruption to air travel similar to the crippling experience of the last few weeks of December 2010 which caused airlines to cancel 35,000 flights during the crisis.[1]

Mr. Kallas expressed his views on the winter 2010 crisis at European airports by saying that clearly, contingency planning for snow at airports needed to be improved, and that the European Commission needed to ensure better co-operation between all those involved—in the air and on the ground and also to ensure the proper functioning of the airline hubs. He also stated that there was a need to provide better and more timely information about delays and rerouting To achieve all this Mr. Kallas suggested that, to achieve all this, minimum service and quality requirements at airports for passengers was needed.[2] The chaos at European airports in the winter of 2010, particularly London Heathrow, wrought by pummelling snowstorms and ice, not only was caused by cancelled flights and stranded passengers but also resulted in the tremendous cost involved for the airport authorities. Airports operator BAA has released the figure of 24 million pounds sterling ($38 million) as the cost incurred by the Spanish owned firm which operates six airports in Britain. These costs included reduction in profit as a result of the decrease in passenger numbers by 11 % over a few days.

---

[1] EU Transport Chief Kallas Wants Common Quality Standards, *Aviation Daily*, January 21, 2011 at 2.

[2] http://www.airtransportnews.aero/article.pl?mcateg=&id=27750.

R. Abeyratne, *Law and Regulation of Aerodromes*, DOI 10.1007/978-3-319-04780-5_8,

From 17 December 2010 for a week or so, heavy snow and ice pounded Europe, grounding air travel across the continent and leaving thousands of passengers stranded as airports struggled to clear a backlog of flights cancelled or delayed by snowfalls. London's Heathrow, the world's busiest international airport, operated a limited schedule as one of its two runways was open and advised passengers not to travel to the airport unless their flight is confirmed. According to airport operator British Airports Authority (BAA) airlines worked to move aircraft and crew back to their normal positions as severe winter weather continued to cause disruption.[3]

No doubt, the winter freeze and the attendant cancellation of flights caused acute inconvenience to the travelling public. Millions of people faced a struggle to get home in time for Christmas as travel plans were thrown into chaos when planes were grounded, trains cancelled and roads made impassable by snow and ice accumulation. Airport authorities blamed the bad weather for the disruption of flight schedules. A senior Emirates official criticized BAA for refusing to allow two of its aircraft to land in the UK, and warned that the airline faced a massive task in coping with the backlog of passengers now stranded in London.[4] Siim Kallas expressed his increasing concern about problems relating to the infrastructure available to airlines—airports and ground handling—and is reported to have said that he was considering forcing airports to provide airlines with a minimum level of infrastructure support during such severe weather.[5]

In the aftermath, some airlines took strong objection to the manner in which airports—particularly BAA—handled the heavy snow. Virgin Atlantic was reported to withhold airport fees until the inquiry[6] into BAA was completed.[7] The British Government, on 26 December 2010 considered introducing new laws to allow regulators to fine airports for travel disruption. Transport Minister Philip Hammond, told the Sunday Times that regulators should have tougher powers to punish airports who fail passengers, after thousands were forced to sleep at Heathrow when heavy snow grounded flights. Mr Hammond was of the view that there should be an economic penalty for service failure and that greater weight needs to be given to performance and passenger satisfaction.[8]

---

[3] Icy conditions also curtailed Europe's train services, left cars skidding through slushy streets and saw major events postponed, including music shows and sporting events. See http://www.ibtimes.com/articles/93795/20101220/travelers-air-passengers-stranded-as-europe-freezes-due-to-heavy-snowfall.htm.

[4] http://www.arabianbusiness.com/emirates-lashes-out-at-uk-airports-body-amid-winter-chaos-368334.html?parentID=368939.

[5] http://www.canada.com/news/European+freeze+haunts+Christmas+airlines+shops/4007697/story.html.

[6] BAA's non-executive Director, Sir David Begg is reported to have launched an inquiry just prior to Christmas to inquire into what went wrong.

[7] Virgin Atlantic Withholds BAA Fees Over Snow Row, *Air Letter*, Monday 10 January 2011, No. 17,147 at 2.

[8] http://www.flyertalk.com/forum/newsstand/1164326-britain-mulls-new-airports-law-after-heathrow-chaos.html.

The fundamental questions that arise are, should airports be held responsible for service failure brought about by a natural phenomenon; and should airports have had, what in modern business parlance is called "corporate foresight".[9] Firstly, in terms of responsibility, the question could be raised as to whether; irrespective of the business status of the airport (whether it is privatized, autonomous or corporatized) the State in which the airport is situated should bear ultimate responsibility. This responsibility devolves upon the State *in limine* by virtue of Article 28 of the Chicago Convention which stipulates *inter alia* that each Contracting States to the Convention undertakes, so far as it may find practicable to provide, in its territory, airports, radio services, meteorological services and other air navigation facilities to facilitate international air navigation, in accordance with the standards and practices recommended or established from time to time, pursuant to the Convention. The provision also requires such a State to adopt and put into operation the appropriate standard systems of communications procedure, codes, markings, signals, lighting and other operational practices and rules which may be recommended or established from time to time, pursuant to this Convention. Obviously, the Convention, through an inarticulate premise requires in Article 28 that States provide *functional* airport services among other services prescribed in the provision.

The airlines–airport relationship is most vital as was reflected in the *Vumbaca* decision.[10] They are each others' closest partners and therefore airlines and airports should work together towards a unified agenda. They have the same aim: to encourage more passengers and freight and achieve improved service quality to their customer. Tom Windmuller, IATA's Senior Vice President of Airport Passenger and Cargo Services puts it best, that this agenda should be based on:

- A mutual understanding that long term sustainability is an issue for both airlines and airports;
- Recognition that the solution to the common challenge faced by both airports and airlines is not to take each other in an anaconda-like grip to squeeze out every last penny from another; and
- Partnership and working together to help airports find new and mutually beneficent efficiencies, infrastructure investment which is aligned to airline needs, as well as new and additional non-aeronautical revenues.[11]

---

[9] The functions and responsibilities of an airport will vary according to its size, type of traffic and areas of responsibility. For example, some airports are responsible for air traffic control as well as for meteorological services, while at most other airports such services are provided by separate government entities. Many airports are involved in security functions in varying degrees and in providing facilities for customs, immigration and health authorities. Ground-handling services for the airlines, including terminal handling or ramp handling, or both, are provided by some airports, while at others they are provided by the airlines or by specialized agents or companies. Certain airports also perform functions that exceed the scope of conventional airport activities, such as consultancy services, public works, construction, and real estate development. See Abeyratne (2009) at 13.

[10] *Supra*, Chap. 1, note 6.

[11] Windmuller (2013) at 24.

The third aspect—corporate governance—is as important as the other two just discussed. Governance is responsibility toward moving in a strategic direction. Airports are subject to both external and internal factors with regard to revenue generation and their cost-benefit equation. The most significant external factors are current and projected traffic levels, global and local economic fluctuations and currency exchange rates, taxes and charges imposed on airports by governments and authorities as well as charges that can be exercised by airports on their users. A large number of factors will influence an airport's ability to maximize its commercial revenues. There are first of all certain external factors, which are crucially important in affecting revenue generation or strategic options but which are largely outside the control of individual airport managements. These include the airport's traffic levels and its proportion of international traffic, exchange rates and the level of taxes or duties imposed on alcohol or tobacco. Then there are a variety of factors which can be influenced directly by management. These are the area and the location of terminal space allocated to commercial activities, the nature of the contracts negotiated with the concessionaires and the quality of the concessionaires themselves.

The responsibility that devolves upon an airport is based on integrity and professionalism and rests with the board of directors. Until the *Enron*[12] fiasco, corporate executives were in a comfort zone of their own, as they believed they had only to act in the best interests of their employer by increasing the profits of their company. The Enron case highlighted the fact that an executive could be exposed for corporate misdeeds and for personal liability for such misdeeds. Therefore the airport executive has to be mindful of his responsibility to the shareholders, creditors and other stakeholders of his company, in terms of his personal liability.

Until fairly recently, executives were of the general belief that only responsibility was to maximize corporate profits and act in the best interest of their organizations. This myth was shattered by scandals such as those involving Enron, WorldCom and Adelphia and indeed several others where liability was imposed for corporate misdeeds by white collar workers resulting in their personal liability. Perhaps the most controversial and shocking was the Enron case. Enron Corporation was an American energy company based in Houston, Texas. Before its bankruptcy, in late 2001, Enron employed around 21,000 people and was one of the world's leading electricity, natural gas, pulp and paper, and communications companies, with claimed revenues of $111 billion in 2000. The magazine *Fortune* named Enron "America's Most Innovative Company" for 6 consecutive years.

Enron was disgraced at the end of 2001 when it was revealed that the corporation's reported financial condition was sustained mostly by institutionalized,

[12] In January 2002, the United States Justice Department confirmed that it had begun a criminal investigation of *Enron*, following the events of the company in October 2001 when Enron reported a $638 million third-quarter loss and disclosed a $1.2 billion reduction in shareholder equity, partly related to partnerships run by its Finance Chief that hid huge amounts of debt as well as write downs in money-losing broadband and water trading ventures. *Enron* went bankrupt on 2 December 2001, putting all its employees out of employment.

systematic, and creatively planned accounting fraud. Enron has since become a popular symbol of willful corporate fraud and corruption. The lawsuit against Enron's directors, following the scandal, was notable in that the directors settled the suit by paying very significant amounts of money personally. Executives have a personal liability to their shareholders, employees, creditors and other stakeholders. This is not only applicable to the private sector but also apples to government departments and instrumentalities of States. The corporate veil that shielded executives from personal liability has now been lifted, often compelling executives to take precautionary measures before they act, particularly by seeking legal counsel.

Another offence, particularly in the United States, is insider trading which is a practice related to the trading of a corporation's stock or other securities (e.g. bonds or stock options) by corporate insiders such as officers, directors, or holders of more than 10 % of the firm's shares. Insider trading may be perfectly legal, but the term is frequently used to refer to a practice which is illegal in many jurisdictions, in which an insider or a related party trades based on material non-public information obtained during the performance of the insider's duties at the corporation, or otherwise misappropriated.

Rules against insider trading on material non-public information exist in most jurisdictions around the world, though the details and the efforts to enforce them vary considerably. Usually, corporate insiders are a company's officers, directors and any beneficial owners of more than 10 % of a class of the company's equity securities. Transactions concluded by these types of insiders in the company's own stock, based on material non-public information, are considered to be fraudulent since the insiders are violating the trust or the fiduciary duty that they owe to the shareholders. The corporate insider, simply by accepting employment, has made a contract with the shareholders to put the shareholders' interests before their own, in matters related to the corporation. When the insider buys or sells based upon company owned information, he is violating his contract with the shareholders.

The above discussion goes to reflect that corporate foresight, cooperation between airlines and airports and corporate governance are the three pillars on which the integrity of the law and regulation of aerodromes are built.

References

Abeyratne RIR (2009) Airport business law. AuthorHouse, Bloomington, p 13
Windmuller T (2013) The foundation for collaboration. Int Airport Rev (4):24–25

Index

R. Abeyratne, *Law and Regulation of Aerodromes*, DOI 10.1007/978-3-319-04780-5,

MIX
Papier aus verantwortungsvollen Quellen
Paper from responsible sources
FSC® C105338

If you have any concerns about our products, you can contact us on
ProductSafety@springernature.com

In case Publisher is established outside the EU, the EU authorized representative is:
Springer Nature Customer Service Center GmbH
Europaplatz 3, 69115 Heidelberg, Germany

Printed by Libri Plureos GmbH
in Hamburg, Germany